COUGHING IT ALL UP

CHRONICLES OF A REMARKABLE LIFE DESPITE CYSTIC FIBROSIS

LUKE PETERS

Sharon,

Thanks for your support. Enjoy the read!

Published by Fitzhinton Publishing 2020

ISBN 978-1-8383068-0-9

CONTENTS

To my wife and two children. You give everything I do a purpose and make everything I go through worthwhile. I love you.

“If the path ahead appears treacherous and your destination impossible to reach, stop for a moment, take a breath and then try looking at that path again from another perspective.”
- Anon.

FOREWORD

PROFESSOR DIANA BILTON

I graduated in medicine from Manchester University in 1984, and it was during my first two years as a trainee doctor that I discovered respiratory medicine was my specialist area of choice for a career in hospital medicine, and that working with people with chronic lung diseases was something I definitely wanted to do and where I could make a difference to peoples' lives by being involved in their care.

At that stage, I was only aware of cystic fibrosis (CF) as a fascinating inherited disorder that was one of the conditions benefitting from evolving research and scientific attention as the knowledge of genetics in science and medicine was rapidly expanding. It is sobering to think that we were still several years from the discovery of the CF gene, which was to be the Holy Grail that would unlock the door to development of new therapies.

I had no idea then about what it was like for someone living with CF – something which you will learn from reading this book. I was lucky enough to meet Dr Kevin Webb, a consultant in respiratory medicine who had just set up the first Adult Cystic Fibrosis Unit in the UK outside London. Dr Webb had trained at the Royal Brompton Hospital in London and then moved to Manchester, deciding to develop not only care services but also research into better care and treatment for adults with CF.

He had attracted funding from the UK-based Cystic Fibrosis Trust ("the CF Trust") and it was as a research fellow that I joined the team and began my 30-year career in CF care and research. With Dr Webb as a clinical mentor, along with a senior lecturer called Joan Braganza as my academic supervisor, I was able to complete the work required to gain an MD research degree which set me up for a future consultant post in cystic fibrosis medicine.

Importantly, I had also spent three years working purely with adults with cystic fibrosis learning the realities of how a small change in the genetic code for a protein that regulates movement of salt and water across cells lining important tubes in the human body could have such devastating consequences on the lives of people inheriting that altered gene.

Whilst Dr Webb and Dr Braganza were inspiring supervisors and teachers, it was the people with CF who became my greatest tutors.

When I first met Luke in 1994, I was just establishing the new specialist adult CF unit at the Royal Papworth Hospital near Cambridge – a hospital renowned for establishing lung transplantation in the UK. The CF development was thanks to the foresight of the Papworth Hospital Chief Executive who had listened to his transplant teams reporting the need to improve care for people with CF way ahead of requirements for lung transplants.

I had been appointed in 1993, but had to engage in long meetings with those opposed to the development with concerns about the costs of CF care, along with regional respiratory physicians who simply did not see the need for a specialist service.

My argument from back then remains the same now, although perhaps nuanced in terminology with the passage of time and advancing technologies. I simply asked, "If you owned a Ferrari and it was not performing, would you take it to the local garage where they did a really good job on all the Ford cars but had no experience or access to Ferrari specialist knowledge? CF is a specialist disease requiring specialist treatment, and people with CF deserve access to that treatment."

There are three themes behind the story that unfolds in the following pages with Luke's advancing years that are worth highlighting.

Firstly, advances in understanding the science of CF have resulted from international co-operation and collaboration. A lesson I learned early on as a CF research fellow was that all of us involved in CF worldwide were working together as a family, and that the principle of 'phone a friend' was an important one to ensure the prize of getting the best results for our patients.

Not only did Luke's mysterious and devastating illness in 2003 require me to make use of that 'phone a friend' facility, but it also became the spark that ignited international research to characterise the emerging strain of nontuberculous mycobacterium or NTM (which we now call '*M. abscessus*') and to identify new therapies to tackle the problem. Luke was the first UK case of the *M. abscessus* syndrome, now recognised as being associated with the particularly vicious strain. The CF Trust are today funding research for new therapies and clinical trials to improve treatment for *M. abscessus* in CF and to reduce the side effects of treatment.

The theme of science-based recommended therapies designed to improve survival is particularly pertinent at a time now when the whole population is experiencing lockdown in order to prevent the spread of COVID-19. As people express the view that the solutions to prevent deaths in the pandemic seem to be creating side effects in unintended ways, I hear the playback of so many conversations in CF clinics with people like Luke as I recommended a course of intravenous antibiotics to treat infection causing lung damage, based on sound scientific evidence but also resulting in cancellation of that long awaited holiday or a delay in starting that new job or university course. The publication of this book in this year of lockdowns feels timely as I hear a collective voice from patients past saying, "Welcome to our world."

Secondly, care in specialist centres dedicated to those with CF has been developed and given appropriate funding and national standards by the NHS with the advent of specialist commissioning. These developments lifted CF care for adults out of a postcode lottery and established the principle of fair care for all advocated and campaigned for by the CF Trust over many decades.

It is a real advance in Luke's lifetime that families with children with CF can expect their children to receive specialist care in childhood and then graduate to a designated appropriately funded adult centre at a planned transition age. Luke's story is both inspiring and moving, and our hope remains that the current generation of people with CF joining the adult clinics will have an easier path in terms of attaining their life ambitions.

Finally, there is now real hope of achieving the CF Trust's aim of people with CF living 'a life unlimited'. Understanding the CF gene and its function has facilitated, albeit taking over twenty-five years, the development of therapies that correct the underlying cellular defects. These therapies (known as CFTR modulators) are now available as simple tablets and prescribed in NHS clinics. There is already evidence to suggest that they truly are reducing the need for intravenous antibiotics and hospital admissions.

Furthermore, they are likely to reduce the requirement for the onerous daily inhaled therapies which, though designed to reduce infections and enhance survival for people with CF, have undoubtedly been a burden with consequences for quality of life. Thus, the introduction of CFTR modulators to routine CF care makes the reduction in the burden of treatments an important and achievable goal whilst ensuring continued improvements in survival.

It strikes me that the beauty of this book is in the sheer lack of bitterness or self-pity, coupled with the humour and sheer resilience which I have witnessed first-hand in so many people with CF and their families.

I have come to believe that the gene change that causes CF also seems to confer an associated gritted determination to live life to the full with both positivity and purpose. Those qualities are what attracts so many of us working in the field of CF and explain why we have made it our life's work. The descriptions of Luke's battle to balance living some kind of 'normal' life with performing the daily treatments that we on the CF team threw at him in our efforts to prevent the disease ending his life earlier than necessary, are a perfect display of that determination.

I am sure this book will encourage anyone involved in CF support or care to continue to make a difference. With that in mind, I will be recommending this book as mandatory reading for anyone looking to work on a team providing care for those with CF. Additionally, I hope it will also inspire those who had no idea what CF was all about to get involved.

Professor Diana Bilton Bsc. MBChB MD FRCP

Adjunct Professor, National Heart and Lung Institute, Imperial College, London

Honorary Consultant in Cystic Fibrosis, Royal Brompton Hospital, London

BEFORE WE GET STARTED...

I just want to clear something up.

This book is not intended to be a treatise specifically about cystic fibrosis, or even lung transplantation. Such subjects have been covered in great depth in other books, and if you have come here to obtain a detailed knowledge of either, then you are reading the wrong book.

Nor is it a medical journal of any kind, although medical terminology makes regular appearances throughout. I could not possibly cover the multitude of physiological and mental nuances that cystic fibrosis inflicts on those who have the condition – at least not with a degree of accuracy that wouldn't make anyone with a decent level of medical training wince – and so I won't even attempt to do so.

It is certainly not solely about illness or being unwell, although illness does form the backdrop to many of the events that happen throughout my story.

Rather, it is a chronicle of a life lived *despite* having cystic fibrosis, a chronic medical condition that when I was born was likely to prevent me reaching my teenage years. Yet almost fifty years on, I am still alive, still going (relatively) strongly and as determined as ever to keep pushing the boundaries that my wavering health imposes upon me. Having faced a steady stream of setbacks along the way, this book examines how I strive to live my life to the full; to overcome those setbacks and to vehemently pursue my wish of being just like everyone else.

Throughout my life, my steadfast determination to defy the odds has seen me achieve so much more than I could ever have hoped for, or that most medics would have predicted when I was born back in 1972. Yet I have also spent large swathes of time in hospital, taken almost a million tablets over the course of my lifetime, and reached the very darkest depths of hopelessness. On more than one occasion, too, I have almost lost my life.

I had talked about writing this book for years. I have always believed that there is a book in everyone, and that the trick is simply finding the trigger to release it. For so long, I have made remarks about anecdotes, people, and places that I would include should I ever get around to putting pen to paper. Yet, up until now I have found ample excuses not to start writing. I have confined those anecdotes and experiences to my memory; safely tucked away and completely inaccessible to anyone else – lost forever should something ever happen to me. Not so long ago, however, a certain set of events forced me to show my hand. With those events came an overriding sense that it was the right time, if ever there was to be one, to get those memories written down. My future was uncertain. And that was my trigger.

What follows is my version of how I have reached the age I am and what I have done in that time, living in the shadow of a chronic disease. A disease that has shaped my life but one that has not determined how I have lived. This book is an account of what I have been able to achieve despite the impact of that illness, rather than because of it. In these pages, I share my story – of living life with this thing of darkness hanging ominously over me, yet finding a way to keep going, keep living, and keep enjoying the time I have rather than dwelling too much on the time I might not get to have.

As much as my memory will allow, I have set out to try to describe the main events of my life as I experienced them. Some of them will have been caused by my health condition but others were not affected by it in any way. And that is the juxtaposition I wish to convey; I am one of many people who has been forced to mould and shape the direction of their life by the limitations and obstacles that having a serious health condition imposes. Yet as someone who would rather find ways around such obstacles than be beaten by them, I have kept on going. I have strived to take what I want from life before the effects of my deteriorating health take the life from me. Whilst such obstacles may cause stumbles and even falls from time to time, over many years I have learned that it is not the fall itself that is important but rather the manner in which you pick yourself up, dust yourself off, and keep going.

It would be disingenuous to say that there haven't been (and continue to be) dark days where the scale of what I have been through and the ongoing difficulties I may face temporarily displace my positivity and optimism. But so long as those days are the minority, then I go on and life goes on with me. My journey, which started so long ago, will continue and I will carry on making memories.

This book was not written to instruct, inspire, nor to teach. Neither is it intended as a source of reference or a manual to live by if you have a chronic condition such as myself. It is about my relationship with my own chronic illness. An illness that, despite its pervasive existence, I have never allowed to define me as a person.

This book aims to achieve nothing other than to tell my story as honestly as I can and to detail how I have gone about living my life. I have written this account for me and to use the writing process as therapy to assist me with navigating through the tricky times I am currently facing. Should others wish to spend a little of their precious time reading about the memories and occasional silly stories contained in the following pages, then I am honoured to be able to share them.

If anyone reading this draws even the tiniest glint of anything which causes them to think about matters in a slightly different way or forces them to look at their own life from another angle, then that would be a good thing. By sharing this book, my hope is that others will enjoy reading it of course, but that they also might possibly learn something. That something may simply be about me, but also possibly about them or perhaps a family member or someone else they might know.

There is nothing particularly special about me nor what I have done with my life. I simply harbour a desire to do as much as anyone else whilst knowing I probably can't. I have spent a lifetime feeling just the same as anyone else but at the same time different. My journey through life has been one of ups and downs; both plain sailing and the very roughest of seas. It has taken me from exhilarating highs to the depths of despair. Yet I am still here, still playing as well as I can with the cards I have been dealt, forever wishing for more but with untold levels of gratitude for what I have.

Join me as I embark on the most difficult stage of my life to date, as I am placed on the waiting list for a double lung transplant; a medical procedure of such magnitude that it could possibly save my life but conversely could end it. Will I survive the wait? How will I cope with a seemingly endless amount of time spent on the transplant list and will I ever receive the call that could just result in me receiving a new pair of lungs, a whole new existence and the ultimate in second chances?

Strictly speaking, I shouldn't still be alive to tell you my story, and the book you are now reading should not exist. Yet thanks to pure luck, good fortune, resilience, determination, medical excellence – or perhaps even divine intervention – I am and it does.

So, that being the case, let's get started on this story of my life. A life that has been eventful in so many ways, but 'remarkable'? Well, I'll leave that for you to decide...

HOW DID IT COME TO THIS?

ONE
THE DAY THE WAITING BEGAN

It has just turned five p.m. on Monday 16th January 2017. I am sitting on my bed with the home telephone receiver in my hand. I'm alone and the house is quiet. Moments ago, I finished the most important telephone call I have ever had to make. A call which will have dramatic repercussions for me, my wife, and my young children for the rest of our lives. A call that will shape the way our futures play out from this point on.

Despite lasting only a minute or two, the exchange of words between myself and the person at the other end means that nothing can ever be the same again. I am utterly conflicted; I don't know whether to be angry, scared, sad, or disappointed with the situation that I find myself in. I suppose, given the circumstances, I would be perfectly justified in feeling all these emotions simultaneously.

I allow myself a bit of time to settle my head. I draw a few deep breaths to slow my heart rate. Tears well up as the sheer magnitude of the situation overwhelms me. But then I wipe my eyes, gather my thoughts, and set about the task of informing those closest to me about what I have just done. Because, now, I am officially waiting for a double lung transplant.

At the time of writing, the UK lung transplant list includes the names of at least three hundred and fifty people. Some of those on the list will be fortunate enough to only wait a few months before receiving their new organs, but others will have much longer to endure. Some will not survive their wait at all and will die before a suitable donor can be found. In fact, approximately seventeen percent of those listed for a lung transplant will not survive a year on the list.

The stark reality of the transplant list is that the number of people waiting for new lungs far exceeds the number willing, or able, to provide them through donation.

And there lies the problem.

According to official NHS statistics[1], the number of people waiting for a lung transplant in the UK has risen by forty-six percent in the past five years. This is attributed largely to demographics (an ageing population) and an increase in referrals for the procedure (the benefits of lung transplants are now much more widely known). The sad truth of this, however, is that, despite the ever-growing need for donor lungs, supply cannot keep up with demand.

Organ donors today are mostly aged fifty and over and are more likely to have pre-existing health problems, thus making successful transplantation of such delicate human organs less likely. More concerning is the simple fact that family refusal remains the main obstacle to organ transplantation. While increasing numbers of the population are in support of organ donation in principle, one in three families still refuse to honour their loved one's wishes and to donate their organs at the critical time.

As I write this, legislative plans are afoot to switch England to an 'opt-out' system of presumed consent, following the example set by Wales in 2015[2]. However, expert opinion remains divided about whether this will have a real effect on the number of organs becoming available for donation; families will continue to have a veto in the opt-out system, and the limited data available remains inconclusive.

But even when lungs *are* donated, they must be assessed for suitability. Firstly, the donor and recipient must be of the same blood group type. Despite improvements in anti-rejection medication, organ rejection is still the primary risk in carrying out any transplant procedure. You can have the best surgeons in the world performing the operation itself, but the human body is a complicated machine and, when parts are being taken out or replaced, it needs assistance wherever possible. Being of the same blood group type means the recipient body is being given at least a fighting chance of accepting the new donor organs and allowing them to take the place of the old, worn out ones.

Having said that, even when the blood group between donor and recipient are a match, some organs remain unsuitable for transplant. Some may have been damaged by illness or injury to the donor during their lifetime, or may simply be of insufficient quality for transplantation, thus compromising the chances of the recipient surviving the operation.

One of the other key factors that determines how donor organs are used is the size of the organs themselves. Donor organs clearly have to be able to fit into the space being vacated within the body of the recipient; the lungs of a large adult male are not going to fit into the chest cavity of small child and, conversely, a small child's lungs would not be transplanted into a fully-grown adult as they would not be developed enough to adequately perform in the much larger body. Whilst small surgical adjustments can be made to lungs through a procedure known as a *lobectomy*, this increases the chances of further complications downstream.

Incredulously, one of the lesser-known factors that prevents an organ transplant is that the recipient may have decided not to accept donor organs from a particular demographic, such as smokers or those from particular ethnic backgrounds. While this may seem foolhardy, perhaps even bordering on reckless, individuals must legally have their rights and wishes respected – regardless of the rationale behind them. Just for the record, however, I consented to accept lungs from *anyone*; if I am lucky enough to be offered of a pair of working, medically acceptable lungs that are a good fit for me and are from a blood-matched donor, could I really reject them? Could I reject something that might just save my life, and that might be the only offer I ever receive? No. For me, to refuse those lungs would be an act of pure folly.

In the UK, on any day, when a set of lungs become available for transplant, a highly complex yet well-refined procedure is set in motion to find the most appropriate recipient from those who are currently on the waiting list. Whilst this procedure gets underway, the donor organs are tested, both inside and outside of the donor's body, before any decision is taken as to whether the transplant operation should go ahead.

In around sixty percent of cases where a potential recipient is called to a hospital to await their life-saving transplant operation, the organs are, in the end, deemed unsuitable for transplant and the patient is sent away. Disappointed, to say the least, they must then simply take their place back on the waiting list and hope for better luck next time.

For the avoidance of doubt, the recipient doesn't simply go to the bottom of the list as if they have just missed an appointment at the dentist; the waiting list is run on the severity of recipient need and the suitability of the donor organs. You do not move up the waiting list over the course of time, as with a conventional waiting list, although you do if your condition worsens, as there is also an 'urgent list' for those whose life is in grave danger and who may not survive many more hours without new organs.

For me, as a person born with the congenital lung condition cystic fibrosis, the prospect of requiring a lung transplant at some point in my life has been a possibility since the day I was born in 1972. However, in the last three months of 2016, this possibility became a reality.

Following a difficult period of recurring chest infections, combined with a steady loss of lung function, my medical team and I first discussed going on the waiting list in September 2016. Ironically, only a short time prior to this, I was being told if I kept myself well, I should be able to avoid needing a transplant for a few years at least.

Unfortunately, though, over the past few months, conversations about my condition have taken on a more pessimistic tone, and the requirement for a transplant has now become very real. The chats where I was being told that there were still other options available – other medications to take and other treatments to try – have been replaced by conversations where I am told that those 'other options' have now run out and that things may not be *okay* after all.

This shift has been hard to accept. It would be hard enough for anyone to listen to, yet it is made even more difficult when feeling tired and unwell, struggling with simply keeping going on a daily basis, and doing all that's possible to stay out of hospital. It is very difficult to reconcile that all the hopes and aspirations I had for the future must be put on hold for an undetermined period of time while I wait my turn on the transplant merry-go-round.

The reality of the situation is stark.

Of course, I may survive the wait. The transplant may be successful, and I may be given the priceless gift of having a new life with new lungs to go out and enjoy; a real second chance to fulfil my dreams. However, the other side of that coin is that – by the very nature of needing to go on the waiting list – I am being advised that the state of my health is delicate and deteriorating and, frankly, that things are not looking good.

The only hope I can focus on now is that the call comes quickly and that I get my second chance. We all know we are going to die, of course. But being told you are closer to dying than even you had feared doesn't get any easier.

Given the immense risks involved, the decision to go on the list is not one to be taken lightly. The statistics are sobering. Seventy-five percent of people who are placed on the waiting list die before they are given new organs. Even if the call comes, and you are one of the lucky forty percent for whom the transplant goes ahead, surviving the first thirty days post-transplant is fraught with complications and danger; one in every ten recipients does not survive this period.

Post-transplant complications are wide-ranging and serious, from damage being caused to other organs, to a heightened risk of developing certain types of cancer, to organ rejection at any time. With this minefield of dangers ahead, even following a successful transplant, my long-term survivability remains a huge area of uncertainty.[3]

With all of that information swirling around in my head, it would be fair to say that I am terrified by the whole prospect; there are few surgical procedures that outstrip a lung transplant in terms of the sheer risks involved. But if I want to live a long and prosperous life, and see my children grow up, a transplant is my only viable option.

Even knowing that, whether or not I should join the waiting list has been a monumentally difficult decision to make. In the end, though, it feels like the right decision for me. Others decide that the whole prospect of a transplant is too much for them and opt not to go on the list at the crucial time. I have known several people who felt this way, and I have always respected that this is very much a personal decision. Anyone who decides a transplant is just one step too far should be given, in my view, the utmost consideration, empathy, and respect. However, in my case, despite all the statistics and the fear, I know this is something I *have* to do.

In the last three months or so, leading up to the phone call I just made, procedures and tests required for acceptance onto the list have been carried out. I have had meetings with various medical teams and discussions with many different doctors and other specialists. I have been scanned and x-rayed to the point where I must now glow in the dark. I have had so much blood taken that I'm surprised I have any left, and I have been prodded and poked in just about every way imaginable.

After all of that, the experts have decided that now is the right time for me to be listed.

In a way, it feels too soon. Despite the medical evidence indicating otherwise, I feel too 'well' for all of this. But if we do hold off, I may not have enough fight left in me to survive a potentially long wait on the list.

If I delay, there's every possibility that I will be deemed to be too ill to go on the list at all. This is crunch time – it could well be now or never.

Having said that, the process of getting on the list is not just based on my physical condition; I have spent an awfully long time working through the implications of my decision in my own mind and, in doing so, it has become patently clear that the mental and emotional hurdles are at least as important as the physical ones.

In fact, it would be fair to say that the physical assessment has been easier to deal with than the mental tug-of-war that's been played out in my head. And, for however long I am forced to wait for new lungs, I know that this emotional tussle will carry on.

In order to remain pragmatic during this time, some form of coping mechanism will have to be found. At this stage, though, *coping* seems far off and improbable.

Despite the fact that Christmas has only just been and gone, I have spent the past month performing particularly un-festive tasks such as updating my will, writing letters to my wife and family (to be filed away and opened in the event of my death), formulating a statement of wishes for my end of life care (just in case the transplant should not go as planned) and getting other financial and legal matters in order. Throw into that cocktail a high-speed road traffic accident between Christmas and New Year (our car was destroyed but we were, mercifully, unscathed), and it strikes me that the journey I've undertaken over the past three months – leading up to taking up my place on the list – has been a mental health minefield.

I keep telling myself it's all right to be a mess; to feel like I am drowning with the emotion of it all and that I'm unable to see a clear path forward. But I am torn between wanting to put on a brave face for those around me and needing to carry on so that I don't collapse under the weight of the anxiety I feel.

Nevertheless, I am here, and it is done. The call has been made and I am now 'live' on the list. I may have survived sixteen thousand, three hundred and twenty-nine days alive without officially needing new lungs to live but, as of today, that particular clock has stopped and a new one is ticking in its place. Like a stopwatch, the numbers on this new clock will increase as the days and weeks pass by until, eventually, my turn comes.

It strikes me as bizarre that there can be no formal countdown to such a monumental event taking place in one's life. After all, other major events such as milestone birthdays, weddings, and children being born all happen once a pre-determined waiting period is up. Thirty years. Two years. Nine months. However, with the waiting period for a transplant operation, the clock just continues ticking and there is no way of knowing when – or if – it will stop.

Even the most experienced and well-trained medical professionals cannot give any real estimate of when my transplant might happen. Even when pushed, they are very reluctant to hazard little more than a pure guess, relying simply on national averages. I was told during the preparation talks leading up to today that one of the worst things you can do whilst on the waiting list is to count the time that you are waiting. As someone who has always been fairly methodical and structured in my approach to things, and who likes living with good order and organisation, this will probably be one of the hardest things for me to come to terms with.

People who know me will agree that I love lists, timetables, and structure. So, going forward without knowing when my transplant may take place will be almost intolerable. That said, it is a part that I must now learn to play for as long as I am required to.

Because I have a 'rare' blood group type, rather than the average twelve to eighteen months waiting time, I have been told to expect a wait of at least eighteen to twenty-four months. I am not sure whether knowing this nugget of information makes the situation easier or harder to deal with.

From today, I will be living with the knowledge that the phone could ring at any time, day or night. Should the call come, I will be required to present myself at the transplant hospital as quickly as possible so that I'm ready if they decide to proceed with transplantation. I am required to inform the transplant team immediately if there is any change in my condition, medication, or treatments. I must also let them know if I travel anywhere that will increase my journey time getting to them should lungs become available. While on the list, I am not permitted to travel overseas and should do all I can to keep as fit and well as possible. I must stay contactable at all times and always ensure that I am in range of a mobile phone signal.

Some of the nicest and most caring people I have ever met have looked after me over the past three months and have held my hand, both virtually and physically, through the process leading up to officially listing. I have been told that there are people I can call if I need to talk about the transplant process, and that they will always be there to help.

Yet I feel so lost and so lonely.

Something about being on the transplant waiting list feels so intangible and uncertain. The future life I have always aspired to now seems distant and unobtainable, and the aspirations I once held a distant memory.

Over the weeks and months ahead, I know that it will be important to find a way to reconcile these feelings; to learn how to manage them and to store them away without disregarding them completely. After all, they tell the story of what makes me who I am and my approach to life (and equally I suppose to death).

As I sit here, alone and afraid, I try to reassure myself that things will work out.

I think about my life, about how far I have come and what I have achieved – even when others said it wasn't possible. Without warning, my mind fills with the image of my smiling wife and the sound of laughter from our young children. And, despite everything that is happening, I am consoled by an overriding sense of hope and optimism. A sense that, after this particularly difficult stage of my life is over, however far away that may be, things *will* turn out all right.

Because, despite all that life has thrown at me, they have done so far…

TWO

CYSTIC FIBROSIS AND ME

A QUICK TOUR

Before I go any further, some explanation of how I find myself in the position I have just described would probably be useful. After all, almost forty-eight years and a lifetime's worth of events took place prior to finding myself on the waiting list for a double lung transplant.

I fully appreciate that chronic lung disease is not the lightest of subjects for a book; describing a life blighted by it is likely to be, at best, rather dry and, at worst, miserable in the extreme. But I promise to lighten the mood where possible.

You see, my life hasn't been simply a gradual, and sometimes painful, downward spiral – my health declining to a point where my lungs have had enough, are waving a white flag, and are now on the verge of giving up entirely. On the contrary. In fact, it would be fair to say that there have been far more highs than lows in my life, and that I consider myself extremely fortunate to have had the opportunities I have.

Grabbing life firmly with one hand whilst fending off a serious medical condition with the other is the approach I have taken throughout my forty-eight years. But, for all of that to make sense, it must be framed against the backdrop of cystic fibrosis – what it is, how it affects those who have it, and what living with it means for me and my daily routine.

So, let me take you on a whistle-stop tour of cystic fibrosis, using as little medical jargon, and as much plain English, as possible. Ready? Then kindly strap yourself in and brace yourself because, during the journey ahead, we will undoubtedly experience some turbulence (the aviation references will become obvious/humorous in later chapters).

Although events leading up to going on the waiting list accelerated rapidly during the latter stages of 2016, the prospect of me requiring a double lung transplant could not be considered as 'unexpected' in any way. This was always how things were going to transpire for me, and a lung transplant being a milestone in my life, whilst not inevitable in the true definition of the word, was certainly *probable*. That said, simply knowing that it was likely to happen has not made arriving at this point any easier, nor has it made the deep sense of uncertainty I feel for the future any more palatable.

But we are where we are, and I try to frequently remind myself that, strictly speaking, I shouldn't still be around. And that, actually, I am extremely fortunate to have all these years of memories to lose myself in when the need to escape from the present situation becomes overbearing.

When I was born, the chances of me reaching the age I am now were thought to be almost zero, Improvements in healthcare and medication have allowed me to get to this point, and further improvements in both will hopefully continue to work in my favour while I wait for my lung transplant and in the future.

As a person with cystic fibrosis, I regard myself as extremely lucky to be the age I am, living how I am living, and with enough of my marbles left to be able to sit down and write about my life. Whilst many would find the concept of being born with a serious lung disease anything but lucky, my version of luck is different to most people's.

Yes, there have been times when that luck nearly ran out. But I am still here, writing my story, and harbouring hopes for what the next chapters of my life will bring.

It is this overriding sense of good fortune that makes me get up and keep going each day– this, and the knowledge that any day could be the day the call comes through from the transplant team and things change forever.

I was born 3rd May 1972 in Ashford Hospital, Middlesex. Twenty months prior to my arrival, my older sister Louise had been born with no abnormalities or identifiable health defects of any type. However, as I grew older, my parents noticed that I was struggling to gain weight. These concerns came to a head just after my first birthday, and I underwent tests for conditions that might explain my 'failure to thrive'.

These tests revealed a much higher concentration of salt (chloride) in my sweat than the normal amounts seen in children of a similar age. In conjunction with my inability to gain weight and with being quite an unwell baby throughout my first year in terms of digestive problems, this made it clear to the doctors exactly what my condition was.

At thirteen months of age, I was diagnosed with the genetic condition cystic fibrosis (CF). My parents were told I would be lucky to make it to double figures in terms of life expectancy. They were devastated, but having a name for my condition meant that my symptoms could at least be brought under some semblance of control, and that the correct course of treatment could begin in order to prolong my life as much as possible.

It also meant that, from that point on, my life would take a very different path to most children. My health would effectively have to be micro-managed for the rest of my life with hospital visits, medication, and physiotherapy becoming part of my everyday routines.

But what exactly is CF?

CF is a genetic condition which affects nearly eleven thousand people in the UK. In any given week, two people will die of CF-related illnesses and five babies will be born with the condition. Only half of those born with CF are expected to reach forty-seven years of age and the median age of those who die of the condition is just 31[1].

The gene affected by CF controls the movement of salt and water in and out of cells throughout the body. This movement is compromised in the cells of people with CF resulting in a build-up of mucus in the lungs, digestive system and other organs within the body, particularly the pancreas, liver and kidneys. This mucus, if left untreated and allowed to accumulate, can cause infection that damages the organs affected. In people unaffected by CF, the body retains the ability to regulate the production and build-up of mucus so that the organs remain clear and can function normally.

CF can neither be caught from someone with the condition, nor can you develop it if you don't have it from birth. One in 25 people carry the defective CF gene, and for someone to be born with CF, both parents must carry this defective gene. If this is the case, then there is still only a one in four chance that their children will be born with CF. Everyone with CF has two faulty or 'mutated' genes (one inherited from each parent). There are currently over two thousand known mutations and these two faulty genes can be either the same type or two different ones. The specific mutation combination is known as the 'genotype' and it is this which dictates the exact range of symptoms that a person with CF will experience and to what degree or severity. It will also affect some of the treatments and medications that those people can take.

Any given person with CF will have a different range of symptoms to the next, so any two individuals can have very different experiences of living with CF and of how they are required to manage the challenges that the condition brings.

Great strides have been made in medical research over recent years to provide early diagnoses for those suspected of having CF. Whilst the heel prick test and the sweat test are used regularly to diagnose CF in new born babies, modern medical science now enables screening for many genetic disorders (including CF), so the process can start well before the child is even born. An increasing number of couples now opt for antenatal testing for genetic disorders such as CF before even getting pregnant. In couples where one person is likely to be a carrier of a faulty gene, the other partner's blood can be screened early on for the most common CF genes in order to assess whether there is an enhanced risk of their future children being born with CF. If the other partner's test is clear, then their future children will not have CF. If the partner is also a carrier of a faulty gene, there is a one in four chance that any children they have will be born with the condition.

The most common symptoms for those with CF are related to the lungs and respiratory system. Issues such as recurring chest infections, a persistent cough and restricted breathing are part and parcel of daily life for those with the condition. Over the course of time, the lungs become increasingly damaged through infection and, as lung damage progresses, the scarring process (known as *fibrosis*) leads to a loss of lung function. It is this loss of function that can eventually result in the requirement for a double lung transplant.

A healthy pair of lungs is coated with a thin layer of mucus which aids in the removal of bacteria and other pollutants. In lungs affected by CF, this mucus is thicker and stickier. It can accumulate on the lungs and within the airways themselves, which creates the perfect environment for bacteria to thrive, causing infection and damage to the lungs and the airways. Such damage results in a progressive loss of lung function with the associated increase in shortness of breath, tightness, and wheezing.

Most people with CF will take some form of preventative or 'prophylactic' antibiotics (which fight off bacteria before they can take hold). Additional antibiotic treatment will be required when the bacteria is of a particularly stubborn type that gets through this first line of defence.

Antibiotics can be either taken orally in tablet form, by way of a nebuliser or via an intravenous (IV) line direct into the patient's blood stream. The toxicity of the drugs administered, particularly by IV, is such that they can damage the liver, kidneys, and hearing. Toxicity levels are measured whilst the patient is on these drugs so that such damage can be avoided wherever possible. Tinnitus, more commonly known as ringing in the ears, is just one example of an unwanted side effect and, unless use of the drugs is stopped and alternatives are sought, a complete loss of hearing is a strong possibility.

Exacerbations in chest infections are most commonly dealt with by antibiotics that are given in combinations. This reduces the risk of bacteria becoming too familiar with just one type of antibiotic and therefore less responsive. They are generally given to the patient in IV form as effectiveness is lost if they are given in an oral tablet form. Whilst some IV antibiotics can be administered to patients solely in a hospital setting, CF patients are encouraged wherever possible to self-administer their own IV antibiotics at home (what we refer to as 'home IVs') as this reduces the need for inpatient hospital stays and frees up limited healthcare resources.

While the availability and range of IV antibiotic treatment has developed greatly in recent times, the prevalence of antibiotic resistant bacteria has become a real issue and is now considered to be one of the biggest threats to humanity in the 21st century. Antibiotic resistance is the process by which bacteria become immune to a particular antibiotic. Over-use of antibiotics in the past, particularly for illnesses against which they have little effect (such as the common cold) has only exacerbated this situation.

Now, older, less developed antibiotics are having to be used. They are generally less effective and can harbour unpleasant side effects. A matter of specific concern to CF practitioners is that there is an increasing number of CF patients being diagnosed with certain types of bacteria that can be suppressed through combination IV therapy but that cannot be eradicated entirely. But we will revisit these later, with reference to a certain bacterium called non-tuberculosis mycobacterium (NTM) abscessus which, through bitter experience, I have become something of an expert in over my CF career.

Once damage to the lungs has progressed to the point at which the patient's quality of life is severely compromised, the only remaining course of action available is a double lung transplant. But life post-transplant presents its own range of challenges too; while CF is not eradicated in those who have had a lung transplant, many symptoms synonymous with CF are replaced by others that require equally careful monitoring and management.

Complications with the digestive system are common in those with CF too; we are unable to process fat normally and efficiently. In healthy people, the pancreas creates natural enzymes which assist in the breakdown of fat, proteins, and carbohydrates in food. In people with CF, the small tubes that transport those natural enzymes from the pancreas can become blocked with mucus, preventing the enzymes from reaching the digestive system. Consequently, people with CF need to take pancreatic enzyme supplements with food to replace those natural enzymes and to aid digestion. These drugs help to ensure that fat, along with vitamins and other nutrients, is absorbed from food in appropriate quantities.

Due to difficulties in breaking down fat, people with CF often suffer from digestive symptoms such as difficult bowel movements, constipation, nausea, a swollen abdomen, bowel blockages, and a loss of appetite. Many people with CF will also be of a lower average weight than others of the same sex and height. It is therefore important that we eat a high-fat diet to compensate for the loss of absorption. Low body weight can lead to complications and can increase susceptibility to infection and illness.

It can be a daily challenge for those with CF to match the appropriate number of enzymes to what types of food are being consumed, although most of us become experts at it eventually.

As the pancreas becomes inflamed and scarred, the production of insulin by the pancreas is affected. This can result in CF-related diabetes, or CFRD for short. CFRD is common; around thirty percent of adolescents and adults with CF are also being treated for CFRD, and those with CF are regularly tested for CFRD through routine blood tests and blood glucose monitoring.

This means that CFRD tends to be picked up before any of the main symptoms present themselves (weight loss, increased thirst, and the need to pass urine more frequently). It is treated through the careful management of blood glucose levels and through regular insulin injections. If left untreated, however, CFRD can lead to other health complications such as low body weight, chest infections, reduced lung function, kidney damage, and eyesight problems.

CF can also cause the blockage of the small ducts within the liver, which can lead to liver damage and, if left untreated, liver failure. Around forty percent of people with CF will have some form of liver abnormalities, although, through the improvements being made with diagnostics and screening, this figure is increasing. Regular ultrasounds and blood tests are used to closely monitor the performance and appearance of the liver in CF patients, and medication can be used to slow the rate of deterioration in liver function. Should the liver become too damaged to work properly, then the patient may require a liver transplant.

In people with CF, bones are less well developed than in those without the condition and begin to thin at a much younger age. Osteopenia and osteoporosis (where the bones are of a lower mass than they should be) mean that CF bones are more fragile and more likely to fracture. We are more prone to developing bone disease primarily because calcium and other nutrients from food are not absorbed properly. The use of oral steroids, although a useful tool in reducing inflammation of the lungs and prolonging lung function, can also have a detrimental impact on bone mass and those CF patients who are exposed to long term or regular steroid treatment are more likely to exhibit signs of bone disease.

Sinusitis is also common in CF patients, caused by a build-up of mucus in the sinuses. Symptoms include facial pain, chronic nasal congestion, nasal polyps, loss of taste and/or smell, headaches, and a constant need to clear the throat. Nasal polyps, too, must often be surgically removed to ease the discomfort they cause.

I hope this gives you a flavour of what having CF means to those with the disease. CF should not be considered a single condition, but rather a combination of various health complications caused by a single underlying genetic fault. On any given day, any one of the issues raised above can flare up and cause pain and discomfort requiring immediate medical intervention. If you are lucky, it will be *just* one, but often it is more.

With CF, the concept of feeling 'well' is possibly very different to that held by most people. On a 'good' day with CF, I might just have a bad chest, or a tummy ache, or feel incredibly tired and generally washed out. On a bad day, it can be all these plus other symptoms too, putting me in a hospital bed for an indeterminate amount of time and away from my family and friends.

CF is often described as an invisible disease. To many, I might look 'normal' on the outside, but the truth is that I am anything *but* normal. Bits of me are decaying, failing, and becoming increasingly unable to perform their function. Medication can slow the rate of my decline, but there is no 'silver bullet' that will save me from CF in the end. A double lung transplant might reset the clock in terms of my lungs, but CF will eventually attack my new lungs too.

However, if we leave all of that aside just for a moment, it is of utmost importance as you make your way through the following chapters that you try your best to see things from my point of view. Yes, life with CF is tough and there are no easy days, but this does not mean that you should feel sorry for me. After all, I do not feel sorry for *myself.* I have CF. I will always have CF. And nothing will ever change that.

Having CF means that I have lived a different life to most. Yet I don't consider that my life has been worse because of having CF. For all the pain and distress that CF has put me through over the years, it has also made me who I am. I am proud of the way that I have lived and the way I have dealt with CF, and *that* is what I'd like you to remember as you read on.

THREE
SPINNING PLATES

As you have seen, CF presents a multitude of symptoms and dealing with these is a daily struggle that affords no let up at all. It has always been my view that the effective management of these symptoms is rather like spinning plates; regardless of just how many plates are spinning at any one time, each plate must be watched, managed, and manipulated to avoid them dropping to the floor and smashing, thus spoiling the whole show.

In much the same way, in order to manage my CF, I am required to take multiple medications, perform physiotherapy (perhaps several times a day), eat well and exercise, rest when required to, attend hospital appointments, and manage stock levels of numerous drugs so that I never run out of, perhaps, up to twenty different types of medications.

These activities, like each spinning plate, have to be performed daily, even if I am feeling unwell, short of breath, tired and washed out, or suffering from the side-effects of the medication I take. Quite often, it will be several of these simultaneously.

Whilst treatments of the symptoms of CF are constantly developing, the burden on those with CF is high. We can be required to take typically around fifty tablets a day to manage both our primary and secondary symptoms. These can be in the form of antibiotics, pancreatic enzymes, mucolytics (to assist in the breakdown of mucus), steroids to reduce inflammation in the airways, vitamins, iron and calcium supplements to aid nutrition and bone development, and other medications to reduce damage to the liver and kidneys. This is over and above bronchodilator drugs (normally in the form of inhalers or dispensed via a nebuliser) to open the airways by relaxing the surrounding muscles thus relieving tightness and shortness of breath.

Though some people living with CF have families, partners, or friends who assist them with some or all these activities, many don't. And this makes the burden of treatment even greater.

I am extremely fortunate to have a wife who ensures I adhere to my treatment regime every day, and I am very conscious of how difficult it must be for those who do not have such support around them.

It would not be an over-exaggeration to say that most people with CF spend several hours each day managing their version of the condition. This can be laborious and demoralising. I have heard the daily treatment of CF being likened to brushing your teeth for several hours every day of the week, every week of the year. Except, the consequences of not sticking to your routine are much more severe than a build-up of plaque.

In as much as anything is 'typical' with CF, I will try to describe what a typical day means to me.

Percussion

The day starts with waking up feeling chesty and clogged up. As my lungs have largely been inactive overnight, save for shallow breathing as I sleep, this inactivity allows for mucus to build up. Before anything can happen, my lungs need clearing so that they can function better throughout the day. So, straight after waking up, I undertake an hour-long physiotherapy session. On a particularly bad day, it can take longer.

I start by using an inhaler loaded with the drug *salbutamol*. Many people will recognise these inhalers as the blue-coloured ones that are given to those with asthma. Salbutamol relaxes the muscles around the airways, widening the airways themselves and making it easier to breathe.

Following this, I spend ten minutes breathing in what is effectively salty water. This salty water, or hypertonic saline, to give it its medical name, has a very high concentration of salt in every water particle (seven percent), so it is very effective in hydrating the lungs. Upon inhalation, the vapour forms a thin film in the airways which makes it harder for the mucus to stick. It can also help to break down any mucus that has already built up in the lungs and surrounding airways.

After breathing in the hypertonic saline, there then follows something that, in any other area of life, could be classed as physical assault. When carried out on a CF person, however, it is given the rather more positive sounding and medically acceptable term of 'physiotherapy'. Put simply, the person undergoing the physio sits or lies down and is patted or slapped on their sides and back in order to physically dislodge the mucus from the lungs (a process known as 'percussion', the irony of which will become clear in later chapters). Once dislodged, the mucus has then to be cleared through a variety of breathing exercises (known as Active Cycle Breathing or ACB) and/or through coughing.

When I was younger, my dad would perform this ritual for me every morning before I left for school. Each time, he would pull the curtains to the window in my bedroom which overlooked the pavement and street below. It was many years before I eventually asked him the reasoning behind this curious action. "Well, Luke," my dad responded with his usual dry, Yorkshire-style of delivering humour, "the sight of a grown adult beating a small boy, seemingly, within an inch of his life, regardless of how innocent the reasons behind it may be, could be quite alarming to a passer-by down on the street below. So, I always closed the curtains to protect myself from receiving a call from the authorities at some point!"

As the years rolled on, I was shown how to carry physiotherapy out on myself and still do so now, every day, twice a day. When in hospital, a member of the physiotherapy department will assist with the percussion, as they are trained in particular techniques and can apply it to parts of my back that I can't reach, thus shifting the sputum quicker and more easily than if I were just to do it myself. The process continues until either it feels like the lungs are clear or, more commonly, I have simply run out of energy from coughing and need a good rest. This is typically after thirty to forty minutes, depending on the severity of my congestion on that day.

Once the lungs are as clear as I can get them, I then spend a further ten minutes breathing in an antibiotic drug via the nebuliser. This allows it to get into the very small airways of the lungs and get to work on the bacteria that thrives there. Once this final part of the process is completed, the nebuliser needs to be cleaned, dried, and put away for the next physiotherapy session.

I try to fit in my first round of physiotherapy as soon as I get up. This is largely to get the lungs cleared and make my breathing easier before I can start to try to do anything. But I have also learned the hard way that trying to do the physiotherapy too soon after eating never ends well. With all that percussion and coughing, breakfast rarely wants to stay in the stomach and is likely to make an unwanted re-appearance. I therefore have a rule of thumb not to do my physiotherapy session within two hours of eating unless it cannot be avoided. I tend to have a second round of physiotherapy in the late afternoon and before dinner in the evening. Once again lasting about an hour, this second session will see me through the evening and the into the night, ready to start all over again the following morning.

It is not that long ago that I only needed to perform this ritual once a day at tea-time. This would see my lungs cleared enough to last through to the same time the following day. But as the damage to my lungs has progressed, particularly in the past three years, twice a day has become the minimum number of sessions that I can get away with if I want to function anywhere near *normally*. Occasionally, I will perform a third round of physio in the middle of the day if I am feeling particularly clogged up or if I'm struggling, possibly due to the start of an infection taking hold. The monotony of all this is hard to put into words, as is the demoralising feeling I get when, at the end of the day, I feel like I have done some really good physio and chest clearance, only to wake just a few hours later needing to start the process all over again.

The physio required of those with CF is a vital element in the arsenal used to fight the condition. But it is also tiring, laborious, and can leave you feeling battered and bruised. I'll admit that there are times when these feelings take over and I end up missing a session. Sometimes, though, I miss one simply because I am out and about for the day and finding an appropriate place, or time, to carry out the physio is just too difficult. In such cases, I simply have to accept I have missed a session and that the next session is likely to be more difficult and, consequently, longer than usual.

Pills

Apart from the physio, CF for me means taking tablets, almost by the bucket load, at regular intervals throughout the day. I take up to ten pancreatic enzyme tablets ('Creon' capsules) with main meals, and slightly fewer with snacks. A typical day will therefore see me take somewhere in the order of forty of these capsules. I also take tablets for vitamins, calcium, iron, and to prevent acid reflux from my stomach. Occasionally, if feeling nauseous, I will take anti-sickness tablets too.

I take four different antibiotics in tablet form, to suppress the bacteria in my lungs, in addition to the one antibiotic that I take via the nebuliser after my physio.

I take another tablet to protect my liver, and a further tablet to relax my airways and reduce chest tightness. Occasionally, I take steroids too.

Finally, I take capsules to thin the mucus in my lungs. So, over and above the forty-or-so enzyme capsules I take with food or drink, I take a further twenty tablets a day to cover everything else.

I often say that the management alone of all these different medicines is a full-time job; ensuring that I have enough of each drug to keep me going until my next prescription is ready. At least I have something else to do whilst not carrying out my physio, I suppose!

If you're now starting to think, '*Blimey, this must be costing the NHS a small fortune*,' then, for the sake of completeness, you also need to factor in the three different inhalers that I use twice a day, and the drug I take via an injection three times a week to boost my immune system. Which, perhaps, is why every six months my GP invites me to come in and have a friendly chat about what I am taking, why I am taking it, and whether I *really* need to be taking everything on my prescription list.

So, in addition to taking all this medication and performing the twice-a-day physiotherapy, a life with CF means keeping myself as well and as fit as I can.

Food

I aim to consume somewhere in the order of three to three-and-a-half thousand calories per day to maintain my weight. Whilst I am not as heavy as I would like to be, I am just within the 'healthy' Body Mass Index (BMI) range for an adult male. I have always struggled to gain weight and have been much lower than this in the past. Thankfully, I have been stuck around this level for several years now. I was told that a minimum BMI of eighteen was required to be on the transplant list, so I have a little bit of wriggle room to play with at my current weight. But I need to remember that the heavier I am, the stronger my body will be, and the better it will be able to see me through the transplant operation and support me during my recovery.

In addition to managing my calorie intake on a daily basis, I also get hooked up overnight to a machine three or four times a week. This machine pumps a litre of what can only be described as gloop via a tube, through my nostril and down into my stomach. The gloop provides an additional two thousand calories each time I do it. Whilst invasive and unpleasant in equal measure, it is an easy way to take on board a lot of calories quickly, and ensures that my BMI stays in the acceptable range for transplant – just another unpleasant but necessary part of life with CF.

Rest and activity

Physical activity is important for those with CF as exercising the lungs, causing repeated cycles of expansion and contraction, can help to remove mucus and hence reduces the likeliness of infection. Exercise also improves strength and general health. Those with the condition are encouraged to undertake as much physical exercise as possible but also to keep within their limits as over-exercising can lead to weight loss and damage to the lungs. We also have regular consultations with physiotherapists who advise on the best form of exercise given the extent to which we are affected by CF and help us to set personalised targets of what we should aim to achieve through exercise.

As the damage to my lungs progresses, physical activity becomes harder. I am still fortunate enough to be able to get around without the need for supplementary oxygen, although I am aware that those days are probably fast running out.

On particularly tough days, I become short of breath just climbing the stairs at home or putting the rubbish out. I have always tried to see such mundane activities as part of the process of keeping active and whilst performing such tasks can be exhausting for a time, they are good at getting my lungs working.

A couple of years ago, my wife bought me a fitness monitor watch for Father's Day. I now use this to try to achieve 10,000 steps each day, roughly the equivalent to five miles of walking. While most other activities and sports are no longer available to me because of my lungs, I do endeavour to keep moving as much as my body will allow. Occasionally, I will venture on to the treadmill we have at home (bought a few years ago when I had good intentions to use it regularly but which, in reality, saw little use). I try to walk for twenty or thirty minutes with a slight incline, but this is hard work and the need to rest at the end is inevitable.

Speaking of rest, us CF patients are always being reminded to listen to our bodies and to take rest when we need to. After all, running your body into the ground is the best way to encourage infection to take hold and you're likely to find yourself being treated for a chest infection, at best, or even ending up in hospital.

Those who know me best will agree that I have always been rather obstinate when it comes to identifying the need to rest. For this, I blame the little CF voice in my head that tells me if I don't stay active and busy, I will start to fade away.

Since going on the transplant waiting list, however, I have been more open to the importance of resting and I do try to rest during the day if I can. It was explained to me recently that I should see my energy for any one day like a glass of water. You can drink it all in the morning, but if you do you'll have nothing left for the rest of the day. Conversely, you can drink a little throughout the morning and have enough to keep you going into the afternoon and evening. If you have something big going on later in the day that will need a lot of energy, then just take small sips to ensure you have enough left over for later. Others refer to 'spoon theory', which is very similar to my imaginary glass of water (do look it up, but don't confuse it with how you and your partner may sleep in bed together – different sort of 'spoons' entirely).

Now that I have a way to visualise my energy levels through the image of this glass of water, I have got better at managing my activity and rest so that I can contribute to family life as well at the end of the day as I can at the start. And whilst that little voice in my head has not been silenced entirely, its volume has been turned down a few notches in recent times.

As my condition has deteriorated, and as treatments and medications have changed, my daily routine has changed over the years. Going on the transplant list has not added anything new to that routine particularly but has made the adherence to it much more important; I know I must keep myself as well as possible for when my chance comes.

When people ask how it feels to have lungs like mine, I tell them to imagine themselves doing everything they normally do but with a heavy cold and with a damp flannel fixed over their mouth and nose while they do it. Others have described the feeling as spending life breathing through a straw. Either way, you get the picture.

Measurements

As anyone with CF will tell you, my world often seems to revolve around lung function and the relentless measuring of it. At every clinic appointment as an outpatient, and often when hospitalised too, there is a real sense of enthusiasm for measuring lung function in order to put numbers against how I am feeling.

While those numbers are, obviously, important and can give the medical practitioners a great deal of information, they do not always tell the whole story. Many a time, I have been feeling reasonably well and the best I have felt in a long while, yet my lung function has shown a drop since the previous recording. The CF team that looks after me, however, is very good at considering other factors and using those in conjunction with the lung function figures before deciding on any course of action.

At each clinic appointment (which, for me, occur every four to six weeks when I am well), and before the real conversations get started with the consultant, I am required to blow into a plastic tube attached to a computer that records my lung function so that the doctors have a general idea of where I am and how I might be feeling.

It is not that long ago that this tube was connected to a device which pneumatically forced a pencil down a piece of graph paper. Where the pencil line stopped, this was visually interpreted to be your lung function on that actual day. This rather Heath-Robinson contraption has since (thankfully) been replaced by computers, software, and automation with the associated improvements in accuracy.

When measuring lung function, the respiratory physiologist will tell me to take a deep breath in and then to blow out as hard and as fast as I can for as long as I can.

For someone with normally functioning lungs, this may sound easy, possibly even bordering on fun. For a person with CF, however, this ritual is, at best, hard work. At its worst, it can instigate seemingly unstoppable coughing fits and dizzy spells.

The purpose of this breathing test is to measure what is known as a patient's FEV1 value (forced expiratory volume over one second). Put simply, FEV1 gives you an indication of how well your lungs are working compared to similar people in the general population.

Only a few years ago, doctors involved in the treatment of CF used a threshold of thirty percent FEV1 predicted in deciding when a patient should be considered for transplant. Such rigid thresholds have been side-lined in recent years to incorporate a broader scope of thinking, such as how declining lung function is affecting someone's quality of life and what that patient is still able and not able to do.

For many years, my FEV1 had bobbed around the thirty-seven to forty percent mark, dipping occasionally when a chest infection was taking hold and requiring a course of IV antibiotics to bring me back to my baseline level. But, looking back now, there was a watershed moment in late 2015 when this cycle started to change. At first, these changes were subtle, but they eventually progressed to the point where I was having to decide whether to go on the transplant list.

Throughout the second half of 2015, slight fluctuations in lung function were being recorded at each of my clinic appointments at Royal Papworth Hospital ('Papworth') and at the Adult Cystic Fibrosis Centre I attend. This was nothing spectacular at first; certainly not enough to attract anything other than a passing comment by the consultants before being sent on my way for another month.

Initially, these fluctuations were put down to me being tired, feeling under the weather, or simply having an 'off day', all of which were perfectly plausible conclusions to reach given that there was no other evidence of infection.

However, I have always been a stickler for even the finest details regarding my health, and by the end of 2015 I'd started to become a little more concerned about the instability in lung function that was being recorded.

By the tail end of 2015, my lung function was consistently registering around the mid-thirty percent mark and it was at this point that I was asked to start considering whether I would be open to going on the transplant waiting list when the appropriate time came.

The CF Team at Papworth were also keen to introduce me to the transplant team there so that they were aware of me and my medical history ('on their radar screen' as it was put to me) long before they would be called upon to actually do anything with me. As it turned out, following my referral to the transplant assessment team, I was deemed to be outside of the boundaries of acceptable risk at Papworth (for reasons I will go through later) and the process ended there.

Thankfully, and following a second referral to the transplant team at Harefield Hospital ('Harefield') northwest of London, I was accepted as a possible candidate for a double lung transplant there, subject to passing the transplant assessment tests. From then on, I would be in the privileged position of having not one but two specialist medical teams looking after me and my wellbeing, albeit located one hundred miles apart from each other.

By early 2016 it was becoming apparent that the fluctuations in my lung function were starting to morph into a gradual but steady decline. As each month ticked by, my concerns were listened to and discussions were had at Papworth about what else I could try in terms of treatment that would help to increase lung function, reduce chest tightness, and, if not improve my quality of life, then maintain it at its current level.

Even up to the middle of 2016, the prospect of going through the transplant assessment process and the possibility of requiring a double lung transplant, whilst getting closer than it once was, remained a distant one. In fact, my consultation with the specialist transplant doctor at Harefield in April 2016 took the form more of a friendly chat ending with his optimistic sign off of, "You are still a long way off needing a transplant, so I'll see you in a year's time for your next check-up."

What a difference a few months can make!

After the way the second half of 2016 played out, it would be very easy to feel frustrated, even angry, at those seemingly throw away comments. But I am one of those people with CF whose descent towards the transplant process was a rapid and chaotic one, rather than a slow decline over a period of years. "Dropping off a cliff," is how another practitioner described it to me, and a more accurate description is hard to find.

After spending the latter half of 2016 in and out of Papworth with numerous elongated inpatient stays, the decision was finally taken – by Harefield and Papworth collectively – that the time was right for me to begin formal assessment for transplant listing.

Most of the tests were carried out at Papworth whilst I was incarcerated there during September and October 2016, which meant that I could be on site and available as spaces became free on the CT scanners and other equipment that would provide the vital information required by the team at Harefield.

By November 2016, with my FEV1 percentages now firmly stuck in the low to mid-twenties, I received the news that I had been provisionally accepted as a transplant patient at Harefield and that I could be placed 'live' onto the waiting list as soon as I was ready.

It is very hard to describe how it feels to receive such news. On the one hand, I knew that a transplant offered me the best chance I might get of prolonging my life, spending more time with my wife and children, and doing so many of the things that I still want to do. On the other, it was hard not to dwell on the stark reality of the situation; my lungs were now so badly damaged that they would not keep me going for too much longer without a transplant and, without sugar-coating the situation, death was a much nearer prospect than I had considered it to be just a few short months previously.

No breaks

Having CF is pervasive. No matter what I do, it is ever-present.

If there is one thing I would like you to bear in mind when reading what comes next, it is this; everything that happens to me in the forthcoming chapters occurs against a backdrop of all that CF throws at me. Whether this is feeling unwell or tired, or having a chest that feels constantly clogged up and tight, these the things that anyone with CF faces every single day.

From the seemingly endless rounds of physiotherapy to taking cocktails of medication sometimes multiple times each day, CF can be oppressive. Its effects never take a leave of absence, and I really do mean *never.*

There is no let up. There are no 'mini-breaks' from the symptoms and no holidays from the feelings and emotions that having CF creates.

Sometimes, I catch myself thinking about how wonderful it would be to have a few days off from CF; a few short days just to step away from the drugs and the treatments, to take a few breaths, and to enjoy some time for respite. But such breaks never come and finding a mechanism to cope with this fact is just as important as those drugs and treatments are in order to stay on an even keel.

CF is always there – like an overbearing hand on my shoulder attempting to hold me back from getting on with life. But this hand also acts as a reminder that, despite its presence and its influence, I deserve as much of a life as anybody else.

It is this train of thought that has motivated me throughout my life and that has allowed me to experience so many wonderful things.

My outlook has always to been to get on with life as best as I can *despite* having CF rather than because of it, and to not let the condition define me and what I can do. After all, I see myself as just 'Luke' – a complete person in my own right with my own thoughts, feelings, and aspirations. CF just happens to come along with me like an uninvited hanger-on that I just can't seem to shake off.

A life with CF is all I've known. Everything I do to manage my condition is part of me and it is just what I need to do so that I can spend the rest of my time each day on more rewarding and enjoyable activities.

I fully accept that life would be very different without the burden of CF hanging over me and my family. Yet, living with CF constantly reminds me to appreciate what I can do, to value what I have, and to make the very best of each day. And if I cannot silence that little voice of CF in my head entirely, then what better way to drown it out with a much louder one which tells me to get up, grab each day with both hands, and – most importantly – enjoy life for what it offers rather than to dwell on what CF might take away.

THE EARLY YEARS

FOUR
MEMORIES OF A CHILDHOOD WITH CF

For the first three years of my life, my family lived in a modest Victorian semi-detached house in Sunbury-on-Thames, to the west of London and close to Heathrow Airport. My dad, a tall, dark, self-assured Yorkshireman who was never backwards in coming forwards – in either words or actions – worked as a researcher and lecturer in molecular biology at the Middlesex Hospital Medical School. My mum, a blonde-haired, politely-spoken West Londoner stayed at home with my sister and me. Having been diagnosed with CF at thirteen months of age, my parents felt that it was appropriate for one of them to stay at home to keep an eye on me, certainly during my early years. The treatments and medication for CF were far more primitive back in the early 1970s than they are today, and having a child diagnosed with the condition meant a steep learning curve for them both. Being a parent now myself, I can only imagine the emotional rollercoaster of being told that your child has a serious and life-threatening health condition. My diagnosis caused my parents a huge amount of stress and many sleepless nights. It had come as even more of a shock to them given that my elder sister Louise (born twenty months before me) was a fit and well little girl with no health issues whatsoever.

In early 1975, my dad was offered a new position with the Medical Research Council. It was setting up a clinical oncology research unit in conjunction with the University of Cambridge at Addenbrooke's Hospital, the main hospital just outside Cambridge in the east of England. This unit would work towards developing treatments for a wide range of cancers and would investigate how and why cancer attacks healthy cells within the body the way that it does

A move to the fresh air of rural Cambridgeshire must have seemed like a good idea for all of us because my dad accepted the position. I'm sure it didn't hurt, also, that Addenbrooke's was one of the world's leading teaching hospitals (conveniently, with a renowned Paediatric Health Unit for sick children).

So, in the spring of 1975 my parents, my sister Louise, and myself left Sunbury and moved to the village of Stapleford, just to the south of Cambridge, to begin our new lives in semi-rural East Anglia.

We moved into a newly built three-bedroom house with a small back garden in a quiet cul-de-sac. The whole street was new, having just been built on former farmland. As the building work progressed along the street, and as each house in turn was completed and occupied with new owners, many of which were young families like ours, there was a real sense of community and lots of other children close by for my sister and I to play with.

In an age when the roads were largely empty and you could still guarantee how long it would take to get anywhere by car, my dad could be at work in his laboratory at the hospital in less than ten minutes, and we could be in the city centre of Cambridge in less than fifteen.

Not long after moving to Stapleford, my parents – who had always wanted a third child – started looking into adoption. I have since been told that, following my diagnosis, they ruled out having a third child naturally as they did not want to run the risk of having another child born with CF.

Given my age, I would have been too young to be particularly involved (or probably even interested) in the process going on around me or the stress that it must have caused my parents. Yet I can recall, as if it were yesterday, the day my parents returned, after a long day away in Birmingham, with a small girl in their arms, telling my sister and I that this child was our new baby sister, Faith.

Faith was six months old, from an Afro-Caribbean background, and had been put up for adoption by her birth mum in Birmingham who was very young and unable to cope with the rearing of a baby at that stage of her life. So, from that day on, our family was made up of five members, and I was outnumbered by my sisters, two to one.

My childhood was generally happy, and I managed to survive it largely unscathed from the effects that CF would have on me later in life. There was the occasional absent day from school for colds or tummy problems but no more so than my sisters nor any of my peers. And as a child, although I recall being aware that I was slightly different to my classmates, I don't think I ever really understood why or even took much interest in the situation.

One thing I can be clear about, though, is that – as a child – I certainly didn't know that, as I grew older, my deviation from the path of a *normal* healthy life would begin to increase. Maybe it was never explained to me in a way that I could properly understand, or perhaps my parents simply didn't want me to be troubled with it at such an early age. Either way, life went on and I just concentrated on being a happy and generally healthy little boy.

As my first year of school progressed and 1976 became 1977, things were going well for me. CF in these early years did little more than just lurk in the background. Given that this was the case, and unknown to me at the time, my early school career was going to be interrupted massively in the summer of 1977. Although you may be expecting CF to have dealt me some form of devastating blow health-wise, what took place could not be further from that.

As I was keeping well, and my CF was largely under control, my dad applied to take a sabbatical year from his job in Cambridge to work overseas. Initially, it was discussed between my parents that my dad would go on his own and shuttle backwards and forwards as often as he could to visit us. After all, it was only to be a year. However, somewhere along the line, this plan changed – probably after he secured a prestigious position in the USA. It was then decided that we would all go, renting our house out in Stapleford and travelling to somewhere where we had no family and no friends; quite a dramatic change for a five year old boy! So, in the summer of 1977, once the academic year had finished in the UK, we packed our lives into suitcases, said goodbye to our friends and family, and set off on a six thousand mile journey to begin our new, albeit temporary, lives in San Francisco, California, USA.

Whilst I am sure that setting off on this journey must have been a daunting experience for the whole family, I have to admire the fact that my parents saw an opportunity to expand our horizons and to let us experience something that, in those days, few other children got to do.

I also believe that the whole experience instilled a real spirit of adventure in me and a realisation of the importance of going out and doing things whilst you can. These are attributes I have returned to time and time again throughout my life and, even though I am much more limited these days in what I can do, I still hold those values dear. Regardless of my limitations, I continue to pursue them as much as my body, with my dodgy lungs and other parts, will still allow.

Our adventure began on 15th August 1977 when we drove from Stapleford down to my grandparents' house in Hounslow, West London. Incidentally, 15th August would become a very significant date in my life for other reasons too, but we will come to that later.

I loved being at my grandparents' house as they lived just a couple of miles from Heathrow Airport. From early morning until late in the evening each day, aircraft from far flung corners of the world would come roaring over their back garden as they prepared to land just up the road at the airport. This was back in the day when the aircraft were dirty and noisy and those machines, arriving from exotic locations I'd never heard of, fascinated me. Watching them from my grandparents' back garden imparted a love for aviation that continues to this day.

We stayed the night in Hounslow so that we could be driven by my grandad to the airport early the following morning. After breakfast, we all piled into my grandad's navy-blue Triumph Herald estate and headed for the airport to begin our great odyssey.

I can still recall the buzz I had that day; a mix of adventure and excitement knowing that I would soon be sitting on board on one of those huge, shiny metallic machines hurtling above the clouds. All concerns I may have had about leaving my home and my friends were quickly dispatched as we checked in at Terminal Three and headed to the departure gate.

I was almost bursting with excitement as I caught my first glimpse of the aircraft that would fly us to Miami for a stopover before we headed further west the following day. The McDonnell Douglas DC-10, operated by the now-defunct US company National Airlines, was adorned with beautiful sweeping orange and yellow cheatlines along the length of its fuselage and had a smiling sun logo in the same two colours emblazoned across the tail.

As our turn came to board, we took our seats in the seemingly enormous cabin and settled in for the nine-hour transatlantic leg of the journey to our new home. The cabin crew handed my sisters and I fun packs with the airline's smiling sun logo printed everywhere, they even included a small wings badge, like the badges being worn by the crew, except made of plastic rather than metal.

After nine or so hours, we touched down at Miami International Airport and were met by one of my dad's acquaintances. Almost as soon as we were introduced to our host, he exclaimed, "I don't suppose you'll have heard the news?"

It turns out that the so-called 'King of Rock and Roll' Elvis Presley had been found dead at his home in Memphis, Tennessee a couple of hours before we landed. As a five-year-old, I had no idea at all of the significance of this man, nor of his legacy, but as an avid enthusiast of music from the 60s, my dad was visibly shocked.

In the car, as we headed away from the airport that afternoon and the stifling Florida sun burned down, little did I realise that for the rest of my life I would be able to tell people exactly where I was when the news broke that that Elvis had died.

The following day, we were back at Miami Airport for our onward flight via Houston to San Francisco. By the end of the day, we would be touching down at San Francisco International Airport and heading south to our new home; a rented house in the idyllically named suburb of Mountain View, right in the heart of an area of California where numerous computing and technology companies have since thrived, colloquially referred to as 'Silicon Valley'.

Mountain View, situated at the heart of Santa Clara county and its surrounding towns, is now famed for being the home of technology giants such as Apple, Google, and Hewlett Packard, amongst many others. Santa Clara County is also the location of the world-famous Stanford University, where my dad would be working for the next year or so.

Our year in California was momentous and a real adventure. At weekends and other times when my dad took time off work, me and my sisters would be packed into the back of our Ford Pinto estate car (known in the US as a 'station wagon') and we would head off along the highways and byways of California, Nevada, and Arizona to explore the whole new world right on our doorstep.

Our car would become a regular visitor at National Parks across these western states as we ticked locations off a seemingly endless list of places of interest that my dad insisted we visited whilst we had the opportunity to do so.

From Yosemite to Death Valley, from Big Sur to Redwood National Forest, and from the Sequoia and Kings Canyon National Parks to Joshua Trees out in the Mojave Desert. One weekend we could be camping in misty forests amongst the huge redwood trees of Northern California and the next we could be standing in the burning sun on huge salt flat dried lake beds out in the desert.

For a small boy, these weekend trips were more adventurous than I could have ever possibly imagined living back in rural Cambridgeshire and I loved it. I have been fortunate to have returned to many of these places in the years since 1977 and can only imagine how impressive and exciting they must have been to my five-year-old self.

During our time in California, we visited other amazing places such as Las Vegas, San Diego, and Los Angeles. One memorable weekend, we drove south down the impossibly picturesque Pacific Coast Highway to near Los Angeles to stay with an English family my parents knew from back home. That weekend would see us kids get taken to Disneyland (despite my dad having told us that morning that we would be spending the day at 'a museum'). It would also see one of the only times in my life that I have been forced to seek medical attention for anything other than a CF-related issue.

One afternoon, we were playing by our hosts' swimming pool when I ran along the edge, slipped, and gashed the underside of my chin as I tumbled into the pool. Having been fished out, crying and bleeding, my parents decided that my chin wound would require stitches and so off we went in search of the nearest Emergency Room. Some hours later, I returned with eight stitches in my chin and a huge plaster covering the lower half of my jaw.

My recollection of the whole incident largely ends there, except that I remember, for the next few days, constantly dropping bits of food down into the plaster on my chin which would subsequently have to be scraped out by one of my parents.

Some days after that, once back home in Mountain View, my stitches were removed by one of the grumpiest and most aggressive physicians I have ever had the misfortune to come across. To this day, I still have the scar on my chin from the swimming pool incident, although the mental scaring from spending thirty minutes of agony at the hands of this butcher runs far deeper.

During my time living in California, my older sister and I attended our local school in Mountain View – Monta Loma Elementary. I only found out recently that the very same school was once attended by Apple's founder Steve Jobs, who lived in Mountain View with his parents as a child.

As I had already started school in the UK, I was put in the kindergarten (pre-school) year group as children in the USA didn't start school until they were six years of age. I was therefore slightly older than the other children in my class and was taken aside regularly for reading lessons so that I might keep up with my cohort back in the UK.

One other activity that would occur regularly was the 'earthquake drill'. This being the Bay Area of California, we were in a zone particularly prone to seismic activity due to the proximity of the San Andreas fault. Every so often, an alarm would sound around the school, upon which we were basically required to go and hide under the nearest table and stay there until told to come out again. To me, this seemed like little more than a fun game and what protection a small wooden table would provide as the entire classroom collapsed and disappeared into a large crack in the ground seemed to be one of the finer points overlooked by the authorities. But, regardless, this was the drill we were required to follow when the alarm of impending tectonic Armageddon sounded.

In the December of 1977, the film Star Wars was released in the United States. I was taken to see it at the local cinema (or 'movie theatre') by my dad soon after its release and I recall it being simply the most incredible thing I had ever seen. Images of epic space battles, dusty landscapes on far away planets, and the overriding story of good triumphing over evil was enough to take me to bursting point.

Over the next few months, I persuaded my dad to take me to see it another three times, including once at a large drive-in movie theatre for my sixth birthday in May 1978. This is where you would sit in your own car, alongside several hundred other cars, in front of a huge outdoor screen and with your windows down so that you could hear the film's audio being played over a scratchy little speaker on a stand next to your parking space (I can't imagine why these don't still exist!). Watching the film today with my own son and seeing how he drinks in the excitement of it whilst avidly absorbing every detail and line of dialogue reminds me of exactly how I felt seeing the film for the first time some forty years ago.

By the summer of 1978, our time in California was up and it was time to return to the UK for the start of the new academic year that September. We left Mountain View and flew out of San Francisco International Airport, leaving behind the Golden State and the sunshine, heading home with a year's worth of incredible memories and a desire for further travel and exploration that has stayed with me ever since.

Life soon got back to normal in Stapleford and I returned to school. At this stage, although CF continued to dictate what I ate and kept me on a low-fat diet, my lungs were behaving well and I was troubled very little by the disease that would become such a major part of my life as I got older.

Every six months, I would be collected from school early by one or both of my parents and taken to the Paediatric Outpatients Clinic at Addenbrookes Hospital. In fact, it was often my mum who would collect me and we would meet my dad there, as his laboratories were rather conveniently located straight across the road from the main entrance to the Outpatients Department at the hospital. As this was the paediatric clinic (catering solely for sick children) there were colourful murals adorning the walls and children's books and toys scattered around the place to keep youngsters occupied before being called for their consultation with the doctor. My main recollection of being in this place was the seemingly endless waiting around. Whilst possibly not too long in reality, for a child any waiting around seems like a lifetime!

Upon arrival at clinic, I would be taken to a side room to be weighed and measured and to be given a general once-over, just to make sure I was still breathing and that no bits had fallen off in the preceding six months, that sort of thing.

It would then be back to the waiting area to eventually be called by the lady on the desk to see the Consultant. The doctor I saw throughout my childhood was a lovely gentleman by the name of Dr Roberton.

I can still hear his soft voice, with his gentle northern English accent, and recall his wispy greyish/white hair and beard even now when I think about him.

Although I remember Dr Roberton as an older gentleman, it turns out that when he passed away in early 2018, he was seventy-eight years of age. When I was a patient of his, he would have been in his late thirties and early forties! It's funny how the young form a distorted perception of the age of adults, and this example aptly illustrates a beautiful sense of innocent naivety.

My six-monthly appointments with Dr Roberton continued for many years from the time I would have first seen him in 1976, before going to live in the United States, until I transitioned up to the more general chest clinic for adolescents and adults at Addenbrookes in the mid-1980s.

Although I have no recollection whatsoever of what was discussed in those appointments with Dr Roberton, I am sure that they provided much needed reassurance for my parents.

From a practical standpoint, they also kept me on the hospital's radar should CF start to have an adverse effect on me at any stage. As one of the lucky few whose childhood was largely unaffected by CF, these visits were largely routine, and I am sure I saw them simply as a way of getting out of school for the afternoon rather than anything more.

At the end of the appointment, we would be duly dispatched by Dr Roberton for another six months and make our way to the hospital pharmacy to collect any medication that I required. This involved more waiting around but, as the pharmacy dispensing counter was conveniently located adjacent to the hospital shop and cafe, I was often treated to an iced bun or a small packet of sweets while we waited for the drugs to be dispensed. And that was it. The NHS's monitoring of my condition was over for another six months, and we would head home to resume our normal family routine.

As *normal* a family life could possibly be with one member having CF, I suppose!

FIVE

THE SAME, BUT DIFFERENT

I am acutely aware that, as a child with CF, I led something of a charmed life. Many children with CF spend countless weeks, if not months, in and out of hospital being treated for CF-related complications.

Children's immune systems are underdeveloped, making them particularly prone to any coughs and colds going around. Although generally harmless for much of the population, coughs and colds for those with CF can escalate into something more sinister in a relatively short space of time. As we all know, children are snotty, unhygienic little creatures who spread nasty germs around as a matter of routine. Whilst it is important for children with health conditions such as CF to mix with and be schooled alongside other children as much as possible, this does rather put them in the firing line for anything nasty going around. Consequently, children with CF are likely to spend more time fighting illness and having to take time off from school than their peers. But, thankfully, such an existence sounds alien to me. I was rarely absent from either primary or secondary school, was never in hospital, and was a virtual stranger at my local GP surgery.

My first real memory of being different from other kids comes from my early years at primary school. Back in those days, every child would be given a small bottle of milk to drink during the mid-morning break. These small bottles, which each held half a pint of milk, were made of glass and had a silver coloured foil lid over the top of the neck to keep the milk fresh. Amongst the thirty or so silver topped bottles, laid out neatly in rows in the crate in which they were delivered to the classroom, was a solitary bottle with a red foil top instead of silver. Before the rest of the children were allowed to push, punch, and jostle their way to the crate to take their silver-topped bottles, retreat to their seats, and devour the contents, this red-topped bottle was always handed out to me first.

The red top on the bottle meant that the contents was skimmed milk, rather than the full-fat version handed out to everyone else in the class. Given that I was on a low-fat diet throughout my childhood, as pancreatic enzymes were still in their infancy, my intake of fat had to be carefully managed; drinking full-fat milk like the other children was simply not an option for me.

Upon reflection, I may as well have had a big sign around my neck with 'different to you' written on it; nothing gets a group of six-year-old children asking complicated questions, which I wasn't really equipped to answer, quicker than being the sole child out of a group of thirty drinking something that was clearly different from what they were having. For the first time in my life, I remember feeling embarrassed about being different and, rather than enjoying the feeling of being special because I was different to the other kids, I felt abnormal and confused.

This pattern of events and feelings became an increasingly common theme as my childhood progressed; I had packed lunches that were prepared by my parents rather than the hot school meals that everyone else enjoyed. And when attending birthday parties held at friends' houses – rather than being able to indulge myself in crisps, chocolate, and cake like the other kids – I would either have to miss out or sit to one side with my specially prepared and very safe jam sandwiches (without butter or margarine, of course). I was permitted to indulge in the jelly part of dessert, but I was the only one who wouldn't have the obligatory ice cream accompaniment.

Occasionally, I was allowed to try a crisp or two, or the odd Jaffa Cake or chocolate finger. But I quickly learned that it was better to abstain from consuming treats like these in such tiny quantities, as the frustration caused by being allowed just one of something when there's plenty more available was simply too much to bear.

I still refer to this rule today (known to no one else but me as the 'Luke's None Is Better Than One Rule').

As a small child, this whole situation was not easy to accept. Not only was I being kept away from the sorts of things that most children my age would eat by the bucket-load, given half a chance, but increasingly, and in more and more situations, I was starting to stand out as the kid who was different. Worse still, as the boy who had something wrong with him.

By seven or eight years old, I was becoming increasingly conscious of this and found being labelled in this manner quite distressing. Far from feeling like a novelty, I was starting to feel that I just didn't quite fit in.

These feelings increased over the years, although I kept them mostly to myself; the resounding memory I have of being a child with CF is being incredibly secretive about having the condition.

I never told anyone about having CF, disingenuously relying on a belief, formulated purely by myself, that as I was so mildly affected and there were no visible signs of anything being wrong with me, I could get away with adopting such an approach. However, as I grew older, I began to realise that this was all about people's perception of me and that, to a large extent, I was able to manage that perception.

I developed a very strong sense that, although I may be different from others, I didn't want to be treated any differently. I didn't want to receive special treatment, and I certainly didn't want or need sympathy from anybody either.

Perhaps the roots of these feelings came from the embarrassment I felt at not being allowed the same milk as the other kids at school or having to eat different things at birthday parties. These small events, however innocent they must have been at the time, must have led me to decide subconsciously that I would try to hide my condition as much as possible. By hiding it, I could reduce the number of events where I felt uncomfortable or embarrassed about having CF and find a way to mitigate the feelings of being different to others.

I am sure that had I been sat down by a psychologist as a child, I would have been able to explain these feelings and why I acted the way I did. But no such service was ever offered to me, so the determination to make myself appear normal became something of an obsession.

As I grew older, and became increasingly more self-aware, the desire to integrate with my peers and to be treated as an equal took over and made me effectively pull down the shutters on my condition to just about all of those around me. Me having CF was contained within the confines of my immediate family and a few select others – strictly on a 'need to know' basis for many years. I wouldn't explain to people where I was going when I was picked up from school to go to see Dr Roberton, although I was clearly having far more trips to the 'dentist' than anyone else in my class.

My dislike for school dinners was constructed as an excuse for having to have packed lunches, and my regular bouts of coughing were passed off as a touch of asthma or hay fever.

The bottom line is that I felt more comfortable telling people a bunch of lies about what might be wrong with me than simply telling the truth. But, as misguided as this approach may seem to me now, it worked at the time. So, I persisted with it throughout my childhood.

For me, even small events like taking my Creon enzyme capsules with my packed lunch became an issue; something that could not be done in front of others. Often, if not secretly swallowed down after lunch with the aid of the water fountain in the boys' toilets, they would be flushed down the lavatory or simply discarded in the nearest bin.

Aside from these small inconveniences, however, the mildness of the CF I had as a child allowed me to live a close-to-normal life. I played and enjoyed sports like other children and, in fact, developed something of a reputation as a rather adept cross-country runner, representing my school in various inter-school competitions. I enjoyed football too and played as a forward for the school football team. I played a lot of tennis in my spare time, joining Stapleford Tennis Club and spending many a school holiday morning or afternoon engaged in countless grudge matches against my nemesis Simon, with whom I grew up. From an early age, I took regular swimming lessons on a Saturday morning at the Addenbrookes Hospital's staff leisure centre pool with my sisters, and would return there most Sunday mornings for general pool time with my family.

My dad also regularly took me to watch Cambridge United play football on Saturday afternoons at the Abbey Stadium in Cambridge, which I enjoyed immensely. These were the days when the team was flying high in the upper echelons on the English Second Division (now referred to as 'The Championship') and they hosted several of the bigger teams from around the country.

I always enjoyed these afternoons with my dad, and the talks we had on the way to the ground about Cambridge's prospects for the game ahead. On the way home afterwards, we would conduct a full post-mortem of how the team had performed and analyse whether our predictions for the final score had been accurate. Normally, my dad was closer to the final score than me (much to my constant frustration), although I am sure that even he would have admitted that the day that Cambridge beat Newcastle United six-nil caught him by surprise.

As I grew older and reached my teenage years, my entrepreneurial spirit began to show its face and my desire to earn some cash came to the fore. At around the age of thirteen, I took myself off to the local newsagents and signed up for a Sunday morning paper round. Following a chat with the manager, I understood that my assigned round would be twenty papers to be delivered close to the street where I lived and that it would pay the princely sum of £1.70 per week. Despite the frankly inhumane starting time of six thirty on a Sunday morning, this seemed like easy money to me, especially as I reckoned that if I got a move on, I could be back in bed by eight thirty!

On that first day, I set off for the mile-long ride to the newsagents with my shiny new fluorescent paper bag swinging at my side, already planning how I would spend my first few weeks' wages. My bubble was to be burst within the first minute of arriving at the newsagents, however; rather than being a round consisting of just twenty newspapers, I had been assigned round number twenty, which in fact consisted of about sixty papers! On a Sunday, almost all of these contained what were referred to as colour supplements (glossy magazines). Some of the papers, such as the Sunday Times or the Observer, consisted of multiple sections and were the equivalent size and weight to a volume of the Encyclopaedia Britannica.

With about fifteen of the sixty papers being either one or the other of these two publications, my dreams of making a quick buck and being back in bed before the rest of my family were even up were shattered; it took two trips to transport the full load back to my house (four miles in total) and that was before I had even started any deliveries. With my delivery bag full of heavy newspapers, staying upright on my bike became something of an art form and often gravity would get the better of me. But I was determined not to be beaten by such adversity and persevered with that paper round for years, even adding a second round after a while – I was up early anyway, so I might as well maximise my earning potential.

On the odd occasion, my dad would be up early on a Sunday and would drive me to the paper shop early to collect my full load of papers and get them back to our house in a single trip. Or he would meet me half-way round my route in the car and bring the second half of the papers to save me cycling home and having to set off again.

Whether he was mindful that for a boy of my age and size, and given that my lungs were not the best in the world, this was all rather a large undertaking, or whether he was up anyway and just wanted to help, I was never entirely certain. Either way, it was help gratefully received, particularly on freezing cold winter mornings when I teetered along on my bike, precariously negotiating frosty pavements and driveways with a newspaper bag that probably weighed more than I did.

My other great scheme for earning cash as a youngster followed something of a more spiritual route, although it also involved getting up early on Sunday mornings. Word went around that the local church choir was looking for new recruits and, more importantly, that small cash payments were made for each service that a chorister sung at. Not being from a religious background, this was not the most conventional route to take in order to make a few quid, but the opportunity to make money from sitting about singing a few songs seemed too good to be true.

That I had to do this whilst sitting through a church service, ostensibly wearing a purple dress, was of no consequence compared to the bounty that awaited. As a few of her friends from the village were already in the choir, Louise signed up at the same time. But while she saw it as something of a social club for her and her mates, I saw it as a covert way to hang around with teenage girls.

I stuck out the choir for three years or so, until I realised that it was really not as lucrative an enterprise as I had initially hoped, although getting paid £1.50 for singing at weddings was a little more like what I had in mind on signing up.

That said, the one wedding I sang at – where the bride fainted and had to be carried out, only to return a while later in order to resume the nuptials and vomit all over the floor and her shortly-to-be husband – provided so much entertainment value for a Saturday afternoon that, frankly, I would have been happy to provide my vocal services for free that day.

Once the novelty of being in the choir and close to the same set of girls each Sunday had worn off, and continuing meant that I was unable to expand my more lucrative newspaper delivery enterprise on Sunday mornings, I decided to hang up my cassock and focus my cash-making efforts elsewhere. That, plus the fact that, as a teenager, it was becoming increasingly uncool to be in church choir and was starting to conflict with my aspirations for mega-stardom as a rock drummer.

That said, I still get the shivers when I hear a large choir echoing around a cathedral or church. The hairs still stand up on the back of my neck as the sheer magnificent beauty of that particular sound washes over me.

Throughout my childhood, I was aware of CF but I had the luxury of being able to largely ignore my condition and what it might mean for the future. By taking this approach, and by trying to constantly prove to people that I was just like them, I realise now that the person I was fooling most was myself; I lived in something of a bubble, surrounded by a web of half-truths and, indeed, downright lies. I did whatever I could to ensure I wouldn't stick out from the crowd, would be treated equally, and so that no one would be any the wiser as to my condition. Largely, I believed that I was getting away with it. However, in hindsight, I realise that this approach to life left me hugely underprepared for when CF would finally catch up with me in my twenties.

I have had people who knew me when I was younger tell me since that they suspected there was something 'not quite right' about me, but could not say exactly what. All that effort I put in to covering up my condition may perhaps have been in vain. Yet, feeling the way I felt as a child, and managing the situation to a level where I felt comfortable enough to get on with life, clearly worked for me at the time. I have so many happy memories of being a child, very few of which are overshadowed by anything to do with CF. And that is the one legacy from my childhood that I will always have.

My childhood was much like anyone else's and I could do as much as any of the other boys I knew. As I have grown older, things have obviously changed for me, with CF taking hold and bringing me to the point of transplantation. Yet I take a great deal of solace from remembering a time in my life when I could go days at a time without giving any thought at all to being different from others, being considered as 'ill', or – worse still – 'suffering from a condition'.

CF is like that, though; it is hard, painful, and frustrating in equal measure.

Today, there are times when I can still switch off from CF and its endless daily rituals and requirements, and just be a version of myself unencumbered by those things, even if only for a short time. When I do, I am always conscious of my younger self standing alongside me, smiling back as if to reassure me, and nudging me along ready to meet whatever may come next.

SIX

SCHOOL DAYS AND DRUMMING DISPLAYS

One of the earliest memories I have as a child is my first day of primary school. It was a dry day and must have been quite warm as I can vividly recall that no one was wearing a coat. This would have been the first week of September 1976, at the end of what had just been (and remains to this day) the longest and hottest UK summer since records began.

My school was the local village primary, about a six or seven minute walk from our front door. Stapleford Primary School was built in the style of one of those old red-brick Victorian school buildings that you often see in historical TV dramas, with a small house for the incumbent headteacher built alongside. In fact, the small village school that my two children attend today bears an uncanny resemblance to that first school I went to some forty or so years ago.

I was in Mrs Arnold's class along with thirty or so other four and five year olds. Mrs Arnold was a friendly older lady who, as it turned out, also ran a local grocery shop in one of the nearby villages with her husband when she wasn't performing her duties as a full-time teacher to thirty snotty little kids from Monday to Friday. I am not sure how such moonlighting would be viewed these days by the educational authorities, but this was the mid-70s and I guess attitudes were a little more relaxed back then.

I settled easily into school life and was a contented little boy. I was generally well, and CF placed very few limitations on what I could do. My parents ensured that I ate the appropriate food and took the medication prescribed at the right time in the right doses. Given that pancreatic enzymes were still very much in their infancy back then, my diet remained low fat if not *no fat*. Foods such as chips, chocolate, butter, and ice cream remained strictly off limits for me, but we ate healthily at home and I didn't really miss such things too much (except when at birthday parties).

It was during the summer of 1977, after only a single year in the infants' section of Stapleford Primary School, that my family had uprooted itself and headed to California for the year. We returned to the UK, and our house in Stapleford, in the summer of 1978, with my dad resuming his cancer research job in Cambridge.

On our return, I dropped straight back into the same class of children that I had left the year before, although we were now beginning the last year of being Infants before moving on to join the 'big children' and the heady heights of the Juniors. There were a couple of new children in the class, and some had left, but largely the cohort remained the same, and was now under the watchful control of Mrs Holt, the wife of our headmaster.

I was a good and diligent pupil at primary school. Whilst I feared getting on the wrong side of the teachers (and worked hard on being the teacher's pet) this was nothing compared to the fear I felt of getting on the wrong side of my parents. I have always been the sort of person who is eager to please others, and at school I was no different. That said, over-exuberance would occasionally get the better of me. One lunchtime, for example, when a small-scale food fight kicked off in the lunch hall between the adjacent table and mine, a rogue boiled potato landed unceremoniously in the centre of our table. Unable to resist, I took it upon myself to hurl the offending potato back in the general direction it had come from. I did this just as Mrs Peverel – a stern, no-nonsense dinner lady – cast her gaze upon me and, as quickly as I had despatched my potato grenade, I myself was despatched to spend the rest of lunchtime standing outside the Headmaster's office (in tears).

That incident taught me a lot about the inequity of life, and the harshness of injustice. Most, though, as a normally well behaved seven-year-old, it taught me not to chuck food about in the dining hall (or, if I did, to be more careful not to get caught).

For a while, at school, I took piano lessons. I am not too sure whether this was my idea or something that was inflicted on me by my parents. Mrs Finlayson, the school music teacher, was a small, dark-haired, thin lady whose spindly long fingers unnerved me, probably even more so after hearing the well-circulated rumour amongst the other children that she was, in fact, a witch in her spare time. Ironically, she had just the sort of fingers one needs to be a great pianist. However, the way she would grab my fingers whenever they landed on the wrong keys and rearrange them angrily onto the correct ones clearly did nothing to endear me to her.

By the time I was eight years old, this was all just too much for me to put up with and my piano playing career was over not long after it started. Although I was hugely relieved, I imagine this came as quite an annoyance to my parents (who had just bought a second-hand piano for me to practise on). Maybe they hoped that I would go back to it at some point, and indeed I did – many years later – once the fearsome Mrs Finlayson was well out of the picture.

Whilst my piano playing career may have been short lived, my primary school years were my introduction to other forms of music and, in particular, to one range of instruments that I still indulge in today.

Each Friday morning, we would have an extra-long assembly in the main school hall. As the whole school filed into the hall, and as it left, the school orchestra would perform. This was largely, I suspect, a futile attempt to drown out the raucous din made by two hundred or so over-excited school children. Children who were ecstatic to being freed from the confines of their classroom for forty-five minutes and overwhelmed with the knowledge that it would soon be the weekend with no more school until Monday.

I would listen to the orchestra as it screeched out versions of well-known classics from the musicals and other, rather less identifiable, ditties. And, as I listened, I wondered whether I would ever be able to play an instrument well enough to be invited to join that merry band of musicians. What really focussed my attention on joining the orchestra, however, was my sheer dislike of reading. I realise that the link between the two activities isn't immediately obvious, so let me explain…

Friday mornings were designated as reading time. This would take place once we returned to our classrooms after assembly and would continue until morning playtime at ten forty a.m. For someone who had no interest in reading books of any genre, this hour represented sixty minutes of misery which I would spend daydreaming and pretending to read while, secretly, just looking at the pictures in the books and making my own stories up instead. Yet, whilst reading time was being inflicted on ninety percent of the school's attendees, the other ten percent who were fortunate enough to be able to play instruments, and who were in the orchestra, stayed behind in the school hall for practise time. I soon realised that if I could get into the school orchestra, then my Friday mornings would be free of reading hour and I would be liberated. All I had to do was get myself into the orchestra. So, I started to hatch a plan.

The only other instrument that I had any experience of up until this point was the recorder. Although I was also in the recorder group at primary school, I had no idea how to play the wretched thing or how to read music, both of which you would imagine would be prerequisites to being in a recorder group. Given my blatant inability to string two decent notes together on a recorder of any type, I have no idea how I blagged my place in the group. However, I soon realised that if I always ensured I stood next to my friend William (who was something of an accomplished recorder player and whose finger movements I could emulate to a degree on my own instrument) I could create the impression that I had some vague idea of what I was doing. This illusion carried on for years, and I performed in that recorder group in many school concerts and village fetes over the years. The fact that I had no idea what I was doing seemed to elude everyone. Alternatively, if they realised that I was clueless and was just winging it, they were simply too apathetic to do anything about it.

As the recorder group was separate from the school orchestra, however, I needed a plan.

One Friday, as we filed into assembly and I watched the orchestra bash out painful and barely recognisable versions of tunes from Lionel Bart's hit musical 'Oliver', my gaze wandered over to the far corner of the musical ensemble. There, I spied two boys who spent most of the time sitting and doing not very much except for occasionally standing up to bang or hit things of various shapes and sizes. These actions seemed to be totally uncoordinated with what the rest of the orchestra was doing at any point in the music. I knew the two boys carrying out the hitting and banging, and I also knew that, if possible, they had even less musical talent than me. I know world-renowned scientists and inventors always recall the 'light bulb' moments when the penny drops in their brain and they discover something magnificent and life changing. Well, although it may fall short of the moment when the apple dropped on Sir Isaac Newton's head, this was to be my very own light bulb moment. This was the moment when I finally saw my route to joining this motley crew of musicians. The moment that would finally get me out of the dreaded Friday reading hour.

This was the moment I decided to become a drummer.

Within days, I had plucked up the courage to ask Mrs Finlayson if I could join the percussion section of the orchestra. It just so happened that one of the boys who was currently incumbent in that particular section had grown bored of spending his Friday mornings slapping a tambourine or tapping a triangle wildly out of time to music; he had decided to hang up his guiro and return to reading hour, presumably with a renewed sense of literary vigour. So, at precisely the right time, there was a vacancy. And I was just the person to fill it.

I started with the school orchestra the following Friday, teaching myself to read percussion music and learning how to hit, bang, tap, or ring a variety of drums, cymbals, bongos, and a whole host of other instruments, in the correct manner and generally in time to the music. For a small village school, ours had a surprisingly eclectic collection of instruments for a budding percussionist to cut their teeth on. And I did just that, finding – with some surprise – that I began to enjoy the experience for what it was rather than just because it got me out of reading hour.

This started a passion for drumming and percussion that stayed with me throughout my whole school and university careers, and which still keeps me occupied today (when I find the time) as I try to teach my children how to play the set of drums we have at home.

The rest of my time at Stapleford Primary was happy and, despite CF, I got on as well as any other child there. I got involved in school clubs and attended sports days and school discos just like all the other kids. One disco, however, was to teach me an important life lesson and would see an incident so shocking that it would set my confidence back at a time when I was desperately keen to be normal and to fit in with my peers.

Usually, our school discos had a relaxed dress code, but one in particular was declared a fancy-dress disco. Unable to decide on what to go as, I eventually settled on dressing as my hero at the time – the lead singer of the band Adam and the Ants, namely Adam Ant himself, who was going through the 'Prince Charming' alter ego phase of his career. I rummaged around at home and came up with what I considered to be a suitable costume. It included a white frilly blouse borrowed from Louise (this was the 1980s 'new romantic' period of pop music after all) and I had my Mum replicate Adam's full face make-up, copied from an edition of Smash Hits magazine that Louise had in her bedroom.

I left for the disco thinking I looked amazing and could not wait to see the reaction of the other kids at school. But my world came crashing down when, a couple of hours later, I found myself surrounded by a group of bigger and older boys in the boys' toilets, taunting me for wearing 'girl's clothes and make up'.

After being knocked about and roughed up a bit, I was left slumped on the floor of the toilets, crouching in a puddle of urine (possibly, but not definitely, my own) and with my mascara rolling down my cheeks and onto my pristine white blouse. I eventually picked myself up and ran out of the toilets to find Louise and to tell her what had happened. "Oh Luke, that's awful," she said sympathetically. But just when I thought she was on my side, she rolled her eyes and added, "Just look at the state of my blouse!"

Two particular days at Stapleford stick in my memory for their historical significance.

Late on the morning of 12th April 1981, when I was nine years old, we were ushered out of our classroom mid-morning and into the main hall where the rest of the school was already assembled, sitting quietly and patiently in front of a television (which seemed large at the time but was minuscule by today's standards).

On the screen was an all-white space plane named *Columbia*, pointing vertically skywards with a puff of white smoke drifting from underneath it. We were told by the commentator on the television that this was to be the first ever mission of the NASA space shuttle program. After a few minutes and an expectant countdown, there was a loud roar, a huge plume of smoke and, with that, *Columbia* was airborne and heading for the stars. We watched in awe as the little white spacecraft, piggy-back mounted on the back a huge white fuel tank, shot into the dawn skies over Florida (this was at midday our time but seven a.m. at the launch site) and headed away.

This was the most spectacular thing I had seen since viewing Star Wars back in 1977, and it lit a spark inside me that never went away; the dream of one day being a flyer myself. I went home that day and drew picture after picture of *Columbia* on its launch pad, *Columbia* rising into the air, and *Columbia* orbiting the earth. I was entranced by what I had seen that day, the memories of which have never left me.

On the back of the excitement of the first time we were shown into the hall to watch something amazing happening live on television, the second occasion was somewhat less spectacular. It was on 11th October 1982. We were told that this would be a momentous day as King Henry VIII's Tudor flagship, the Mary Rose, was being lifted from the bed of the Solent, where it had laid for several hundred years.

The entire school sat patiently as John Craven (he of 'Newsround' fame in the 1970s and 1980s, now of 'Countryfile') narrated over the rather small and grainy shots taken from a boat bobbing around on the surface of the sea, focussed on a crane mounted on a ship with its ropes dangling in the water. In our childish naivety, we sat muttering with excitement and hoping to get a glimpse of a real-life galleon, resplendent with its sails billowing in the wind and its cannons primed and ready in its gun ports. However, after what felt like hours, words simply cannot convey the feelings of disappointment that fell across the room – as if, somehow, we had been short-changed by our teachers – when the lifting unfolded before us. As we sat increasingly impatiently, the sight of a yellow metal cradle with what appeared to be a plank of soggy, seaweed-covered, old driftwood emerged from the waves at a lifting rate of about a centimetre a minute. In hindsight, even the teachers seemed a little disappointed, and could sense the boredom rising in the air amongst their charges. As we were quickly ushered back out of the hall, we muttered amongst each other what a waste of a morning that had been, although – looking on the bright side – it had got us out of PE.

As I reached the age of eleven, it was time to say goodbye to Stapleford Primary and to head to the local comprehensive school, Sawston Village College, some five miles and a bus ride away from our house. We had moved a couple of years before this, from the house in Stapleford to a very old semi-detached house in the neighbouring village of Great Shelford. This house had once been quite a grand single property but had been divided into two houses at some point in the last century. We lived in the smaller of the two sides, which was brimming with what an estate agent would now describe as 'period features'; open fireplaces, ornate brass door handles, and a real doorbell (when you pulled and pushed the handle on the outside, the wire through the wall would tip a small bell backwards and forwards on the inside, making it ring). All very Downton Abbey!

Sawston Village College was massive and completely different to anything I had experienced before. There were five year groups, each with around two hundred and fifty children in them. I joined Form 1D in the September of 1983 along with my friend William (yes, the same William who was adept at playing the recorder). Before the transition to the bigger school, we were asked who we would like to be paired up with so that we would know at least one other person in our class when we started at Sawston. William and I picked each other, so on that first day we found ourselves sitting side by side in a room full of strangers from other local primary schools, wondering how we would survive spending the next five years in this seemingly monolithic fortress of learning.

Looking back now, we were extremely fortunate to be going to such a well-run and well-equipped school. The sports facilities were magnificent, with a sports field big enough to accommodate several football, rugby, and hockey pitches all at the same time. There was also a heated indoor pool, a sports hall with a separate gymnasium as well as multiple tennis courts. More importantly for me perhaps was the excellent music department which, amongst its various assets, had two gleaming brass kettle drums (or timpani) as well as a shiny black five-piece drum kit with a dazzling array of cymbals and other hardware. Getting involved in the music scene at this new school was like a Sunday amateur league footballer joining a Premier League team. I simply couldn't wait to get stuck in.

For the first three years, we would stay with our initial classmates for every lesson, travelling between the science block to the languages department, and from the history to the geography departments as our timetable dictated. It felt like much of the day was spent in transition, either walking around the site between lessons, getting books out at the start of a lesson, or putting them way again at the end. These small intervals in the school day always allowed for a short period of respite to let off a bit of steam, with a game of tag or a quick 'bundle' along the way. The final two years, once you had taken your 'options' (which meant whittling the down the array of subjects currently taken into a more manageable amount in preparation for GCSEs) were spent in ability groups ranging from one to five. I sat out my final two years in classes either one or two, except for music because there were only enough of us to make up one class, regardless of our ability.

They say your school days are the happiest days of your life and, although reluctant to adhere to such a cliché, my time at Sawston Village College was largely very enjoyable and I look back on those days with fondness. I worked hard, was well behaved, and was regarded as a good student throughout my time there. I had quite a range of friends, some who I am still in contact with, and one with whom I still regularly go out for a beer and a curry some thirty years later.

There was, however, the odd occasion when the desire for light-hearted japes would get the better of me. Whilst we are not talking about setting fire to classrooms or locking teachers in store cupboards, rather small moments of larking about to relieve the boredom of certain lessons.

My favourite example of having a little fun at school was the hijinks we would carry out at the expense of our Religious Education (RE) teacher, Mr Sylvester (affectionately referred to as 'Bone-Head' by just about the whole school on account of him having a bald head and sporting a, frankly, ridiculous comb-over). Mr Sylvester was an older gentleman whose best years of teaching were patently behind him, and who was cruising through to his retirement by trying to teach a bunch of disinterested teenagers something about religion. It was clear to us all that this was a man who didn't care whether we paid any attention to his paltry attempts to teach us.

We were sat in pairs throughout the classroom, with Mr Sylvester's desk at the front, conveniently adjacent to a book cupboard to his side. It became something of a ritual that whenever Mr Sylvester went into the cupboard to bring out textbooks, myself and William – who was sat next to me – would switch seats with our mates Neil and Gwilym. Like a Formula One pit team, we became quite adept at carrying out this manoeuvre in the few seconds we had available and would often perform the trick several times each lesson. I can still recall the enormous effort it took not to giggle as poor old Bonehead came out from the cupboard and glared at us with a confused expression on his face before handing out the books and continuing with the lesson.

It would also be in RE where me and the same three friends would pull off the greatest prank of our school career.

By this time, Mr Sylvester had retired (or possibly gone off on long-term sick leave as the result of a breakdown) and we were now graced with the presence of a newly-qualified member of staff by the name of Miss Darlington. Whilst Miss Darlington was a breath of fresh air compared to her predecessor, even her youthfulness and enthusiasm for teaching would not grant her immunity from our juvenile silliness.

On a particularly hot day, we decided that the boredom of a double period of RE was more than we could stand. This was at a time when we had to endure our RE lessons in a mobile classroom which had no air conditioning and which would heat up like a sauna in warmer weather. My three comrades and I concocted a plan whereby I would pretend to faint and need to be excused from the class to recover.

When Miss Darlington's back was next turned, I slipped forwards off my seat and slumped in a heap on the floor beneath my desk (with suitable levels of dramatic effect thrown in).

In the ensuing commotion, William and Neil leapt to their feet and came to my aid, checking my pulse and fanning my brow with a rather conveniently located copy of the Bible. After reassuring Miss Darlington that, in fact, this was a regular occurrence and that I was prone to such fainting events, my accomplices were instructed by the visibly shaken teacher to remove me from the classroom and escort me outside so that I could get some fresh air. With tables and chairs hastily removed from around my lifeless body, and with pencil cases and rulers strewn around the general area like a crime scene, my accomplices threw my arms around their shoulders and dragged me, as if wounded in combat, from the classroom and out into the bright sunshine.

This was all done with the four of us stifling the huge guffaws of laughter rising inside us. I even recall giving one or two reassuring comedy winks to some of my classmates as I was being carried away from the scene of chaos we left in our wake.

Once out of view from the classroom and, of course, Miss Darlington, we found a nice bench to sit on, eventually composed ourselves, and wiped the tears of laughter from our faces. As we congratulated each other on our marvellous acting abilities, we relaxed in the warm air and enjoyed what remained of the lesson sitting in the warm summer sunshine. Halcyon days indeed!

Throughout my time at secondary school, I was heavily involved in playing drums and percussion in a whole range of musical groups from the main school orchestra to the brass band, and from playing in small groups of other musicians for school plays to being selected to play in the orchestra for the annual Sawston Youth Centre drama productions (renowned for their high quality and professionalism throughout Cambridgeshire at the time). The school also entered various musical groups into local inter-school music competitions, and it is with a small degree of pride that I can say that I have played in such auspicious venues as the Cambridge University Concert Hall, Cambridge Arts Theatre, Norwich Cathedral, and – quite amazingly – the Royal Albert Hall in London when one particular musical group I was involved with reached the final of a nationwide school orchestral competition.

However, the drumming I probably enjoyed the most was with the rock band that I played in, initially called 'Ahead of Time' but whose name was changed at some point and for some unknown reason to 'Eleventh Hour'.

Regardless of our moniker at any given moment, me and some like-minded mates would take over the music room at lunchtimes and blast out cover versions of whatever we liked the sound of in the charts at the time. Believe me, and regardless of all the toxic antibiotics I have taken in my life, nothing brings on the onset of tinnitus faster than spending your lunch hour in a relatively small room surrounded by amplifiers at full volume whilst smashing away on a drum kit with all the finesse of Animal from The Muppets. Our own versions of White Wedding by Billy Idol or She Sells Sanctuary by The Cult were legendary (in our own minds at least) and as we bashed out these, and a range of other heavy rock classics of the day, the spare space in the room would fill with other kids coming to listen and watch. Whilst some of our spectators perhaps were of the view that we sounded okay, I suspect the vast majority were wondering how four spotty lads could make such a ridiculous amount of horrible noise with just three guitars, a drum kit, and a microphone.

Quite often, and just for variety, we would switch instruments and I would become the band's bassist, as one of my band mates took up position 'in goal' on the drums. We would then attempt the same tunes albeit with some of us in different positions to the ones we were used to. We even carried this lark off at a couple of gigs we did, and I became quite adept at playing the bass guitar during my time off from being not only the band's but also the whole school's resident rock drummer.

Two highlights of my early career as a rock star were as part of this group.

In the third year at Sawston, we managed to persuade somebody or other that we were the next big thing and that we should be allowed to have a half-hour slot at the next school disco, at which we would perform a set of eight songs for the attending masses. With permission inexplicably granted, we set about rehearsing in earnest and perfecting those eight songs until we were operating like a well-oiled machine (albeit a very noisy one with acne and bad hair).

On the night of the *gig* (referring to it as a 'school disco' was simply no longer cool enough for us), we fought against multiple technical issues and terrible acoustics and made it through to the end of the set. Generally, we were well received and, as the DJ took over, we spent the rest of the evening being slapped on the back and were grateful to receive such kind and generous compliments as, “Yes, you lot were not as bad as I thought you were going to be.”

I am sure similar compliments were paid to John, Paul, George, and Ringo back in their early days too.

Whilst the school disco gig gave us our first taste of being rock stars, we were launched to a whole new level of ‘superstardom’ just a few short months later; during a GCSE music lesson, we were told that a group of one hundred school children from Japan would be visiting our school for the day in a few weeks’ time and that it was up to *our music class* to provide entertainment for them by way of a concert during the afternoon. After some discussions amongst ourselves, a running order was worked out and, after various individual recitals, small ensemble performances and some choral renditions of popular English songs that Japanese visitors may recognise, Eleventh Hour were permitted to play three songs to bring the proceedings to an end and to close the show ‘on a high’.

As the day of the visit arrived, we were all ushered into the assembly hall by our music teacher, Mr Adams, to sit and await the arrival of our guests. Not long afterwards, the doors at the back of the hall opened and in filed around one hundred immaculately dressed Japanese teenage girls, resplendent in their smart navy-blue uniforms, white knee-high socks, and bright red school ties. As the concert got underway, our visitors sat quietly and politely, and following each performance would show their appreciation with quiet, almost choreographed, rounds of gentle applause.

My Eleventh Hour buddies and I started exchanging comments amongst ourselves along the lines of, “Tough audience, this lot,” and, “Do you think they’ll be ushered straight back out of the hall as soon as we turn the amplifiers on?”

With the main concert approaching its conclusion, we left our seats and went to tune up in the music room behind the stage area. As the drummer with nothing to tune up as such, I just stood around occasionally hitting stuff with my drumsticks, trying to look busy.

When the penultimate performance drew to a close on stage, the curtains were drawn so that the stage could be reconfigured for Eleventh Hour’s headline performance, with amplifiers at the front, the school drum kit at the back, and – most importantly – the band’s backdrop, which I had knocked up at home a few days beforehand, suspended behind the drums. This was, in fact, an old white double bedsheet with ‘Eleventh Hour’ emblazoned across it in black paint, and with a clock face with the hands pointing to eleven o’clock in the centre of the ‘O’ of ‘Hour’ – inspired, eh?

As we took our places behind the curtain and switched on the amps, we could hear Mr Adams giving a short speech, thanking the various performers for their efforts and the audience for showing their appreciation for what they had seen so far. He finished by saying that he hoped they would enjoy the final act of the afternoon, which was to be, "Something a little different," from the rest of the concert.

The hall fell silent. There was a palpable level of anticipation in the air, and the curtains were drawn back to reveal the visual and aural splendour of Eleventh Hour to our unsuspecting audience.

For the past hour or so, the visitors had been the epitome of courtesy and good manners. However, when we struck the initial chords of our first number, any semblance of order and decorum was replaced by anarchy and chaos. One hundred Japanese school girls leapt out of their seats and rushed to the front of the stage, climbing over each other and jostling for the best view whilst many decided that screaming was now how they should be conducting themselves.

On stage, we were gobsmacked. But we quickly began to revel in our fans' reactions.

The school assembly hall now felt like Wembley Stadium and, as the four-song set took on a life of its own, we felt like we could play all afternoon (although with only about ten songs in our repertoire, this would have been rather repetitive). As our fourth and final number came to end with one of those long rock and roll song endings where the last note is played and replayed until the drummer finally brings proceedings to a close with one last crash on the cymbals, the audience erupted. I managed to resist throwing my drumsticks into the audience like all my boyhood hero rock star drummers did (given that drumsticks cost money and I wasn't prepared to fork out for new ones) and the four of us made our way to the front of the stage to greet our adoring audience.

After spending twenty minutes or so signing autographs (yes, really) and having our photos taken with huddles of giggling Japanese schoolgirls, it was time for them to leave and, as we made our exit backstage, we felt on top of the world. We may have been just four school kids playing bad cover versions, but on that afternoon, and for one day only, we felt invincible. And we made memories that still make me smile when I think back to that day half a lifetime ago.

SEVEN
GOING UP, UP...

In the summer of 1988, as my five years at Sawston drew to a close, it was time to sit our final exams – the ones that would determine what we would all do next in terms of our school careers. For reasons linked to putting more emphasis on coursework and less on the final examination, the Government had decided some years prior to this that the class of 1988 would be the first year group in the UK to sit the new General Certificate of Secondary Education examinations (or GCSE for short). The shift in emphasis seemed to make a lot of sense at the time, as the old O-Level exams were fully biased towards the final examination, thus prejudicing those who were perhaps better at coursework and who performed less well under the pressure of exam conditions. Luckily, I didn't suffer from this shift and in June 1988 I left Sawston with eight decent GCSEs (one of which I am proud to say was in music) and headed off to begin the next stage of my school career – Sixth Form College and A-Levels.

That summer was spent working at a couple of temporary jobs I had found for myself. I spent much of the summer behind the counter of the local convenience shop, which was just up the road and a minute's walk from my house. The shop was owned by a lovely chap called Jerry Brown who was something of a local celebrity. His participation in numerous local groups and community activities alongside running a fine wine company had left him little time to run his own shop, so this function was largely handed over to me for the summer.

Jerry was an extremely friendly and funny man. He was full of charisma and was entirely wasted running a corner shop; he was much more suited to a career on the stage as an entertainer or stand-up comedian. Regardless of this, he ran his little shop and had previously been employing me to work on Saturday afternoons when he would decamp from our little corner of South Cambridgeshire and head to north London to watch his beloved Tottenham Hotspur play football.

My family had used his shop since moving to the area and every time I entered it, for as long as I could remember, Jerry would welcome me with a smile, always (for some reason) referring to me as 'the King of the village'.

As I paid for my stuff, he routinely sent me on my way with the phrase, "See you on the beach!"

I have no idea why he said this, what it meant, or the genesis of this nifty catchphrase. But it always made me smile and I loved it for its positivity and for the tropical images it conjured up in my mind. I have never forgotten that phrase and, every time I think about it, I vow to use it more often myself.

Jerry's shop felt like my own little kingdom and I spent my days selling groceries, renting out videos, managing dry cleaning, and sorting out the newspapers and magazines that were also on sale. Much of my time in the shop was spent chatting to old ladies whose sole activity that day would be to head out for a pint of milk and a natter with anyone who would stop to listen. Being stuck behind the counter rendered me something of a captive audience in that regard, and I got highly adept at discussing the weather and listening to chat about the state of 'young people today' multiple times daily.

When not in the shop, I worked with a guy called Keith who ran his own painting and decorating business. I oversaw rubbing down surfaces and undercoating, leaving the more advanced parts of the job, such as wallpapering or gloss painting, to Keith himself. However, for a couple of weeks, I was let off on my own to rub down and repaint our local cemetery's entire perimeter fence. A more tedious task would be hard to find; if you can imagine a fence with a total length of three hundred metres, which is completely identical the whole way around, you'll get some idea of the scale (and monotony) of the task. The only way I got through those two weeks was with the companionship of BBC Radio One on a small transistor radio and by enjoying the sunshine which, fortunately, shone the entire fortnight I was assigned to the job.

The summer of 1988 flew by and soon enough it was time to start back at school. Sawston Village College was already a distant memory and the daunting challenge of a new school and A-Levels lay ahead.

I spent the next two years attending Long Road Sixth Form College in Cambridge. The college itself is situated alongside Addenbrookes Hospital where both my parents worked (by this point, my mum was working as a midwife at the Rosie Maternity Hospital alongside the main hospital on the same site). I spent two years studying geography (which had been one of my favourite subjects at Sawston) as well as economics, mathematics, and French.

Those two years were equally as enjoyable as my time at Sawston and, once again, I applied myself well and worked hard. On Tuesday evenings, after college and homework were over for the day, I would cycle three miles to the nearby village of Trumpington where I would spend from six p.m. until about midnight washing up in the kitchen of a Beefeater restaurant. Needless to say that, in hindsight, spending this amount of time in a hot, sweaty, and damp environment was probably seriously detrimental to my health and wellbeing, yet my parents were adamant that if I wanted money, I would have to go out and earn it myself… so I did.

Free handouts of cash were rare from my parents growing up (rightly so, I believe) and having cash in my pocket seemed much more important than incurring damage to my lungs. Not being particularly well-paid, whilst also being mind-numbingly tedious, I hated this job with conviction and would spend my Tuesdays at college dreading the evening ahead. The money came in handy, though, particularly on Friday nights when we would head as a crowd to one of a handful of pubs in Cambridge city centre which were known to be *flexible* about asking for ID when one was purchasing alcohol before reaching the age of eighteen.

Looking back, I don't remember there being a particular career direction that I wanted to follow at this stage. I'd always had a keen interest in aviation and would have loved to have become an airline pilot, but I already knew that CF would prevent me from achieving that goal. I therefore needed to set my sights on something more ground based.

It was around early 1989, whilst studying for my A-Levels, that my first job in aviation came about. A small airline had just started flying out of Cambridge Airport, running scheduled flights to Amsterdam and Manchester on weekdays and operating the odd charter flight at weekends. The airline was called Suckling Airways, eponymously titled after its founders (husband and wife Roy and Merlyn Suckling) who had started the airline in 1986, flying just one eighteen-seat Dornier 228 turboprop aircraft.

The airline had originally run its operations out of Ipswich Airport, but had been forced to move to Cambridge after waterlogging of the grass runways at Ipswich rendered them unusable for an aircraft as large and heavy as Suckling's Dornier. The company was very much their 'baby' and, whilst they were the owners of the company, the two of them were totally hands-on with the day-to-day operations. Mrs Suckling, a former barrister, ran the whole of the office and administrative functions of the airline whilst Roy took charge of operations, engineering, and pilot training. He also flew the occasional passenger flight to keep his hand in. The airline and its charismatic owners even became the stars of the show in a BBC television documentary in 1990, amusingly entitled 'Darling, Let's Start an Airline'.

I hoped that Ipswich's loss would be my gain and I wrote to the Sucklings, asking them if they had any weekend or school holiday jobs available. I heard nothing for a few weeks until, one Friday evening in May 1989, I was at home when the phone rang. I picked it up to find Mrs Suckling on the other end of the line. She wanted to know whether I'd like to come to the airport over the weekend to help their full-time ground services guy (a pleasant enough chap called Ashley) wash and clean the aircraft. HRH Diana, Princess of Wales, was opening a new domestic terminal at Manchester Airport the following Monday and Mrs Suckling (keen to exploit a good marketing opportunity) wanted her aircraft looking as clean and shiny as possible for the numerous television cameras and press photographers that would undoubtedly be there on the day.

Cleaning an aircraft may sound like a relatively simple task to anyone who hasn't done so before, but even an eighteen-seater turboprop aircraft is much larger than you would expect. In much the same way as washing a car, we soaked the aircraft in fresh water before scrubbing it with brooms soaked in a special aviation cleaning fluid which was really rather useful in getting rid of the bug splats, hydraulic fluid traces, and engine exhaust that had all caked themselves to the normally pristine white fuselage and wings. This task took most of Saturday, and we returned on Sunday to turn our attention to the lower half of the fuselage, which was red and lined with a pale grey stripe. Once waxed and polished, these coloured sections came back to life and by the end of the weekend, the aircraft was gleaming from nose to tail as if just out of the factory.

Once the interior had also been given a freshen up, with all the seats and carpets vacuumed, and the interior wall panels and drop-down trays wiped, it was time to call it a day.

At the end of a long weekend, the aircraft was looking amazing and both Roy and Merlyn arrived at the airport to give it the once over before Ashley and I knocked off. They both seemed very impressed at the job we had done and they asked me if I would like to return on a casual basis for other tasks that needed an extra pair of hands from time to time. I gladly accepted their offer and so, over the next few months, I was back at the airport helping Ashley out with other miscellaneous tasks.

One weekend, Roy Suckling had taken a call from a freight company at Stansted Airport some thirty miles down the motorway from Cambridge. The regular aircraft that they used to transport all of Guernsey's Sunday newspapers from the mainland to the island was unavailable as it had a technical fault and Roy had agreed to provide the Suckling aircraft as a replacement.

Ashley and I spent the whole of the Saturday afternoon unfixing and unloading all the seats out of the aircraft so to maximise its payload for the overnight newspaper transportation to Guernsey. After a spot of dinner, Roy arrived at the airport and invited me to join him on the positioning flight down to Stansted and onwards to Guernsey 'to keep him company'. I jumped at this amazing opportunity and couldn't quite believe my luck. A short time later, we were lining up at the end of the Cambridge Airport runway, with me sitting in what normally was the co-pilot's seat. I gazed out of the front windshield in wonder as Roy advanced the throttle levers and we shot down the runway. With the aircraft being empty, and therefore very light for this positioning hop to Stansted (whose runway lights we could make out as soon as we were airborne), we soon leapt off the tarmac at Cambridge and climbed away into the darkening night sky.

The rest of the night was a pure *Boy's Own* adventure. Roy and I nattered in an office at the freight terminal at Stansted as the newspapers were loaded and the aircraft was refuelled. Soon enough, we were off again. It was just after midnight, and we were airborne and heading for the Channel Islands. Our route took us over central London and down towards Southampton before heading out of the English Channel towards Guernsey. There was only Roy talking to London Air Traffic Control at that time of the morning and the radio was quiet until we approached Guernsey. It was still dark as we landed and taxied to our allocated parking stand, but the first signs of daylight were beginning to show as Roy and I climbed out of the aircraft and headed to the airport terminal cafeteria to get some breakfast before the return flight back to Cambridge.

After an hour or so on the ground in Guernsey, we were back in the air and heading home. An hour later, the familiarly flat landscape of Cambridgeshire spread out under the nose of the aircraft and we started our approach into Cambridge. We could see Stansted Airport, where we had been supping on cups of tea just a few hours before, off to our right and the M11 motorway below was just coming alive with Sunday morning motorists. With the soft reassuring squeak of the tyres kissing the tarmac back on the Cambridge runway, we taxied to the apron and shut down. I thanked Roy for taking me on the adventure and headed home for a few hours of sleep.

By early afternoon, I was back at the airport helping Ashley fix all the passenger seats back in the aircraft ready for the first flight out to Amsterdam at seven o'clock the following morning.

By the time the summer of 1989 had come around, a few months later, I had passed my driving test and had been granted the occasional use of my mum's Mini. The Sucklings had asked me if I could spend two weeks that summer filling Ashley's shoes whilst he was on holiday; another opportunity that I grabbed with both hands. Each day involved getting up at four thirty a.m. to be at the airport by five a.m. Once there, I had to go out to the aircraft to power it up, check the fuel quantities and other items on the cockpit instruments, and check that all external lights on the aircraft were in working order. Once the aircraft had been 'woken up', as the Sucklings called it, I wandered over to the control tower to collect the latest weather for the flight crew that would be arriving at about six a.m. for the first departure at seven a.m.

Having briefed the crew on the state of the aircraft, fuel and weather, my task then turned to aiding the passengers who started arriving for their flight to Amsterdam. I would assist with the check-in process and provide them with tea or coffee and a newspaper before they boarded at about six fifty a.m. Once the aircraft left at seven a.m., I would stand outside and watch it take off before heading back into the tiny terminal building to tidy up, have a sit down, and wait for the next set of passengers for the nine thirty-five flight to Manchester start drifting in at around eight thirty a.m.

At about nine o'clock, the radio would come alive with the inbound flight returning from Amsterdam. The co-pilot would pass on details of how many passengers they were carrying and how many required taxis into Cambridge upon arrival (yes, really!).

I would also take the requirements for additional flasks of coffee and cartons of orange juice to be loaded on the turnaround between the inbound and outbound flight. These turnarounds were the most adrenaline-inducing parts of the day as the aircraft needed to be unloaded of its passengers and bags from Amsterdam, cleaned, restocked, and then reloaded with the passengers (and their baggage) heading to Manchester, all in the space of ten minutes. Often, with only a handful of passengers, this was easy but a relatively full flight on either the inbound or outbound leg could see this slip a bit, although the aircraft would always seem to pick up a bit of time and land on schedule into Manchester.

Once each week, if space allowed, I would jump on at the last minute to fly up to Manchester where I would disembark, run into the terminal to the ticketing desk to top up the Suckling Airways marketing material and pocket timetables then run back down to re-board the aircraft for the return flight back to Cambridge.

By eleven fifty a.m., and approaching lunchtime, the aircraft would land back at Cambridge and the morning crew would knock off. I would head home for a couple of hours before being back at the airport for the afternoon departure to Amsterdam at three fifteen p.m. This sequence of flights repeated in the afternoon, with the last flight arriving back into Cambridge at seven fifty p.m. Upon closing the aircraft up and saying goodnight to the airport security staff, I would head home for a spot of dinner before going to bed and starting the whole process all over again the following morning.

I performed this two-week stint filling in for Ashley for three summers and loved every moment of my time working for the Sucklings. I grew very fond of them and, as strange as it sounds, I also grew rather fond of their aircraft, having spent many happy hours in its company over my time at the airline. Sadly, however, that aircraft was destroyed in a landing accident in Chile in 2013 in which the two pilots died.

The airline itself expanded throughout the 1990s before changing ownership in 1999 to become known as Scot Airways before being sold again to large Scottish regional airline Loganair, in 2011. Although the Suckling Airways name no longer exists, it will always be remembered as the airline which was set up by a husband and wife team around their kitchen table, and which was run more like a family than an airline. It was an incredibly fun place to work and I will always look back on my time there with a happy heart.

EIGHT
AND AWAY!

Back at Sixth Form College, as the spring of 1990 began, it was time to start making decisions about what I would do with my life after A-Levels. By this stage, I had decided that – despite CF meaning I couldn't be a commercial pilot – a career in aviation was where my true passion lay. So, I embarked on a series of visits to such glamorous higher education institutions as Cardiff University, Huddersfield Polytechnic, and London City University, all of which offered more generic courses in transport and logistics management, rather than being specifically aviation related.

My last visit was to Aston University, located in the centre of Birmingham and about two and a half hours from Cambridge by car. With its multimodal approach to transport studies plus a good level of business studies thrown in for good measure, the course offered by Aston (a Batchelor of Science degree in Transport Management) seemed the most akin to what I wanted to study. I had also enjoyed my open day visit, and I found the prospect of living amongst the bright lights and bustle of Birmingham (often referred to as 'Britain's second city') quite alluring. There was also the option of taking a year out from the degree course after the second year for what was then called a 'sandwich placement year' (more commonly referred to as an 'internship' these days). This would involve working as a paid employee in the industry for a year before returning to university for the final year of study. I found the proposition of breaking up the degree course with a year of earning a proper salary a particularly exciting one.

Therefore, around the Easter of 1990, my application went off by post to UCCA (the University Central Council of Admissions) for a place at Aston that

October. They responded with an offer of just three C's (or eighteen points in the old points-based system) being required in order to be successful. All I needed to do was to knuckle down, put the revision hours in, and pass my exams that summer. I had done reasonably well during my mock exams, so I hoped to replicate that performance come June.

As the spring of 1990 turned to summer, the college put on a range of activities, from which we could choose one – presumably to allow us to let off some steam before settling down to some serious revision. Me and three good school mates (all of whom I knew from my Sawston days) somehow managed to wangle four out of the ten places available on a four-day train trip to Paris. Actually, I say 'somehow', but a fair amount of badgering and cajoling was involved! We were to be accompanied by a younger, rather attractive, female French teacher, which may or may not have had something to do with why we were so keen to secure a much-coveted place on the excursion.

The journey started at Cambridge railway station at lunchtime of the day of departure, boarding a train to London followed by a chaotic journey by tube to Victoria Station, where we got on a second train to Newhaven on the south coast. Upon arriving at the ferry terminal at Newhaven, some time late in the evening, we got on the ferry that would take us on the two-hour crossing to Dieppe in Northern France. In Dieppe, we would finally board a train bound for Paris.

After what seemed like the longest night of grabbing twenty minutes of sleep here and there on a variety of transportation, we finally arrived at the hotel in Paris the following morning. We were dirty, probably smelly, and undoubtedly exhausted from the epic odyssey that had got us there. But, after a couple of hours to rest, we embarked on a two-day whistle stop tour of the sights of Paris.

Whilst I recall sharing many laughs and having a thoroughly enjoyable time with my three mates on that trip (the main objectives of which seemed to be the procurement of alcohol and trying to chat up as many French girls as we could), the arduous journey there and back did perhaps take the shine off it a little. But we were eighteen, about to have the hardest month of our lives so far sitting our toughest exams yet, and would then be leaving Cambridge to start our new lives scattered around various Universities around the country. So, a couple of crushing hangovers induced by too much cheap French plonk, book-ended by two sleepless nights on public transport, seemed like a small price to pay for a final hurrah.

The four-week period in which I sat my A-Levels was tough going. In addition to the various papers I had to take in each of the four subjects I'd studied, for some inexplicable reason I also elected to sit two of what were then called S-Levels; sold to me as supplementary papers that would allow supposedly gifted students to display their knowledge of a particular subject in greater depth. This was before the invention of A* grades, which effectively aimed to achieve the same thing.

Whilst I was not seeking a place at Oxford or Cambridge, the main institutions to give credence to S-Level papers, I was somehow talked into taking the two extra exams in economics and geography. Whilst I did have to attend classes on how to master exam technique, there was no additional curriculum material to learn. So, I must have thought that it was a good way to get something that my fellow pupils didn't have and, as it only involved sitting one additional three-hour exam in each of the two subjects, it seemed worth it.

Later that summer, it was A-level results day and my grades duly arrived by post. In those days, before leaving college, you had to go to the office with a stamped and self-addressed plain brown envelope in which they would place your results slip and post out to you on a set day. So, when it clattered through the letterbox, as soon as I saw my handwriting on the front of the large brown envelope, I knew what was inside.

In my dad's study, I nervously opened my self-addressed envelope, exactly as I had done so for my GCSE results two years previously as some bizarre nod to superstition. Despite my nerves, I was delighted to discover that I had obtained well in excess of the eighteen UCCA points required, and the reality quickly hit me that I would be off to start a new life in Birmingham in just six short weeks' time.

Looking back, I don't have any recollection of a major sit-down discussion where my parents and I went over how I would manage my health while I was away from home. Maybe they saw me as mature enough to deal with things on my own, or maybe they simply trusted that I would find a way to manage my CF without the safety net of my home environment around me.

Either way, I set off for Birmingham at the start of October 1990 with my dad, two suitcases, my stacking stereo system, and my bedding piled up in the family car. It was time to grab the next chapter of my life firmly with both hands and to deal with whatever came my way – the good, the bad, or the Brummie...

NINE

UNIVERSITY LIFE

NO MORE SAFETY NET

I arrived at Aston University on Saturday 6th October 1990. I had spent the first half of the summer since finishing my A-Levels working several different jobs, earning as much money as I could to see me through the next four years away from home. I'd worked from Monday to Friday in the Holiday Inn hotel in the centre of Cambridge as a linen porter, which basically involved shuttling around the floors of the hotel with a huge plastic tub on wheels, collecting dirty towels and bedsheets from the room attendants' trolleys. Not a particularly taxing job intellectually, and rather tedious at times, but me and my fellow porters made the best of it, jollying each other through our shifts by swapping jokes and with the occasional prank thrown in for good measure. Although I didn't give too much thought to it at the time, all that racing around the floors of the hotel, pushing tubs full of heavy linen, must have been fantastic for my lung function.

At the weekends I would either pick up extra work with Keith and his decorating business or in Jerry's village shop. This was all in addition to my now regular two-week summer stint for the Sucklings. In the ten weeks from mid-June through until the end of August 1990, I took just two days off from all these jobs. But even my quest to become the country's richest student required taking a break now and again.

Following the relentless working schedule that I inflicted upon myself for much of that summer, I then spent the whole of September 1990 travelling by myself around the western USA. I first flew from London to New York on a Virgin Atlantic Airways Boeing 747. Virgin Atlantic had been set up some six years earlier by a British millionaire businessman called Richard Branson, and I harboured a dream of working for his airline. I admired both Branson and the cheeky, upstart approach the airline had taken towards the incumbent airlines flying the air routes across the Atlantic Ocean at the time. Amongst other things, the airline was the pioneer of having personal video screens in Economy class (albeit very small ones) and marketed itself as having the best economy class product between Europe and the USA at that time. The fact that it only had four rather old aircraft in its fleet was hidden away through clever marketing and the seemingly regular appearances of the airline's charismatic owner onboard its flights.

Upon my arrival in New York, I stayed the night in a rather dodgy, low budget hotel somewhere near the docks close to Newark Airport. This was certainly somewhere that once you had arrived at the hotel, you stayed in the hotel and didn't wander out for a late-night stroll. The following morning, I boarded another flight from Newark to Phoenix, Arizona with a refuelling stop in Denver along the way. By the time I arrived in Phoenix, it was late afternoon and the novelty of flying by myself was already wearing rather thin. I was staying with a friend of mine from both Sawston and Long Road College days, Hayley, who had left the UK at the start of the summer and had gone to the USA to live with her American father and her English stepmother.

I gave no consideration to Hayley's domestic arrangements before I left but, as I landed in Phoenix and Hayley's stepmother drove us back to the house, I soon got a sense that all was not quite as I was expecting. To put it in stark terms, I spent the next week or so listening to Hayley and her stepmother screaming at each other with her father occasionally stepping in to try and calm things down 'before the cops turned up'. It was immediately obvious that there was a distinct loathing between the two women, and I had just unwittingly landed straight into the crossfire.

The original plan had been that after a few days in Phoenix, Hayley and I would head to Los Angeles and do a bit of travelling around, although after a week of listening to slamming doors and things being broken, I decided that enough was enough and it was time to leave. Having rung home and told my parents of the situation I found myself in, my father hastily arranged for me to stay with some people he knew in Los Angeles and I asked Hayley whether she still wanted to come with me.

Inexplicably to me at the time, she said that she needed to stay to try and work things out with her father and stepmother. Consequently, the following day, we found ourselves back at Phoenix Airport saying our goodbyes. This was the last time I would see Hayley. We wrote for a few months after my visit (using good old pen and paper back in those pre-email days) but we eventually lost contact. I sat on the plane as it headed west on the hour-long flight to Los Angeles feeling tired and rather shell-shocked. I hoped that Hayley would indeed be able to work things out with her parents and settle down, although, given what I had experienced over the previous few days, I wasn't holding my breath.

The rest of my summer, however, was memorable for much more positive reasons. Thanks to my father, I had a wonderful time staying with my hosts Kathy and Fred in Los Angeles. They lived in the very upmarket district of Palos Verdes, an exclusive estate of huge houses set on a leafy hillside to the south of the Los Angeles basin, with awe-inspiring views of the Pacific Ocean and downtown Los Angeles. They showed me huge kindness, and great generosity, both of which I really appreciated after my rather rough time in Phoenix. They took me to Universal Studios for the day and took me to hire a bike at nearby Redondo Beach, where I cycled the beachside path northwards to Santa Monica – a distance of almost twenty miles – before having lunch on the pier there and then cycling all the way back again. Not bad for a kid with a chronic lung disease, I suppose.

After a few days in Los Angeles, I flew up to San Francisco and had a week staying back in Mountain View with Ann and Ed, a couple my family knew from our time living there and whom my parents were still in touch with. I spent my days being a tourist in my old hometown and loved every minute of it. San Francisco is such an amazing, beautiful city; it is truly one of those special places where you could spend days exploring and feel like you have not even scratched the surface of it. Visiting the former US jail island of Alcatraz, exploring Chinatown, and walking across the Golden Gate bridge were just some of the ways I spent my time during those few days. And I remember telling myself during that visit that I must try harder to return more often in the future.

One morning back in Mountain View, I asked Ann if I could borrow a map and one of the bicycles in her garage as I wanted to explore the local area and try to find my old family home along Diablo Avenue and my former school. Ann provided me with all I needed, and I duly set off in the morning sunshine to take a very personal trip down memory lane.

My route took me to the heart of the area of Mountain View where I had lived back in 1977–78. I first passed by my former school, Monta Loma Elementary. I took a bit of time looking around and peering through the windows of my former classroom where, no doubt, those potentially life-saving earthquake drills carried on being rehearsed just as they were during my time there.

It was still the summer holidays and the school was deserted, so I could explore the campus without being challenged. But, having taken a few photos, it was time to move on.

I could recall the walking route my sister and I used to take with our mother from home to school every day, so I simply reversed it and, with my bike, headed towards our former house a couple of blocks away. With little trouble, I found myself cycling down Diablo Avenue and pulling up outside number 248. I took a few photos and had a drink from a bottle of water given to me by Ann but, before I set off, the front door opened and out of it walked an old lady. She was very friendly but, quite understandably, asked who I was and why was I taking photographs of her home. I explained that I was from England but had lived in her house in 1978 and was simply back so thought I would drop by to see it again.

The lady immediately said she recognised my name and remembered me as a child. I was put at ease by her demeanour and kind words and was thrilled when she invited me into the house to look around and take some more photos of the interior. I walked through the front door and went into the large open plan kitchen and living area, which I remembered as vividly as if I had just left the day before. The lady's husband was also home and I sat and chatted with him while she made some cold drinks and prepared a light lunch for the three of us.

We talked for a while, and I told them about my family and what we were all doing now. They both nodded and smiled at the appropriate places, and I had no reason to doubt that these people were the folks that we had rented the house from some twelve years previously. During our chat, my love of aviation came up and so, once lunch was over, the husband and I set off in his car for Palo Alto Airport, the local airfield where his son owned an aircraft overhaul and maintenance company. I spend the next hour examining some amazing aircraft, obviously owned by some very wealthy individuals, and talking about aviation-related matters with both the husband and his son.

Sometime later, we were back at the house and it was time for me to say goodbye to this kind old couple who had been so friendly and who had looked after me so well that day. As I cycled off back down Diablo Avenue, I remember being struck by the hospitality they had shown me and how lucky I had been that the couple in the house remembered me and my family.

It wasn't until the following evening, when I rang home to update my parents on what I had been up to, that the reality of what had happened the previous afternoon in Diablo Avenue became patently clear; my dad told me that the house had been unoccupied when we went to live there and that the true owners had put it on the rental market because they had gone travelling overseas for a year.

We had never met the actual owners of the house as it was rented through an agency and, indeed, the owners may not have ever known our surname or anything about us as a family. So, the couple who had been so hospitable to me the day before, couldn't possibly have known my name, recognised me, or known anything about me prior to when I turned up outside their house. They certainly didn't need to give up their time to make a stranger lunch and entertain him for the afternoon as they had done. And so, the return to my former home was not all as it seemed and remains shrouded in mystery to this very day.

I still like to think that this was simply two kind-hearted, and possibly lonely, individuals who tried their best to do the right thing when a relatively young teenage traveller from overseas appeared on their doorstep.

I remain of the view that there was nothing sinister about what happened and don't recall anything that rings any alarm bells. Yet that didn't stop me getting a stiff talking to from my dad about the foolishness of wandering into strangers' houses unaccompanied and failing to tell people where I was and who I was with.

I might have been eighteen, full of confidence and adventure, and trying to see the good intentions in people, but I was still young enough to get told off for letting my guard down. And rightly so. Thankfully, an afternoon that could have ended in so many mays, and not all of them good, simply left me with further fond memories of that house and of the time I had spent in that sunny little corner of California.

I returned to the UK a few days later, still buzzing from an amazing trip and with a head full of memories. Yet there was no time for getting over the jet-lag or enjoy any post-holiday recuperation; it was time to get myself organised, to pack up all my things, and to head to Birmingham to start the next chapter of my life as a university undergraduate.

Starting at Aston was a major milestone for me, as for any student living away from home for the first time, and I wasn't sure whether to be excited or nervous about the whole prospect. In the end, I settled on allowing myself to feel a bit of both. Having CF didn't make me feel particularly more nervous about the whole experience, but I recall being very aware that I would now be solely responsible for managing my condition and my health on a day-to-day basis. The days of having my parents acting as a safety net, looking out for me, running me to medical appointments, and making sure I took my medication were no more. I was now fully in control; not just for the next four years but for the rest of my life.

My dad drove me to Aston on a Saturday morning, and we arrived on campus around lunchtime. We soon established that I would be spending the first year of university life living on the second floor of Stafford Tower, one of three twenty-storey tower blocks built on the campus in the seventies. Given that the Aston campus is confined on all sides by parts of Birmingham city centre, the only way that the huge increase in student numbers in that decade could be accommodated was by way of using the vertical space available, and by building these three towers for student accommodation. When built, the towers were among the highest student accommodation in the UK, giving their residents far-reaching views over the centre of Birmingham. Back in the seventies and even in the eighties, however, following the death of large-scale manufacturing in the West Midlands and the resulting austerity experienced by the whole region, I am not sure whether these views would have been particularly enticing or inspiring!

Birmingham was in a rather sorry state by the time I arrived in 1990 and in desperate need of inward investment and rejuvenation. Conversely, if you visit Birmingham nowadays, the place is largely unrecognisable even from the early nineties and my time there. Much of the city centre has now been transformed into a thriving business, commercial, and leisure destination for the heart of England. The campus at Aston has been similarly transformed, with Stafford Tower (along with its two sister towers) having been demolished in 2014 and replaced by swanky new student accommodation.

I had arrived at the end of what turned out to be freshers' week at Aston. The other nine guys living on my floor of Stafford Tower had spent the previous few days getting to know each other and getting incredibly drunk, but I had forgone the opportunity in order to stay as long as I could in the USA. Whilst not giving it a second thought at the time, this meant that by the time I arrived on campus, I was already playing catch-up in terms of getting to know people and finding a social group in which I felt comfortable. But the others on my floor were all nice enough; they came from a huge variety of backgrounds and were all doing different courses to me. We would spend the next nine months conversing in the communal kitchen, playing the tactical world domination board game Risk in each other's rooms until the early hours, and going across the road (or rather, through the dimly-lit underpass beneath the expressway which linked the campus to the city centre) to our local Indian restaurant, Royal City Tandoori, for our regular fix of Balti chicken (a hot and spicy curry dish famously invented in Birmingham).

The waiters in that establishment were blessed with levels of patience far greater than I have experienced anywhere else on earth; in the early hours of Saturday and Sunday mornings, the place would be packed out with gangs of hopelessly drunk, rowdy students, barely conscious enough to remember their own names let alone order and consume a meal. Yet the waiters dealt with such groups with courtesy far beyond what was deserved, and always managed to maintain their dignity while all those around them surrendered theirs. If going to university was all about life experiences, then sitting in Royal City at two a.m. watching hordes of students, worse for wear after spending a week's worth of grant money on beer in one evening and falling asleep face-first in their lamb bhuna, was certainly one of them.

After a few days of being at Aston, and conscious that I was now responsible for looking after myself, I went and registered at the campus medical centre. Thankfully, however, in the whole time that I was in Birmingham I never had cause to return to the medical centre other than to collect repeat prescriptions for my regular medication. I also made sure that I followed up on a referral made on my behalf by Addenbrookes Hospital to the local CF team, which was based at East Birmingham Hospital, since rebranded as 'Birmingham Heartlands'. I received an appointment letter soon afterwards and within a couple of months would be heading there for my first consultation with them.

As the first term progressed, I knuckled down and got on with studying. I took being a student seriously, in the most part, and worked hard. It must be said that my chosen degree course in Transport Management was not the most challenging thing I had ever done, nor did it place particularly onerous demands on my time with only around twelve hours of lectures a week. Wednesday afternoons were always clear (as this has traditionally been the slot when all UK students participate in some form of sport) and Fridays were supposedly 'study days'. Ask just about any of my cohort what they understood by the term 'study day' and their answers would largely involve lying in bed all morning then heading to the pub or Student Union around lunchtime for a few beers before going back to bed to 'rest' before the weekend's entertainments really kicked off. Having Fridays free also meant that those who wanted to head out of Birmingham for the weekend could do so on a Thursday evening, thus availing themselves of cheaper fares on trains and coaches before the Friday price-hike kicked in.

On arriving at Aston, I had signed up for membership of the Musicians' Society, stating that I was a 'drummer and percussionist' on the application form. It wasn't too long before I was contacted about playing in a band that was to accompany the Christmas drama production being put on by the University Drama society. I saw this as a good way to get to know a wider range of people other than just those on my course or those that I shared floor two of Stafford Tower with, so agreed to join. This was the spark that I felt needed as up until that point, I had been feeling a little lost and with only limited lecture time during the week, my life at Aston needed filling up a bit. Doing the Christmas play was great fun and the after-show party was particularly memorable, with a free bar laid on for all those involved in the production. I made good friends with the other musicians in the band and had got back into the one thing I really enjoyed and was quite good at – drumming. What I didn't know then, was that agreeing to do the show would result in me being gainfully employed as a drummer in one form or another throughout my university career.

My first visit to East Birmingham Hospital came shortly into my first year at Aston. The hospital was located in the Bordesley Green area of the city some twenty minutes by bus from Aston. As it was my first visit, there were various forms to fill in and a few extra tests to be carried out before I got to see the consultant. I was attending in the days when the hospital ran only a general chest clinic rather than a specialist CF clinic (which was to come later), and this was before the time when CF patients also got to have chats with dietitians and physiotherapists at their hospital appointments.

On this occasion, I had my initial consultation with the registrar rather than the consultant, who was elsewhere that day. The registrar thought it wise that whilst I was away from home, I attended clinic once a term just so that they could, "Keep an eye on me in case things started to decline."

I remember asking what he meant by this, and he told me that I was now of the age when, typically, things started getting harder for those with CF and that I should start to expect more frequent hospital visits.

This was the first time that I recall any doctor *ever* pointing out in such stark terms that CF is a progressive condition. I also recall realising, for the first time, that CF was not something that would just stay in the background for the rest of my life and that it was something that needed much more constant monitoring than I had been used to.

I headed back to Aston following that appointment feeling rather melancholy and despondent; while I probably still didn't fully understand how significant CF would become in my life as I got older, for the first time that day I began to get the smallest sense of what might lie ahead.

This minor wake-up call had the opposite effect on me than one might expect. Despite having set out at Aston with the intention to keep myself well and to ensure I took all of my medications and carried out my treatments, those best intentions were soon forgotten in some sort of misguided act of defiance against CF.

Being brutally honest, thirty years on I have no memory of being particularly diligent about taking my medications whilst at Aston or, indeed, of doing any physio. So, I can only conclude that I was very bad at doing so. How I remained so well remains something of a mystery to me; I pushed my body hard, didn't sleep very much, and – like most students – drank far more than was good for me. Yet somehow, I got away with it (although I suppose there is an argument that it all catches up with you in the end, whether you have CF or not).

In the lead up to Easter break in the spring of 1991, I went to a band night at the Students Guild. There were ten bands playing that night, but it was the penultimate band that would catch my eyes and ears the most. The Confession had male and female joint vocalists, played a mix of their own songs and cover versions, and seemed to have the biggest following out of any of the bands performing. I vaguely knew the bass player, Andy, who had also performed in the band for the Christmas show with me. I watched them play their set and the way the crowd reacted, and could only hope that soon I would be playing in a similar band and be able to take part in future band nights rather than just be a spectator.

Within just a couple of weeks, my wish would come true; I was checking my post box one day after lectures and I found a handwritten note from Andy saying that the drummer of The Confession was retiring from the band to concentrate on his final exams and asking if I would like to take his place? Within twenty-four hours, once I had tracked down Andy, I had accepted the position and a couple of days later I was rehearsing with the band in the Student Guild music room.

We played a few gigs in the remainder of that first year and continued throughout my second year at Aston. Our finest hour came when we were asked to play on stage at the main University May Ball (the biggest night in the student year). We were on the bill that night alongside a host of other acts such as Bad Manners (famous UK ska band featuring larger than life frontman 'Buster Blood Vessel'), Bomb the Bass (who had just reached number seven in the UK charts with their single 'Winter in July') and Bjorn Again (a well-known Abba tribute band). And I thought that performing in front of a bunch of Japanese schoolgirls in a secondary school hall in rural Cambridgeshire would be the pinnacle for my rock and roll alter ego!

It was also at the May Ball in 2001 that I met Jo for the first time.

TEN

STARK REALITIES AND NEW HORIZONS

Jo was also a first-year student studying for a degree in Management and Administrative Studies, and she just happened to live nineteen floors above me in Stafford Tower. Jo was five years older than me and, before returning to studying, had been a qualified nurse at a hospital on the Wirral in Merseyside. We got on well from the outset and spent much of the rest of that first academic year in each other's company. My relationship with Jo was the first serious relationship I had been in, and little did I know in those early days that we would stay together for the next four years, throughout our time at Aston and beyond.

It was Jo who was the first person in my life to spot that I was harbouring a secret and to call my bluff on it. She had noticed how I coughed in the mornings a bit, was a little underweight, and how my fingers were a little oddly shaped at the ends. One evening in my room, she simply asked outright whether I had CF.

I knew that the game was up and that there was no way I could keep the pretence up any longer, so I admitted having CF and we spent the next couple of hours talking through it all.

Jo had spent a lot of her time as a nurse looking after children who had CF. Some of this experience had been with children who were very sick but some were very well and she only saw them in hospital every now and then.

We didn't get into the gritty details of what the future might hold for me during that conversation as we largely talked about how I had managed up until that point. In a way, I felt relieved that I finally had someone who I could confide in about CF. But at the same time, I was very conscious of not turning Jo into some sort of medical advisor, carer, or counsellor.

Inside, though, I was angry that I had been caught out and realised that the veil I drew over my condition was not as bullet-proof as I thought. I was also angry that someone who I had developed serious feelings for might now treat me differently because of CF, something I had always feared and had protected myself from. I wanted our relationship to develop without CF coming between us and spoiling what we had.

When looking back on the early days with Jo, I have considered at what point I would have told her about CF had she not confronted me about it. The truthful answer is that, knowing how I felt about everything back then, I would probably have delayed it for as long as I possibly could.

My way of thinking had only been upset because Jo knew exactly what was wrong with me and wanted to get it out in the open. And the same situation would arise again, some years later and with someone else, when I reverted to that person who thought that he could keep CF from those who loved him most.

In the summer term of 1991, I returned to see the consultant at the hospital. For the first time in my life, I let someone else who wasn't one of my parents come with me to this appointment.

Jo and I hopped on the bus and set off for my appointment, but I had not told her about the way I felt after my last visit or about the chat with the registrar that had upset me so much. On this afternoon, however, after all the preliminary tests were completed, we did actually get to see the consultant running the chest clinic.

I discussed the chat that I had shared with his registrar a few months previously and how it had made me feel. Nothing, however, could have prepared me for the consultant's response and if I thought that my previous appointment had been tough, I was in for a nasty shock. Whether the consultant listened to me and thought I was rather naive in my knowledge of CF, or that I was reckless in my approach to it, I am unsure. But he clearly decided it was his duty to give me the full speech about CF, how it was likely to eventually kill me, and would do so even quicker if I did not look after myself.

The conversation reached its most upsetting pinnacle when I asked him how long he thought someone with my severity of CF could expect to live. Pausing to look me up and down before answering, the consultant finally proudly pronounced that if I kept myself well and took my medication, then I could expect to live until my 'mid to late twenties'.

Being nineteen at the time, this brought me instantaneously to tears. I was speechless and shaken by how grave and cruel CF really can be – a concept that I'd never really, until that moment, allowed myself to absorb.

To this day, those words still reverberate in my mind.

Now, as I look back on that day, I wonder whether the consultant was simply trying to scare me or whether that was his *actual* professional opinion at that time. It certainly did scare me, and it made me realise that his words would become reality if I continued to mistreat my body as I was at that time.

It took me a few days to get over the trauma of that hospital visit, and many emotions went through my head during that time. Eventually, anger and despair gave way (with help from Jo) to a determination that I would do all I could to defy that consultant and his doom-ridden prediction, and that this process must start immediately.

That hospital visit, and the subsequent mental processes that I went through, were a pivotal moment in how I look at CF and, furthermore, how I learned to look after myself; I had finally realised that the days of me treating CF as an insignificant sideshow in my life had to end. If they didn't, I would never live a full life or achieve the things that I had always hoped for.

The remainder of my first year at university, and much of the second, was spent studying hard when required but enjoying myself too. Jo and I visited her brother and his wife in New York over the summer break in 1991 and I continued to play in The Confession throughout my second year.

At the start of the second year, in late 1991, I also secured one of the coveted positions of being a member of the bar staff at the various bars around the Students' Guild. These were highly sought-after positions and competition was always fierce whenever a spare slot came up. The queues to get served at the bars on Fridays and Saturdays at the Guild were horrendous and there would always be a sea of people, sometimes three or four deep, right along the bar awaiting their turn.

We, as staff, would always look after our own first, such was the camaraderie amongst us. As such, if you were on a night off and you made your way towards the front of the queue (and occasionally not even that far), you would always get served quicker than others around you. It was an unwritten rule, of course, but all the staff seemed to abide by it.

I worked two nights a week behind the bar throughout both my second and final years, which provided me with a modest income and a few extra pounds to assist me in my efforts to graduate from Aston with as little debt as possible. Back in those days, when smoking was permitted in pubs and bars, I would end the night with the stench of cigarette etched into the fabric of my clothes and my lungs filled with other people's smoke, yet the extra income was handy and pulled a fiscal veil over the harm I was doing to myself by spending so much time in a smoke-filled environment.

Having decided that I would, indeed, take up the option of spending my third year at an industrial placement, I spent a huge amount of time completing application forms for a dazzling array of firms that offered such places.

Around Easter-time in 1992, I was successful in securing a placement with the aviation department of Esso, part of the major American oil corporation Exxon who had just built a huge new head office in the leafy Surrey commuter belt near Epsom, just outside London. It was a major relief to have the placement finalised and left me to concentrate on my studies. I felt very fortunate to have not only secured a placement in a field I was particularly interested in, but also to have bagged one of the best paying placements available that year, much to the chagrin of my classmates.

Typically, students on my course tended to spend their placement years working in draughty warehouses and for haulage companies, so I counted myself lucky that I would be spending my year in a bright, new, warm, and very spacious office complex.

During the Easter holidays of 1992, Jo and I went to California to visit my sister Louise, who happened to be spending the third of her four-year American Studies course at the University of California in Santa Barbara. I had decided that this trip would be a productive way to spend my student loan for that year (rather than to spend it on anything useful like textbooks or feeding myself). So, Jo and I spent three weeks touring around California in a rental car, visiting many of the landmarks and national parks that I had previously been to as a child. We had a fantastic time, went to some amazing places, and really enjoyed being in each other's company and away from Aston.

Sadly, a couple of weeks or so into our trip, however, things took a rather dramatic turn; Jo called home and received some worrying news from her mother. Her father, who was in his eighties, was very ill. He had been unwell, on and off, in the months before our trip but had always rallied and made something of a recovery. However, this time it would be different. He had been told that he had stage four lung cancer and that it had spread to his other organs.

He had been treated for cancer some years previously, but it seemed that this time, given his age and the extent that the cancer had already spread, there was nothing further that anyone could do. Jo was distraught, as was her mother, and it was hard to get a sense of what we should do. I rang my dad to see whether he would ring Jo's mother to ascertain just how urgent the situation was. A few days passed until we rang my dad again. He told us that following his discussion with Jo's mother, he understood the situation to be grave and, from what little detail he had been told, it was his view that Jo's father probably had just a very short time left to live.

After a very short discussion, Jo and I decided that we would curtail our trip and get back to the UK as fast as we could. Jo was heartbroken and I felt completely emotionally ill-equipped to deal with the situation at hand. While I did my best to comfort and reassure Jo, I knew that whatever I did or said, it could never be enough. I just had to do everything I could to get us back to the UK as quickly and as safely as possible so that she could be with her father.

We drove overnight from Sacramento in northern California down to Los Angeles so that we could go and find the downtown ticket office of Virgin Atlantic the following morning, hoping to change our tickets and fly out that same day back to London. This was in the days before ticketless air travel, and you had to be in possession of a hard copy, paper ticket to be able to fly.

We eventually located the airline's offices in Santa Monica and managed to secure two of the last remaining seats on that evening's flight back to Heathrow. Jo was terrified that we would not get back in time for her to say goodbye to her father, and the flight back felt like it lasted double the twelve hours it in fact took.

We didn't speak much on the flight home and neither did we sleep, despite it being an overnight flight. We both just sat quietly, hoping that Jo would get home in time to see her father, possibly for the last time.

Our flight landed the following morning at Heathrow. Jo's brother Brian had driven down from his home in Cheshire early that morning to pick her up and take her straight up to the family home near Liverpool just over 200 miles away. After twelve hours of struggling to find the right thing to say, but also knowing that there was nothing I could say that would make this situation any easier, Jo and I said a hasty goodbye. She was then whisked away towards the car park and I was left on my own in the arrivals concourse, very tired from the last thirty-six hours of travelling, and emotionally exhausted. I just hoped that Jo would make it home in time.

After a cup of tea and something to eat, I got myself to the airport coach station and was soon on a National Express coach heading out of the airport and onto the motorway for the two-hour journey back to Cambridge. I slept on and off as the miles wore on and, as I got closer to home, familiar sights started to appear out of the windows. It was at this point that the dramatic events of the past few days really started to catch up with me. We came to a halt at the coach station in Cambridge and I climbed down the steps with my bags, seeing my dad waiting for me. He came over to me and, without either of us say anything, he hugged me and I simply cried my eyes out, the pent-up emotions of the past few days escaping at last.

Later that evening, the house phone rang. I picked it up to hear Jo's voice. She was upset but she also sounded composed, almost relieved. It did flash through my mind that maybe her dad was feeling a bit better and that she had, perhaps, managed to spend the afternoon chatting away with him, or even that there had been a mistake and that somehow he wasn't quite as ill as we had all thought. Without thinking and simply through habit, I asked how she was. She didn't answer my question, but simply replied, "I made it home in time to be with Dad when he died. I'll call you tomorrow."

The last term of the second year started a week or so after Jo's father died. I had returned to Birmingham to continue my course and Jo returned to Aston a few days later. Her father's funeral had been held in Ireland and he had been buried there too. Jo felt she was ready to get on with studying and so had decided to come back to Birmingham. She told me that she intended to go back to see her mother at the weekends to make sure she was coping without her father, and so we spent the rest of the year seeing each other only during the week.

That term passed quickly and following the end of year exams, it was time to leave Birmingham for the year and move to Epsom in Surrey for my placement year at Esso.

Jo was also taking an industrial placement year and would be working for a large multinational snack food company based in Leicestershire. So, the next twelve months were spent working at our day jobs from Monday to Friday and then traveling at the weekends, either me to see Jo in Leicestershire or her coming to stay with me in Surrey. Occasionally, we would meet at her mother's house near Liverpool, but these visits remained awkward and I continued to feel that perhaps I shouldn't really be there.

One thing that I am not particularly proud of during the year I was away from Aston is that I, once again, took my eye off the ball in terms of managing my CF.

As I was no longer in Birmingham, I had no more appointments lined up at East Birmingham Hospital. However, as I had not been seen at Addenbrookes for a considerable time by this point, I was not under their care either. I let myself fall into the gap somewhere between the two hospitals and, although conscious of the fact that this was not an appropriate approach to be taking, did little to resolve it. Simultaneously, I also became very bad in keeping up with my tablets and physiotherapy sessions. I went running in the evenings and played a lot of five-a-side football, which kept my lungs clear and, thankfully, kept me well. But the fear I'd felt when the consultant in Birmingham reminded me of my own mortality had faded into the background.

I was fortunate, therefore, to get through the year without needing to seek medical advice or assistance from anyone but I had become lazy and had taken on a rather lackadaisical approach to my CF.

I was now in my twenties, yet I was resuming the attitude that I had held towards CF in my childhood. I have no doubt, looking back, that this behaviour will have had some effect on how my life has been affected by CF since then. It was my responsibility to ensure I took care of myself but (not for the first time in my life) I was not taking this responsibility as seriously as I should.

Any person with CF will be quick to tell you that their required daily treatments can be tiring and mundane, and just how nice it would be to occasionally take a break from having to deal with CF. Yet I had taken this to the extreme, and I gave CF very little consideration at all during my twelve months away from Aston, almost certainly to my detriment in later life.

Upon completing my year working in Surrey and returning to Birmingham in Autumn 1993, I settled back into studying and we were encouraged to turn our thoughts towards the following summer when we would be graduating. I still hoped that, with my interest in aviation and travel, I would be able to get a job working for an airline. The fact that almost no one from my course had secured such a lucrative position in years, and that the closest thing to it was a junior role offered by the planning department of Birmingham Airport, did not deter me. In addition to filling out numerous applications for graduate training schemes across a range of industries, as well as also expressing an interest in returning to Esso down in Surrey, I wrote to around twenty airlines, hoping that just one of them would be able to offer me something.

By the following Easter, just a term away from graduating, I still had nothing lined up and the very real proposition of heading back to Cambridge, living at home, and signing on to the unemployment register was starting to loom large on the horizon.

My first visit back to East Birmingham hospital didn't go well either. If I felt that I had had a bad time at previous appointments, that was nothing compared to what I had to go through this time. On learning that I had not seen anyone about my CF in the sixteen-or-so months since I had been at East Birmingham previously, the consultant clearly did not know what to do with me.

His options were either to give me an absolute roasting or to roll his eyes, shrug his shoulders, and wash his hands of me. As it happens, I got a bit of both, although I promised both him (and, I suppose, myself) faithfully that I would stop being so foolish and start taking CF much more seriously in return for him agreeing to continue to have me as his patient. Unlike before, I knew that this time I would comply with his instructions.

Jo and I continued seeing each other throughout that final year and spent much of our free time together. Studying was taking up rather more of our time than in the earlier stages of our relationship and, as 1993 became 1994 and the prospect of dissertations and final exams appeared on our respective radars, we both agreed that getting to the end of our degree courses and doing well in our final exams should take priority.

Jo had already secured a place on a graduate training scheme for a large national logistics and warehousing company, which left just me without a job to go to after graduation. The pressure of this, along with the stress of the final exams was a lot to take and I started to struggle a bit, mentally.

Nonetheless, I revised hard over the Easter holidays and got through a fortnight of exams unscathed. There then remained just three weeks of term, which were largely taken up with parties, pub crawls, and spending time with friends before we all headed off to start our new careers or – as in my case – headed back to our parents' houses to come up with ideas as to how we might find a career.

The band I was playing in at the time (curiously named 'Chuff') had a few final gigs around campus and I enjoyed every one of them. Little did I realise at the time that the last of these gigs, held in the postgraduate social centre, would be the last time I would play the drums in a band and that I would be hanging up my drumsticks and finishing my fifteen-year drumming career thereafter.

It was on a warm afternoon in early June 1994 when things took a miraculous turn. I was sitting around the campus lake (more like a glorified duckpond with a large 'A' fountain structure in the middle) with some friends, enjoying a cold beer and relaxing in the sun. We had received our final degree results a few days earlier and had all achieved, largely, what marks we had expected.

I was feeling relieved to have passed with a respectable 2:1, but also a little disappointed as I had missed out on a first-class degree by just three percentage points. This was no time to worry about such matters, though; my main concern was finding a job, and I had no idea how I was going to do that. I certainly wasn't going to achieve it by sitting about in the sun drinking beer. But it is strange the way things turn out sometimes.

As I relaxed in the warm afternoon sunshine with Jo and some friends, Tim (one of the guys on my course) came rushing over to find me. He had a piece of paper in his hand and explained that he had just run over from the University's career advice office. The piece of paper was a photocopy of a fax sent to the University, and I immediately recognised the logo of the company that had sent it. The document was an advert for the role of 'Commercial Planning Executive' with Virgin Atlantic Airways, based down near Gatwick Airport in West Sussex.

I grabbed the piece of paper, read it, and re-read it. Without putting too fine a point on it, the position could not have been more tailor-made for me if I had written the job description myself. Without hesitation, and despite having sunk a few pints of beer, I set about drafting my application letter that same afternoon, keen to get it sent back to Virgin as soon as I possibly could. My letter and accompanying CV were in the post a couple of days later, finely tuned to the job on offer and explaining why I was their ideal candidate. The whole thing seemed like a dream and I found it hard to concentrate on much else for the next few days.

Within a week or so, however, I found myself on a train heading south towards London and then another from London down to Gatwick Airport. On the back of my application, I had been offered an interview with Virgin and was due to meet with the Commercial Manager and a lady called Jane from their Human Resources department later that morning. I shared the journey to Gatwick with Tim, who had also applied for the job and had been offered an interview just after mine that same day.

Tim and I were good friends and had been throughout our time at Aston. We came from similar backgrounds and, although he was from Oxford and me from Cambridge, the only rivalry we had that day was for the job we both desperately wanted.

We shared a taxi to the airline's office in Crawley town centre. Tim sat in reception while I had my interview and vice versa. Afterwards, on the train journey back to Birmingham, we had plenty of time to compare notes on our respective interviews.

The most striking thing we had both experienced was that our interviewer, a nice chap called Martin, had curiously spent the entire time wearing sunglasses. We had expected that Virgin Atlantic might be quite a cool place to work, but the fact that people wore sunglasses around the office was beyond even what we were expecting. (It would later transpire that Martin was suffering particularly badly from hay fever that day, and that his eyes were badly swollen and sensitive to light as a result. Or at least that was his story.)

There were five interviewees that day for the one job, but both Tim and I felt as though we gave strong interviews. We returned to Birmingham where we had our course graduation ceremony a few days later, and then it was time to leave Birmingham once and for all.

I packed up my stuff and swapped contact details with all of my friends. These were still pre-email days, and a long time before mobile phones or social media of any kind had been invented. Contact details therefore consisted of a home address and a landline telephone number.

Jo and I were due to see each other throughout the summer but as for many of the others, I was unsure when and if ever I would see her again. My parents drove me back to Cambridge the day after my graduation ceremony at the start of July 1994, to await a response from Virgin Atlantic and whatever lay in wait for me beyond that.

It was only a couple of days before I received a telephone call inviting me for a second interview back down at Virgin Atlantic. It turned out that Tim had also been invited back and, in fact, it was down to either him or me for the job. On the phone later that day, Tim and I laughed off the fact that we would be battling it out for the much-coveted position, although it was clear that we were both as desperate as each other to get it.

So, a few days later, I was back at the same office in Crawley being interviewed once again by Martin (this time *sans* the comedy sunglasses routine) and his boss Ian. Tim was being interviewed the next day and so we didn't see each other the day I was there.

I gave that second interview everything I had and headed back to Cambridge knowing that I simply couldn't have done any more in my attempt to get the job. The next day, Tim called to say that he too felt that he had done as well as he could have, and we then entered a waiting game to see which one of us would be the successful candidate.

The following lunchtime – as I pottered around at home, having just returned from a trip into Cambridge to talk to a nice lady at the Job Centre and to apply for Unemployment Benefit – the telephone rang. Being the only one at home, I answered it.

To my complete shock, it was Jane from Virgin Atlantic, the Human Resources lady I had met at the first interview a couple of weeks prior.

I was shaking and sweaty as soon as I heard her voice, but this soon turned to sheer elation as she told me that I had interviewed strongly, that both Ian and Martin liked me and thought I would fit in, and that, as a result, they were offering me the job.

After running through a few details about starting salary, number of holidays per year, and so on (none of which I paid any attention to due to my excitement), Jane said that Martin would call me later that day to sort out a start date. She wished me well and hung up. I spent a few moments drinking it all in and calming down before I picked up the phone again to ring my parents at work and tell them the good news – that I had been offered the job, that they wanted me to start as soon as possible, and that as a result (and probably much more importantly for Mum and Dad) that I wouldn't be spending the rest of my adult life living with them after all.

Tim called a short time later to offer his congratulations. He had arranged to work on a project at Birmingham Airport for a while and I told him that, once I had settled in, I would do my best to get him into Virgin Atlantic should any suitable jobs come up – a promise that, happily, I was later able to fulfil.

And so the next stage of my life was set out and was ready to start.

I had survived four years at university and, as CF had started to raise its head more frequently, I was more aware than I ever had been of the importance of keeping myself well.

Being a student with CF was one thing, but I would now be expected to work thirty-five hours a week (and often more), only having twenty days of leave per year, and possibly travelling overseas at short notice. Looking after myself would now be of paramount importance.

ELEVEN
FLYING HIGH AND LIVING LIFE

On Monday 18th July 1994, I walked into an unremarkable office building known as Ashdown House in the centre of Crawley, West Sussex. Crawley was built as a new town in the post-war era as a project to re-house people from overcrowded Greater London, where a shortage of affordable housing was becoming a critical issue. The proximity of Gatwick Airport, which was being developed as London's second major international aviation hub, was to provide a wide range of employment opportunities for those willing to make the move out of the capital, with the surrounding Sussex countryside and adjacent south coast resort towns such as Brighton and Worthing providing ample recreational activities for leisure pursuits.

However, it would be fair to say that Crawley was not the most scenic or picturesque of towns in the summer that I arrived to start my working life.

The initial Government investment back in the 1950s was, by 1994, a distant memory and many of the buildings and housing stock were now proudly displaying their vintage. You could quite imagine coach loads of design students or architectural historians pulling up in the high street to marvel at the iconic building designs, notably the police station, the town hall, the library, and the central shopping precinct that was arranged neatly in a rectangular shape around the rather precociously named 'Queen's Square'.

Whilst there were small signs of some limited investment being made to the town centre and its amenities, there appeared to still be an awfully long way to go. Nonetheless, 'Creepy Crawley' (as it was referred to by many of my new colleagues) was to be my home and for the next four years, so I would have to grow to enjoy it for what it was.

For my first week, I had arranged to stay in a bed and breakfast in the town centre. This was a bungalow owned by a middle-aged couple whose kids had obviously flown the nest, leaving the parents to rent out their bedrooms for a bit of extra cash. It was only a few minutes' walk from the bungalow to Ashdown House and, being July, this provided some welcome exposure to sunshine and fresh air before being confined to a sweltering office building without air conditioning for the remainder of the day.

Given that this Monday was my first day, and whilst I didn't expect any fanfare or grand welcoming committee, I thought at least my new boss would have showed up to greet me, but Martin (the 'sunglasses-at-interview' guy) was off sick with a chronic migraine brought about by (yes, you've guessed it) hay fever again. So, I was told that another chap – by the name of Adam – who worked with Martin would be showing me the ropes and introducing me to people until Martin himself returned the following day. That first day was spent undergoing some IT training to learn the various in-house systems that I would be using and getting to know the building and the people that I would be working with.

After a morning of introductions, it must have been nearing lunchtime when Adam asked me to follow him up the corridor as there was one last person that he was keen for me to meet. Not twenty steps from my desk was an older guy in an open shirt and no tie, sitting at a small desk. As soon as I saw this person, I recognised him from the television and the media. His wavy hair and beard gave his identity away well before Adam had the chance to introduce us formally.

"Richard, may I just introduce Luke? He's just joined us today in the Commercial Department," Adam said politely as I stood before the owner of the airline (and the *very* famous, multi-millionaire businessman) Richard Branson.

"Nice to meet you Luke and welcome aboard." Richard grinned warmly and nodded his head as we shook hands.

Now, whilst I am not one to suffer from being star struck, this was rather a momentous moment for me and I couldn't believe quite what was happening; not only had I just started my dream job working at the one company I wanted to work for over any other, I had also met and shaken hands with one of my heroes on my very first morning in the job. I immediately knew that, for however long I worked for this company, my time here was going to be special.

Martin and I made up the company's Commercial Planning Department, which meant we were responsible for planning out the operation of the airline from week to week and from season to season. At the time of my joining, the airline had fourteen aircraft in its fleet, flying to six US cities as well as Tokyo and Hong Kong in the Far East. These fourteen aircraft had to be organised so that each route was covered each day by an aircraft that had the right capacity and range, as well as allowing for maintenance to be carried out on each aircraft in turn as the schedule dictated.

We were also responsible for managing the landing and take-off slots required by the airline for the congested airports into which they flew, and we were also heavily involved in new route development.

Richard Branson's goal was to have his airline flying on the twenty busiest routes from London (in terms of passengers travelled per annum) as soon as practicable, whilst also maintaining Virgin's reputation as being an innovative, fun-yet-safe airline for both business and leisure passengers alike.

Martin and I made a good team. We were both aviation enthusiasts at heart, enjoyed our work, and got on well together. Martin's tolerance for anyone who didn't see things the way he did was limited, however, and this reputation was legendary around the various departments with whom we had dealings. That said, Martin's dedication to his role was total. He would be in the office at seven thirty every morning monitoring the operation as '*his*' aircraft would land back in the UK after their overnight trips to far flung destinations. He would often be in the office at weekends too, performing this self-appointed paternal role.

After a couple of weeks of getting to know the job and what was required of me, Martin decided that I needed to see the company's operations first-hand. So, after finishing work early on the Friday of my second week, we travelled from Crawley up to Heathrow to catch the late Virgin Atlantic flight to New York JFK airport. If this was not exciting enough in itself, Martin had cleared it with our boss (the Commercial Director of the airline) that, should space allow, we could travel in Upper Class both ways. Upper Class was the airline's version of business class, although it was pitched as more akin to the first class service offered by the competition.

As a young graduate in the second week of his first job, relaxing in a huge red armchair seat in the nose section of the 747 that would take us to the USA that evening, I had to pinch myself to check it wasn't all just a dream.

The flight to New York was wonderful, with fantastic food and drink and amazing service from the crew throughout. I compared it to my first experience of flying on Virgin Atlantic some four years previously (when I had flown on the *very same aircraft*) to New York at the start of my ill-fated trip to visit

Hayley. This thought made me smile, given the change in my status and the very fortunate situation I now found myself in.

We landed in New York that evening and headed to one of the fairly unremarkable hotels situated on JFK Airport's perimeter, in an area known as Jamaica Bay. Again, and as I had discovered four years previously, airport hotels do not tend to be situated in the most glamorous of locations and, whilst possibly sounding enticing, the taxi journey to the hotel quickly revealed that Jamaica Bay was not the sort of place where you would wander out of the hotel for a late night stroll.

The following morning, Martin and I were picked up by the Virgin Atlantic JFK station manager and driven back to the airport to spend the day with his team before catching the flight back to London that night. The highlight of the day, undoubtedly, was a specially authorised visit to the top of the newly constructed JFK Airport control tower, offering incredible views over the whole of the airport and beyond. We could see across Jamaica Bay itself and had amazing views of the Manhattan skyline; an experience that money simply cannot buy.

Before we knew it, though, we were landing back in Heathrow early on the Sunday morning and were back in Crawley by breakfast time. I said cheerio to Martin and headed home for a few hours of sleep, my head still spinning from everything I had experienced since leaving the office not even forty-eight hours previously. Such jet-setting was completely alien to me yet would soon become normal during my time working at the airline.

During those early months of living and working in Crawley, I felt as though I was leading something of a charmed life. I found somewhere more permanent to live, bought a second-hand Mini to drive, and simply loved my job.

After six months of working at the airline, every employee became entitled to concessionary travel on Virgin Atlantic operated flights and, after a year, to cheap travel on flights operated by other airlines too. Whilst the salaries at Virgin Atlantic, like much of the airline industry, may not have been at levels that would make you rich, the concessionary travel benefits were probably the best in the business. You, and up to five named individuals, were entitled to five free of charge (FOC) return flights per year (where you only paid the applicable taxes) followed by unlimited flights at just ten percent of the published fare plus taxes (known in the industry as 'ID90' fares).

All of these flights were on a space available basis; that is, if there was space on the flight after all the revenue-paying passengers had boarded, you flew. But if there was not, then you didn't. Depending on your seniority and length of service, you could also upgrade these flights to either Premium Economy or Upper Class should space be available in those cabins on your chosen flights.

Having access to the airline's booking system from my desk meant that it was a relatively quick and easy process to discover which flights would have space on them for staff travel and which ones were likely to see you not getting a seat and being stranded half-way around the world without a way to get back.

Once I had completed six months at Virgin, me and a colleague – who had also just reached his six-month mark – decided we would take ourselves off for the weekend to celebrate reaching this momentous milestone. Having browsed through the flight schedules and loads for that weekend, we selected Boston as our chosen destination and contacted the staff travel department to organise our tickets.

By three o'clock on the Friday afternoon we were sitting on another Virgin aircraft at Gatwick Airport ready to depart for the seven-hour flight to Boston. After this, Boston soon became a favourite destination for weekend trips as the flight left Gatwick (just up the road from the office) at three fifteen on the Friday afternoon and arrived in Boston in the early evening, local time. This meant that we had Friday evening (if we could stay awake), all day Saturday, and all day Sunday in Boston before catching a flight back to London at eight o'clock on Sunday evening, arriving back at Gatwick just before seven on Monday morning.

Although the flight back to the UK was often very quick (my fastest being just five hours and five minutes) it provided just enough time for a few hours of sleep before dashing home from Gatwick, having breakfast and a shower, and heading straight into the office for nine a.m.

Whilst Boston was the most convenient city to travel to for weekend breaks, New York, Washington, and Miami on the US East Coast were also popular destinations for such trips. For people outside of the airline industry, I appreciate that all this sounds like pure decadence and the stuff of fantasy, and just a few months prior it would certainly have sounded like that to me too. But for us, it was unusual to come into the office on a Monday morning and for someone you worked with *not* to have been somewhere far away over the weekend. Moreover, once you reached a year's service, you became eligible for reduced travel on other airlines too, normally also using ID90 fares. Suddenly, the range of options for weekend getaways became almost limitless and Europe, in particular, opened like the pages of an atlas, inviting you to taste all that it had to offer.

Regretfully, and like many of my work colleagues, my rather limited salary at the time restricted my indulgence in the airline's concessionary travel scheme. That said, I made good use of it throughout my time at the company – as did several members of my family and friends. Amongst them was my old friend William (the legendary recorder player from Stapleford School), who took one of the coveted places on my travel list. I had stayed in contact with Bill (as he was now known). Like my sister Louise, he had spent a year attending university in the USA and had met a girl (who would become his wife some years later). I therefore put Bill on my list so that he could visit his girlfriend far more often than he otherwise would have been able to if he'd been forced to pay full price each time. After providing me with some insight into the correct way to play a recorder all those years before, it only seemed right to offer something in return!

So, my weeks were spent at work, organising which aircraft would fly to which cities in the weeks and months ahead, attending meetings, and working on other ad-hoc projects. My weekends were spent trying to find reasons not to be in Crawley, whether this was trips up to London or down to Brighton (both thirty minutes away by train) or occasionally further afield by aeroplane – as and when my budget allowed.

I continued to rent a room in a house owned by a flight attendant for another airline and – while trying to resist falling into the trap of promulgating stereotypes – my landlady knew a lot of other flight attendants (both male and female) who certainly knew how to let their hair down and enjoy a good party. Life was going well and I was enjoying myself, possibly sometimes a little too much.

TWELVE

WHAT'S YOUR NAME AGAIN?

In the early days of working for Virgin Atlantic, I met two people who would become very important to me; one of whom would eventually become the most important person in my life.

The first of these people was Steve.

From the very first day in Crawley, the name Steve was mentioned in conversation on a regular basis. He seemed to hold legendary status, certainly in the Commercial Department in which I worked. Steve worked in Flight Planning at the Virgin Atlantic Flight Operations Centre down the road, close to the airfield boundary of Gatwick Airport. He was known as the man who knew airline operations inside and out, and what he didn't know about the performance of heavy modern airliners such as the Boeing 747 and Airbus A340 (that Virgin had in its fleet) simply wasn't worth knowing.

But Steve was also known as a fixer and could arrange amazing things at short notice through his contacts with the airline and beyond. In fact, it was Steve that had fixed up mine and Martin's trip to the top of the JFK Airport control tower.

It was on just my second day at Virgin that I met Steve for the first time. Martin had escorted me into Crawley town centre to buy sandwiches at Marks and Spencer for our lunch when we happened across Steve and another chap, Mark, who worked with him in Flight Operations.

Steve was a little older than us, in his late thirties, and was friendly from the outset. Upon being introduced, Steve jovially asked what terrible crime I had committed in order to have been assigned to work for Martin and told me that if I ever needed a 'proper job' in aviation I should give him a shout. On a more serious note, he also told me that I couldn't possibly do my job without getting to know other parts of the airline. Magnanimously, he then offered to give up a morning of his time to show me around the Flight Operations Centre, introduce me to the team there, and help me get a better insight into how the airline operated across each twenty-four-hour period. Of course, I jumped at the chance and the following week I spent a day in Steve's company learning about what he did and gaining a valuable insight into all of the things he *thought* I needed to know (many of which I clearly didn't) about life at the airline.

Steve, originally from Birmingham, was a clever and very knowledgeable man. He was funny and always had a humorous story to tell, aviation-related and otherwise. He had worked for British Airways before joining Virgin and his airline knowledge was astounding.

As I got to know Steve better over the weeks and months ahead, I formed a close friendship with him. There was a group of us that went out from work regularly in those early days and Steve was always in that group, enlightening the rest of us with his extensive knowledge of music, identifying bars and clubs we must visit on our next trip to whichever Virgin Atlantic destination we were discussing at that particular moment, and generally being a fountain of knowledge on just about any topic that came up. He was one of life's all-round good guys and would always stop for a chat and a laugh whenever our paths crossed, often over a beer or two (another subject on which Steve was something of a connoisseur). Steve and I remained great friends for many years, long after we had both moved on from Virgin Atlantic.

After meeting Richard Branson on the first day of my new job and Steve on my second, one might think that my first week couldn't possibly have been more memorable. But the person I met on the Wednesday of that week eclipsed both of those encounters with ease.

That Wednesday, 20th July 1994, I was being shown around Sussex House – another pretty unremarkable office block on Crawley High Street in which Virgin rented several floors.

Sussex House was a horrible building even by Crawley's startlingly low standards. Built in the 1950s, the building itself was now dirty and terribly run down. There was a local government benefits office on the third floor, so it was not uncommon to read in the local paper about a dispute of some description breaking out in Sussex House between staff and a disgruntled customer/client and that the police were in attendance.

The upper floors, however, were occupied by Virgin Atlantic who used the space to accommodate the reservations centre for the airline (in the days when people used a telephone to book a flight instead of the internet) as well as other departments such as Inflight Services and Customer Relations.

I had been sent by Martin over to Sussex House to meet up with a guy called Andy who would show me around. Andy was another person who had worked for Virgin for a few years, having previously worked (like many at Virgin Atlantic) for the now-defunct airline Dan Air. I spent a couple of hours with Andy touring the departments, shaking people's hands, and getting a brief insight into what went on in this quiet little corner of the Virgin Atlantic machine.

Before I headed back up the road to Ashdown House, I was sitting and chatting with Andy in his office until he suddenly sprang up and told me to follow him. Just outside his office was the photocopier for that floor, and using it was someone I had not yet been introduced to.

Andy ushered me over and, muttering words to the effect of, "Right, you two are both new to the company and new to Crawley, so you should probably become friends," he introduced me to a girl whose name sounded like 'Ashley' but, I eventually discovered, was actually the beautiful Irish name 'Aisling'.

Aisling was petite with long, brown hair and brown eyes. She was also rather pretty and displayed a warm, friendly smile as she put down her papers to shake my hand. We glanced briefly at each other, exchanging awkward greetings and, hearing her accent, I realised that she certainly wasn't from my side of the Irish Sea.

Andy told me that Aisling worked in Inflight Services and was responsible for catering and other aspects of the inflight services on several US routes that Virgin Atlantic flew.

With our brief shake of the hands and with nerves rising rapidly within me, I told Aisling that I was working in the Commercial Department at Ashdown House. She quickly explained (so that I was under no illusion) that everyone in the commercial team was considered – by just about everyone else in the airline – as nothing more than frustrated plane-spotters and that we, consequently, carried little credibility in the great scheme of things.

Furthermore, she intimated that she'd prefer that I did nothing in terms of aircraft planning that might unsettle her meticulously organised arrangements for the routes for which she was responsible. With that, she casually threw a, "See you around, plane spotter," quip in my direction and smiling once more at me, picked up her copying from the machine, and walked off.

And that was it. Our introduction was over as quickly as it had begun and I never could have realised, in that brief moment, the significance of what had just happened.

Whilst I accept that the life that I was living in Crawley may sound fanciful, the spectre of CF was never that far away. Although much seemed to be going my way, and my postgraduate life had quickly become becoming both exciting and enjoyable, it would be accurate to say that by this time, CF had placed a hand firmly on my shoulder – reminding me that it was never that far away and, more importantly, that it shouldn't be forgotten or ignored.

Up until the summer of 1994, I had remained under the care of the medical team at Birmingham Heartlands Hospital and had been attending clinic there every three to four months prior to my graduation.

During the Easter holidays of 1994, however, I had an appointment at the Thoracic Outpatients clinic back at Addenbrookes. At this appointment, my future care was high on the agenda because the team in Birmingham would shortly be discharging me from their services. The consultant that saw me that day was clearly buzzing to tell me about a major development in the care of CF in the East of England – one which could have a profound effect on me and my treatment going forward.

He explained that there would be a new Adult CF Centre (for patients aged sixteen and over) opening during the summer of 1994 at Papworth Hospital near Cambridge and that patients for this service were currently being recruited. I had no idea what this meant for me, but as the care of people with CF in my age range was being divested to this new unit, I was compelled to agree to a transfer.

Papworth Hospital was in the small village of Papworth Everard, about twenty minutes to the west of Cambridge and was somewhere I had never visited. I had only heard of this hospital because it would occasionally appear on the local television news when the breakthrough of some new surgical technique was being announced or upon it reaching a particular medical milestone. I had never paid too much attention to its mention as I had no reason to, never anticipating that I would become a patient there one day.[1]

The hospital was originally set up in 1918 by a local doctor, Dr Pendrill Varrier-Jones, who had developed something of a specialisation in the treatment and care of those suffering from tuberculosis (TB) in his catchment area west of Cambridge. This disease was prevalent throughout the general population in the years immediately following World War I, yet the condition was not well understood and treatment was rather primitive. Many discharged soldiers from the battlefields of France and Belgium suffered from the effects of tuberculosis, swelling the numbers of cases in the UK to alarming post-war levels.

Dr Varrier-Jones, through a personal donation from a wealthy local philanthropist, was able to purchase land and buildings at Papworth Hall and to set up a dedicated tuberculosis colony to treat patients with the disease on a larger scale than he had been able to up until this point. Along with more traditional techniques, Varrier-Jones' new hospital was designed to address what he described as the 'after-care' problem; fresh air and natural light were believed to be central to recovery (even in the colder months of the British winter) and so the first hospital building was designed in a large south facing crescent shape, with rooms that opened up so that patients' beds could pushed outside onto balconies, regardless of the prevailing season or the outside air temperature.

From the colony's opening in 1918, and for the next three decades, new treatment buildings were developed on the site around Papworth Hall and in 1948 these treatment blocks were passed to the newly established National Health Service. The facility subsequently began to expand its services and develop expertise in other areas of chest medicine under the new name 'Papworth Hospital'. As surgery started to be used increasingly as a treatment for tuberculosis, Papworth began to attract renowned chest surgeons to come and work there, who over the course of time moved into other types of heart and lung surgery, for example transplantation.

Over the decades that followed, surgeons at Papworth Hospital went on to pioneer several 'firsts' in the field of human medical transplantation including the first successful heart transplant in the UK in 1979 and the world's first heart, lung, and liver transplant in 1986. These ground-breaking procedures helped Papworth to become known as a centre of excellence for heart and lung medicine throughout the world; a reputation it retains and is fiercely protective of even today.

Further services were added to the hospital's portfolio throughout the 1980s and 1990s, and in 1994 CF became the next focus of the hospital.

The plan was to open a new eight-bedroom ward specialising in the care of those with CF in the East of England and to bring together staff from other disciplines already working at the hospital such as physiotherapists, pharmacists and dieticians to create a multi-disciplinary team to treat those with the condition. A young doctor by the name of Dr Diana Bilton had been recruited to lead the new CF centre and was relocating down from Manchester to take up her new role. A dedicated team of nurses would staff the ward, led by a specialist nurse, all with an enhanced degree of experience in treating those with the condition.

I attended my first clinic appointment at Papworth Hospital in July 1994, just before I started at Virgin Atlantic. I met with Dr Bilton and found her most pleasant, with a friendly demeanour and a gentle voice, tinged with the slight hint of a northern accent. We got on well and she congratulated me on being one of the first patients to be enrolled at the new CF centre. I was seen in one of the general clinic rooms downstairs before being taken (along with my dad) up to the new CF ward directly above, to be shown around and to meet some of the staff who worked there.

Accommodated in the western end of what was Varrier-Jones' original building on the site, the ward had been completely refurbished, and everything looked and smelled new. The single patient rooms were large and airy, yet still benefitted from floor to ceiling glass doors and access to the external balcony that had been crucial to the treatment of tuberculosis so many years before. It was an interesting few minutes looking around, although my arrogance (and quite possibly my ignorance too) was telling me that I had no intention of spending any time in this place as an actual patient. After all, I was far too fit and well and enjoying life way too much to ever spend a night there. I was infallible! Wasn't I?

Despite an unwavering belief in my infallibility, not long after starting my job with Virgin Atlantic, I noticed that on my walks to work in the morning, I was getting just slightly more short of breath than I had been used to, and that my lungs had more sputum to shift in the mornings. I had always been a fast walker, but this felt slightly different. Having had a long and frank chat with Dr Bilton just a few weeks earlier, I was now far more educated in what to look out for with CF and the sorts of changes that I may start to see over the course of time.

Shortness of breath and the production of sputum in the lungs were two things that had been mentioned during that conversation, and it quickly dawned on me that this was probably CF making its presence felt for the first time in my life. I decided there and then to take this moment of enlightenment as something of a wake-up call and to act swiftly. After all, I didn't want anything to disrupt the new way of life that I was enjoying so much, or to start a decline that I would not be able to control.

I started running regularly in the evenings, several miles at a time from the house in Crawley, past the local golf course, and onwards down the local country lanes that laced this little corner of West Sussex. Whilst I ran, I would be accompanied by the soundtrack of aircraft taking off from Gatwick Airport as I pounded along. Occasionally, I would stop, take in some air, and have a cough to clear my lungs. By the time I got back to the house, I would either go in and carry out some physiotherapy on myself to make sure my lungs were as clear as they could be or, if I knew my landlady Margaret was going to be in, I would walk around the block a couple of times before returning to carry out the same process but out of earshot. After all, and true to form, I had not disclosed my CF to Margaret and didn't wish to give the game away in such a crude and obvious manner.

Occasionally, I would get to work in the mornings and head straight for the toilets to have a physio and coughing session in order to shift any deposits that had loosened from my lungs on my walk. Whilst perhaps not the most hygienic of places to carry out lung clearance, at least I could do this in relative privacy and without drawing attention to myself in the workplace.

Throughout my life up until this point, CF was *my* condition to deal with and was only disclosed to others on a need-to-know basis. Given that I remained well (for the time being at least) and didn't require time off work through sickness at all, it remained my view that no one else needed to know about CF.

The only concession I made to this was that I told Martin that I had a lung condition and that I would require the occasional Friday afternoon off to attend hospital appointments in Cambridge. Martin accepted this without delving any further into the exact nature of my condition and so that was the approach I decided to adopt for as long as was practicable.

I would keep CF to myself so that I would not attract any unwanted attention, and I would do what I could to avenge the further onset of CF by keeping well, exercising, and eating as much as I could as often as I could in order to pursue those goals.

I travelled to Papworth for Friday afternoon CF clinic once every three to four months and chatted with Dr Bilton to make sure I was keeping on top of things (often turning up late after the two hour drive from Crawley and still in my work suit and tie) and I took the medication that I was told to take to maintain the level of health that I was at that time benefiting from.

I was determined that CF was not going to derail my life at the point I had just started having fun, was doing a job I had always dreamed about, and when everything was going so well for me.

THIRTEEN
FOUR CORNERS

I worked with Martin in the Commercial Planning Department for around a year. I was largely office-based, although I had been able to accompany him to a week-long airline conference in Miami where we stayed at the legendary Fontainebleau Hilton Hotel right on the white sands and crystal blue waters of Miami Beach.

Whilst this was ostensibly a biannual conference where world airlines and airports would come together to talk about business development opportunities and to trade landing and take-off slots, the week seemed to be rather more about who could drink the most margaritas at lunch time and then still be able to attend the nightly cocktail parties – hosted by some aviation-related company or another – either in the hotel ballroom or down on the beautifully cultivated lawns adjacent to the outdoor swimming pool.

One night, at one of the outdoor events, a Virgin Atlantic 747 stopped everyone sipping their cocktails for just a moment as it roared overhead on its way over the beach and departed out to sea on its smoky, noisy way back to London. This earned Martin and I a round of applause from the gathered masses and the unofficial award for having arranged the 'fly-by of the week'.

My main job for the week, however, was mostly to carry and distribute a vast range of Virgin Atlantic merchandise (t-shirts, pens, aircraft models) to anyone we were trying to impress, while Martin got on with the more serious business of trying to secure the airline better landing slots at key airports that Virgin either flew to already or wished to start flying to in the future. The conference was a good mix of work and play and was my first real experience of representing the company on a truly international stage. The week went by in something of a jet-lagged, tequila-fuelled haze but was a great experience for someone just starting out in their career.

Although my short encounter with Aisling would occasionally enter my mind, I remained in a relationship with Jo from university for a year or so after moving to Crawley. We would see each other at weekends as often as we could, although the distance between us had become an issue. Jo had secured a place on the graduate training scheme of a large logistics company (ironically this was normally the domain of those graduating from my degree course) and was based at the company's distribution centre in Stoke-on-Trent.

Getting from Crawley to Stoke by train on a Friday night and back again on a Sunday afternoon was possible but time consuming and expensive, and the available time that Jo and I had together at weekends was only around thirty-six hours. She would also often come down to Crawley but would head back after lunchtime on a Sunday to be back at work on the Monday morning. After a few months of this, our weekend visits started taking on more of an irregular schedule and often two or three weeks would pass between each visit.

This was a time before the internet, email, and social media. So, we would chat by phone in the evenings as much as possible but it was becoming clear to me as time passed that our relationship was perhaps not as strong as it once was and could be entering its final phase.

We spent the Christmas of 1994 together at Jo's brother's house in San Francisco with his wife and young daughter, taking advantage again of my newly-acquired concessions and flying Upper Class together for the first time. Although this was supposed to be a trip for us to spend some 'quality time' together, and to perhaps get things back to where we had been before leaving Birmingham, it all felt very different – verging on awkward at times – and I don't think that trip was anything like either of us had hoped it would be.

Following that Christmas, and during the first few months of 1995, our lives continued to branch off in different directions and, admittedly, I did little to turn things around. I had let myself get carried away with my lifestyle in Crawley, and my ego was perhaps running away with me somewhat. In the end, although our relationship limped on until the early summer of 1995, it eventually became obvious to both of us that, despite our best efforts, it was time to end things.

Over one weekend in Crawley in June 1995, the time had come to bring things to a close. We spent the whole weekend together just talking and crying. We went over the five years that we had been together and remembered the many good times that we had shared. I was feeling very unsure of the future and of no longer being with Jo, but we had simply grown too far apart, and separating felt like the right thing for us.

The things that we had once had in common were no longer there and our lives were taking us in different directions. Jo wanted further commitment from me that I was unable to provide; rather selfishly, I wanted to be able to do as I pleased. Our diametrically opposed positions had progressively brought us to this point and had finally become too great a barrier to overcome.

The weekend was as difficult as it was sad, but I didn't want to waste any more time allowing Jo to wait for something I was not going to be able to provide. Of course, we agreed that we would remain friends (as breaking up couples always do at times like this) but that weekend in Crawley was the last time that Jo and I were ever to be in each other's company, bringing a significant chapter of my life to an end.

Other aspects of my life changed during 1995 too. Back in Cambridge, my parents got divorced around the same time that mine and Jo's relationship was ending. For a while, I'd had a sense that things at home weren't too good and I had stopped going back to visit, so the news of the divorce didn't come as too much of a surprise to me. It seemed that since my sisters and I had left home, my parents had also discovered that they had little in common anymore and wanted different things from their lives. Rather than stay together and be unhappy, they had decided to go their separate ways and to start afresh.

After our experience of living as a family in the United States in 1977, my mother had always harboured a hope that she would go back and live in the US if she ever had a chance. Consequently, she left the UK and went to live close to the city of Raleigh in North Carolina. My father stayed in the family home in Cambridge for a while before selling it and moving to a smaller property in the same south Cambridgeshire village my parents had moved to whilst I was at university.

I have always found that life has a way of balancing things out and the events of 1995 were no exception. Whilst the year may have been difficult in several aspects of my life, one particularly remarkable event took place, which had a huge impact on how I would spend the next few years and which would ultimately set the course of the rest of my working life.

After a year or so working with Martin in the Commercial Department at Virgin, I was asked whether I would like to apply for a new position being created in a newly-formed Airline Alliances department, which basically consisted of just one person, Andy, whom I had met in that early visit over to Sussex House and who had introduced me to Aisling.

The leading trend in the worldwide airline industry at the time was for airlines to enter into joint ventures with other airlines in order to gain access to new markets and to increase global presence. Virgin Atlantic had just one alliance, with a small Irish airline by the name of Cityjet that operated between London City Airport, in the Docklands of East London, to Dublin. These flights, although being about as far from the Virgin Atlantic model of flying large aircraft on long haul routes from Heathrow and Gatwick as they could be, were just the start of a range of joint ventures that Virgin would enter into over the next couple of years, and Andy – with me as his assistant – would initiate and manage those relationships going forward. After interviewing with Andy (who by this stage I had got to know quite well), I was offered the job and started in my new capacity as Airline Alliances Co-ordinator at the beginning of May 1995.

Within a few brief months, Andy and I had responsibility for seven alliance relationships with airlines in the USA (Midwest Express and Delta Airlines), Ireland (Cityjet), Malaysia (Malaysia Airlines), Australia (Ansett Airlines), and South Africa (Sun Air). The nearest alliance to home was with British Midland Airways, based at Castle Donnington in the English Midlands. The nature of these relationships and the degree of complexity varied but given their very nature (and that technology in terms of inter-company email was only in its infancy) the requirement to travel to meet our counterparts at partner airlines was high. So, throughout the second half of 1995, and both 1996 and 1997, I spent an increasing amount of time away from the office and, indeed, the UK.

At one stage during 1996, I found myself in Kuala Lumpur in Malaysia every few weeks for several days at a time. I would leave the UK on the Sunday evening, arriving in Malaysia on the Monday afternoon, and would work on the Tuesday, Wednesday, and Thursday before leaving at eleven o'clock Friday morning to be back at Heathrow by tea-time on Friday evening.

I grew very fond of Malaysia, Kuala Lumpur, and the Malaysian people I would meet, and there was even talk at one point of me being stationed in Kuala Lumpur on a semi-permanent basis to oversee the partnership from down there. Thankfully, this proposal never came to anything as it was decided easier just to fly there and back as and when required rather than to station someone there full time. I say thankfully as I still have no idea now how I would have managed having CF had I been sent to live there for a while and, in fact, may have been forced to pull out on this basis alone.

I particularly enjoyed my trips to Kuala Lumpur as they involved nights out with Harvin. Harvin was a young Malaysian in his early twenties who had been taken on by Andy along with three other locals to act as airport representatives for Virgin Atlantic at Kuala Lumpur International Airport. Virgin planes didn't actually fly to Malaysia in their own colours. Instead the airline would buy blocks of seats on the double-daily flights between Kuala Lumpur and London that were operated by Malaysia Airlines and then sell them on as their own. Strictly speaking, therefore, Virgin Atlantic would have its own customers at the airport, so ground representatives were required to look after them.

On my early trips to Kuala Lumpur, it quickly became apparent to me that Harvin was something of a 'party animal' who loved clubbing and was well-known on the social scene in the bars and clubs of downtown Kuala Lumpur. After spending my days working in the stuffy head offices of Malaysia Airlines, Harvin would always be keen to meet me at my hotel and take me to one of his regular nightclub haunts around the city.

Under Harvin's bad influence, my visits to Kuala Lumpur soon became marathons of endurance; working all day and partying into the small hours drinking pitchers of Jack Daniels and Coke with Harvin and his mates. On one occasion, I was in a nightclub in the city when I spotted a guy wearing an Aston Villa Football Club replica shirt. Aston Villa were my local team at university, who I had been to watch on the few occasions when I could afford to, and so armed with an over-eager sense of enthusiasm (caused by a heavy combination of jet-lag and exhaustion, mixed with several Jack Daniel's and cokes) I decided to go over for a chat. It turned out that not only was this guy from the UK and an Aston Villa supporter, his sister worked in the Staff Travel department of Virgin Atlantic and I knew her quite well. It's amazing how small the world can be sometimes, even if you think you are alone and a long, long way from home.

I enjoyed the two and a half years that I worked for Andy in Alliances immensely. In the Alliances department, I got to travel to some amazing places and do some amazing things. Side trips from my regular journeys down to Johannesburg in South Africa to meet with Sun Air saw me travel to Namibia and Zimbabwe to meet up with representatives from their national airlines and I would often tag a weekend in Cape Town on to a week of working in Johannesburg. I would be in the United States so frequently that upon entry, the immigration official greeting my arrival would often question (with more than a hint of suspicion in their voice) why my regular visits to the country were limited to a day or two on each occasion.

One trip took me to Paris and onwards to Mexico City for a two-day meeting with Aero Mexico, and one of my regrets is that I didn't take time out after that trip to see more of that particular country, but duty called me back to London straight after the meeting concluded.

In general, Andy allowed me a great deal of autonomy, and I went where I liked and for how long I liked; if the work was justified and got done, Andy was happy.

My passport rapidly filled with stamps from a variety of exotic destinations and I got to stay in some terrific hotels in fantastic cities, and to see some incredible sights. Having kept well up until this point, and continuing to look after myself, had allowed me to live a life that I would never have envisaged as possible for a person living with a chronic disease such as CF.

The good fortune of my situation was not lost on me and I felt extremely lucky.

CF may have been waiting in the wings, ready to jump out at me at any time, but I was determined to live life to the full before it did.

The social scene at Virgin was a lively one. On the Thursday after pay day each month, many of the younger employees in the various elements of the Commercial department would go on a wild night out in Brighton. This would normally involve a rowdy meal in our favourite Italian restaurant in The Lanes area of the city, followed by a pub crawl before heading back to the station for the last train back to Crawley just before midnight.

The following day in the office was always noticeably quieter than normal, as people sat at their desks nursing monumental hangovers. As the day wore on, stories would begin to emerge of what japes people had got up to the previous night and nominees for the fictitious, but no less important, 'MPP' prize (the 'Most Pissed Person') would be voted on and awarded. As the afternoon drifted towards the end of the working day, those who had been on the night out would skulk off home for an early night and to start their weekends.

These Thursday nights out became legendary in the Commercial department and everyone looked forward to the next one just as soon as they had recovered from the last. There were also other nights out with work colleagues to local pubs and clubs in the area.

Having got to know Steve from Flight Operations well, I often found myself at some remote pub in the Sussex countryside watching a gig by some band I have never heard of but who came highly recommended by Steve himself. True to form, Steve would often know some of the members of the band performing and always had a chat with them at the bar afterwards – whilst pointing me in the direction of which of the local ales on offer was the best to sample that evening.

On occasion, I would meet up with people from other departments and, with increasing frequency, my path began to cross with that of Aisling, the curiously alluring Irish girl from Inflight Services who I met in my first week at the company.

Over time, Aisling and I struck up something bordering on a friendship. And over the course of 1995, and through 1996, we began to see each other more often, although always with other people and never as anything more than as just friends.

In the summer of 1995, while my landlady Margaret was away working in Birmingham for a few weeks, I decided to have a party at her house. Although it was a small house, I invited everyone I knew and, on that Friday night, the house was packed with people. It was a warm night and even the back garden was full of partygoers as loud music blared out from Margaret's stereo system in the house. Although the party was loud and boisterous, everyone was well behaved and the house was largely left intact, much to my relief.

The following day, a few people came back to help me clear up and within a couple of hours the house was spotless. I even took all the rubbish to the local municipal refuse centre so as not to overwhelm the bins on Monday when the council refuse collection was due.

To my absolute horror, however, as the last of my friends disappeared in their cars around the corner, Margaret's car came into view. It soon became very apparent that one of the neighbours had tipped her off about the party. Upon being questioned as to how the house was so spotless and why the bins were all completely empty, I quickly came clean and confessed to using her house as Crawley's newest pop-up party destination the previous night.

After a chat, it was decided that it would be best if I found somewhere else to live.

Coincidentally, however, I had already been planning to move into a two bedroomed flat in Crawley town centre with my university friend Tim. True to my word, I had put Tim's name forward for a position in the Revenue Management department at Virgin when it came up in early 1995 and, upon getting the job, Tim had been working in the same office block as me ever since.

I agreed with Margaret that I would leave as soon as I had somewhere to go and within a fortnight I was moving into the flat with Tim where our beer drinking, partying, and general larking around continued from there.

As a footnote, on the evening before I moved out of Margaret's, she cried and told me that I had been the best lodger she had ever had and that she didn't want me to leave after all. But the contract was signed with the letting agent and the deposit had been paid. So, two years of flat sharing (and laddish larking around) with Tim awaited. Whilst I remained on good terms with Margaret, there was no going back.

Tim and I had a great couple of years in that flat. We came and went as we pleased, and often one of us would be there on our own as we both travelled a lot with our respective jobs at Virgin Atlantic. The flat often became the rendezvous point for 'pre-drinks' prior to nights out with friends in Crawley or for a venue for post-closing-time drinks after the pubs had all shut.

For the time that we lived there, Tim and I ran various challenges between us to keep things lively, the most notable of which was our 'airline sector challenge'. This was simply what it sounds like – a competition to see which of us could fly on the greatest number of commercial airline flights during that year (for either work or leisure purposes). We had a log sheet pinned to the notice board in the hallway on which we recorded our respective flights, and the competitiveness was intense.

During 1996, I managed one hundred and ten flights to Tim's ninety.

This was my busiest period of travelling and I was flying, on average, just under once every three days that year. There was no prize for this, or for any of the other silly contests we engaged in, yet this did not diminish the healthy competitive spirit that existed between Tim and I.

It also became something of a habit that after a night out – and coming home slightly worse for wear – I would pick up the phone and ring Aisling for a 'chat'.

Aisling had rather foolishly once told me that she always stayed up late in the evenings and so, for reasons that still remain unclear now, I would call her up and ramble down the phone at her, laughing at my own jokes, and wittering on about nothing in particular.

I am convinced now that Aisling was probably sitting at the other end of the phone (having placed it on 'speaker' mode) reading a good book or doing the ironing rather than listening to me. But unfathomably, she never hung up on me. I quite liked that about her and continuing to enjoy 'a bit of craic' (as Aisling would put it) whenever we spoke, our friendship developed over the course of 1995 and into the following year.

Looking back now, I can see that I pushed my body to the limit during this period of my life. And although it cannot be said with any certainty, everything that has happened to me since may have been triggered by how I lived my life during those years. After all, I worked hard, played hard, and spent an awful lot of time on aeroplanes breathing in recirculated air and other people's coughs and colds.

But simultaneously, and unlike when I was at university, I worked hard to keep myself well by running, doing my physiotherapy daily, and eating properly.

I continued to attend Friday afternoon clinics at Papworth every three to four months and got very good at picking my medicines up from the local pharmacy in Crawley on a monthly basis.

Despite all that I threw at my body, it held up well and did not let me down once.

By the age of twenty-four, other than when I was born, I had still not spent a single night of my life in a hospital bed and had no experience of treatment for CF-related chest infections other than occasionally taking a few extra oral antibiotic tablets.

I was fully aware that I was living a charmed life and I hoped that this would always be the case. Simultaneously, though, something within me was telling me that this could never last. The information I was learning from my regular trips to Papworth – from my chats with Dr Bilton at clinic appointments and the knowledge imparted to me in no uncertain terms from the doctors in Birmingham – were building my awareness of what CF was *really* like and what the disease would do to me as time went on.

Yet, with my arrogance and optimism keeping me going and with nothing more than good fortune preventing me from entering a downward slope with my health, I remained cocooned from the harsh reality of CF, protected from what lay in wait for me ahead.

I was enjoying myself, had good friends, and in the most part loved my life. It would be another couple of years before my body would finally crack and succumb to the awful effects of CF for the very first time.

FOURTEEN
REACHING FOR THE SKIES

I had always wanted to learn to fly. For as long as I could remember, I had dreamed of taking the controls of an aeroplane and flying myself around the sky. From those very early days of my childhood, watching the aircraft passing low and slow over my grandparents' back garden in West London, I had harboured a desire to join the ranks of those who no longer considered the earth's surface their single domain of existence and had often looked to the skies for further adventures.

Throughout my life, through flights I had taken on both small and large commercial aircraft, flying with Mr Suckling on the Dornier to Guernsey, and other flying activities, I knew that obtaining my private pilot's licence (PPL) was the single most important thing that I wanted to achieve, above almost any other.

Towards the end of 1995, I was in a good place.

I had a good job at Virgin Atlantic and was earning enough money to save a reasonable amount each month. So, it was my hope that one day this would become enough to enable me to take flying lessons. My health was good and I was keeping myself well. Working in aviation and being surrounded by aviation-minded people had really stoked my interest in flying, and I had started to read an increasing number of articles and publications on a wide range of aviation-related matters.

I would often chat with the airline's chief pilot when he came into our offices for meetings and, through my colleague and friend Steve, often found myself being invited onto the flight deck of Virgin Atlantic aircraft for the take-off or landing (and sometimes both) at some of the world's busiest airports should I happen to be on that flight for a business trip.

I have fond memories of dawn landings at Heathrow, of landing at Los Angeles Airport in the mid-afternoon sunshine, and of taking off from New York's JFK airport at night in a snowstorm. These were all from the spare seat in the flight deck of a Boeing 747 and, believe me, nothing awakens a dormant yearning to learn how to fly than experiences such as these.

It was a normal working day, late in 1995, when I was in town for my usual lunchtime walkabout. I had stopped at the local newsagents in the town centre and had spent a few minutes flicking through the pages of Pilot magazine when an advertisement towards the back caught my eye. Taking up the whole page, the headline of the advert read 'UK PPL in 21 days for £1990'. I read and re-read the advert before purchasing a copy of the magazine and rushing back to my desk at the office to examine the advert in minute detail.

I should explain at this point that normally, in the UK, obtaining a pilot's licence would cost around four thousand to five thousand pounds and could take anything from a few weeks to a few months to complete, due to the unpredictability of the British weather. As flying training for a basic UK PPL requires good clear weather conditions throughout, most student pilots suffer from extreme frustration as flying opportunities are frequently lost due to inclement weather on the days booked for lessons. But this advert offered something that no other had ever done, and reading it again revealed exactly why; it was based in Florida, where the weather is almost ideal for aviation and where the price of aviation fuel was significantly lower than that in the UK.

As the establishment was run by a British flight instructor and registered examiner, it had special dispensation from the Civil Aviation Authority in the UK to teach the UK PPL syllabus and to issue a UK licence to those who successfully completed the course.

For the rest of that afternoon, I remained distracted by the contents of the advert and the magazine lay open on my desk on the relevant page for the rest of that day. My mind wandered over and over as to how and when I might be able to take advantage of this offer. From that point on, I had my mind set on spending the money, going to Florida, and finally obtaining my PPL. There was no question in my mind that CF would prevent me from doing this and, even if it tried, I would simply have to find a way around it.

A couple of days later, I was at home and decided to ring the number shown on the advert. Curiously, it was a freephone number in the UK. I dialled and waited. After a few seconds and a few clicks on the line, I heard the unmistakeable sound of an American ring tone at the other end. Almost instantly, a lady answered who had an English accent, introducing herself in that typical American way by saying, "Hi, this is Jackie."

Jackie explained that she was the co-owner of Ormond Beach Aviation, the flight school in Florida, and that her husband was her fellow co-owner and the in-house examiner. Although I had called a UK number, the line had connected straight through to the office at the flight school in the USA and this was where she was speaking from.

We spoke for about twenty minutes as I extracted as much information as I could from Jackie about the school, the location, the training, and just about anything else that came into my head. Jackie told me that she would put some information into the post and that it would be with me in a few days. Really, though, there was no need for anything further; my mind was already made up. I was going to Florida to learn to fly in three weeks. I would go as soon as I could. I just needed to sort out the details, book the time off, and I would be on my way.

With a little research, I had found out that Ormond Beach was a small town on the north-eastern side of Florida, on the Atlantic Coast. Its nearest large city was Daytona Beach, with Orlando two hours' drive to the west and Miami five hours south. Ormond Beach was also located close to the Kennedy Space Centre, further down the east coast and home to the NASA space shuttle programme (more of that later). Ormond Beach, like so many small towns throughout the US, has its own municipal airport, taking up acres of land with three huge tarmac runways and numerous aircraft parking areas and hangarage. There were no scheduled commercial flights to the airport as there was no passenger terminal (Daytona International Airport nearby catered for the local airline traffic) but there were several flight schools and other aviation-related businesses located on the airfield.

Given that this was late in 1995, and that my leave for that year was just about exhausted, it was clear that I would have to wait until early 1996 before I could head to Ormond Beach Aviation. I discussed it with Andy, who was happy to allow me the time off. Three weeks' leave in one go was unusual in the office (unless you were getting married) but this was different and, as I agreed to leave it for a couple of months so that Andy and I could arrange our work and travel schedules accordingly, I was permitted the time off.

The travel to Florida would, of course, be easy and cheap as I could simply use my Virgin Atlantic concessionary travel benefits, and accommodation was included in the excellent price of the training; students lived in one of several houses that the flight school owned just around the corner from the airfield in Ormond Beach. All I had to do was to apply to the US Embassy in London for a special student visa, which could be done in writing (by using the fax machine in the office) and I was all set, except for one thing. And that one thing was the big one – I had CF.

Jackie had explained that upon arrival at Ormond Beach Aviation, the first morning is spent in the company of a local doctor who issues temporary medical certificates to those learning to fly at the school. This was the only aspect of my plan that I had concerns about. I just could not take the risk of paying my money and arriving in the US, only to be turned away by someone who in all likelihood knew very little about CF (for the risk of being sued should something happen to me, or worse still, to one of Jackie's aircraft).

I had to take some action to mitigate that risk, so I asked around at work and obtained the details of the Aeromedical Division of the Civil Aviation Authority (or 'CAA'). This was the department that issued medical certificates to every holder of a UK pilots licence, whether they were amateur weekend pilots flying small propeller planes around for fun or those who flew Concorde faster than the speed of sound across the Atlantic Ocean for a living. I rang the number and booked myself in for what was called a Class Three medical. Should I be successful in passing the medical and obtaining a Class Three medical certificate, I assumed that I could take this with me to the US and I would be ready to strap an aeroplane to my backside and take to the air without having to trouble the nice American doctor chap at all.

Rather conveniently, the Aeromedical Division of the CAA was located in an office building between Crawley town centre and Gatwick Airport. So, I trotted out of the office one morning in early January 1996 and made my way to the appointment.

I had decided that there was too much at stake to not be full and frank about my condition with whoever I met there, but as I remained fit and well (and from the little research I had done into the matter) I was not too concerned about the outcome. As it turned out, I passed the Class Three medical with flying colours (excuse the pun once more) and I was issued with a stamped piece of paper that I could take with me to Florida when the time came.

As I headed back to the office, my relief was palpable. Rather than focussing my attention back on work, all I could think about was getting the diary out, identifying the three weeks that I would take off, and sorting out the final details. My dream of learning to fly was within touching distance. I had the money saved to pay for the training, the means to get to Florida, somewhere to stay when I was there, and the medical clearance in my hand. All I had to do was tell Andy when I was leaving for the US... and inform my parents of my latest escapade.

That evening, I rang and left a message for my Mum. I knew she would not be keen on my plan as she hated 'little aeroplanes' and avoided them at all cost. In fact, she had never been the greatest fan of flying in any shape or form; I recall when me and my sisters were young, her and my father went on a couple of trips together related to his work, but she insisted on flying on a different plane to my dad, "Just in case something should happen."

Given that my attitude to flying was the opposite to hers, it was perhaps a welcome relief that I was able to give just the sugar-coated, edited highlights of my news on her answer machine without any comeback on that occasion.

Conversely, my dad's reaction was as astounding as it was welcome. He listened with interest as I explained my plan. I went into detail about the course, the location, what was involved, and the costs. I was able to answer his numerous questions about all aspects of the trip and my enthusiasm and excitement must have clearly been detectable over the phone line. All that said, it still came as an absolute shock when Dad paused, obviously thinking for a second, and then said, "Well, it all sounds quite exciting. So, maybe I'll come with you."

At this time, my dad was in the twilight of his career as a medical scientist and was working three days a week as the editor of a cancer journal in London. He had some time on his hands and had already begun planning some major adventures for when he would retire completely within the next couple of years. Yet the news of my plan had obviously stirred something within him, and I could not have been happier; not only was I going to fulfil a lifelong ambition in the very near future but I would have my dad as a travelling companion and fellow student!

Over the next few days, we decided on our date of departure. We would leave at the start of February 1996 with the hope of being back around three (or thereabouts) weeks later. I liaised with Jackie at Ormond Beach Aviation for the two of us. I booked the outbound flights at work and got my leave signed off by Andy.

Dad and I decided that we would leave the date of our return open in case we either finished the course early (which seemed at that time highly unlikely) or overran the advertised twenty-one days. We paid our respective course fees to Ormond Beach Aviation by international bank transfer and applied for our student visas from the US embassy in London (a matter from which my dad drew much amusement, having not been classed as a 'student' for over thirty years).

By early January 1996, everything was in place. It was almost time to go and strap ourselves in for this amazing journey, reach for the skies and to earn our wings.

FIFTEEN
GOING SOLO

My dad stayed with me in Crawley the night before we left for the USA and, on the morning of Friday 2nd February 1996, we departed Gatwick Airport on the Virgin Atlantic flight to Miami. From there, Dad had arranged to hire a car and drive us two hundred and sixty miles up the eastern coast of Florida to the city of Ormond Beach, the location of our flight school and our home for the next three weeks.

Completely unlike him (as he always planned everything meticulously and to the last detail), I am not sure that he fully considered that this drive would done at night, in the dark, and after having just flown ten hours across the Atlantic Ocean. Nonetheless, after several hours of driving, we safely arrived at Ormond Beach late at night and rang Jackie from a pay phone at a BP service station just off the I-95 freeway. She came along to meet us and we followed her to the house in which we would be staying for the duration of our time there. It was a large single-storey house with four big double bedrooms, each with two single beds and its own bathroom.

Dad and I were sharing a room and Jackie subsequently left us, telling us to be at the office at the airfield by nine o'clock the following morning to complete the paperwork and to be taken to our medicals. We shared the house with a bunch of other students at the school, all of whom seemed to be like-minded youngsters (I exclude my dad from that description) and all keen to take to the air. Some were newbies like us who had never flown anything before but had spotted this unique way to obtain their PPLs quickly, whilst others were more serious fliers, either building hours or gaining extra licences on their way to forging a career in the airline world of tomorrow.

Either way, everyone seemed friendly enough and as I lay down that first night, buzzing with excitement as to what the next three weeks held in store, I was fast asleep no sooner than my head had hit the pillow.

The next morning, through a combination of eagerness to get going and the time difference between Florida and the UK, we were up bright and early and headed to the airport. Ormond Beach Aviation was based in a multipurpose building that acted as an office, classrooms, a small cafeteria, and an aircraft hangar for maintenance. As we parked the car and walked across the apron, we caught our first glimpse of the fleet of aeroplanes that we would be flying. All of Ormond Beach Aviation's aircraft were sitting together out on the ramp in neat rows. There must have been twelve to fifteen aircraft in total, mostly single-engine, propeller-driven Cessnas with a couple of twin-engine Piper aircraft for those whose preference was for two engines versus one. The aircraft were all together outside the flight school's offices and sat like a flock of birds, just waiting for someone to throw a few crumbs in their general direction.

We were met by Jackie and were quickly introduced to her husband Andrew. Andrew was a loud, brash Yorkshireman who had a penchant for swearing at will and who clearly didn't suffer fools gladly. He shook our hands and asked where we were from.

In our first conversation with Andrew, he set out his stall early. He was jovial but firm and wasted no time in explaining that if we knuckled down, worked hard, and put in the study time required to pass the six ground examinations required for the PPL, we would get our licences and be on the plane home as qualified pilots in three weeks' time. However, if we had come for a holiday, to explore all the delights that this quiet little backwater of Florida had to offer, and to do a bit of flying on the side, expecting to be handed a PPL on a plate, then we may as well leave straight away (although the language he used to relay this warning was somewhat more colourful).

Following our introductions, we had a quick tour of the building and a briefing about the rules of the flight school and how things were run. We could expect to fly two, possibly three, hour-long training flights a day, generally with the same instructor but not always, and would methodically work through the UK PPL syllabus. If all went well and the weather remained kind to us, we would fly solo (without an instructor) in about ten days' time after which we would continue to build our hours of training up until we reached the magic number of forty hours – the minimum amount required by the Civil Aviation Authority in the UK to issue a PPL.

On completion of the required hours, we would have to undergo a General Flight Test (GFT) with Andrew and a Navigation Flight Test (NFT) on our own to pass the practical side of the syllabus. There was also the matter of six written exams to pass, on various subjects from radiotelephony, meteorology, and air law to a paper on (believe it or not) how an aeroplane flies. We were encouraged from the outset to get the ground exams out of the way early on to concentrate on the flying as the course progressed.

After our briefing, we were hustled into a minibus and driven out into the sticks to a doctor's office in what seemed like the middle of nowhere. I had explained back at the office that as I had a brand-new, shiny, UK Class Three medical certificate in my possession, perhaps I could sit this bit out as I didn't want to waste anyone's time. It was at this point that the difference between what I thought I would manage to avoid versus what was actually required became reality; as we were flying US-registered aircraft in US airspace to Federal Aviation Administration (or 'FAA') rather than CAA rules, I was required to have a medical certificate issued by the FAA certified doctor. My heart sank and the drive to the doctor's office was spent with my dad reassuring me that as I was fit and well, there shouldn't be a problem.

As we pulled up at the doctor's office, I just hoped that he was right.

Doctor Rundles (the physician we saw that day), was a gentleman probably well into his seventies, who clearly did FAA medical examinations simply to supplement his retirement fund. Upon examining the medical questionnaire that I had filled out on the minibus en route to his office, he exclaimed that he probably knew far less about CF than I did and proceeded to ask me whether there was any reason that I could see for why I might not be fit to undergo the flight training. After the briefest of conversations (in which it became abjectly clear that I indeed knew far more about CF than Dr Rundles), we mutually agreed that I was in acceptable physical shape and I was sent on my way with the necessary paperwork. Job done!

Ironically, it was my dad who almost came unstuck that morning. As he was over the age of fifty, he was required to have an ECG of his heart to check that he wouldn't keel over at two thousand feet in a light aircraft above the Florida countryside. As historically there was something of a history of heart problems on my dad's side of the family, I could tell that this prospect unnerved him. Thankfully, however, the ECG result was fine and he too was given his medical certificate and sent on his way.

We returned to the airfield with our little cream coloured cards, telling Andrew that we were medically fit to fly his aeroplanes and that at last we *really* were ready to go flying.

We spent the rest of that Saturday afternoon at the flight school, sitting in the warm afternoon sunshine and watching our fellow students come and go from their lessons.

The sky around the airfield was peppered with small light aircraft flying in the circuit (a racetrack pattern flown by aircraft around and overhead the airfield) and practising take-offs and landings while others flew off to or returned from other airfields around Florida.

We chatted to those further into their course to learn what to look out for and to garner any hints that our fellow budding aviators may be able to convey. We were down to take to the air ourselves for the first time the next day and so, with my head full of excitement and trepidation simultaneously, we headed away from the airfield once the sun began to get low in the sky and went to get some dinner in town.

We woke early and returned to the airfield around eight a.m. Although this was a Sunday morning, the flight school was already a hive of activity, with instructors and students checking the operations schedule – a large whiteboard mounted on one of the walls showing who would be flying when that day and to which aircraft they had been assigned. I was down for two separate flights that first day with an instructor called Dave.

Dave and I met and shook hands and he took me out to the line of aircraft parked out on the ramp. I was shown how to carry out a pre-flight external check of the aircraft, where you walk around checking the whole aeroplane, making sure it is fit to fly and looking for anything that might prevent it from doing so safely or that may become a problem either before or whilst you are in the air.

I was shown how to check the engine oil quantity and the state of the fuel in the wings to ensure that there was no water mixed in with it. With the high humidity in Florida, condensation can build in the fuel tanks and can contaminate the fuel causing the engine to fail if serious enough. The flight school's policy was to fill each aircraft up with fuel at the end of the day to prevent there being air space in the tanks in which condensation could build up, thus eradicating the risk of water contaminating it. Nonetheless, we were told to always take this precautionary step. Like a lot of things in aviation, it is good to get into a 'safety-first' mindset early on (especially as I wouldn't always be flying an aircraft that the previous pilot had filled the tanks to the brim).

Once the external pre-flight check was complete, we climbed into the aircraft and strapped in. I had been in small aeroplanes a couple of times before but the sheer lack of space in this Cessna 150 still took me by surprise. Being a classic training aircraft, there were just two seats next to each other facing the banks of clockwork dials and switches laid out (to my untrained eye) in a confusing jumble before me.

Dave was a big guy and he filled two-thirds of the cockpit area himself, leaving just enough space at the side for my slender frame. I pulled my seat forwards, ensuring that I could reach the pedals on the floor in front of me and could manipulate the control column freely in all directions. As Dave talked me through what everything was and its function, I could not quite believe that in just a few days I would be flying on my own in a machine just like this with no Dave (or anyone else) to help me. Despite this being a chilly Sunday morning, with the sun still hanging low in the February sky, my palms were already clammy as I tried hard not to be overwhelmed by the prospect of the challenges of next three weeks.

After twenty minutes or so, it was finally time to get the training started and begin earning flight time, building towards the forty hours I required for the PPL.

After talking me through the procedure, Dave let me push the master switch to 'on', prime the engine with fuel, making sure my feet were firmly on the foot brakes, and turn the ignition key. After a few seconds and a cough or two (the engine, not me) the propeller leapt into life. With a puff of white smoke, the engine was running and the clock was ticking; my first ever flying lesson had begun and I was bursting with excitement.

As I gently took my feet off the brakes, the aircraft started to roll forward, and we were moving. With a quick tap on the brakes to ensure they were working correctly, and following Dave's instructions, I steered the aircraft away from the parking ramp and onto the taxiway, heading out to the active runway. With palms still clammy and my heart racing, I could hear my heavy breaths being captured by my microphone and played back to me over the earphones of my headset. Dave reminded me to, "Just relax, take deep breaths, and enjoy the moment." And as we approached the holding point to wait for our turn to take off, I allowed myself a brief smile which itself allowed my nerves to settle just a little.

After a few minutes of waiting and running through the pre-take of checks, it was our turn. I slowly advanced the throttle and we rolled onto the huge white 'piano keys' at the end of the runway and lined up. I turned us around so that the enormous arrowhead painted on the tarmac in front of us pointed straight ahead. With a final deep breath, and a reassuring look from Dave, I pushed the throttle fully forward. The aircraft gave a slight jerk and we shot off down the runway. At the appropriate speed, I gently pulled back on the control column and our little aeroplane leapt into the air.

After years of dreaming about this moment, I was finally flying.

That first lesson lasted thirty-five minutes. We headed away from the airfield and out over a sparsely populated area where Dave gave me a general demonstration of how the aircraft handled. We made some turns, climbed a bit, descended a bit, and discussed spins and stalls. We went through how we would find our way back to Ormond Beach and the procedure for the approach and landing.

Throughout the lesson, we could hear chatter over the radio and Dave instilled in me the importance of keeping an ear out so that you have a general idea of who is doing what and where.

At these lower levels there was no air traffic control to tell you where everyone was, which made listening and, of course, keeping a very good look out of the windows even more important.

The voices over the radio were mostly American accents – various instructors making the radio calls while their European students concentrated on keeping the aircrafts the right way up. You would hear other accents too – in stuttered, broken English – as slightly more advanced students got to grips with using the radio for the first time, using the strange radiotelephony language and terminology that aviation both here and in the USA insists upon.

All too soon, we were making our approach back to Ormond Beach. After just that first little taste of flying, I already felt that I could have stayed up in the air all day.

As we came in on our final approach, the runway stretched out ahead of us for what seemed like miles and Dave plonked us back down gently onto solid ground.

We taxied back to the parking area, completed the shutdown checks, and I turned the key to stop the engine. Once again, the engine gave a cough and a splutter, and the propeller finally stopped turning. We opened the doors on either side to let some fresh Florida morning air into the aircraft and we talked about what I had just learned. After a few more minutes, we climbed out of the aircraft and strolled across the apron back to the flight school building where Dave would complete the paperwork and write up the lesson in my flying logbook. And with that, my training was officially underway, and I had completed my first flying lesson. Only thirty-nine-and-a-half more hours of flying stood between me and my long-coveted pilots' licence.

Over the next five days, I flew two or three times a day for around thirty-five to forty minutes each lesson. We covered basic handling, flying around in 'the circuit' and practising 'touch-and-go's', where you land the aircraft on the runway, throttle up, and take off again without ever coming to a full stop like a normal landing.

Between that first lesson on the Sunday and the following Friday, I completed fifty-four successful landings on the various runways at Ormond Beach. An old aviation adage states, "Any landing where you can walk away from it and use the plane again can be classed as successful."

Some of my landings were sublime (more down to good fortune than skill) whilst others were bone-rattlingly awful. Luckily, the small Cessnas in which I was undergoing my training were designed for trainee pilots like myself and were built to withstand being dropped onto a hard surface at seventy miles per hour with all the finesse of an elephant performing a ballet routine.

After just six days and twelve-and-a-half hours of training, the first major obstacle of the PPL course was now bearing down on me – the dreaded first solo flight.

Saturday 10th February 1996 started like all the others that week, except on this day I was full of nerves. Dave had indicated the night before that he thought I was ready to 'go solo' and it was likely that I would be doing so that day. My dad and I headed to the airfield, and upon arrival I checked the operations board. I was assigned aircraft number N704XQ (or 'Cessna Four Xray Quebec' as I was known over the radio) to fly that morning.

I met with Dave and he told me to go out and pre-flight the aircraft. Knowing that this little aeroplane might just be flying me around on my own shortly meant that I was probably a little more thorough with my checks than I had been up until that point and, once I was finished, I strapped myself in and waited for Dave.

I looked over all the instruments again and again, talked through my procedures and mnemonics for flying in the circuit, and revised the speeds for take-off, approach, and landing. I felt sharp and wide-awake. The sky was clear-blue, and the sun was shining with just a very gentle breeze blowing across the airfield. If there was to be a *right day* for one of the most significant moments in my whole lifetime, surely this was it.

Dave climbed aboard and strapped in. We discussed what was going to happen (like we had done every other day that first week) and we set off to the runway. Over the course of the next hour, I completed five circuits of the airfield, with four touch-and-go's and two full stop landings.

After the second of these, Dave instructed me to vacate the runway and park on the adjacent taxiway for a moment. Having spoken with other students who had just been through this themselves, I knew this was it. Dave told me to taxi back round to the start end of the active runway and to carry out one take-off, one circuit of the airfield, and one landing then return to the parking area. And, with that, he disembarked, leaving me on my own.

Looking back, I was fully aware of the significance of what I was about to undertake. I had an overwhelming sense of being on my own and glanced briefly over to the empty seat where Dave had been sitting a few moments before. My dad was already in the air with his instructor, building up to his first solo later that day and so I had no audience watching me. I glanced out and saw Dave making his way on foot back to the flight school where he would be on the radio to assist me should it all get a bit tricky. I tried to settle my mind and took some deep breaths. I knew exactly what I had to do and how I was going to do it. Yet nothing could take away the fact that the next six-or-so minutes were going to be some of the most terrifying of my life.

I pushed forward on the throttle and headed slowly back out to the runway, my heart beating hard in my chest and my breaths coming faster than ever.

I cleared my throat, adjusted myself in my seat, and announced over the radio, "Cessna Four X-ray Quebec taking off runway three-five Ormond Beach." And just like the previous fifty-four take-offs I had performed already that week, me and my little blue and white aeroplane lifted off from the runway and headed upwards into the big blue Florida sky.

At five hundred feet above the ground and above the local baseball ground with which I was now so familiar, I turned the aircraft ninety degrees to the left and continued my climb to one thousand feet. As I approached this height, and with the shopping mall car park below me, I turned another ninety degrees onto the downwind leg of my circuit.

So far, so good. Everything was looking as it should.

The aircraft was behaving as I expected, and I was already almost at the halfway point of my first ever solo flight. One again, I glanced over at Dave's empty seat and allowed myself just the faintest of smiles. I was really flying by myself, with no one giving me instructions or telling me how to do it. This was just me, on my own, flying my aeroplane around the sky.

Within a minute or so, I was abeam the end of runway three-five – on which I would hopefully be landing in the next couple of minutes – and so I carried out my pre-landing checks from memory. Once above the freeway intersection, it was time to turn another ninety degrees to the left and start descending back down to five hundred feet. Once there, one more turn of ninety degrees saw me on my final approach, with runway three-five laid out before me just a couple of miles ahead.

I now had about one minute left to get my flaps down and to reduce my speed to the required landing speed of sixty knots. With every ounce of concentration

I could muster, I repeatedly alternated my focus between the view of the runway and my airspeed.

Having done this so many times before, I now knew what the runway should look like if you were in the correct profile for landing and so examining the altimeter to see how high you are becomes less relevant during these last crucial stages. As the end of the runway passed under the aircraft, I slowly pulled the throttle right out and kept my eyes fixed on the far end of the runway, pulling back on the control column slowly and feeling my bottom sinking down towards the tarmac beneath me.

With a shudder from the airframe and a reassuring squeak from the tyres, the aircraft settled back onto the runway and began to decelerate. As the aircraft approached the first taxiway, I turned towards it and vacated the runway. Before heading back to the parking apron, I brought the aircraft to a halt just for a few seconds to complete the after-landing checks. It was then that an overwhelming sense of elation took over. I had done it! In just six days, I had gone from someone who had never flown a light aircraft before, to taking off and flying myself around this little part of the USA before landing safely again with both me and my aircraft in one piece.

And, as if this all happened just yesterday, I can clearly recall realising the significance of that moment; it was precisely at this point that I knew CF might not always be so kind to me and that it may prevent me from doing everything I might want to in life. But, for as long as I was able, I vowed to grab opportunities with both hands and make the most of what I could do rather than dwell too much on what I could not.

I parked up and Dave came out to greet me, shaking me warmly by the hand as I climbed out of the aircraft. We went inside to complete the paperwork of events for that day and I scurried off to get some fresh water from the water cooler to refresh myself.

It had become a warm day once again and my shirt was still damp with sweat from having spent the last ninety minutes in the hot, cramped environment of a Cessna 150 cockpit under the most pressurised of situations. I went outside to get some fresh air and to let the blood start to circulate around my body once more. Just as I did so, I saw my dad taxiing back in in his aircraft on his own, without an instructor. Once his engine was shut down, I went over to make sure everything was okay to find that he too had just successfully completed his first solo flight.

Typically, his demeanour was not so much 'I have done it, aren't I great?' (like mine, I suppose) and more 'right, that's done, what's next?'. But, graciously, he let me have my moment and it would be rather an understatement to say that I felt awfully pleased with myself for the rest of that day.

After a few beers out at a beachside bar that evening, the day ended as it had begun with us back at the house wondering what lay in store for us next on this amazing adventure.

We had both just successfully negotiated the first hurdle, but there were several more to come before we would successfully reach the end of the course.

SIXTEEN
EARNING MY WINGS

Our flight training became more varied and significantly more interesting as the days passed by. The sorties with Dave became longer and we started heading away from Ormond Beach and landing at other airfields around our part of Florida.

The USA is peppered with airfields large and small and Florida is no exception. We headed to small airfields with just a single runway, and to large international airports like Orlando and Sanford where multiple runways and acres of tarmac spread out across the landscape. We landed at Titusville (also known as 'Space Coast Regional Airport') located adjacent to the space shuttle landing facility at the NASA Kennedy Space Centre, and the airport at St. Augustine (Northeast Florida Regional Airport) some fifty miles up the coast to the north. Interestingly, this historic town is the site of the oldest continuously occupied settlement of European origin in the United States, founded in 1565 by Spanish explorers.

These flights gave me valuable practise for what lay ahead; as part of the PPL course, we were required to complete what was known as the 'cross-country qualifier'. This involved flying away from our 'home' airfield, navigating our way to two other airfields in a triangular pattern, performing a landing at each, and then returning to our starting point. This would all be done solo, with me having complete responsibility for planning the route beforehand and handling all the paperwork myself.

The day before my actual cross-country qualifier, I was sent off on a practise mission. My task was to take off from Ormond Beach and to carry out a circuit and a touch-and-go there before flying up to St. Augustine, landing, and then flying back.

Setting off just after lunchtime, the flight up to St. Augustine was uneventful and, rather than feeling nervous, I rather enjoyed it. I had been there with Dave a couple of days previously, so knew what to look for in terms of waypoints along the route and where to find the airport itself, just north of the town and landside of the inlet from the Atlantic Ocean.

As I approached, the radio got busy with other aircraft flying in the vicinity and I worked out where in the traffic pattern I would slot in order to make my approach and landing. The runway at St. Augustine was like those at Ormond Beach; long, wide, and forgiving to a novice pilot like myself.

There were several other light aircraft in the circuit as I approached the airfield and I joined the traffic where there was a gap in the circuit. I followed my drills and completed my pre-landing checks as the aircraft ahead pulled off the runway to the side. I announced over the radio that I was landing at St. Augustine and, within a few seconds, was touching down on the hot tarmac of runway twelve.

I had the option of either parking up and shutting down or just taxiing round back to the end of the runway and heading straight back to Ormond Beach. Due to a hefty headwind, it had taken just over an hour to get here although the flight back was due to be quicker. As it was a warm afternoon, I decided to find a quiet corner to park up, shut down and take a few minutes to get some air and to brief myself before the flight back to Ormond Beach.

After sitting in the aeroplane with the side door open, it swinging in the warm afternoon breeze for a while, it was time to head back. This was February, after all, and the sun would still be going down relatively early, so I needed to get back at Ormond Beach well before sunset.

I sat in the cockpit of my blue and white Cessna, arranged the paperwork for my flight back, and took out my route log. This broke the flight back into sections, each bookended by waypoints, and told me how many minutes it should take to each point, on what heading, and at what height. As it happened, this was probably the easiest cross-country route from Ormond Beach that there could be. You simply took off, followed the beaches along the coastline for fifty miles, and before long your destination should appear off the nose. That said, taking such a lackadaisical approach to the journey back would not help me on later trips that would not involve simply following the coastline.

As I made my way back to Ormond Beach that afternoon, the magnitude of what I had achieved not only that afternoon but over the past two weeks really hit me for the first time. From arriving in Florida having never flown before, here I was flying myself alone from one airfield to another with no-one to rely on for any form of assistance or support but myself.

As the sun began to lower, the now familiar shape of Ormond Beach Airport appeared up ahead and I almost felt like I was 'coming home'. I joined the pattern and brought me and my aircraft in for a safe landing. With a sigh of relief and a real sense of pride, I taxied in and parked up. Another small milestone accomplished.

There was only a week or so left of the course and I had already accumulated almost thirty hours of flight time by this point. The following day it was time to do it all again, but for real this time on my cross-country qualifier. Rather than flying up to St. Augustine and back, though, the route I was given that day took me from Ormond Beach to Keystone Air Park, a small airfield located near the town of Starke, in amongst the swamplands of northern Florida and some eighty miles northwest of Ormond Beach. From there I had to navigate my way to St. Augustine and finally back to Ormond Beach. At each intermediary point, I had to shut down, get out, and find someone who would sign a document to say that they had seen me and my aircraft – proof I had completed the assigned route.

The flight to Keystone was uneventful and I was there just an hour after take-off from Ormond Beach. The route was relatively straightforward, climbing away from Ormond Beach in a north-westerly direction until I was above the huge chimneys or 'smoke-stacks' of the Palatka power station, followed by a left turn on a heading which would take me straight to Keystone. Once I was safely on the ground at Keystone Airpark, which consisted of little more than two runways and a few hangars dotted around, I disembarked and set off to find someone to sign my document.

I followed the distant sound of a radio playing and wandered into a hangar where an old gentleman was tinkering with a wrench over the open panel of a light aircraft's engine. After a brief chat with the gentleman and the customary, "Gee, what accent is that? I love it," comments from him, he signed my form and, before long, I was airborne again on the forty-five minute flight to the now-familiar territory of St. Augustine airport.

On this occasion, however, things would not be as straightforward as they had been the previous day. Some way out from the airport, I noticed that the radio was quiet; *very* quiet. Given that this was early afternoon on a warm clear day, there would undoubtedly have been other aircraft in the vicinity, but I could not hear them and started to wonder if anyone could hear me. There was no control tower at St. Augustine and everyone in the area would simply transmit their position and intentions over what is called a 'Unicom' frequency.

It soon became clear, having issued a couple of transmissions reporting my position and requesting responses and receiving no response, that my radio was on the blink. I couldn't hear a soul, and I had to assume that they couldn't hear me either.

I told myself not to panic but my heart began to race and my breathing became shallower and more rapid. The only thing I could do was to keep a very good look out around me and try to watch what was going on as I approached St. Augustine.

A few miles out, I identified which runway was in use and, as far as I could tell, there were only two other aircraft in the traffic pattern over the airfield itself. I decided to join the pattern as far behind these two as I could and slowed down to slot in behind them.

At regular intervals, I transmitted my position, prefixing each of my reports with, "Radio failure," just in case anyone could hear me and wondered what I was up to. It took all my concentration not to get too overwhelmed with my radio problems and instead to just fly the aircraft and get on the ground as safely and as quickly as possible.

I followed another brightly coloured Cessna around the circuit and onto final approach. He was carrying out a touch-and-go, but there was ample distance between me and him to allow him to get on and off the runway and for me to land behind him. As I bumped down onto the runway surface, as if by magic, the radio sprang back to life and radio calls from other pilots on and around the airfield filled my headphones once more.

I taxied in and parked up. I was a bit shaken, although I was never in any real danger. More than anything, I was angry. Questions like *Why did this happen to me?* started to consume me but I did my best to put them to one side and headed into the airport building to find a pay phone so that I could call Ormond Beach and ask for advice. It took a few minutes to calm down and settle myself before making the call as I didn't want to come over as flustered and possibly unable to complete my afternoon's flying.

I rang the Ormond Beach Aviation number and got hold of one of the instructors. I was told that there might have been a loose connection or that some humidity could have affected the radio whilst airborne but, given that the problem cleared upon landing, I might have no further issues.

I was told to go out and try the radio again before taking off. If it worked normally and there were no further adverse signs, I should head back to Ormond Beach. If there were any signs that the radio still had problems, I should call back and they would somehow come and rescue me (and my aircraft). There were other airfields to divert to en route if I needed them, and I made a mental note of these as well as marking them on my map.

After a cold drink and a check of my route plan, I found a lady at the airport desk to sign my form and headed back out to the aircraft. Upon starting the engine, the radio sprang into life and gave no further problems that afternoon.

As I walked back into the flight school office at Ormond Beach, one of the school's resident engineers took the aircraft keys straight off me and headed out to the apron to check my aircraft. I had made it safely back in one piece, but somehow still felt rather annoyed that a slight technical problem had overshadowed my day and taken the gloss off my first epic solo adventure.

One of the first rules you are taught as a trainee pilot is to 'aviate, navigate, communicate'. That is, always fly the aeroplane first and foremost and keep yourself safe. Secondly, always navigate in such a manner that you always know where you are. And thirdly, communicate by using the radio to let others know who you are, where you are, and what your intentions are.

That evening, as I reflected on the issues that I had encountered that day, my dad was on hand to remind me that I had clearly relied on aviating and navigating to make sure I got on the ground at St. Augustine in one piece. But the whole experience had shaken me slightly and my confidence –which had been growing exponentially over the previous few days – had taken a knock.

With hindsight, I now consider that to be a good thing. Fate had played a part in reminding me that what I was doing was new and dangerous and it did me no harm to be taught that things can go wrong regardless of what you are doing, and that it is how you deal with the situation that largely dictates how you will come out of it.

The lesson I learned that day was one that I have applied time and time again throughout my life since, and perhaps is particularly relevant in how I have dealt with the numerous issues that CF has thrown at me over the years. After all, I am still here, twenty-four years on from that day, living my life and still enjoying it.

The following morning was another bright sunny day and marked the two-week point of my training. It was time for my first of two practical flying exams with Andrew along for the ride in his capacity as Chief Examiner.

This was the Navigation Flight Test (or 'NFT') which involved departing Ormond Beach, flying to another airfield but not landing there, flying to a third – again just overflying it – and landing back at Ormond Beach. Andrew told me the details of the route we would be flying and sent me away to plan it out considering the weather and any landmarks to look out for on the way, and to calculate how long the whole flight would last.

These days, various software packages do this for you in a matter of seconds and send the results direct to your tablet or phone to use as your primary navigating tool. Unfortunately, no such niceties were available in 1996 and a calculator, a slide rule, and paper and pencil were the order of the day.

Once planned, I headed out to the assigned aircraft to await Andrew's arrival. I had heard various stories about how he conducted himself on such flight tests and so it came as no surprise when he arrived at the aircraft with his cup of coffee and the local Sunday newspaper. He promptly announced that I should consider him as a passenger for the purpose of this exercise (rather than an examiner) and simply to let him know when we were approaching each of the two assigned airfields along our route. Other than that, he would just let me get on with the flying and would sit quietly and read his paper unless I did something 'bloody silly', in which case he would fail me on this part of the course and would take over the flying to get us back to Ormond Beach.

Thankfully, I managed to avoid doing anything 'silly' and, just over ninety minutes later, we were touching down back at Ormond Beach, having overflown the airfields at New Smyrna Beach and Spruce Creek along the way. Andrew had finished his coffee and his paper by the time the wheels kissed the tarmac on runway seventeen and, as we taxied back to the parking area, he announced that I had passed the NFT.

I knew that I was now within touching distance of completing the course and the sense of achievement was palpable once more. However, the knowledge that sometime in the next few days I would be back in an aeroplane with Andrew for my General Flight Test (GFT) kept my head out of the clouds, at least for the time being.

After three more days and another eight hours of flying to hone my general flying skills and different landing techniques, the time had come. I had completed exactly thirty-nine hours of flight training, some with an instructor but also many on my own, and had completed one hundred and twenty-eight successful landings.

Andrew once again met me at the aircraft, and we spent the next hour and a half out over the sparsely populated landscape to the west of Ormond Beach performing stalls, steep turns, and other general handling exercises called out by Andrew.

He was a lot more vocal than on the NFT a few days earlier and acted more like an instructor than a passenger this time. It was a very warm afternoon and the sun glared through the windshield, heating the confined space of our cockpit to an uncomfortable temperature. This, added to the extreme level of concentration I was expending, meant that my whole GFT was spent with a damp brow and sweat-ridden shirt.

After heading back to Ormond Beach and carrying out five landings and take-offs, Andrew announced that I had passed and that my training was complete. We spent a few minutes back in the office where Andrew signed off my log book and placed a large stamp in the centre of my last page with the wording:

UK CAA Group A syllabus completed with all flying and instruction certified correct.
Signed: A.Thompson
21st February 1996

After seventeen days and forty hours of training, I had reached the end and was now a qualified private pilot. My dad went up with Andrew straight after me and I spent the time they were away chatting with my fellow students on the picnic tables outside the office and overlooking the airfield.

As per usual, the monotonous buzz of numerous small light aircraft was ever-present in the background. But that afternoon felt different; I was no longer a student pilot (although many say with flying that you never stop learning). I had completed something that I had wanted to achieve for such a long time, and I was proud of it.

Three weeks prior, I had never taken the controls of a light aircraft, and now here I was, having demonstrated that I was able to fly myself around Florida safely and with the requisite paperwork to attest to this fact.

A short time later, my dad returned from his GFT and duly received his stamp from Andrew in his logbook. And that final action marked the end of our time at Ormond Beach Aviation.

The following morning, we packed up our luggage and set off on the long drive back to Miami. We had a couple of days before our flight home and stopped at various locations on the way back down the coast to enjoy the last of our time in Florida. Given that the previous seventeen days had been anything but a holiday, it was nice just to take some time without having to think about either flying, the next challenge on the PPL course, or the subject of the next written examination we were due to sit.

During those last few days, Dad and I got to spend some real time together and to enjoy each other's company. This was something we had not done in years and was something that I had really, truly missed. The highlight, undoubtedly (and in fact one of the highlights of my whole life), was having the opportunity to witness the launch of a NASA space shuttle from the Kennedy Space Centre, located just to the east of Titusville, Florida and just sixty miles south of Ormond Beach.

By pure coincidence, there just happened to be a launch planned for the day after we had completed our PPL course.

Ever since watching the first shuttle launch with complete awe as a nine-year old boy, I had hoped that I would have the opportunity to see a real launch in my lifetime. But I had never believed that it would actually happen. Yet I was now merely an hour's drive from where this exhilarating event was to take place.

It was a bright and sunny day, and everything looked good for a launch. This was something I simply could not miss and it was to be made even more special by the fact that the shuttle assigned to this mission (the 75th space shuttle launch) was to be *Columbia* – the very same spacecraft that I had watched fifteen years previously in my school assembly hall.

That morning we set off from Ormond Beach early, having been forewarned by others at the flight school that things could get very crowded in the area around Kennedy Space Centre on launch days and to get there to claim a viewing spot early. The launch was scheduled for three eighteen p.m., so we had ample time to make our way back towards Titusville.

We stopped and had an early lunch close to Patrick Air Force Base. It was late morning by this stage and, already, the whole of the surrounding area was becoming gridlocked with traffic, with very few remaining opportunities to legally and safely park our rental car.

We decided to leave the car in the restaurant car park and to walk as far as we could along the beach to get as close to the launch as possible. As it turned out, this walk ended up being about six miles, through Cocoa Beach and to Jetty Park on the banks of the Banana River estuary, which separated us from the Kennedy Space Centre boundary fence on the opposite bank. From this viewpoint, we could clearly see the unmistakeable white profile of space shuttle *Columbia* on launch pad 39A, pointing skywards, poised and ready for lift-off.

It was now about three hours before the scheduled launch time and the crowds were building.

The wait passed in a flash, probably due to the sheer excitement of the occasion. There was something of a party atmosphere and people who had never met before shared barbecues and passed soft drinks around, united in their common interest in the spectacle that was about to unfold just across the water.

The excitement was compounded by a truck emblazoned with 'NASA FM' down the side giving a running commentary on the events taking place over on launchpad 39A.

"The astronauts are now in their seats," and, "The pre-launch computers will be checking all of *Columbia*'s systems three million times each second," was the type of information we were drip-fed over that time, only adding to the tension. To cap it all off, a giant digital clock counting down the hours and minutes to launch time ticked ever downwards, heading steadily towards the time when the spectacular main event was scheduled to occur.

Launches were timed to the second, although everyone there was aware that proceedings could come to a sudden stop at any moment. The slightest change in the weather or the most minor of faults on the spacecraft could bring a postponement to the launch, and a delay of probably several days, by which time Dad and I would be long gone and back in the UK.

If I was ever to see a shuttle launch in 'real life', this was going to be the day I would see it.

As the last hour before the launch ticked by, the tension was almost unbearable. I'd had some adrenalin inducing moments over the previous three weeks and yet this was equal to any of them. As NASA FM continued to whip the increasingly impatient crowd into a state of frenzy, the clock worked its way down through the fifteen-minute mark, and then ten. White smoke could be seen drifting from the bottom of the shuttle as the spacecraft prepared for its launch.

As the countdown reached one-minute. I felt almost breathless with the excitement. I had longed for the day when I might experience what was about to occur, and now it was finally happening.

The crowd counted down the remaining ten seconds in unison, all eyes fixed on the small white spacecraft located a mile or so ahead of them on the opposite bank.

In all my wildest dreams, I could have not possibly imagined the visual and aural spectacle of the next couple of minutes. The first thing I saw was a gargantuan release of white smoke as the rocket engines were ignited just before launch. This was followed shortly afterwards by the thunderous sound of those engines roaring into life and pushing against gravity to get the spacecraft to which they are attached airborne and heading skywards.

Within a couple of seconds, the shuttle had cleared the launch tower and was heading upwards at tremendous speed, leaving a thick trail of fluffy white smoke in its wake as it climbed into the bright blue afternoon sky. The crackle of the engines was deafening and shook the ground around us, adding to the sense of wonder at what was unfolding.

All eyes remained on the orbiter as it headed through five thousand then ten thousand feet on its ascent above the Florida coastline.

We finally lost sight of it as it entered a thin layer of mist about two minutes after launch and just after the white side-mounted booster rockets detached themselves from the central fuel tank in order to drop into the Atlantic Ocean.

For those two minutes or so, it felt like the whole world stopped and it reminded me of just how amazing humans can be. Long after the shuttle had disappeared, the plumes of white smoke left by *Columbia* hung in the cloudless afternoon sky. In fact, they were still visible long after we had started to make our way back to our car.

Despite the long walk back, I had a spring in my step like never before. We had witnessed one of life's most amazing displays of science and engineering and, of course, a feat which pushed the very boundaries of aviation to the most extreme levels.

By the time we reached the car, the shuttle had already entered its orbit and the astronauts would have been out of their seats and setting about their business. As we set off, heading southwards towards Miami, I smiled to myself; I would remember that day for the rest of my life.

As something of a postscript to this story, whilst I never saw taking flying lessons or obtaining my PPL as a way to stick two fingers up at CF, the significance and perhaps the magnitude of what I achieved over those seventeen days in Florida has never been lost on me. The whole episode still sits as a testament as to how I viewed having CF in my twenties and the resolute approach I took in order to not let CF get the upper hand.

Obtaining my PPL remains one of my proudest achievements, and a reminder of what I can achieve in the face of adversity. I fully appreciate that so many with CF do not get to do such amazing things because the condition simply prevents them from doing so. Yet, I am so pleased that I managed to fulfil this dream before CF took me in its grip and rendered me unable to do so.

Although it is many years later now, and my health is much more fragile than it was back then, the desire for accomplishment has never left me. Although my aspirations and dreams have been tempered by CF in recent years, I remain hopeful that one day, assuming I live to benefit from the double lung transplant which I long for so much, that I will again achieve some of the great things I still hope to.

In the meantime, the waiting for the transplant call continues and with it, so does the time I spend continuing to dream about other great challenges and adventures that may await me, or that I might set for myself, in the future. For the time being though, my current situation is all the challenge I need.

EVERYTHING CHANGES

SEVENTEEN

HIDING THE TRUTH

Following my great adventure earning my PPL in the USA, I returned to the UK and to my job at Virgin Atlantic. After a momentous three weeks away, returning to my normal routine seemed rather an anticlimax. But work continued to keep me busy, and I headed away from the UK again almost immediately on another of my regular overseas work trips.

Having been issued with a shiny new PPL by the CAA, I was keen to keep the flying up and to build my experience. Having not flown in the UK up until this point, I joined a flying club based at Shoreham Airport, close to Brighton on the south coast. One of their instructors happened to be a Virgin Atlantic pilot in his day job, and so I arranged to spend a Saturday afternoon with him going over the differences between flying in the UK and the USA.

Whilst the laws of physics and aerodynamics obviously do not change from country to country, and an aeroplane largely flies the same way wherever you are, the type of language used over the radio and certain flying procedures differ. We spent the afternoon flying around the Kent and Sussex countryside learning these differences and practising certain flying skills, so that I could be signed off to fly the club's aircraft any time I wanted to.

Sadly, the guy I flew with that day was to be involved in a horrific flying accident at Shoreham Airport some nineteen years later, when the Hawker Hunter vintage military jet he was flying at an air show crashed onto the main A23 road alongside the airfield. Although he escaped with his life, eight others lost theirs on that terrible afternoon.

Throughout the remainder of 1996 and into 1997, my life continued at the same frenetic pace. When I wasn't travelling with my job, I would be out socialising with friends or flying from Shoreham at the weekends, often taking other people with me for short sightseeing hops along the south coast.

I was still largely in control of my CF at this point. I still took my medications and exercised regularly. But the days of feeling slightly more 'chesty' than normal were becoming more frequent and it was clear to me that I was producing more sputum on those days, making my daily physiotherapy sessions longer and harder work.

I continued to attend the Friday afternoon CF clinic at Papworth Hospital, but the frequency of these visits had increased to once every eight weeks. There was the odd occasion when I would have to take extra oral antibiotics to counteract a flare up that I was experiencing, but as I was now familiar with these drugs, and the required dosage recommended by Papworth, I could obtain them from my local GP and they, largely, did the trick.

I was very aware, however, that CF was making its presence felt for the first time in my life, although I was certainly not going to let it stop me from doing anything and felt (albeit mistakenly) that as long as I respected it and followed all of my treatments, that it would largely leave me alone. How wrong I would turn out to be.

Unfortunately, CF is not as kind a condition as I clearly considered it to be back in those days. All the while I misguidedly ran my life with this 'work hard, play hard' mentality, I was bringing forward the date on which CF would really bite back for the first time. Although I had been lucky enough to live my life up until this point largely unscathed by CF, the days that this would continue to be the case were numbered. However, with my steadfast desire to live my life as I wished, and perhaps through a degree of ignorance, I was unwittingly setting a time bomb within me that, regardless of how much physio I did or what medication I took, was bound to go off in the not-too-distant future.

While I was in Crawley getting on with life, my dad had returned to his home near Cambridge and to my surprise had continued with his flying too. He had joined the flying club at Cambridge Airport and flew fairly regularly from there, also taking friends and acquaintances for sightseeing trips over Cambridgeshire and the neighbouring counties of Norfolk and Suffolk. I say 'surprise' as it would not have come as any kind of shock had my dad had finished his PPL and then, considering the task completed and the goal achieved, had never taken the controls of a light aircraft ever again. However, he clearly enjoyed the mental exercise that flying presented along with the sheer enjoyment of it, so was flying a few hours each month in aircraft he rented from the club at Cambridge.

Dad and I returned to Ormond Beach for a week the following February to build some additional flying time together. So, on 2nd February 1997 I was back flying Cessna 150, registration number N6237K. This was the very aircraft in which I had performed my cross-country practise flights to St. Augustine – and almost exactly a year later, I was doing what was known as a 'check ride' with an instructor to ensure that I remained capable of flying one of Andrew's aircraft without damaging either it or me.

Upon passing the check ride, and my dad doing likewise, we were free to spend the next week exploring the charms of Florida's numerous airfields. We dropped into Gainesville Regional Airport and went out for lunch with an old work colleague of my dad's who lived close by. We landed at Titusville, the airport adjacent close to the Kennedy Space Centre and flew over the NASA launch pads where we had seen *Columbia* launch.

We also spent a day crossing the northern part of Florida to land at a charming little airstrip in the quiet art and fishing community at Cedar Key. With sea at each end of the runway, and a much shorter length than we were both used to, landing at Cedar Key was certainly a challenge. There is, in fact, a plaque at the airfield which states that the runway at the George T. Lewis airport in Cedar Key (at just 718 metres) is the shortest paved public runway in the state of Florida.

As we approached the airfield, we called up on the radio and spoke to an old gentleman (who also just happened to double up as the local taxi driver). He passed the latest weather information and the wind direction to us and asked whether we required transport into town upon landing. Not knowing the geography of the town, and not wanting to appear ungrateful or discourteous, we accepted. The approach into Cedar Key was exhilarating and incredibly scenic. Thankfully, our landing was uneventful and upon taxiing and parking up, we were met with the sight of an old 1950's era Buick taxi which, with its black and white paint job, looked like it had probably been a police car in a former life. It was driven by the gentleman we had spoken with over the radio, and he took us on supposedly the 'scenic route' into the centre of town. The journey took a matter of just minutes, and we were dropped by the driver at the fishing pier and quayside, where we found a nice restaurant overlooking the harbour for a hearty breakfast.

Following breakfast, we walked through the quiet streets of this quaint old Floridian fishing town and sat on the pier watching the locals fishing for a while. We chatted to a few people who had caught our accents and wondered what 'a couple of Brits' were doing sitting on Cedar Key pier at this time of the day in early February. We got one of the local fishermen to take a photo of us sitting on a bench on the pier; a photo that remains on display in my study at home to this day.

Before too long, it was time to head back to the airfield and make our way back to Ormond Beach, some one hundred and forty miles to the east. As we took off, flying directly over the fishing pier as we turned on track to Ormond Beach, I promised myself that I would have to return to Cedar Key one day.

During this time (between 1996 and early 1997), I had a few short-term relationships. But none amounted to anything serious, which suited me fine. After the years that I had spent with Jo, and the rather difficult way in which the relationship had ended, I was enjoying being single and only having myself to consider. There were a few people that I kept crossing paths with during this time, though, one of whom was, of course, Aisling from Inflight Services.

Whilst her approach towards me in public remained professional, behind closed doors we actually started to get on and we were becoming quite good friends. I enjoyed her company and I could tell that, through the banter we shared, we were quite alike in certain respects. Even my late night, drink-fuelled phone calls didn't seem to annoy her quite as much as I expected they might. Although I think it would be fair to say that neither of us realised it at the time, we were becoming closer as friends and, very slowly, I was beginning to see Aisling in a whole new light.

Not long after returning to the UK from Ormond Beach, I was out after work with my flatmate Tim and we had invited Aisling to join us for a drink. I had not seen her for a little while as she had been travelling in the US with work, and so we spent the evening catching up on what we had been up to.

I had previously told Aisling about doing my PPL in Florida and, for once, she had shown more than a passing interest in what I had to say. So, in a thinly veiled attempt to impress her, I took the opportunity to tell her of my latest flying adventures.

After that, the interest in aviation that must have been burning quietly away inside was awakened and, within a few days, she informed me that she had taken the decision to go, along with three friends of hers (all flight attendants for British Airways), to Ormond Beach and obtain her PPL too.

She had organised the time off work and was all set to go, so I spent that evening imparting all the knowledge and handy hints I had that would assist her upon arriving in Florida – as well as things to watch out for when dealing with Ormond Beach Aviation, Andrew, and the PPL course.

Before she left, Aisling and I agreed that I would take her to Shoreham Airport to show her around the controls of a Cessna 150 so that they would be familiar upon her arrival in the USA. If the weather was good, we would also go for a short hop along the south coast to give her a feel for what flying a small aeroplane was really all about. Aisling was due to head to Florida at the beginning of April 1997, so we arranged to take our trip to Shoreham the weekend before she left.

On that Sunday, 23rd March 1997, the weather was doing its best to upset our arrangements. It was cold, raining, and the cloud base was low. Aisling and I set off on the thirty-minute drive from Crawley to Shoreham, hoping that the weather might improve by the time we got to the airfield but, given the forecast for the day, we already knew that it probably wouldn't. We arrived at the airfield and, quickly resigning ourselves to being grounded for the day, we decided to go and sit in one of the aircraft and talk through what all the dials and switches did.

We spent about an hour in the aircraft going through everything, with me exhausting my repertoire of hilarious flying-based anecdotes. Then, as there was to be no actual flying that day, Aisling and I decided to head into Brighton a few miles up the coast to grab something to eat before returning to Crawley. We had dinner in a restaurant at Brighton Marina, which Aisling offered to pay for in return for me giving up my Sunday afternoon. Forever being the true gentleman, I gladly took her up on her offer (something I have never been allowed to forget). After dinner, we headed back to Crawley and I dropped Aisling back at her house in the Pound Hill area of the town.

All week, it had been in the news that on Sunday evening, the UK would be treated to the best possible view of the Hale-Bopp comet as it passed overhead, assuming the skies were clear. So, after a quick cup of tea, we ventured out for a stroll around Aisling's neighbourhood to try to catch a glimpse of what had been termed the 'Great Comet of 1997'.

Many of the clouds from the day had cleared by this time, but the much-heralded comet was to prove elusive and we were to be left disappointed once more. After heading back to the house and drinking another cup of tea to warm up, it was late and – as we both had work the following morning – it was time for me to head home. I got up to leave and headed for the door. As Aisling thanked me for the trip to Shoreham and I thanked her for dinner, we gave each other a hug that turned into a peck on the cheek. Before I knew it, the peck on the cheek somehow turned into a proper full-on kiss, and I left Aisling's that evening with my heart beating just a little faster and with a slight spring in my step.

What had started almost three years previously as a brief introduction over a photocopier, had since developed into whatever was now happening between us. But as I went to bed that night, it would have been impossible to imagine what lay ahead or what would happen on the journey we had just embarked upon.

Aisling left for Florida a week later, and we kept in contact while she was away by phoning one another every few days. After so long of having been just friends, I felt that I already knew her quite well and I certainly missed her while she was away. But the three weeks flew by and, of course, she too successfully completed the course and came home with her PPL, ready to begin her flying back in the UK.

After that, Aisling and I started seeing more and more of each other and spending more time together at the weekends. We both travelled a lot with our jobs, so occasionally were out of the country at the same time. But we fell comfortably back into each other's company on our return.

By this time, the different offices that Virgin Atlantic occupied around Crawley had been amalgamated into one purpose-built office building located on the industrial estate just outside the town centre. Aisling and I were therefore now located in the same building for the first time. Being fully aware that our relationship would quickly become the 'talk of the town' and the subject of salacious gossip were news of it to get out, we would occasionally meet in the back stairwell during work hours for a chat. We were both unified in our opinion that no one needed to know about us and that, if our relationship was to have any chance of flourishing, then the longer we kept it to ourselves the better. I told my flat mate Tim, but he was a safe pair of hands; I knew he could keep it to himself.

At this point, in mid 1997, Aisling was completely in the dark about me having CF. I still hadn't told anyone at work about it (except for Martin, my previous boss) and I was managing to hide it well from everyone, or so I believed.

With Aisling, however, I was faced very early on with the dilemma that most people with CF will probably face at one point or another in their lives. Being attracted to someone and starting a relationship with them is all well and good, but how do you go about telling them that you have a degenerative condition that may eventually kill you and that, even before it does, your life will revolve around endless physio, tablet-taking, and regular trips to hospital?

Having given the matter serious thought and being truly petrified of scaring Aisling away in those early days of our relationship, I decided to keep CF to myself for the time being. If I had known then what I know now, I would never have taken such a decision and, with hindsight, it still stands as just about the silliest and most selfish thing I have ever done.

What I thought I would achieve by not coming clean from the outset I cannot imagine, other than not wanting to rock the boat or jeopardise what I thought might develop into something wonderful between us.

This misconceived decision to keep CF a secret would, though, eventually come back and bite me – in a very dramatic and rather emotional way, just a few months into our relationship.

Through the rest of 1997, Aisling and I would go flying at weekends when the weather allowed and spent increasing amounts of time together. A few months into the relationship, she decided that she would like me to meet her parents. This is a frightening enough experience for anyone, but for us there were added complications; Aisling's family were Catholic and she had grown up in Northern Ireland through the height of what were, and remain, known as the 'The Troubles'.

During the 1970s, 80s and 90s, a sectarian war between Catholics and Protestants prevailed, with the occupation of Northern Ireland by the British Army and with direct rule from the British Government being at the heart of it. Although largely ignorant as to the political minutiae of Northern Irish politics over the previous thirty years, I harboured concerns as to how an English non-Catholic might be received by Aisling's parents and family. I might even be perceived as a Protestant, which could throw fuel onto what I thought might already be a volatile situation.

We flew from Gatwick to Belfast one Saturday morning in September 1997 and hired a car to get us from Belfast City Airport to the family home in County Tyrone, an hour's drive away. Before too long, we were off the motorway and heading through the winding lanes towards Aisling's parents' farm, on the top of a hill with amazing views of the surrounding countryside and the Mourne Mountains off in the distance.

As we came down the lane on the approach to the farm, Aisling pulled over the car close to where some guys were working away with shovels in an adjacent field.

It soon became clear that these guys were, in fact, Aisling's dad John, and two of her three brothers. They greeted Aisling warmly and peered through the driver's side window at me. As if I was a caged animal in a zoo, the three of them stared intently at me and the confidence I had struggled to maintain that day suddenly melted away. Nonetheless, I smiled politely back and introduced myself to my audience. With that, Aisling's dad welcomed me to his home, told us to pull up in the driveway and said that they would be right down.

We headed down to the house where Aisling's mum Josie greeted us and, within seconds, I was made to feel completely at ease; I could not have wished for a warmer welcome. Aisling's parents have always been the kindest and most welcoming of people – the very epitome of Irish hospitality. Despite all my early concerns, it soon became apparent that this was going to be a good weekend and that I had probably been a bit of a fool to expect anything different.

The couple of days we spent at Aisling's parents' home was an enjoyable time and far less stressful than I had been expecting in the days leading up to our trip. The only event to somewhat overshadow the conviviality was my attempt to shoot Aisling's dad with a shotgun. (You may feel that you have to re-read that sentence although with a deep sense of shame, this did actually happen).

After we had returned from mass at the local Catholic church on the Sunday morning, and had been fed a plentiful breakfast by Aisling's mum, her dad and two of her brothers decided that I was rather wet behind the ears when it came to matters of a countryside nature and that the best induction to country life was to set me loose with a double-barrelled shotgun.

Just to set the scene a little, I had never even seen a real gun up until this point in my life, let alone had to aim or fire one at anything. With me suitably equipped in a pair of borrowed wellies, we set off into the field behind the house where a clay pigeon sling was set up. Aisling was despatched to load and fire the clay pigeons, while I was tasked with shooting them out of the sky. That was the theory, at least.

After almost thirty minutes of aiming, firing at, and missing each clay pigeon that flew past, it had become abundantly clear that perhaps shooting was not going to be my forte. Gathering up the numerous clay pigeons that now lay bereft and fully intact in the neighbouring field, Aisling's brothers then set them up right along the top of the hedge that divided the fields. They clearly thought that, as my shooting skills didn't yet stretch to hitting a moving target, I may have more luck hitting a static one. Whilst I think I might have hit a few, I had by this point become rather despondent with the whole experience.

Had a drum kit been set up in the field that morning, I could have pulled off a mean demonstration of my musical abilities, but I was clearly going to need a lot more practise before any clay pigeons had anything to worry about. Thankfully, though, my poor ability to hit anything was just about to save Aisling's dad's life… and spare me life imprisonment.

After firing what I believed to be both cartridges from my gun, I turned around to where John was standing just a few metres behind me, watching my dismal shooting abilities with incredulity. As I went to lower the gun (to, ironically, not have it aiming at anyone) my finger flinched and pulled the trigger. A split second later, as a loud bang rang out into the fresh air, I recall John diving for cover as huge clumps of earth and mud shot out of the ground just in front of him and over his head.

As he pulled himself together, and as I stood there aghast, I think we both knew it was time for me to be relieved of my firearm and to find something slightly less potentially-deadly to do.

Back in the safety of the family's kitchen, we were able (after a while) to laugh at the close shave that had just occurred. But I think we were all happy to agree that giving a gun with live ammunition to a novice 'townie' like me was not the best idea, and that I should stick to other – less dangerous – pastimes instead. I was happy to concur, and Aisling was even happier to have her dad still alive and, although shaken, still relatively unscathed after his ordeal.

Ironically, it was me who – a couple of days later – was sitting in front of a doctor; I had not worn any kind of ear defenders throughout my morning's shooting experience in Northern Ireland and the resulting ringing in my ears when I returned home started to cause me a little concern.

After a brief look in my ears with his little torch device, however, the doctor remained largely unsympathetic with my plight. I was told in no uncertain terms to ensure I wore something over my ears the next time I decided to take up a pursuit involving firearms and that the ringing should subside over the coming days. Thankfully, he was right but that (along with almost shooting another human being) was enough to put me off guns for life, and I have never held one since.

As 1997 wore on, and with both Aisling and I having a lust for travel, we started planning our first holiday together. We both fancied going island hopping around the Greek Islands and had talked about doing this several times both before and since getting together. So, we decided that we would take a couple of weeks off work in the early summer, with the aim of seeing as many islands as we could within that time.

Before we left for Greece, we had a 'practise run' by way of a weekend in Edinburgh, just to ensure that we would not tire of each other's company whilst in Greece and to verify that we made good travel companions. We may have known each other for three years, but going on holiday together for the first time was still a big step for us and Aisling, in particular, wanted to make sure that she would not be sick of the sight of me after twenty-four hours in my company. As it turned out, the weekend in Edinburgh was very enjoyable and we had a really nice time. We visited the castle and Holyrood House, and spent Saturday evening on something of an improvised pub crawl around Princes Street. Our warm-up trip for Greece was a success and we were confident enough to head off a couple of weeks later with the knowledge that we probably wouldn't kill each other while we were away.

We flew to Athens with just a vague idea of an itinerary and a guidebook on Greek island hopping in our possession. We had two weeks to come and go as we pleased with no accommodation pre-booked and our return flight from Athens as the only constriction we had. I hadn't for one moment considered how I would conceal my CF from Aisling during this trip or how I would keep up with my medications and physio sessions. Nonetheless, I was determined to keep up the pretence and to enjoy the holiday without CF spoiling it for us.

During our two weeks away, we stayed on a number of the islands in the Cyclades and Dodecanese island groups, arranging accommodation upon our arrival at each place. Luckily, on stepping off each of the inter-island ferries we took, the harbours would be dotted with travel and tour offices advertising accommodation, car hire, and tours, as well as onward ferry tickets and timetables to other islands. Our accommodation during those two weeks ranged from some quite nice small hotels (Santorini) to basic holiday apartments (Naxos and Paros) but it was on the small island of Amorgos where our rather ad-hoc travel plans unravelled.

Having arrived on the mid-afternoon ferry, we headed to the local tourist office to discover that the island only had one hotel on it and that it was likely to be fully booked, given the time of day. Nonetheless, we took a local bus to the village where the hotel was situated to enquire as to our chances of a room for the night. Soon enough, however, our worst fears were confirmed; the hotel was indeed already full. With no further ferries leaving the island until the following morning, our fate was sealed, and we had little option but to sleep on the adjacent beach for the night.

After an early dinner and watching the sunset over the island, we found a spot under some trees at the back of the beach. Using the towels in our backpacks as blankets and the backpacks themselves as pillows, we settled down for the night. Early the following morning, we were woken by the sound of a ship's horn sounding out in the bay in front of us. We quickly gathered our belongings, threw our backpacks onto our backs, and walked the short distance to the jetty where the ship was docking.

The vessel turned out to be one of the 'flying dolphin' hydrofoils that zigzag across the seas in that part of the world during the spring and summer months. We quickly bought a ticket and a short time later we were queueing up to board the curious looking vessel that would speed us away from Amorgos (hopefully, to a neighbouring island and, preferably, a cosy hotel with hot and cold running water, a shower, and a comfy bed).

Our first holiday together largely went very well, apart from the 'Great Amorgos sleeping arrangements cock-up'. Each morning, I took myself off for an early walk alone, during which I would carry out some form of physio to clear my chest before the day's events.

I also, largely, managed to keep up with taking my tablets without drawing attention to myself. Looking back, I feel ashamed of the level of deception I went to in order to hide my CF from Aisling – in the misguided belief that, for as long as she didn't know about it, she would somehow be protected from it.

Knowing Aisling as I do now, it would have been far better to come clean from the outset and spare us both a lot of heartache further down the line, but in my blinkered and rather selfish approach to life, I felt that protecting her from the truth was the kindest thing to do. And if that meant more stress for me by doing so, then so be it.

EIGHTEEN
IT'S CERTAIN WITH CF THAT NOTHING IS CERTAIN

As 1997 neared its end, things began to change for both me and Aisling at work. In September of that year, I had been on an Airline Marketing course where I had met a couple of guys who worked in the Marketing Department of Airbus, the multinational passenger aircraft manufacturer based in Toulouse in Southwest France. They had told me that Airbus were actively recruiting and that they were particularly keen on people applying from commercial airline backgrounds.

I had always harboured a desire to work abroad at some point in my career, but was always mindful as to how this might be compatible with having CF. The proposition of me working in Malaysia a year or so before had come to nothing, but France seemed – on the face of it – to be more viable as a destination; not too far from the UK and somewhere from which I could return home from if I became ill.

The more I considered the prospect of going to work in France, the more it interested me.

Simultaneously, at Virgin Atlantic, my boss of the past two years Andy (who had introduced me and Aisling three years previously) had been told he was moving to work for the airline in Greece and that I would now be working directly for the Commercial Manager, a guy who was new to the airline and someone I was not particularly keen on working for.

The opportunity at Airbus was looking increasingly attractive as time went on, and I decided to put in an application to see how far it went. I was invited to go to Toulouse for an interview, which seemed to go well, and it felt like everything was looking promising. It took a couple of months for Airbus to get back in contact with me, informing me that I had been successful at interview and that I was being offered the position of Marketing Executive, but the salary was good and Toulouse seemed like an exciting place to go and live and work.

The only difficulty in all of this was Aisling; things were going so well between us that to jeopardise our relationship seemed rather foolhardy. But with emotions set aside, the prospect of moving to France was an attractive one and, given that our relationship was still only a few months old, it seemed churlish to pass up such an opportunity now that an offer was on the table and the possibility had become a reality.

At around the same time, however, Aisling had also concluded that it might be time to move on from Virgin Atlantic and that she was also ready for a new challenge.

Aisling had seen in the trade press that British Airways were recruiting for Inflight Catering Executives at their Heathrow head office and decided to apply. Within a few weeks, she had been for two interviews and had been informed that her application was successful. Thus, within a few weeks of each other, we both knew that we were set to leave the comfort and relative security of Virgin Atlantic, with Aisling heading around the M25 to British Airways and me rather further afield to Southwest France.

We had discussions at that time as to how our relationship would continue despite the distance. This was still way before the days of Skype, WhatsApp, and other internet-based ways of communicating, leaving just the landline phone as the main way of keeping in contact and with the more traditional handwritten letter serving as a very old-fashioned alternative.

Nonetheless, given the way we felt about each other, we both believed that our relationship could manage the distance. One of Aisling's well used phrases, "If it is meant for you, it won't pass by you," seemed particularly appropriate to the circumstance in which we now found ourselves.

So, after much discussion and reassurances, we both accepted our respective job offers. Separately and collectively, we started to prepare for the new opportunities that life was presenting us with.

We would be heading in opposite directions to each other and would now have over seven hundred miles between us. But we felt confident that our relationship had blossomed into something that could survive us being apart; it had taken us three years to finally get together and so, with a little effort and determination, we were not about to let a mere seven hundred miles come between us.

We both decided that we would leave Virgin Atlantic on the same day, Friday 12th December 1997. That would give us a few days after finishing work before Aisling was due to go home to Northern Ireland to spend the Christmas holidays with her family. Before then, however, we resolved to use up our remaining staff travel concessions for that year.

In October 1997, we headed to Florida for a few days, flying to Miami and hiring a car to drive to Key West, the furthermost island of the Florida Keys. The Keys, the archipelago of outlying islands spread out from the southernmost tip of Florida, are linked to the mainland by the 'Overseas Highway' (or Highway One) which – by way of multiple bridges – links all of the major islands (or 'keys') and also provides what must be one of the most picturesque drives anywhere in the USA.

We had a great time in Key West, mixing time on the beach with exploring and a little sightseeing. One afternoon we even headed to Key West Airport and, along with an instructor, hired a four-seat Cessna 172 to do some sightseeing from the air for a couple of hours. Even though we each had a turn at flying the aircraft, we took an instructor with us as our UK PPLs would not allow us to just turn up and fly a US-registered aircraft alone. Plus, it was useful to have someone with some local knowledge of the area to double-up as our tour guide for the afternoon.

A few short weeks after our trip to Florida, Aisling and I found ourselves in Hong Kong, which had just returned to Chinese rule after being ruled by the British for the previous one hundred and fifty-two years. Neither of us had been to Hong Kong before, but everyone we had spoken to about it told us what an amazing place it was and that it was somewhere we should try to get to before we left the company.

Our trip to Hong Kong was filled with activity and sightseeing. We travelled by the funicular railway to the top of 'The Peak', a viewpoint with the most extraordinary views over Hong Kong Harbour towards Kowloon Island, and spent an afternoon hiking across Lamma Island, a small offshore island hosting an intriguing mix of Chinese fishing communities as well as an eclectic range of Westerners, many of whom followed an alternative, 'hippy' lifestyle as artists, writers and musicians.

Back in the city, after a few nights doing our best to embrace the local culture and to eat as the locals do, our delicate (and some would say rather unadventurous) western palates were starting to get the better of us. After all, there are only so many one-hundred-year-old eggs you can eat before craving roast beef, burgers, and chips.

Like in most cities of the world, it didn't take too much effort to seek out the nearest traditional Irish pub, located in the Wan Chai area of the city. You could almost hear the relief from our stomachs as we gobbled down Irish Stew and mashed potato that night, giving our digestive systems a much-needed hiatus from Chinese food.

We also came across the legendary 'Flying Pig' pub – a bar and bistro with the walls bedecked in airline memorabilia where you sat enjoying your cocktails whilst lounging in former Cathay Pacific business class seats. As both airline employees and aviators, the pub obviously appealed to the two of us and we pondered whether such a place might work well in London. It was just one more highlight of an amazing few days in this fascinating city. Like Cedar Key in Florida, I made a promise to myself (and to Aisling) on our last night that we would return to Hong Kong at some point in the future.

As the weeks ticked away, December slowly came around and it was time to leave Virgin Atlantic. Aisling and I made a quick reconnaissance trip to Toulouse one weekend in early December to have a look around and to start thinking about places to live and how I was going to get to work every day.

There happened to be an Ibis hotel just outside the gates of the Airbus office complex and I decided that I would stay there until I found myself an apartment closer to the city centre. We also met up with a woman who acted as a relocation specialist for those moving to Toulouse from the UK. She said she might be able to find me somewhere to live and that she also had a range of used furniture that I could rent from her company until my own furniture arrived from the UK.

As it happened, given that Tim and I had rented the flat in Crawley fully furnished, I had no furniture of my own, so I would need to purchase just about everything when I arrived in Toulouse in early January of the following year.

Toulouse was cold and bleak that weekend and, with a light covering of snow on the ground, was not particularly enticing. But my decision had been made and, the following week, I would be leaving the offices of Virgin Atlantic for the final time (or what I believed would be the final time) and, just three short weeks later, landing in Toulouse to start my new job.

Our respective departures from Virgin Atlantic were somewhat muted, with no real fanfare and no leaving parties or even drinks after work (at our request). One thing that Aisling and I had in common was not wanting to be the centre of attention, so we had decided against throwing any kind of event to mark our leaving. There was a small presentation for me in the Commercial Department that Friday afternoon, where I was handed the requisite card signed by all my colleagues and a few largely unmemorable mementoes marking my three and a half years at the company.

By five thirty that Friday afternoon, everyone had drifted home to start their weekends, leaving me in relative peace to clear my personal belongings from my desk, to tidy up, and to sign off from the company's email system for the final time. I didn't regret leaving as it felt that the timing and circumstances were right to move on and to try something somewhere else. I had enjoyed an amazing forty-two months at Virgin Atlantic and had experienced so many things that the other fifty or so graduates from my degree course could only have ever dreamed about.

I still think back to my time at the airline very fondly and, of course, it was where I met Aisling for the first time. I may have left with so many great memories from my time at Virgin, but I also left with Aisling who, alone, was worth all those memories put together. It was with her that I would begin this next chapter in my life, and that prospect was all the reassurance I needed.

What was to come next, however, would rock me to my core.

It was finally time for CF to make its presence felt and to remind me, as I headed off to France, how delicate a life with CF can be.

Given that I was now twenty-five years old, CF was about to remind me that I could no longer push myself to the limit, like I had been, without consequence. Nor could I head off to Toulouse without giving due consideration to what this might mean for me and my health, regardless of how much I hated the notion.

After a few days together, Aisling headed off to Northern Ireland for Christmas with her family. I had a couple of days in Crawley before returning to Cambridge to spend Christmas with my dad and his new partner. On that Friday, 19th December 1997, it just so happened that my next appointment at Papworth was due and my dad decided to come with me for company. It was almost as if he had foreseen the outcome of that appointment and knew that I would need someone there to support me that day.

I recall heading to Papworth feeling rather tired and chesty, and my respiratory tests that day indicated a worrying dip in lung function. Some blood was taken from a vein in my arm to be sent away for immediate testing so that the results would be back for Dr Bilton to review prior to seeing me later that afternoon.

Given that this was the last CF clinic before Christmas, the outpatients area was rammed with other patients hoping to be seen before the holidays began. The wait to see Dr Bilton was, therefore, a particularly long one. By the time she entered the consultation room, accompanied by Pam the CF specialist nurse, it was dark outside and most other patients had already left.

My conversation with Dr Bilton took an ominous tone from the outset, and I knew almost immediately that she had concerns about my lung function and the raised infection levels indicated by my blood test results. This concern was clearly exacerbated by the fact that, in just over two weeks, I was setting off for Toulouse, rendering myself several hours from Papworth should I need urgent hospital treatment.

After listening to Dr Bilton for just a few minutes, it was clear that she was not going to let me leave the hospital that day without some form of medical intervention and a sudden – and rather shocking – lesson in how to treat chest infections in people with CF followed.

One has to bear in mind that at this point that, with a great deal of good fortune (although with some degree of me attempting to look after myself thrown in), I had got through the first twenty-five years of my life without a serious chest infection.

CF had certainly lulled me into a very false sense of security in this respect. So, with this in mind, when Dr Bilton suggested that I should seriously consider a two-week course of IV antibiotics, starting that very afternoon, my world crumbled. The thought of having an IV line in my arm for the next fortnight (and indeed over Christmas) was abhorrent and I found the whole prospect terrifying. Perhaps it was the fear of the unknown that was getting the better of me, or maybe the plain and simple truth that after twenty-five years, CF had finally got one over me. Either way, I fell apart and asked if Dr Bilton could give me a few minutes alone with my dad to consider what I should do.

As she and the nurse left the room, I looked towards my dad with tears in my eyes.

I must have looked to him as much as any lost little boy looks to his dad for reassurance. I felt confused, trapped, and angry. I wanted to lash out at someone, anyone, or to try and show that somehow there had been a mistake. But, as ever, my dad had the words to calm my nerves and make me see what was staring me right in the face; as much I searched for an alternative to what was being proposed, there was none to be found.

My dad, in all his wisdom, and with a greater knowledge of CF than I, simply looked at me and said, "You just need to bloody do this, Luke." And I knew then that the game was up.

The running away from CF, this horrible disease that had been lurking in the shadows for the past twenty-five years, was over. I felt like I had tripped and fallen, allowing CF to stand over me and claim victory. I felt broken and beaten. But, as much as I hated it, I knew my dad was right. I had no option but to agree to Dr Bilton's proposition and submit to CF, something I had never had to do before.

We called Dr Bilton back into the room and I agreed to the treatment that she recommended. I thought that by facing up to it and starting the IV treatment, a sense of relief might take over. but my emotions were all over the place, and no such sense was forthcoming.

Almost like a child watching a scary film from behind the sofa, I sat and listened as I was talked through the procedure and what would happen next. My mind swirled in every direction imaginable and I am not sure how much of what I was being told I really took in.

Before long, we were in a side room with Pam the nurse threading a long IV line into a vein in my left arm. Others with CF who are reading this may recall their own memories of having IVs for the first time but, in my case, it was hard to discern whether the discomfort of having this done or the sheer sight of it was the worst part.

After a few minutes of Pam pushing and turning, the line was in place in my arm and she tested it by pushing some saline through the line to check it was free flowing. The line was then covered in a dressing and a bandage was placed over my arm so that the loose end of the IV line could be secured within it, avoiding the risk of snagging it or, worse still, pulling it out entirely.

It took another thirty minutes or so to be shown how to draw up each of the two different IV drugs, as well as the line flushes, and how to follow protocol for keeping everything sterile as much as possible. Following this (and my dad taking notes, thank goodness) the first dose of the drugs was administered by pushing them through the line and into my vein.

Every time new medication is started (even now, having done this hundreds of times since then) you are monitored for thirty minutes after the last drug is given in case of the onset of anaphylactic shock. This is where the body has a massive reaction to the drugs it has received and in the worse cases can stop the heart (cardiac arrest). Thankfully, such a reaction was not observed or experienced and we were sent on our way with a quick diversion to the hospital pharmacy to collect the first seven days' worth of IV medication. My life with CF had just become that much more complicated. I knew it, and I realised that there was nothing I could do about it.

NINETEEN
DIVERGING PATHS

Hospital rules dictated that, Christmas or not, patients were only issued with seven days of medication at any one time. As Dr Bilton was keen to see me back at the hospital after seven days anyway, to see how my first ever course of IV antibiotics was going, the timing was all rather inconvenient. I say inconvenient as this was 19th December, meaning that my day-seven appointment would be on the following Friday - Boxing Day.

As Dr Bilton would not be at the hospital that day and, in fact, there would be no CF clinic either, it was arranged that I would have a consultation with one of Dr Bilton's junior doctors instead, who would be able to prescribe the following seven days' worth of medication in her place.

The one amazing thing about the treatment I have received at Papworth over the years is how the staff have always bent over backwards to help their patients, and this was a good example of that. It may have been my first dose of IV antibiotics, yet I was already being given something of a bespoke service to fit in with my requirements and to accommodate Christmas.

I have always said that the treatment I have received from Papworth (since first walking through their doors in 1994) is akin to a private health service except it is being provided by an NHS team.

On more than one occasion over the years, I have telephoned the CF team at Papworth in the morning, telling them I am feeling unwell, and have found myself having a chest x-ray and seeing a CF consultant that same afternoon. By the evening of the same day, I have either been started on home IV treatment or, in the more severe cases, have been given a hospital bed to start my treatment as an in-patient.

I don't think that there are many areas of today's NHS where the same could be said and, whilst resources are obviously more stretched than they once were, I have nothing but praise for those at Papworth who have monitored and managed my condition over the years and who have kept me alive while CF did its best to achieve the opposite result.

Over that Christmas period, my dad was up with me at six every morning, helping me draw up the IV drugs in the correct order and making sure that I followed the very detailed instructions that he had typed up on his home computer after returning home from Papworth.

We would reconvene each day at two p.m. and then at ten p.m. to complete the day's three doses and to prepare the IVs for the following day too. It was with his support that I got through that first set of IVs.

Given everything else that has happened to me since, what felt like a momentous event back then seems rather insignificant now. When I think back to how meticulous and slow I was when preparing and administering those first few doses, compared to now, it makes me smile. Yet it was all so new and scary to me that I was absolutely determined to do it right and properly from the outset.

After taking me to the day-seven appointment at Papworth and, satisfied that I'd shown a nice looking improvement in my lung function over the first seven days of treatment, my dad headed off on a trip to Venice leaving me to return to Crawley and finish the final week of treatment on my own. Obviously nervous to do so, given that I no longer had the mental reassurance that my dad's supervision gave me, I pressed on and slowly got through the next few days.

On the Sunday during my second week of IVs, I was due to collect Aisling from Heathrow on her return from Northern Ireland. I knew that I would have to come clean about the line in my arm and doing IVs, but I battled with the dilemma of just how much I should tell her.

Right up until the point when I saw her smiling face walk through Domestic Arrivals in Terminal One at Heathrow, I was still unsure what I was going to say. I was torn between wanting to tell her everything about me and CF and not wanting to put our relationship in jeopardy, especially given that I was leaving for Toulouse in exactly one week's time. At some point within those few critical moments, I decided that full disclosure was not going to do either us or our blossoming relationship any good and that I would come up with some sort of story that would leave the great CF monster undisturbed, at least for now.

As we drove back to Crawley, Aisling noticed the bandage on my arm (covering my IV line) and asked what I had done while she had been gone. Given that I had not mentioned anything to her over the phone, she must have been a little confused.

In my panic, I explained that I had been suffering from a chest infection and, to get rid of it quickly and to prepare me for my imminent departure to Toulouse, the doctor recommended IV antibiotics. At the time, in my crass stupidity, I thought that my explanation sounded plausible. We drove the rest of the way home with me feeling like I had dealt with the issue and that there was little more to be said on the subject.

But by saying what I had said and feeling how I did, I was doing Aisling a huge injustice. I was treating her like a fool. I deserved to be rumbled there and then, and to be caught out for my deceit. For reasons known only to her, Aisling took what I said onboard and didn't question me about it. But, clearly, my explanation left her with many internal questions unanswered and the whole issue very much unresolved. It would be some months, however, before full disclosure would become inevitable and unavoidable.

The events of that morning at the tail end of 1997 have lived with me ever since and lie in my memory as one of my deepest regrets. I had the perfect opportunity to come clean, to explain everything about CF to Aisling and to let her decide whether she was able to cope with the difficulties and stress that being in a relationship with someone who has CF must undoubtedly bring. But through my fear, selfishness, and the trepidation of heading to France to start a new life alone, I robbed her of being able to make that decision herself.

If there is one thing in my life that I would change, it would be the events of that Sunday. I find it raw to think about it even now.

Whilst Aisling has assured me since that she understands why I did what I did, this does little to remove the stain on my memory and my regret will stay with me forever.

The next few days were spent mostly in each other's company. The flat in Crawley was emptied and vacated and my possessions were picked up by a relocation company to be brought to me in Toulouse once I had established somewhere to live. By the end of my last week in the UK, I had two cases of clothes and a rucksack of bits and bobs, and I was to stay at Aisling's house for the last couple of nights before I left. I was due to leave for Toulouse on Sunday 4th January to start at Airbus the following morning.

I headed to Papworth alone on the Friday before for my day-fourteen check and to finish my first ever course of IVs. Dr Bilton gave me the all clear to head to France but under the strict instruction to call Papworth if I felt unwell at any stage. I was due back there in eight weeks in any event, but Dr Bilton – in her wisdom – wanted to keep me on a fairly tight lead, even if geography didn't allow for it.

On our last day together, and despite it being a Sunday, I insisted that Aisling and I set the alarm early so that we could have the whole day together before I headed to the airport. We had a lovely day and went out for Sunday lunch at a nice local pub before sitting in the afternoon sun of that cold January day.

It felt like we had so much to say to each other, but the enormity of what was about to happen hung over us and made talking difficult. As the hours drew on and it got near the time to head for the flight, the reality hit home and what little talking remained was soon replaced by hugs and tears from us both. At Gatwick, we assured each other that what we had was special and that the relationship would survive the distance between us. But neither of us could be sure whether that were true or what the future would bring. We planned for Aisling to head to Toulouse after three weeks, by which time I hopefully would have somewhere to live and would be able to show her around my new hometown.

I felt sick to the depths of my stomach and was barely able to hold myself together. We hugged and kissed for one final time and Aisling stood and watched in tears as I disappeared through the sliding screen doors of Departures. The last memory I had of Aisling that evening was her looking completely crushed, watching me with lost eyes and a tear-stained face.

As the doors closed behind me, I did my best to compose myself. I wiped my eyes, took some deep breaths, and headed through passport control towards my new life in France.

Within an hour or so I was sitting on the aircraft, looking out of the window at the dark night and watching the lights of Brighton and the south coast of England slip away beneath me. I thought about the decisions that had brought me to this point and whether I would ever see Aisling again. After all, it had been my decision to go to France just as our relationship really started to mean something and I had clearly just broken her heart by leaving.

I wondered whether our assurances to each other about the future were truly heartfelt or if they would simply turn out to be empty promises when reality kicked in and the make-believe ran out?

A short ninety minutes later, the aircraft touched down in Toulouse. As I disembarked and walked slowly through the airport, I had never felt more lost and alone. Thoughts of Aisling, Crawley, and the few wonderful months we had just spent together were all fresh in my mind but now seemed so distant and out of reach. And, regardless of how close I was to the UK and Aisling, the way I felt as I made my way through the airport, I may as well have just landed on the far side of the moon.

I made my way to the Ibis Hotel, a short taxi ride from the terminal at Toulouse Airport and literally across the road from the main gates of Airbus where I would be working. I had booked to stay at the hotel for the first fortnight and, as much as I disliked staying in hotels, this seemed like the most convenient place to stay whilst I settled in at my new workplace and found my feet around Toulouse.

I checked in using my passable but rather rusty A-Level French and headed to my room. I shut the door behind me and sat on the bed for a few minutes. The hotel was quiet on this late Sunday evening and it felt like I was the only person staying here. Thoughts of the fun work nights out in Brighton and flying from Shoreham Airport filled my mind but I did my best to dismiss them, turning instead to the task of unpacking and sorting clothes for my first day at Airbus the following morning.

As I emptied the first case, I hung up my shirts and placed everything in neat piles on the limited shelf space in the wardrobe. Opening the second case, however, it immediately struck me that there was something in there that I had not packed myself. It was a shoe box wrapped in colourful wrapping paper with my name written on the top. I had no idea what it was or where it had come from until I lifted the lid and peered in.

The shoe box contained packets of my favourite sweets and a few other items, as well as a short note. I opened it carefully.

In the note, Aisling explained how important our relationship was to her and that she was determined not to let the tiny inconvenience of a few hundred miles come between us.

I discovered later that Aisling had prepared the box during that previous week and had snuck the box into my case before we left her house for the airport. It was a lovely gift, of course, but the thoughtfulness and kindness she had shown me with that gesture was something I had never really experienced before.

I went to bed that first night feeling more alone and apprehensive than I had probably ever felt in my life. But Aisling's shoebox had instilled something else in me too and I felt somewhat reassured that, despite being here in France and away from everything and everyone that I knew and loved, this move was the right thing to do. Suddenly, I felt that – that if I wanted it to – it could work out to be one of the best things I had ever done.

I re-read Aisling's little note one last time before turning out the light, allowing myself the briefest of smiles before falling asleep.

My first week at Airbus was spent meeting people, getting to know my way around, and sitting through various introductory courses across several subjects. I managed to get hold of a couple of property newspapers which I spent the evenings back at the hotel trawling through. The area immediately around Airbus and the airport (a suburb of Toulouse called Blagnac) was particularly soulless and uninspiring, so I set my heart on finding something closer to the city centre (although, of course, this meant that I would be paying more in rent). I arranged to visit a couple of places early the following week and planned to spend my first full weekend in Toulouse exploring the city to familiarise myself with its layout and areas in which I might like to live.

Toulouse is a beautiful Romanesque city in the southwest of France with a medieval city centre dissected by both the Garonne River and the renowned Canal du Midi. It is widely known for its universities and for being a centre of excellence for the aerospace industry, although it is also located on the doorstep of some of France's most famous vineyards and has the Pyrenees mountain range within a relatively short drive. Indeed, the delightful beaches of France's south coast are only two hours' drive down the autoroute.

During my first week at Airbus, I was sent to the Medical Department for a new personnel medical check. Given that I had not mentioned CF to anyone at the company up until this point and having recently just become acquainted with hard core IV antibiotic treatment, I decided that now was the time to come clean about my condition. My medical check was performed by two nurses who appeared older in years and had probably seen and heard everything in their long careers. With my limited knowledge of French medical phraseology and their limited command of English, and after hearing me describe my symptoms and them finding the marks on my arm where the IV line had been inserted, we mutually decided that I had *mucoviscidosis* (which, thankfully, after looking it up later *did* turn out to be CF in French rather than some other rare lung disease). They made a few notes and got me to sign a few forms, but nothing further was said, and I was sent on my way.

That first week at Airbus rushed by and before I really had a chance to catch my breath, I was back at the hotel. Although feeling fairly upbeat, I was fully aware that a full weekend of just my own company was staring me in the face until

Monday morning and this brought back the feelings of loneliness that I had experienced when I first arrived.

I sat on my own at dinner in the hotel restaurant, pretending to be heavily involved in reading some literature I had brought down with me. In fact, I was too busy trying to think about anything else other than spending the next forty-eight hours alone. I decided that the best thing to do would be to return to my room, have an early night, get up early the following morning, catch the bus into the city, and start exploring.

I got back to my room and had just tidied up my clothes from that day when there was a knock at the bedroom door. I was immediately on edge; no one really knew who I was or that I was there, so who would be knocking on my door at that time on a Friday night? Warily, I approached the door and decided that, rather than just open it as I normally would, I should check to see who it was. I looked through the spy hole in the door and simply could not believe my eyes.

Having agreed that Aisling and I would not see each other for three weeks, there she was, completely unexpectedly, standing outside my hotel room in Toulouse!

I immediately flung open the door and welcomed her in with a huge hug. Of all the people I would have most liked to be outside my door that night, Aisling was that person. And to my astonishment and pure delight, there she was.

What had been looking like a quiet and lonely first weekend spent shuffling around Toulouse on my own had just become an adventure for both of us, and an experience we would share together. From feelings of despair and of being alone, I now felt elated and excited, as though I was the luckiest man on earth.

Another significant thing also happened with Aisling's arrival; from worries that our relationship might not survive the test of distance, or that she might find better things to do with her time than chasing around after me, I realised that the bond between us was a lot stronger than I had thought and that perhaps, after all, our relationship was meant to last.

Aisling had dropped everything after her first week in her new job and flown to another country so that she could be there for me on my first weekend away from 'home'. And I couldn't believe how lucky I was.

From that evening onwards, I saw her in a whole new light, having realised just how much she cared for me and me for her. And, although this was only the first stage of the next chapter of our relationship, I knew then that it was something special and that it was worth working hard for, despite the distance that now lay between us.

Despite my newfound excitement about our future, however, there remained the spectre of CF that at some point soon I would have to deal with. I couldn't continue trying to hide it from Aisling and nor did I want to.

Finding the right time and the right way to tell her was never going to be easy and was something I would agonise over again and again. Yet I knew that it was the right thing to do, and that I needed to do it soon if our relationship had any hope of continuing.

TWENTY

COMING CLEAN

With Aisling's visit over far too quickly, I began the task of settling into life in France. After three weeks of living in the Ibis Hotel by Toulouse Airport, I found a lovely two-bedroom apartment by the river right in the centre of the city with views of the Canal du Midi and a small balcony on which I hoped I would spend the warm summer evenings.

Renting property in France, I discovered, is rather different from in the UK. Rental properties are always let unfurnished, to the extent that you need to provide absolutely everything yourself. Indeed, I had been warned that should I be viewing any potential properties after dark, to take a lightbulb with me.

In my first month, I also procured a car; I was now the proud owner of a left-hand drive, white Ford Sierra estate, which I bought from a colleague at work. I had seen the car in the Airbus car park one morning as I walked from the bus stop into the offices and noted down the extension number shown on the '*A Vendre*' (for sale) sign in the windscreen. It turned out that the car was being sold by one of the Marketing Directors in my new department, whose office was just down the corridor from where I sat. By lunchtime that day, the deal was done. I gave that car the nickname 'The Hearse' – a curious choice given its brilliant white external finish, but more related to its ridiculous size, given that it was a huge car for me to be using as a mere run-around.

Aisling's first proper – non-surprise – weekend visit was spent exploring Toulouse, largely on foot, along with dinner on Valentine's night itself at Brasserie Les Beaux Arts, one of Toulouse's finest restaurants right on the bank overlooking the Garonne River.

Toulouse is a particularly beautiful city during the day, and at night takes on a whole new personality, with the medieval buildings lit up and the twinkling lights of the city reflecting on the surface of the river. Aisling seemed impressed at how quickly I had established myself in Toulouse and that I already knew my way around fairly well. Those early weekends spent on my own wandering the streets and getting my bearings had served me well, I suppose.

As the winter slowly turned into spring, Aisling and I settled into something of a routine with our respective visits between Crawley and Toulouse. I would fly to see her one weekend and then two weeks later, she would make the return journey. On the weekends in between, we stayed where we were and made our own entertainment. I would mostly spend these weekends going to the supermarket, catching up on my washing, and walking around the city.

After Aisling's first couple of visits to Toulouse, and having seen most of what the city itself had to offer, we started to venture a little further afield, taking The Hearse on adventures out into the country and beyond.

The countryside around Toulouse offers a great deal for those who are fortunate enough to have their own transport and, between us, we became determined to explore as much of it as we could. There were picturesque medieval hill-top towns once inhabited by the Cathars, along with numerous traditional chateaux and the walled medieval city of Carcassonne to visit. The valley of the River Lot also provided the backdrop for some wonderfully idyllic picnic spots and if you carried out down the A61 autoroute for a couple of hours, you would find yourself by the beautiful sandy beaches and seafood restaurants of the coastal town of Narbonne. Soon, the weekends Aisling spent with me in Toulouse were, in fact, spent largely away from the city with us finding new places to visit each time.

At work, I found settling into life at Airbus harder than I expected. There were plenty of other young British employees in the Marketing Department, as well as French, Germans, Spanish, and Portuguese. The department seemed subdivided into well-established groups, mostly distinguished by language, and I found it hard to infiltrate these cliques, certainly from a social point of view.

In terms of the work, the new starters were held in a training directorate before we were permitted to be let loose on actual airline marketing programmes, which I also found frustrating. I had gone from knowing my job at Virgin Atlantic inside out to starting right at the bottom again at Airbus.

The time spent on the training programme (I found out upon arriving in Toulouse) would last for the first three to four months of my time in the Marketing Department and thus, from the outset, I felt a little duped and annoyed that this had not been disclosed before I signed up. Nonetheless, I decided that for the time being, I should bide my time and learn as much as I possibly could about the Airbus family of aircraft and their respective performance characteristics, so that I would become a more capable marketeer when I eventually graduated out of the training nursery and was allowed to play with the big kids.

On one of my regular Friday evening flights back to the UK in the March of 1998, I sat next to a guy who worked as a lawyer for Airbus in the in-house legal department. We spent the whole flight back to Gatwick talking about his work and I told him about my time at Virgin Atlantic and the work I had been involved in there. A lot of my time at Virgin had been spent in rooms with aviation lawyers like this guy wrangling over contracts of various types and I often wondered whether this was a career path that I should or could have followed. I found the work of these lawyers fascinating and it did flash through my mind that, at some point in the future, I should consider re-training to become an aviation lawyer.

However, the very thought of having to go back into education to obtain the necessary qualifications filled me with dread and the notion of trying to qualify as a lawyer was very quickly parked in the recesses of my brain.

But that weekend was to become memorable for another reason; I had decided that I could no longer hide the fact that I had CF from Aisling. The very fact that I was doing so was eating away at me, exacerbated by the fact that we were not together for most of the time.

I felt that I was living a lie and that this was simply not fair on her; after all, she had stuck by me when I packed up and left the UK, and I was now realising that if we were to have a future together, I had to tell her all about my condition. The time had come. It was the right thing to do.

The nagging thoughts of when and how I should tell her were tortuous, but however hard the prospect of doing so seemed, the prospect of perpetuating the dishonesty was no longer an option.

Over that weekend, we did our normal things and enjoyed each other's company as we always did. On the Saturday afternoon, we had been for a walk on Box Hill in Surrey, about twenty-five minutes' drive from Crawley, and stopped at The Stepping Stones pub in the village of Westhumble.

As we took our drinks from the bar and found ourselves at a table in the window of the largely deserted pub, I knew that this was the time. I cannot recall exactly what was said and by whom, but I started by trying to explain why I really had had an IV line in my arm over the previous Christmas; not just to treat an ad-hoc chest infection.

It soon became clear that Aisling had not really accepted my original account back in December, and that she had suspected something for quite a while, perhaps even before the whole IV situation.

She told me that she wondered why I often seemed to have a tickly cough but had chosen to say nothing. As my explanation went on, both she and I became increasingly emotional as I tried to explain why I had kept it from her for the past year.

She asked whether Jo had known about my CF, to which I responded that she had but only because with her medical background, she had figured it out for herself. This did nothing, of course, to paint me in a better light, as it simply confirmed that I – on more than one occasion now – had concealed my CF from someone that I cared about until I was rumbled or until the tell-tale signs of the condition gave me away.

I tried as hard as I could to explain to Aisling what CF was and how it affected me but I realise, looking back, that my knowledge then compared to now was severely lacking in many respects. Aisling was devastated, torn between feeling sorry for me and being angry with me for taking so long to come clean. I felt terrible too and, having hoped that I would feel the weight lifted from my shoulders, experienced nothing of the kind; I was left feeling guilty, sad, and anxious – but none of these emotions would have even scraped the surface of what Aisling must have been feeling.

We spent the rest of that weekend not really talking about CF or the conversation in the pub. We weren't avoiding it, but the issues and feelings that we spoke about were perhaps just too hard for us to deal with and too raw to go over. Perhaps, too, Aisling needed time to process this bombshell, while I had to learn how to live with my deception.

All too soon, I was heading back to Toulouse on the Sunday evening flight from Gatwick. Just as I had at the start of January, I headed away from Aisling not really knowing when or if I would see her again. I knew that what I had done to her was simply unforgivable and the way I had treated her was grossly unfair. I wanted to turn the clock back and return to 23rd March 1997 when we first got together, to set everything out to her there and then – but life isn't like that.

I now had to live with the consequences of waiting a year before telling her, and to accept that if she found the deceit too much to take, then I only had myself to blame.

We continued to talk over the phone for the next couple of weeks and, to my surprise, Aisling seemed to be handling the CF news rather better than I had expected and it wasn't until a couple of weeks later that I got a true feeling for how she had taken it.

I had headed back to the UK for the weekend that marked the anniversary of Aisling and I spending the day in the rain at the flying club at Shoreham. We found ourselves in a pub in The Lanes area of Brighton on the Friday night, Aisling having picked me up from Gatwick and driven us there for a meal out to mark the occasion.

Whilst in the pub, given that this was the first time we had been together since the weekend I had confessed about having CF, we spoke again about the whole situation and how we both felt about it.

To my absolute amazement, whilst I had spent the past two weeks pondering what I had done and trying to convince myself that it was the right thing to do, Aisling had spent her free time researching CF and learning as much about the condition as she could. In our conversation that night, Aisling asked me questions about certain aspects of CF and indeed could tell me things that even I didn't know about.

Rather than disappear into the distance, her expedience masked by a cloud of dust, Aisling had decided to meet CF head on, to get to know as much about it as she could, and to not let it come between us. We agreed that night that we were in this together and that my experiences with CF would, from that point on, become our experiences.

Once again, Aisling had shown the true strength of her character and how much she cared for me and, that evening, I vowed that I would never doubt her again. I didn't feel reprieved (as that would be doing her a disservice) but I did realise that I was fortunate to be getting another chance and that this was now a real opportunity to acknowledge what CF meant to us and to move on with our lives and build on what we had together.

As the months rolled by, we managed to keep the momentum up in our relationship through the regular trips we made between the UK and France and our nightly telephone calls. A large proportion of my monthly salary was being spent on either flights from Toulouse to Gatwick or my phone bill. On my trips back to the UK, Aisling and I would spend our weekends out and about, making the most of the precious little time these weekend visits afforded.

I enjoyed being in Toulouse but it would be fair to say that I never fully bought into the experience, and the prospect of spending the rest of my life there rarely entered my head. The scare that CF had given me just before I left for France was enough to make me realise that, from that point on, CF needed to be considered in all that I did and could flare up at any time rendering me in need of hospital treatment at short notice. Here I was in France, a long way from Papworth and from people who knew about me and my medical history, and this made me feel awfully vulnerable.

The summer of 1998 saw various visitors come to stay with me in Toulouse. During one baking hot spell in the July of that year, Aisling came with her parents and eldest sister to stay for a few days. We spent the time driving around the area and even took a road trip over the Pyrenees mountains, across the plains of Catalonia, to end up in Barcelona for a couple of nights. Some old school friends from Cambridge came over for a long weekend, which we spent on the beach down at Narbonne, and my dad visited a couple of times too.

Aisling and I went to the USA for two weeks in the September of that summer to visit my mum and to drive up to Pennsylvania for my old school friend Bill (William) and his fiancé's wedding. Bill and Amy had decided to get married, and as I had played something of a part in providing momentum in the early days of their transatlantic relationship (through the provision of cheap flights on Virgin Atlantic) I was keen to be there to see the end result!

But as the long hot summer of that year cooled and faded, I started to give serious consideration as to the direction that my life should take going forward. By this point, I was no longer considered a marketing trainee but was assigned to the A320 aircraft marketing group. My days at work were spent working out performance data for how the A320 aircraft family members would outperform their competitors across a range of different missions both in terms of performance and economics. Yet the reality was that I was using raw data, calculated by Airbus computer programmes, for an airliner that was still on the drawing board and comparing this to other airliners for which we could only estimate performance and fuel burn characteristics.

It didn't take long before I started to feel rather despondent over this whole process and began to question its accuracy. This, along with how I had felt early on about my start at Airbus, was sowing a seed in my head that I may not remain with them for as long as I had originally envisaged.

I was also finding parting from Aisling at the end of our weekends together more and more difficult, and knew that eventually – and before too much longer – something was going to have to change. We had worked at our long-distance relationship for nine or so months by this point, but it seemed to be getting harder rather than easier.

During our holiday in the USA in the late September, we talked about things and I decided that I would start the process of looking for a job back in the UK. We did briefly consider Aisling moving to Toulouse, but as she spoke little French and was doing well in her career with British Airways, it seemed foolhardy to throw this all away. After all, I was the one who was feeling more unsettled and who, of course, also needed the virtual parachute of being closer to Papworth than I currently was should CF start to get out of control; I had managed to maintain a reasonable level of health during my time in Toulouse, but this was purely down to luck more than anything I was doing and the spectre of CF was becoming harder to ignore.

TWENTY-ONE

WILL YOU...?

I spent October 1998 sending out a few speculative letters to airlines back in the UK, asking to be considered for any commercial management jobs that they may have had coming up. In early November, I had an interview in London for one outfit called AB Airlines. I travelled to London for an interview with the Chairman and Managing Director of this relatively small airline that flew passenger flights from Luton Airport but, after a week or two of waiting, they wrote to me explaining that they felt I needed more experience for the role they had available and that I had 'on this occasion' been unsuccessful. However, despite their choice of words, there would not be another occasion that I would find myself having an interview for a job with AB Airlines. Just a few months later, they went out of business and ceased operations entirely. A lucky escape, as it turned out.

Shortly afterwards, I was invited to attend an interview for another of Luton's new resident airlines. EasyJet was still in its infancy, having started operations just three years previously with a couple of leased aircraft. The fleet was now growing rapidly as the airline's network expanded and they required someone to manage the administration around the workforce of approximately one hundred and forty pilots and to support the Chief Pilot and Fleet Manager in their day-to-day tasks.

I attended an initial interview with these two gentlemen who I got on well with from the outset. Mike, the Chief Pilot, was an authoritative and disciplined individual – an ex-Royal Navy pilot who had flown a multitude of different types of aircraft during his career as a naval aviator and was not far from retiring. John, the Fleet Manager, meanwhile was the polar opposite. He was

Australian and as laid back as anyone I had ever met or have met since. He had enjoyed a distinguished flying career flying in Australia before heading to Europe to carry on his flying.

The first interview went well and a week or so afterwards I was invited back to meet with them again. I had managed to arrange to have the interview first thing on a Monday morning at Luton, so spent the weekend with Aisling before borrowing her Vauxhall Nova on the Monday morning to drive from Heathrow.

Having battled the Monday morning traffic on the M25, I was up against time and had to be at Luton for my interview at ten thirty a.m. Just passing Junction 17 of the M25 motorway, and in the middle of the three lanes, I heard a worrying 'clunk' sound from under the bonnet followed by every warning light on the dashboard illuminating in rapid succession.

I freewheeled to the inside lane, on to the hard shoulder, and ground to a halt. I sat quietly for a minute or two to consider my options. I had almost no knowledge of car maintenance and getting out to look under the bonnet was unlikely to prove particularly insightful.

Luckily, I had remained a member of the AA, having renewed my year-long membership a few months before heading to France just in case this kind of situation should occur at some point when visiting Aisling back home.

By the time I had stopped panicking and started thinking about how I might resolve my plight, the flicker of blue flashing lights in the rear-view mirror caught my attention as a police Range Rover pulled up behind me. After the usual swapping of pleasantries with my new uniformed friend, he took a quick look under the bonnet and gleefully informed me that my water pump had completely sheared off and there was no way I would be able to get myself off the motorway without assistance.

I informed him that I was a member of the AA and would use the roadside emergency telephone to summon their assistance. Seemingly happy with my escape plan, the officer returned to his vehicle and duly disappeared into the relentless flow of very noisy traffic beside me. I made the call and about twenty minutes later, a bright yellow AA truck arrived to drag me off the motorway to the relative safety of a lay-by off the exit slip road.

Having assessed Aisling's car as undriveable, I agreed with the AA guy that he would take me and the car to the railway station in St. Albans, where he would leave us in the car park until I could somehow arrange to get the car back to Crawley later that day.

In the meantime, I had also managed to get hold of Aisling by phone and she had arranged to borrow a work colleague's car and to come and pick me up and take me to Luton for my interview. I rang the interviewers at EasyJet, who were very understanding and told me to just get there when I could. I eventually made it to the interview about four hours late.

Just a couple of days later, I had a message to call John the Fleet Manager at EasyJet. He was offering me the job of Flight Operations Support Manager (a job title they had invented just for me) and informed me that they hoped I would start as soon as possible. This was mid-November 1998, and my notice period at Airbus was one month. After some negotiating, we decided that it suited all parties if I started with EasyJet early in the New Year. It was particularly handy for me to delay my start until the January of 1999 as, if I left Airbus within a year of starting, I remained liable to pay back all of the relocation assistance payments they had covered when I first moved from Crawley to Toulouse.

We provisionally agreed that my first day at EasyJet would be Monday 18th January 1999. Now, all I had to do was resign from Airbus, give notice on my apartment in Toulouse, sell my car in France, pay all my annual taxes, complete the paperwork ending my employee status in France, close my French bank account, move all my belongings back to the UK, look for somewhere to live close to Luton Airport, buy a car in the UK, and be at EasyJet offices at nine a.m. on Monday 18th January, just six or so weeks away. Added to this, I had to stay out of trouble with my chest and remain well throughout this whole process.

Anyone who really knows me will say that I love lists and ticking tasks off as they get done, but even I have to admit that this particular list seemed too much to accomplish in such a short space of time.

During my time in France, I had managed to keep up with my appointments at Papworth. Despite having had my first experience of IV antibiotics at the start of that year, my visits to clinic were still far enough apart to be manageable, Papworth only needing to see me once every couple of months or so. In order to attend these appointments, I would head over to the UK on the Thursday evening (having taken the Friday as a leave day from work) and drive up on the Friday lunchtime to Papworth. Thankfully, and again with a large helping of luck, I managed to avoid requiring any further IV antibiotic treatments during the time that I was in France and, as such, my clinic appointments were largely routine throughout that year.

Following Christmas and New Year and as 1999 started, it was time to leave Toulouse and head back to the UK for good. I had enjoyed my time in

Toulouse much more than my time working for Airbus, and I was excited about the new opportunity that lay ahead at EasyJet.

A week or so later, it was time to start my new job at EasyJet. As I had not yet found somewhere convenient to live close to Luton Airport, I had no choice but to stay with my dad and his partner in the spare room of their house near Cambridge. This left me with a rather gruelling seventy-five-minute drive each way between there and Luton twice a day but, as it wasn't forever, I just got on with it. In the week between returning from France and starting at EasyJet, I had bought a car so at least I had my own transport, despite not having somewhere permanent to live.

Since leaving Virgin Atlantic, I had kept in contact with Richard, an old friend of mine who had been one of the in-house lawyers during my time there and with whom I had done quite a bit of work. We had got on well and he too was into flying and other pursuits.

Coincidentally, Richard had just been offered a job as General Counsel with Britannia Airways at Luton and needed to find somewhere to live near the airport. So, after viewing a few properties together, we plumped for a nice two-bedroomed apartment in the highly sought-after town of Harpenden, some six miles to the south of Luton.

Ironically, whilst Luton (it must be said) is not the most picturesque of English towns, Harpenden normally comes very close to the top whenever lists of the 'most desirable places to live in the UK' are published. Its quaint high street, dotted with boutiques and high-end restaurants, combined with quintessentially English pubs and the centrally-located cricket pitch and green make it an idyllic place to live, particularly for those who work in London and could benefit from the high-speed railway line from the town's railway station straight into Kings Cross.

Richard and I made good housemates and we got on well. He didn't mind Aisling coming to stay at weekends and I had no problem when his girlfriend was around either. I tended to head away at the weekends to stay at Aisling's – by now she had left Crawley behind and was living much closer to her work at Heathrow. Richard often worked very long hours, so there would be many a time that I was in the flat on my own during the evenings just doing my own thing.

I settled in at EasyJet quickly and enjoyed my job there a lot. I was largely left to get on with things and, as my position had been created for me, I almost wrote my own job description as I went along. I was fortunate in that, rather than being given a desk in Easyland – the slightly ridiculous name given to the plethora of portacabins that doubled up as the airline's original headquarters – I was given a desk in the

EasyJet Crew Room over at the Terminal building. This was the coal face of the airline, where all the pilots and flight attendants would come and meet up for their preparation and planning before heading out to the aircraft for their day's flying.

I got to know all the one-hundred-and-forty-strong pilot workforce well, knowing just about all of them by their first names early on. We would exchange banter as they came and went, and the atmosphere was much more relaxed in the Crew Room than I experienced whenever I was over at Easyland for meetings.

Around this time, EasyJet had a gaggle of young pilots from Australia flying for them. These guys had found getting a job back home difficult as Ansett Airlines had recently gone out of business and there was a surplus of well-qualified pilots in the domestic marketplace for too few airline jobs. They had, therefore, come to the UK to further their flying careers and had found this young start-up airline at Luton desperate for qualified pilots to fly its rapidly expanding fleet of aircraft.

Whenever the Aussies were in the Crew Room, the volume always increased a few notches and the place would fill with laughter. These guys just seemed to have a knack for lightening the mood of the place and bringing a sense of fun to the very serious business of flying multi-million-dollar aeroplanes filled with human beings around the sky.

The Crew Room was also a good place to be for other reasons; in the August of 1999, the UK experienced its first total eclipse of the sun by the moon since June 1927. Myself and many of the EasyJet pilots, along with the cabin crew workforce, lined up at the windows of the Crew Room to watch as the moon covered the face of the sun, resulting in a strange and rather eerie dark red hue smothering everything we could see outside. A very memorable experience for all those who saw it that day, and probably a little frustrating too for the passengers who were stuck down in the depths of the terminal while this visual spectacle was going on outside. Likewise, one morning in November 1999, we were all stood by the windows of the Crew Room again, watching as the Queen and the Duke of Edinburgh pulled up outside in their burgundy Rolls Royce to officially open the newly built terminal extension located across the forecourt that the Crew Room overlooked.

During 1999, CF dictated that I was again required to have IV antibiotics for chest problems. Once again, I managed these on my own from home, thus avoiding the need for a stay in hospital. I was twenty-seven years old by this stage, and many at Papworth were astounded that I had managed to get through my life so far without the need for a single overnight stay.

This was a record I was proud of, but certainly didn't talk about, simply believing that to do so only tempted fate. It was ironic that I had managed a full year in Toulouse without the need for IVs, yet now living back in the UK I had needed them twice in the space of just a few months. Nonetheless, I was able to carry on my job as normal while on the IV treatment and could escape relatively unnoticed early on a Friday afternoon for my check-ups at Papworth, now only about forty miles away.

During the summer of 1999, I went with Aisling on a work trip to Rome where I spent the couple of days there sightseeing while she performed her day job for British Airways at a catering company that supplied inflight meals to the airline. We also went to Verona on another trip and, on one memorable weekend, to Venice.

Aisling had sent me a single red rose and an email telling me to pack a bag and to meet her at Heathrow at four p.m. one Friday afternoon, but had not told me where we were going. I duly met her at the airport as instructed, but it wasn't until we were in Departures that she revealed where we were going. We had a lovely time away, although throughout the whole weekend, the city of Venice was shrouded in a thick blanket of fog, making sightseeing rather tricky. But we made the best of it and visited all the usual tourist hotspots of the city and around the lagoon during the brief time we were there. Yet it was later that summer that we started to plan our main trip for that year.

During many discussions over our time together, we had talked about going to India, although I had also long held a notion for visiting the idyllic Indian Ocean islands of the Maldives. Images of pure white sand and impossibly blue sea teeming with colourful sea life had always appealed to me, and I had made a mental note that it was somewhere I simply had to visit at some point. Having done some research and looked at some good old-fashioned maps, we both decided that our trip would be to spend four days in the Maldives initially, followed by a week travelling around Sri Lanka. Sri Lanka (whilst not India as per our original plan, terrified as we were at the possibly unfounded prospect of getting very ill) seemed to offer the complete contrast of culture that we were seeking, and our research had shown that there was more than enough there to keep us busy for a week or so. It just so happened that Sri Lankan Airlines were offering irresistibly good deals for airline employees to experience both destinations as part of a package and, with that, our decision was made. In a few days, we were booked to go. So, the countdown began.

Looking back almost twenty years on, I cannot pinpoint the stage of this process when I actually considered that the Maldives would be an ideal location for asking Aisling whether she would consider marrying me.

We had, by this stage, been together for two and a half years and had known each other for over five. The relationship had lasted through me living in Toulouse for a year as well as the emotional turmoil and tears that my CF revelation had caused.

We were enjoying each other's company more than ever, and were spending as much time, every weekend and some midweek evenings, as we possibly could together.

I had always thought that if I was lucky enough to get married at all, it would probably be later in life and certainly not in my twenties. But I had been fortunate enough to find someone I just seemed to click with. Moreover, Aisling hadn't been scared off by CF and, like me, embraced a sense of, "Okay, it's CF – now what are you going to do *despite* it?"

We had the same outlook on life, enjoyed the same things and – without wishing to rely too heavily on well-worn clichés, it all just felt *right*.

As the idea of getting engaged grew on me, I gained a sense that now was definitely the right time. I quickly talked myself into the idea that this was really going to happen. But Aisling and I had never really talked much about getting engaged or getting married, so I had absolutely no idea how she'd react.

We left Heathrow on Saturday 16th October 1999 bound for Colombo, Sri Lanka, where we changed planes to fly onward to Male, the capital of the Maldives. Having left London late in the evening, by breakfast time the following day we were boarding a rather antiquated Lockheed Tristar of Sri Lankan Airlines and heading towards the Maldives. This aircraft was of the vintage that if you were shown it from the departure lounge window, you would probably declare, "Fly on it? I am not sure I would even stand under it!" Nonetheless, we climbed aboard and took off on the relatively short hop across the Indian Ocean.

As we descended beneath the clouds on our approach into Male International Airport, we got our first glimpse of what lay in store upon our arrival. The sight of crystal blue ocean filled the window as our aircraft banked to one side and then the other, with small white smudges marking where each of the coral islands lay. Already, it looked as picturesque as any of the images I had seen on travel programmes on the television, and these early views simply whet our appetites further to get down on the ground and be in amongst this paradise.

The reaction from all on board the aircraft was the same as the sights came into view. The cabin filled with gasps of amazement and squeals of delight as the aircraft descended lower and lower. As the landing gear dropped down beneath us, and the crew prepared the cabin for landing, I just wanted to jump straight into the impossibly blue warm sea below.

On landing in Male, we were met by a tour agent who ushered us onto a speedboat that would take us to our island resort about twenty minutes and ten kilometres away. As we sped away from the airport with the wind whipping up a fine spray of salty sea water into our tired faces, we looked out at views of tropical islands passing by, having to pinch ourselves to check we were not dreaming.

All too soon we arrived at our resort island, known to the locals as Lankanfinolhu, although marketed as 'Paradise Island' to the international travel trade. For those such as ourselves who had never been to the Maldives before, a more apt name would be hard to find.

It was still only mid-morning as we stepped off the speedboat and onto the wooden jetty that led to the palm-roofed reception building. We were met with welcome cocktails and were relieved of our luggage, likely as near as we would ever get to being treated like international movie stars and I, for one, loved it.

After completing the formalities, we were shown to our room – a beach villa with wide opening doors that led directly out to the pure white sand of the beach on the western side of the island. As we lay on the bed, looking out at the exquisite sight of the sand and sea in front of us, it didn't take long for the sound of the waves lapping the shoreline to get the better of us and we were both soon fast asleep.

The island itself only measures nine hundred metres long by two hundred meters wide, and could be circumnavigated in about fifteen minutes on foot. It would be no exaggeration to say that we spent the next couple of days doing as close to nothing as it is possible for a human being to do.

We dozed under the palm trees on the beach or by the pool and occasionally stayed awake long enough to read a chapter or two of the books that we had brought with us. We would manage to raise ourselves from our sunbeds and venture the few steps into the shallows every little while to cool off, sharing the space in the bright blue waters with fish of just about every colour imaginable as they darted around our feet. We could venture quite far out without so much as getting our knees wet and there were even people who would erect their sun chairs in the shallow water to enjoy the best of both worlds, sand and sea, simultaneously.

When not lounging around in the sunshine, we were indulging our appetites at the hotel's restaurant, which every lunch and dinner time served up a simply dazzling array of dishes from around the world that you could simply help yourself to.

Those with CF often will say that due to the condition itself, as well as the numerous drugs they have to take on a daily basis, it is often hard to drum up much of an appetite to tackle the increased amount of calories needed to maintain their weight. Add to that being in the hot sunshine all day and you would imagine that such a combination would sap away any last glimmer of an appetite I might have had on this holiday. On the contrary, however, I left that restaurant after each mealtime feeling like I was just one morsel away from bursting and that I must have doubled my bodyweight just at that sitting alone.

I have always had a reasonable, yet not fantastic, appetite. But when faced when an all-you-can-eat buffet, particularly one of such high quality and as wide a range of food as I found on Paradise Island, I seemed to find an extra gear and consumed much more than I would ever dream of at home.

But when it is free and you don't have to cook it yourself (or clear up, of course) then such dining opportunities are fair game in my view, and no dietician at Papworth has ever told me to eat less or consider losing a few pounds! "If only they could see me now," I would remark to Aisling as she rolled me out of the restaurant at the end of another marathon dining session.

We had only arranged to stay on Paradise Island for four days before we heading back to Colombo and having a week touring Sri Lanka. Having arrived on Paradise Island on the Sunday morning, by the time Wednesday arrived, my opportunity for asking Aisling if she would marry me was slipping away. Forever putting practicality before romance, I had not brought a ring out with me, electing for the probably easier option of Aisling selecting one that she would be happy wearing and to get the right size when we returned to the UK.

I had no experience of buying jewellery, let alone engagement rings, and thought that it would be safer all round for Aisling to do the choosing herself. Strangely, the prospect of her saying 'no' was not a factor in my decision-making process, as far as I can recall, such was the level of self-assurance (or general stupidity) I had back in those days. It also clearly hadn't occurred to me that the remaining days of our holiday would be impossibly awkward if she did say no and that the tour around the sights of Sri Lanka might be a very quiet experience.

Nonetheless, I woke up on the Wednesday knowing that the big day had arrived and that if I was to do it, then this was the moment.

We spent the morning lazing around and had our lunch, as usual, in the restaurant. We drifted back to the beach by our villa and, after resting up to let our lunch settle, went for a wander along the beach and into the sea. With the sun shining off the brilliant white sand and the warm water lapping around our legs, I knew that we were now in the right place and that it was the right time. I took Aisling's hand and knelt in the water. As she looked at me in puzzlement, I simply said that I wanted to spend the rest of my life with her and asked whether she would marry me. No soon as I had managed to splutter out the words, she started crying and, upon seeing her crying, I started too.

I think in that moment, we both realised that our journey up until this point had been challenging, but that what we had was something very special and that we wanted it to continue for a very long time.

We had survived living apart for a year, my revelation about CF and the rather cack-handed approach I had taken over it, and me trying (on more than one occasion, in fact) to destroy her prized Vauxhall Nova. Yet we loved being in each other's company and I certainly seemed to have found not just my soulmate, but someone I wanted to share the rest of my life with.

Aisling wiped her and my eyes and, to my relief, accepted without hesitation. We kissed, hugged, and smiled. I looked around me, wishing to capture this scene and etch it onto my brain forever; if ever there was a time when this island was to live up to its name, this was it. I was, indeed, in paradise with the love of my life and she had just agreed to be with me forever, no matter what the future and CF may throw at us.

The whole experience of asking Aisling to marry me had been as perfect as anything could possibly be and that moment felt a million miles, and a lifetime, away from when we had first met over a photocopier five years previously.

TWENTY-TWO

A NEW MILLENNIUM AND KEEPING CF AT BAY

We spent the remainder of our last day in the Maldives in the bar of the hotel, celebrating and talking about when we might get married and what sort of wedding we would like to have. It became very clear even from those initial discussions that we both wanted the same sort of ceremony; intimate with a relatively low number of guests limited to close friends and family. It is traditional in Ireland to have very large weddings, often with the guest list running into the hundreds. However, we agreed from the outset that this was definitely not what we wanted, and that our search for a venue would be limited to places that would – ideally – accommodate no more than one hundred attendees.

In the meantime, we had a holiday to enjoy, and the following morning we were back on the speedboat heading to Male International Airport for our flight back to Colombo, where we were to spend the following week.

The contrast between Male Airport and that at Colombo was stark. Male is a small airport, and as the aircraft parking area is only large enough to accommodate a couple of passenger aircraft simultaneously, the terminal was largely empty as we passed through on that Thursday morning. Contrast that with Bandaranaike International Airport in Colombo, which was a hive of activity on our arrival – a heady mix of sights and noise filling the warm and humid arrivals hall.

We spent a few days touring around the island, being driven around and visiting all the tourist hotspots. Of particular note was the day we climbed to the summit of Sigiriya, an ancient rock fortress located close to the town of

Dambulla. With the remains of a temple still visible on its peak, this giant column of rock stands nearly three hundred and fifty metres tall and dominates the otherwise flat landscape which surrounds it. On a hot and humid day, and undeterred by warnings that those with chronic health conditions should under no circumstances attempt the climb, we boldly set off, successfully reaching the peak a couple of hours later (exhausted but relieved).

At the conclusion of our tour, we had a couple of days at a beachside hotel in Beruwala on the western coast, a couple of hours from Colombo. The Eden Hotel and Resort was pleasant enough but largely unmemorable until Boxing Day 2004, when home videos of it were all over the television news in the UK.

That Christmas, the hotel was decimated by the huge tsunami that hit various locations around the Indian Ocean, and hundreds of guests staying at the Eden Hotel had been washed away and were missing. It was hard to take in the sheer scale of the horror of that event in any case, but to see somewhere we had stayed caught up in the thick of it seemed surreal.

Identifiable on the videos posted on the internet and being played on the news was the pool in which we had swum and lounged around, now full of dirty green water and debris from nearby buildings and vegetation; deck chairs and sun loungers strewn around like abandoned doll's furniture. The hotel had only just competed a massive refurbishment programme four months before the tsunami hit and had to be closed again indefinitely following the disaster. Thankfully, it did reopen after a second refurbishment, and continues to trade under the Eden Hotel name today.

Upon arriving back in the UK, we had a lot to do. We had decided that the wedding would ideally take place towards the end of 2000, giving us about a year to plan and organise everything ourselves. Without it needing to even be discussed, the wedding ceremony itself was to take place in Aisling's local village church close to her parents' home in Northern Ireland.

As we were living and working in England, geography was already working against us. We made two trips to Northern Ireland towards the end of 1999; the first to reveal the news of our engagement to Aisling's parents in person and the second to start visiting possible venues in which we could hold the reception. After a few visits to several unremarkable and rather soulless hotels, and starting to feel a little despondent, we just happened to stumble across somewhere quite amazing.

It was during our second sortie to Northern Ireland to look at possible venues that we came across Castle Leslie, a large and very old country house close to the town of Monaghan, just across the border in the Republic of Ireland. The property, once the ancestral home of the wealthy Leslie family originally from Scotland, had recently been refurbished by the original owners' great-granddaughter and was now being run as a unique and rather quirky boutique hotel.

The fourteen bedrooms of the main house were each themed differently and boasted their own unique colour schemes and decor. Guests had the run of the house, with meals being served by candlelight in the original dining room and 'lazy' breakfasts being served until eleven a.m. each day. There were no televisions or telephones in any of the bedrooms, the owners preferring to market the hotel as something of an escape from modern day life; a place to relax, unwind, and enjoy comfy beds and excellent cuisine with a 'come and go as you please' attitude. The owners themselves were lovely people and seemed to want to bend over backwards to help us create our perfect wedding reception. They had only held two previous weddings at the hotel since its refurbishment, but nothing we suggested seemed too much to ask. We were told that they could only accommodate eighty people in the dining room and that if we wanted (and could afford it, of course), we could book the whole venue (including all the bedrooms) from the Friday evening of our wedding weekend until the Sunday lunchtime, to ensure exclusive use of the whole property.

From the moment we stepped inside the place, I think that we both knew that we had found our ideal venue. Not only did the capacity of the place suit our requirements, we loved the idea of taking over the whole place for the entire weekend, with our families and friends able to enjoy both the house and the extensive gardens and grounds at their leisure. This was particularly important as my family would be travelling over from England for the entire weekend and needed somewhere to stay.

The most important aspect of it all, though, was that it didn't feel at all like a hotel. Unlike the other potential wedding venues we had visited, whose banqueting rooms were booked months – if not years – ahead for hosting carbon copy weddings week in, week out, Castle Leslie offered something completely different and seemed to be just what we were looking for. Yes, it was quirky, almost bordering on the eccentric but we liked the place a great deal. We got on well with the owners and it just felt perfect. It would hopefully provide our guests (as well as Aisling and me) with a wedding reception to remember and, despite it having very little experience of hosting weddings, we were willing to take the gamble.

Once the decision was made, we set the date and started refining the arrangements for our wedding weekend. Aisling and I had decided that we would take charge of everything (despite having to organise it from another country) and, wherever we could, keep things simple. Both of us hated the very idea of weddings being years in the planning and everything being organised to the very finest of details. Our aim was to do this our way, and with our own ideas; we wanted to stamp our personalities all over our wedding day, and make sure that, unlike so many other weddings I have been to, people really would remember it for years to come. After some discussions with the owners of Castle Leslie, and in conjunction with Aisling's parish priest, we settled on the 30th September 2000 as the day on which we would get married.

We carried on with our arrangements for the big day almost as a hobby; something of a sideshow to our normal, everyday lives back in the UK. It was late 1999 and we had just under a year to prepare, so we didn't feel particularly under pressure or rushed to get things organised. I continued with my job at EasyJet whilst Aisling still worked for British Airways, although she was now living back in Crawley near Gatwick Airport where we had first met. I enjoyed both my job and the people I worked with at EasyJet, yet felt that I was not being particularly pushed in my role as Flight Operations Support Manager, nor was I using the skills that I had developed in my time at either Virgin Atlantic or Airbus. By the end of 1999, I felt that I needed more of a challenge and started to put the feelers out for what other opportunities might be around.

Aisling and I spent Christmas and New Year (indeed the dawn of the new millennium) with her parents in Northern Ireland. As the clock struck midnight and as the twentieth century slipped quietly away, we stood outside her parents' house looking across the hills and fields of County Tyrone to the twinkling lights of towns many miles away. The century in which I had been born, had attended school and university, and got engaged had just ended and I looked towards the future, and indeed the next twelve months, with excitement.

The fact that I had been extremely fortunate to survive to the end of the century only mildly affected by CF and was still going relatively strongly was not lost on me for one second. Nor, however, was the fact that such good fortune was not likely to last and that the next few years could well be harder than the previous twenty-eight had been. I could possibly not have known, however, as I looked down at those twinkling lights and held tightly onto Aisling's hand, quite how hard they might be.

The new millennium started with me actively looking for a new job, hopefully moving to be much closer to Aisling than I currently was. I contacted Tim, my friend from university who had followed me to Virgin Atlantic. Tim was now working in the London offices of United Airlines, the massive US-based airline which flew daily from multiple US airports to London. He advised that their

Marketing Department were looking for a marketing executive at their offices near Heathrow Airport and, liking the sound of the job, I applied. By the end of January 2000, I had been for two interviews and had been offered the job at United to start at the beginning of February. After minimal song and dance, I duly handed in my notice and snuck away from EasyJet to restart the aviation marketing career that I had left behind in Toulouse in my haste to be back with Aisling in the UK.

Within a few days, I was attempting to negotiate my way along the forty miles of motorway that stood between Harpenden and Heathrow Airport, twice a day. It became apparent very quickly that this was not a sustainable proposition and the early starts and late finishes were not good for my health.

I had stopped exercising by this point and was relying on my medication and physio sessions to keep me well. Overall this worked well, although I was starting to see the need for IV antibiotics on a more frequent basis. What had started out as a truly abhorrent experience when I had my first course of IV medication back at the end of 1997 was, by this point, starting to become normality when my chest played up and I couldn't sort it out with just oral antibiotics.

I was now meeting the news from the team at Papworth that I needed IVs with a sigh of resigned indignation rather than tears of fear and the overwhelming sense that I had failed. IVs were just part of the new routine of life and I had to get on with it, whether I liked it or not.

Settling into the new job at United was easy enough as it only felt like the week before (rather than the twelve months it actually was) that I had been the new kid on the block at EasyJet. With a new job, and with time passing away before we got married, Aisling and I set about the task of looking for our first home together. We quickly decided to buy rather than rent, both having spent a small fortune over the previous six or so years renting – paying out money each month with nothing to show for it.

Whilst I was getting up and running with my new job at Heathrow, Aisling had also made a switch and was now working for an airline based back at Gatwick. After a search of various properties in the corridor which straddled the border of Surrey and Sussex between the two airports, we found a small housing development being built on Epsom Downs, just around the corner from Epsom racecourse, home of the world-famous annual Epsom Derby horse race.

The development, on our first visit, was nothing more than a building site, with a solitary portacabin acting as a sales office. Epsom is a pleasant market town in the Surrey Hills, with an affluent population and high property prices given its three railway stations offering easy commuter access direct into central London. It is also close to the M25 motorway that surrounds

Greater London and offers excellent connectivity to surrounding counties. Epsom also just happened to be where our very good friend Steve (from Virgin Atlantic days) lived and that alone seemed a good enough reason to move there.

Having viewed the plans for the two-bedroomed houses (which we could afford) and the three-bedroomed houses (which we couldn't), we went away to discuss the matter. Wearing my 'Mister Sensible, risk averse' hat, I said to Aisling that we should make do with the two-bedroomed house as we had a wedding to pay for and had just started new jobs. Aisling, however, wearing her 'you have to speculate to accumulate' hat responded by saying that it made much more sense from an investment point of view to push ourselves to our limit and to buy the larger property, so that we could benefit more from selling it at a greater profit in the future.

After much discussion I agreed to Aisling's approach and the deposit was paid to the sales lady in the portacabin a few days later. With a proposed moving in date of 1st April 2000, we only had a couple of months to wait before we would hold our collective breath and take our first steps onto the UK property ladder as homeowners.

Those first few months of 2000 were a very exciting time for us both. With a new home to move into, a wedding to plan and new jobs, we had somehow found ourselves trying to simultaneously do three things that often make up the top three in a list of the ten 'most stressful things you can do in your life'. Yet this didn't seem to faze either of us, and we just got on with them.

As it turned out, performing this juggling act would be good preparation for the events that would come down the line over the next couple of years, although – of course – we didn't realise it at the time.

With the house bought, a moving-in date in the calendar, and the wedding plans moving along, everything seemed to be going our way. However, they do say things happen to you when you least expect them, and such was the case just three weeks into my job at United.

I had been sent on a one-day airline marketing conference that was being held at the Institute of Engineering building along Embankment in central London. At the mid-morning coffee break I was mooching about, looking for someone interesting to swap pleasantries with, when a loud voice and laugh from the far corner caught my attention. Instantly, I knew its owner and made my way over in the direction it had originated from. As soon as I saw the person standing there, I couldn't quite believe it; it was Ian, who had been the Commercial Manager at Virgin Atlantic and who had been mine and Martin's direct boss when I worked there. In fact, it was Ian (along with Martin) who had conducted my second interview for the Commercial Department job all the way back in July 1994, and with whom I had always got on really well during my time at Virgin.

After swapping greetings and exchanging verbal resumes of what we were both doing these days, Ian (never a man for mixing his words) came straight out and asked me if I wanted a job.

Dumbstruck, I reiterated that I had just started a new job at United and felt that I should stay, but my arguments were futile. Ian was looking for a new Commercial Manager at the airline he was now running on behalf of the Virgin Group.

Virgin Sun Airlines had five aircraft (with a view to getting lots more) and along with a new branch of Virgin Holidays (another of the Virgin family group of companies) was selling package holidays around the Mediterranean hotspots. Ian was offering me a managerial role with quite a bit more money than I was getting at United (although, ironically, I had not yet received it as I was still in my first month there) and the job was located in (yes, you've guessed it) Crawley, just up the road from where Aisling's offices now were and only twenty-five minutes' drive from our new home in Epsom. Ian was always a good salesman and, for the rest of the day, I paid little attention to the speakers taking the stage at the conference.

My mind was already racing away, thrilled at the prospect of being closer to Aisling, closer to my new home, and earning more money. The job itself was also just what I wanted and back doing what I felt I did best. The only problem was how to tell my new manager at United, who had been good enough to interview and hire me less than a month previously, and who was also picking up the tab for the course on which I had just been enticed away from him.

Still, business is business… right? And whilst I felt awful for resigning from a position in which I had barely warmed my seat, I needed to do what was best for me and Aisling. So, a few days later I handed in my letter of resignation and my very short career in the UK Marketing Department of United Airlines was effectively over before it had really even started.

The first year of this new millennium had started in a truly remarkable way. By April 2000, I had been in three different jobs that year and Aisling had been in two. We had also moved into the new house in Epsom (our first home together) and, with all that behind us, now had just five short months left to organise our wedding, which was effectively being held across two different countries – Northern Ireland and the Republic of Ireland. Between now and then, it was full speed ahead to make sure that everything was in place for one p.m. on 30th

September 2000 when, all being well, Aisling would be walking down the aisle with her dad, meeting me at the altar, and saying, "I do."

Should that all go ahead and, avoiding any hiccups along the way, we would then be starting our married life together.

After all that had happened to get us to this point, and despite CF having made a reasonable attempt to come between us, whoever would have thought it, eh?

TWENTY-THREE

ARE YOU REALLY SURE ABOUT THIS?

With only a few months to go before the wedding, one last obstacle stood in the way of a lifetime of married harmony; the Catholic Church insists on completion of a 'Marriage Preparation Course' – the 'pre-marriage class'. This can either be done one evening per week across several weeks or as an intensive 'crash course' (no irony intended).

As we were unable to find evening classes in our area, and doubting that we could commit to attending every week even if we did find one, we opted for a weekend-long crash course. Although not Catholic myself, I had promised Aisling's local priest in Northern Ireland, Father Martin who was to marry us, that we would attend a pre-marriage course before the wedding, and I fully intended to honour that promise.

I had never heard of anyone attending such a course (other than Aisling's siblings, who were already married), so the whole concept was completely alien to me. I had no idea what to expect but I did my best to approach it with an open mind.

After carrying out some research, Aisling found a pre-marriage class running over a long weekend in June 2000 at a former convent near St. Albans in Hertfordshire. The course ran from Friday evening until Sunday afternoon. You were not allowed to leave the venue during the weekend and had to attend *all* sessions.

I tried to be positive and look forward to the whole experience, but it would be fair to say that my underlying apathy was hard to fight off, particularly as the course drew nearer. And, as much as I tried to look on it as an all-inclusive mini-break in the Hertfordshire countryside, the lack of bottomless cocktails, swim-up pool bars, and all-you-can-eat buffets soon applied a decent helping of realism to that approach.

With the pre-marriage class looming, we made one last trip to Northern Ireland to finalise our wedding plans. We met with the head chef at Castle Leslie to go over the wedding meal and wine selection. Noel the chef was a nice guy, with a clear passion for what he did, and with his input we designed a menu that we could be proud of.

As we were only having eighty guests, we were able to make the meal rather more bespoke than if we had been catering for hundreds and we fully took advantage of this benefit. We chose some fantastic wines to accompany the meal and, once our selections were all finalised, we left Castle Leslie feeling confident that our wedding meal would be as memorable as the rest of the day – both for us and our attending guests.

Back in the UK, the weekend of the pre-marriage course arrived. It just so happened that my chest had started playing up a few days earlier, and so I was in the middle of yet another two-week course of IV antibiotics. So, along with clothes and wash things, I also had to pack three days' worth of IV paraphernalia, along with a big yellow plastic 'sharps' bucket, in which to place my used needles. Not the sort of thing one would usually take on a 'romantic' weekend away!

That Friday, we left work slightly early and negotiated our way through the evening traffic. As we pulled into a long gravel driveway, the sight of a large and rather imposing old building filled the windscreen. It looked rather like a grand old house, with a wooden front door leading to a large, galleried, and wood-panelled entrance hall. As we entered, the musty smell of dust filled our nostrils. We were then greeted and ushered towards a large room where many other couples were sat watching the new arrivals pour in, each nervously holding hands as if some terrible fate awaited them.

Once everyone was in and seated, the priest leading the course introduced himself and his small team of facilitators. The object of the weekend, he told us, was to learn more about each other and to discover what our partners expected from married life. It would have been easy for anyone in the room to scoff at this proposition; to think they already knew all that there was to know about their partner and to walk out. However, the priest promised us all that he would lead us on a real 'journey of discovery' over the next forty-eight hours, so everyone stayed put.

The priest, just in case any of us attendees forgot ourselves or where we were, was also kind enough to remind us that that everyone would be in *single* bedrooms and that there were to be no late-night visits with our partners.

Abstinence from sins of the flesh until after marriage remains a cornerstone of Catholic belief and any breaches of this would 'not be tolerated'.

As is customary in situations where there is a group full of strangers, we had to take it in turns to introduce ourselves and our partners to the group. There was certainly an eclectic mix of folks in the room, ranging from a Nigerian couple from North London, who were very religious, to a couple who had only met a few weeks (yes, weeks) previously. Aisling and I nicknamed these two the 'internet couple' as, given their awkward demeanour, it looked very much like they had just met through an online dating site.

Once everyone had been introduced, we were told to get to know each other over dinner, which was to be served in the refectory. Just the use of the very term 'refectory' tells you a lot about the place we now found ourselves in.

The evening's 'welcome' meal was served up by a gaggle of old-school dinner ladies in the dining hall (sorry, refectory) and we queued up to see what culinary delights awaited us. After nearly three hours stuck in motorway traffic, Aisling and I were ready to eat and hoped for something special. Sadly, our expectations (along with our hunger pangs) had rather got the better of us and it was hard to hide our disappointment when we were offered a slab of lukewarm, rather tough fish of some description.

The fish was drizzled with cold, congealed parsley sauce and served with carrots that looked and tasted like all school dinner vegetables look and taste – soggy and limp.

Having had a quick scan around to make sure there was nothing else on the menu, we accepted our sustenance gratefully and found somewhere to sit. Now, I have had some bad meals in my time. I have travelled extensively and have been offered all sorts of interesting things to eat, but this meal was probably the worst thing I have ever eaten (and I include the one-hundred-year-old eggs from Hong Kong in this statement). Indeed, almost twenty years on, I still shudder at the very thought of it and, if I close my eyes, I can still smell that coagulated parsley sauce. If this was supposed to be a meal that would welcome us all to the venue and make us look forward to the weekend that lay ahead, it fell very short indeed.

After a post-dinner discussion, in which the leader of the course set out what the weekend would consist of, we were encouraged to opt for an early night so that the 'fun and games' could start in earnest bright and early the following morning.

It was at this point the serious stuff started; all the ladies on the course would be in rooms in the West Wing of the house, whilst all the men would be down the East Wing. There was, we were told, to be no interaction until breakfast time. Furthermore, anyone who wished to attend early morning mass was asked to put their shoes neatly outside their bedroom door before they went to bed, so that they would be woken early the following morning.

With that, we were given a few moments to say goodnight to our partners before being led away to our respective wings of the house. With no televisions in the rooms, and having not brought much in the way of reading material with me, never had I been so pleased to have a dose of IV antibiotics to administer – entertainment for the next forty-five minutes at least.

The following day was, indeed, something of a journey of discovery. Throughout the day, we were given topics to explore as a couple. We were each given a subject and then sent back to our respective bedrooms to prepare for the discussion element of the session when we returned. Subjects ranged from 'easy' ones such as, "What do you expect from your partner in marriage?" and, "What would you like to achieve from married life?" to the more tricky, "What annoys you about your partner?" and "What would you change about your partner?"

Once reconvened back in the main room, Aisling and I had to take it in turns to discuss the findings from our solitary break-out sessions in our rooms and present them to the rest of the group. Being fiercely private people, telling a group of strangers about Aisling's most annoying habits didn't come easily at all, and the whole experience was a deeply uncomfortable one. More pertinent, though, was the fact that as the day wore on it was becoming increasingly apparent how different Aisling and I were, to the extent that we started to question our suitability for one another.

By the close of the last session, the excitable atmosphere of earlier on in the day had dissipated and Aisling and I both were feeling terrible.

As the others filed out of the room and headed towards the refectory for another brush with death at the hands of the dinner ladies of doom, we were left in quiet contemplation. Feeling a little shell-shocked, we talked for a while, and reminded each other that the whole purpose of the course was to learn how to be tolerant of our partners and to love them for who they were. Then we decided that there was only one thing for it; draw a line under the day, park our thoughts for the evening, and (in breach of the regulations) go to the pub!

While everyone else was distracted by the culinary wizardry on offer in the refectory, Aisling deflected any suspicion about our intentions and went to the toilet whilst I snuck back upstairs to collect the car keys from my room. We met in the car park and, as discreetely as we could, made our escape.

Having not enjoyed anything even resembling a decent meal for over twenty-four hours, we headed for the nearest food outlet we could find, which happened to be a McDonald's. After enjoying a range of fine delicacies from their menu, we drove out into the country to find a pub where we could drink away the stresses of the day and enjoy a bit of time to ourselves to chat, this time *without* having to report back to the group about our thoughts.

After a couple of drinks, a few laughs, and unwinding just a bit, we decided that it was about time we head back and attempt to break back in without being caught by the nuns who were, no doubt, patrolling the corridors with their machine guns.

I was not feeling too great by the end of the evening and, on the basis that I was on IVs and the whole place had been freezing on the first night, Aisling suggested that I stay in her room that night. Contrary to what it looked like, and against the priest's number one rule, Aisling was genuinely concerned about my welfare and didn't want me to be on my own overnight. So, on the drive back, we decided that should someone catch us making our return to the house under the cover of darkness, our cover story would be that Aisling had to help me with my IVs but that we had left a vital piece of equipment out in the car.

Now, lying to a person of a religious order was not something we would normally do. But the wedding was only a few weeks away and if we didn't complete the course we simply couldn't get married. Being thrown out in disgrace following a flagrant abuse of the rules wouldn't do us any favours, but it was a risk we were willing to take.

Thankfully, the stresses of the day had clearly caught up with the rest of our cohort and everyone was in bed by the time we snuck back in. As I made my way to my room to retrieve my medication, I reached the corridor without raising any suspicions and breathed a sigh of relief as I took my room key out of my pocket. Before I could reach my door, however, I tripped over my neighbour's shoes and had to hurriedly scuttle inside before anyone came to see what the commotion was all about.

I gathered the things I needed, took a deep breath, and set off on the journey to the West Wing. Without any further drama along the way, and managing to evade being sprung as I crept along the darkened corridors of the females' wing, I made it to Aisling's room undetected. As we prepared the IVs in whispered voices, sniggering like naughty school children, we wondered whether leaving both of our pairs of shoes outside the door would be taking things a bit too far. It was best, we considered, to give the following morning's early mass a miss.

The second day of the course started with mass followed by another skirmish with death in the breakfast hall. Once those highlights were out of the way it was back to the course to finish what we had started the day before and possibly to finally take a sledgehammer to finish off once and for all the cracked wreckage of our relationship. To our surprise, and with more than just slight relief, the second day was less brutal than the first and was all about reconciliation and learning to accept that, whilst marriage forms a strong union between two people, you remain individuals with sometimes opposing values and different ways of doing things. We were told that we should embrace these differences, and that doing so would make us stronger as a couple.

Despite these reassuring messages, however, it appeared that the previous day had taken its toll on one of the couples in our group; the internet couple, who we had initially assumed were simply late down to breakfast, failed to reappear. Having looked awkward from the outset, I suppose it should have come as no surprise that the turmoil of the first day stretched them to breaking point. At some point in the night, they had either decided that they didn't want to get married after all or, perhaps, just one of them had decided this and had done a runner. Either way, we would have to conclude the course without their presence.

Contrast this with our Nigerian friends, however, who made absolutely sure that we knew they were very much still in attendance. They arrived down for mass, resplendent in full Nigerian national dress, with bright colours and long, flowing robes. Despite this being a rather dreary, overcast morning in semi-rural Hertfordshire, they brought something a little more exotic to the mix that morning and helped to brighten up people's moods.

By mid-afternoon, the course was over and it was time to say our goodbyes. Everyone wished each other well and made their escapes (sorry, exits). In hindsight, Aisling and I actually quite enjoyed the second day, as we saw the whole process come full circle. Whilst the first half of the course had taken us down diverging pathways, the second half rejoined those paths and at least attempted to show us the route ahead for our upcoming lives together. Whilst we may not have known what to expect from the course, it would be fair to say that we must have taken something away from it. After all, we still talk about some of the things that it taught us about each other (as well as the laughs it gave us) even now.

TWENTY-FOUR
WHEN 'I' BECAME 'WE'

As the wedding approached, we finalised the arrangements. We designed the wedding invitations ourselves and made a late-night expedition to Aisling's office near Gatwick to print them off using the colour printer at her work. Given that the wedding and reception were both in Ireland, there was limited time left to finalise things from the UK, so we decided to go over a few days early to make sure everything was ready. In those few days, we checked with the Castle that everything was in place and had a meeting with Father Martin to run through the ceremony. He was aware that almost half the attendees would be non-Catholic and that this would be the first time many of them had attended a Catholic church service, so he said he would explain each element of the service so that the non-Catholics would feel 'included' in the proceedings, at least to some degree.

In Ireland, there are two traditions that take place in the lead up to the wedding day itself. Firstly, for several evenings beforehand, the home of the bride's parents fills with visitors bringing gifts and good wishes to the happy couple. With me being from out of town, this whole procedure was perhaps more muted than it would otherwise have been but, still, Aisling and I stayed up late for a few evenings, meeting and greeting folks as they dropped by to have a drink and enjoy the pre-wedding 'craic'.

The second tradition of note is that the bride and groom get put in a trailer and pulled by a tractor through nearby villages while 'well-wishers' bombard them with flour, eggs, water, and other unmentionable items to wish them good luck in their married life. Aisling and I managed to avoid the ignominy of this bizarre ritual for a while, but by the Wednesday before the wedding, Aisling's three brothers were chomping at the bit as to which of them could get hold of the tractor keys first. That was until the 'CF card' was played by Aisling, and her dad stepped in to put a lid on her brothers' enthusiasm.

Fearing that I might be struggling with the multiple late nights and the stress of the wedding itself, Aisling felt that sitting on the back of a trailer and shivering in cold wet clothes for a couple of hours was probably exactly what I *didn't* need at this point of the week and that if I was to be at the church in a few days' time, undergoing this ordeal would do nothing to improve my chances of achieving this. So, after some quiet words from my soon-to-be father-in-law, and some disappointed groans from the direction of the farm yard outside, I could at least be grateful that Aisling had saved me (and herself) from an evening of wet, cold 'fun' on the back of a farm trailer.

The lead up to our wedding was a chaotic, rushed affair as we dashed around finishing things off and making sure that everything was in place. Looking back, it was far from ideal in terms of how we had both wanted it to be, and the week had taken its toll both on me and my health. I finished that week feeling completely wiped out and in need of a few really good nights of sleep. But with my family arriving *en masse* from the UK, as well as my mum from the USA, there was to be no let up for the next few days.

Through the course of the Friday afternoon – the day before the wedding – my mum, sisters, and other members of my family arrived at Castle Leslie to be shown to their allocated rooms for the weekend ahead. This was except for my dad, who had driven over from England a couple of days previously with my cousin Mark and his then-wife Debbie.

Mark had spent most of his life living in Australia, having emigrated there in the mid-70s, and had returned to England for the wedding. He was an accomplished musician and had agreed that, along with the band we had booked for the reception, he would perform a forty-five-minute set during the evening, which I was really excited about. Mark and Debbie had flown from Australia to England a week or so before the wedding and had a whistle-stop tour of England and Wales with my dad before catching the ferry to Dublin for a couple of days earlier that week.

By mid-afternoon, however, they had not surfaced at Castle Leslie or at Aisling's parents' house. Until, that is, the phone rang and Aisling's dad John picked up the receiver to hear the voice of someone he knew in a nearby village. The caller explained that there appeared to be three very lost souls parked up in the main street of the village who seemed like they might have something to do with our wedding; it wasn't very often that, on a gloomy Friday afternoon in the hills of

Northern Ireland, a British-registered silver sports car showed up. And this one contained a platinum blonde woman, a man wearing sunglasses and a baseball hat when it wasn't even sunny, and an older gentleman who was wrestling with a map and trying to figure out where on Earth they were.

Now, to say that the arrival of this motley crew had caused something of a stir in that village would be an understatement – if they were trying to arrive inconspicuously, they had failed miserably – so, without delay, John sped off in his car to rescue the lost travellers before a crowd gathered and they got invited into every house in the village for tea and buns (think of Mrs Doyle in the 1990s TV series, *Father Ted*).

By eleven o'clock that night, Aisling and I had become somewhat overwhelmed with all the excitement and decided that we needed a short while alone together before I headed off to Castle Leslie for the night. So, we drove up into the hills overlooking the countryside to enjoy the silence and to spend a few brief moments together.

We reassured each other that we would, indeed, turn up the following day, and we talked about what we had been through to get to this point and what may lay ahead for us. Either because of the crushing tiredness of a hectic week or the stress and anticipation of what the following day would bring, both Aisling and I were overcome with emotion and just held each other as we cried.

On the one hand, I had little doubt that Aisling was ready to get married to me and would be walking up the aisle to meet me the next day. But on the other, I had a niggling doubt that I suppose everyone gets before such a big occasion. Would Aisling finally see the whole 'CF thing' as a life-sentence and something that she did not want to deal with? Would the way I had held back about my CF finally catch up with me and teach me the ultimate lesson? Or would she simply just change her mind, for no reason other than because it was her prerogative to do so?

Aisling has since told me that she held similar fears that night too, but I knew that nothing was going to stop me from marrying her; I recognised the best thing to ever happen to me when I saw it and there was no way I was going to walk away from it.

After gathering ourselves, we drove back down the hill to Aisling's parents' house and said our goodbyes. It was almost midnight and, true to tradition, I had made sure that I didn't see Aisling on our wedding day before meeting at the altar to get married.

As she disappeared into the house, I watched the front door close and took some deep breaths. For the first time that week, I felt so very alone. I made my way slowly through the dark country lanes over the hills of Northern Ireland towards Castle Leslie, a journey that we had made a couple of times that week already. Yet this time I was on my own, with no one to help me pick out turnings in the dark.

I sat in the car quietly, driving alone with the radio off. I tried so hard to concentrate on the route, yet my mind kept on wandering off to other things. The time I had spent with Aisling played out like an old film in my head; snapshots of things we had done and places we had been in the three years since that afternoon at Shoreham airfield when we sat in the cramped space of a Cessna light aircraft. Now, just as it did that afternoon, the rain pattered on the windscreen as I wondered about the future. A future in which I would never be alone again and would always have someone else by my side, fighting my corner, and being there for me. Someone who was so loving they were willing to take on CF with me and share the burden that it brings. Sure, I would be the one who would deal with the physical side of the condition but, as anyone with CF will explain, the mental side of it is just as hard to deal with; putting it back in its box when it tries to leap out and bite you is almost impossible sometimes. Anyone along for the ride experiences the journey just as much as you do, so the impact on them should never be understated.

It was about one a.m. by the time I drove through the gates of Castle Leslie and pulled up in front of its imposing entrance. However, if I had been hoping to sneak in and head straight up to bed, I was very much mistaken. The party was in full swing in the drawing room of the main house, and the bar was still open. My dad and sisters were still up, along with my cousin Mark who was singing songs and playing his guitar. Old school friends who had travelled from Cambridge were there too, along with others from around the UK. Steve, our great friend from Virgin Atlantic days, was holding court in one corner of the room, whilst Aisling's youngest brother entertained the crowds with silly jokes and funny stories in another. Tim, our best man, mingled between the groups of attendees making sure everyone had a drink, and the wedding weekend appeared to have got off to a swinging start.

After thirty minutes of doing my best to enjoy the party atmosphere, however, I was finally beaten and made my excuses to leave. I went upstairs to the 'Blue Room' on the second floor of the Castle. I had selected this room to spend my last night as a single man because it benefitted from beautiful views over the gardens towards the lake, which I thought would be lovely to wake up to on my wedding day.

By the time I undressed and got into bed, it was past two a.m. and all I could think of was sleep. The view would be there in the morning but, for now, there was nothing else to do other than shut my eyes and try to settle my mind. The time for rushing around, stressing about details, and wondering if Aisling would turn up was finally over, and there was no more to be done than to get as much rest as possible before the very long day that lay ahead.

I woke the following morning at around six a.m., long before I had hoped I would and way before the eight o'clock alarm I'd set for myself. As I sat up and looked around the room, the first thing to strike me was how bright it was for the time of the day. I rushed over to the large bay window in the corner of the room and flung back the curtains to be dazzled by bright sunlight.

After a week of cloud and showers, we had given up hope that our wedding day would be any different but there I was, looking out over neatly manicured lawns towards the fishing lake, its surface glistening in the early morning sun. I couldn't believe our luck and just hoped that the fine weather would last through the whole day.

I shuffled around for a while, checking my suit and tie and re-polishing my shoes for what must have been the hundredth time that week. Then, with everything in place, I headed downstairs for breakfast.

Following breakfast, back in the quiet of the Blue Room, it finally hit me – from that day onwards, nothing would ever be the same again. I would always now be one element of a partnership, and I should never think of 'just me' again. I would now have to consider Aisling in everything I did, and whatever happened to me would, from then on, happen to her too. The realisation of this was immense and the moment stopped me in my tracks. Yet I soon settled; this was a responsibility that I accepted willingly, and I knew I was ready for.

In fact, as those few moments went by, the knowledge that I would always have Aisling by my side was incredibly comforting, and I couldn't wait to get to the church and for our married life to start.

Tim and I made our way by car to the church. We were there in good time and before long, the place was full.

Tim and I took up our positions front and centre to await Aisling's arrival and after a short delay, caused by several of Aisling's aunts and uncles remaining outside to chat rather than taking their seats in the church, Aisling finally appeared on her father's arm at the back of the church.

Tim leaned over and whispered in my ear, "She's here." And with just those two words, all the stress of the past few days and the nerves that had been dancing around my tummy, tying me up in knots, fell away. In a pristine ivory dress with a subtly Celtic-styled bodice, her face slightly obscured by a thin white veil that was held in place by a beautiful, shimmering tiara, Aisling walked towards me, gripping her dad's arm. Her smile lit up not only the whole church but, more than that, lit a spark in my heart that I knew would never go out.

Everything we had been through; from the very first time we met by the photocopier at Virgin Atlantic in 1994, through our travels overseas and the year we spent apart, had led us to this very moment. And CF, having been an unwelcome guest through much of our time together, finally had to take a seat at the back, sit quietly, and behave.

CF would surely have its moments in our future lives, when it would take control and send us spinning, but this day was not going to be one of them.

Little more than an hour later, it was all over. On our arrival back at Castle Leslie, we made our way into the building where a long evening of music, dining, and drinking lay ahead.

As Aisling and I were led around the gardens for our official wedding photos to be taken, the guests enjoyed sparkling wine and canapés, either inside the drawing room or outside in the gardens, whilst a harpist played on the veranda overlooking the fountain court. For a couple of hours, the guests mingled and drank whilst Aisling and I made our way amongst them, thanking them for coming and wishing them a lovely evening.

It had always been of the utmost importance to us that we would spend time with everyone who had made it to our wedding. We had both been to weddings in the past where we spent the day in the company of strangers and had no interaction with the bride and groom at all. This was not something we wanted for our own wedding.

With the drinks reception over, it was time for everyone to take their seats in the oak panelled dining room for the wedding supper. And as the doors to the gardens closed and the last of the guests took their seats, the heavens finally opened and the rain, which had been threatened by the forecasters all week, started.

The room filled with the very pleasant sound of guests reading the menu and licking their lips in quiet approval. Smoked Irish salmon followed by fillet of beef (cooked as each person preferred) and, lastly, white chocolate crème brûlée. The food turned out to be even more wonderful than either Aisling or I could have hoped, and we agreed that Noel had surpassed himself in the kitchen, delivering over and above what we could have ever possibly wished for.

With the meal over and the after-dinner speeches made, it was time for the dining room to be transformed into the epicentre of the evening's entertainment. As the guests headed into the drawing room for tea and coffee, they were each handed a piece of wedding cake that had been made by Aisling's mum – Aisling and I had been instructed to ceremonially cut the cake using a sword owned by one of the Leslie clan and used in the Crimean War hundreds of years previously, just to add some spectacle to the tradition.

As the hours wore on, the band played for an hour followed by my cousin Mark, whose set went down a storm with the audience. Meanwhile, the bar was doing a roaring trade. Once Mark had finished, the band took over again for their second set of the night, and many of the older guests who had a long way to travel home started to drift away. As the clock passed midnight, numbers started to dwindle but many of the younger element remained, reluctant for the party to end.

Aisling and I had decided a long time before the wedding itself that we would not follow tradition by heading off to bed at midnight, to be waved off by the gathered crowd. We were aware that people had gone to a lot of expense and a lot of trouble to be at our wedding and we wanted to stay up with them for as long as we could. As it turned out, this had been one of the best nights following one of the best days of our lives and, like the rest of those still awake, we simply didn't want it to end.

As the time wore ever onward, those remaining became either too tired or too inebriated to continue, and sometime the other side of three a.m. it was finally time to wind things up. My last memory of our wedding reception is of sitting around in the dining room, bathed in candlelight with some of our closest and best friends. As Mark strummed the tune quietly on his guitar, we joined in with a communal singalong of the James Taylor classic 'You've got a friend'. With the final chords still ringing out in the darkness, Aisling and I said goodnight and made our way to bed.

Some twenty-two hours after our wedding day began, it was over. Everything had gone to plan, and all those present seemed to have had a wonderful time. Most importantly of all, though, Aisling and I had been able to relax and enjoy the day too, making memories we would be able to look back on and recall with great fondness for many years to come.

TWENTY-FIVE

THE CALM BEFORE THE PERFECT STORM

Following the wedding, we headed home to Epsom. To say that we were both exhausted would be an understatement, but we had a week in the Maldives to look forward to. We had decided, given that we had both only just started new jobs, to limit our honeymoon to just one week, re-branding it as our 'mini-moon'.

The plan was to take just a week, for the time being, and to wait for a few months before taking three weeks off and travelling to Australia; somewhere that we were desperate to visit.

The mini-moon was another week of doing very little in paradise yet, given how I was feeling after the wedding, I don't feel like I was particularly able to enjoy the trip, spending a lot of time sleeping and generally not feeling in great form. Remarkably, my chest had held up throughout the whole lead up to the wedding and the wedding itself but by now (and particularly after the twelve-hour flight to the Maldives) was really starting to play up.

Not long after returning from our mini-moon, I was at Papworth and starting IVs once again to get my chest back to where it needed to be; I had pushed my body to the absolute limit over the previous few weeks, so it was time to start putting it back together and to start looking after myself once more.

As we headed back to our respective jobs following the mini-moon, life slowly went back to normal and we settled into the routine of it, although now doing so as a married couple. I continued to visit the CF clinic at Papworth on Friday afternoons and to undertake the occasional course of IV antibiotics at home.

Apart from the occasional blip with my chest, things seemed pretty stable and life carried on. Those blips led to us developing a notional rating system between us for how I was feeling on any given day. Aisling would find asking me how I was feeling and me responding with vague answers such as, "Okay," or, "Not too bad," deeply frustrating. We, therefore, developed a rating system so that she would gain an accurate picture of how I really was. Under this new system, and based on a scale of one to ten, I would be required to quantify how I was feeling 'in my chest' and also 'in myself'. The first part of this was to give Aisling an idea of how my chest was (with 'one' being at death's door and 'ten' being ready to ascend Everest) and whether my lungs were holding steady, improving, or declining in terms of breathing functionality. The second element of the system was to establish how I felt from a mental health standpoint.

With CF, as I am sure most with the condition will explain, the mental side of things plays a part as much as the physical side, and it is important to keep both in check as one can influence the other. We initially came up with our system as something of a joke, but it soon became part of our lives and helped us both to understand how things were from any given day to the next.

Overall, we settled into married life quickly and, apart from the occasional chest infections, things seemed to be going well. We both had jobs that we enjoyed, we were busy making our new house into a home, and everything seemed to be going our way, so we spent the first part of 2001 arranging our 'real' honeymoon to Australia; talking about where we would go, what we wanted to see, and how long we should stay in each place that we visited. This gave me a fantastic opportunity to fully indulge myself in one of my unofficial hobbies of list-making and planning things, and as the weeks went by our itinerary started to take shape. We carried on with our flying, although we had cut back on this a bit due to the immense costs involved. Aware that the Australia trip was going to cost us a fair bit, we fine-tuned our spending where we could to make the most of the opportunities when we got there.

We did, on occasion, go up and visit my dad in Cambridge and go flying with him. He had kept his flying up since gaining his PPL and still seemed to be enjoying the adventure of it all, setting off by himself for little jaunts to small airfields dotted around the East Anglian countryside when the mood took him. Now fully retired, he had time on his hands to satisfy his strong sense of wanderlust, having trekked in the Andes Mountains (including the celebrated trail to Machu Pichu), island hopped around Greece, spent some time in New Zealand, and just completed a drive across the USA – all within the last twelve months or so!

In the May of 2001, some eight months after our wedding, Aisling and I headed off to Australia for three weeks. As I was still working with Virgin Sun (and was once again entitled to staff travel perks with sister airline Virgin Atlantic) we flew Upper Class from Heathrow to Hong Kong before transferring onto a Cathay Pacific flight to Cairns. Whilst at Hong Kong we met up with my old Alliances boss Andy, who was now working there with Virgin Atlantic and who, of course, had introduced us seven years previously. We enjoyed a few hours courtesy of Andy in the Virgin Atlantic Upper Class lounge before making our way down to the onward flight to Cairns.

Thanks to the delicious range of wines and cocktails available in the lounge, we were both fast asleep by the time our plane had taxied out the end of the runway at Hong Kong Airport. We were eventually woken by the crew to enjoy breakfast and the beautiful sight of the Pacific Ocean and the Queensland coastline passing below us as the plane started its descent into Cairns. Within an hour, we were standing outside the terminal at Cairns International Airport, amongst the palm trees and cockatoos, waiting for a taxi to take us to our hotel. Looking around and blinking in the early morning sunshine, it was hard to take in just where we were. Nonetheless, our belated honeymoon had started and it was time for all that energy spent planning to be put to good use.

The first few days of our trip were spent exploring the Daintree rainforest and the beautiful Queensland coastline. We had a day snorkelling out at the Great Barrier Reef and took a seaplane flight to the deserted Whitehaven Beach, often rated as the most beautiful in the world and with brilliant white sand so fine it 'squeaks' when you walk on it.

We also spent a couple of days exploring the idyllic Whitsunday Islands and the sleepy coastal town of Airlie Beach, a Mecca for beach-loving young backpackers from across the world. But it was at the hotel in Airlie Beach where one of the scariest moments in my life was to unfold; having gone into the hotel bathroom, I removed my wedding ring and put it in a piece of tissue paper for safekeeping while I had a shower. After I was dressed again, I was tidying up the bathroom and upon finding a discarded piece of tissue on the side, threw it in the toilet and duly pushed the flush button. No sooner had I taken my finger off that button when a horrible sense of panic spread right through my body. I knew immediately what I had done and wanted to be sick there and then. I stood in silence, not knowing what to do next, with a cold sweat instantly forming on the back of my neck. As I did my best to compose myself, for some unknown reason I looked back down in to the toilet bowl to see, to my absolute astonishment, that the tissue was still there and that beneath it, lying still at the bottom of the toilet bowl, was my ring. Never was I so pleased to plunge my hand into a toilet, as I quickly grabbed the ring and placed it back on my finger! After washing my hands and thanking my lucky stars more than once, I returned to the bedroom where Aisling was lying on the bed reading a guidebook. "You're never going to believe what just happened," I said...

Following our amazing few days in Queensland, we flew from Cairns to Alice Springs and onwards to Ayers Rock, which by now had reverted to its Aboriginal name of Uluru. We spent forty-eight hours here, doing pretty much everything that you can do with a big red rock sticking out of the landscape. We visited it at dawn and at sunset, we photographed it from one hundred different angles, and even spent four hours hiking around the base of it. Had it not been closed off as a mark of respect for a local Aboriginal tribal elder some days before, we probably would have climbed it as well[1].

On one of the days between visits to the rock and sunrise and sunset, we hired a car and drove the one hundred miles to Kings Canyon, the region's 'other' tourist attraction. The drive itself was an adventure that would be hard to replicate anywhere else on earth; we stopped at a ranch where breakfast was on offer to find ourselves sitting in the farmhouse kitchen of a family who ran a cattle station that encompassed one million acres of this part of the Outback. We also dodged wild camels as they ran alongside the highway and, on some of the straightest roads I have ever seen in my life, drove at one hundred miles an hour for the first time. Probably not the wisest thing to be doing when you're miles away from the nearest medical facility but incredibly good fun.

After the journey itself, the couple of hours spent hiking in Kings Canyon was rather sedate in comparison, although very picturesque. With our hike completed and our picnic lunch eaten, it was time to make the return journey back to Uluru, once again seeing how fast we could make the rental car go without breaking it.

Following our trip out into the Australian bush, we took the three-hour flight to Sydney and spent a few days following the well-beaten sight-seeing trail around the city's landmarks. We booked to go on the newest attraction on any tourist's 'to-do' list, the Sydney Harbour Bridge Climb, and over a couple of hours on one of the mornings we were there, we achieved our goal. I was determined that CF or not, and even if it took me all day, this was one experience I was not going to miss out on and felt an enormous sense of achievement upon reaching the summit of the arch. Whilst not being something you would want to do every week, it is certainly something that any visitor to Sydney should attempt (if they are able, of course).

After taking in the sights of the city for a few days, we flew from Sydney to the outskirts of New South Wales and a town called Leeton. This was where my cousin Mark – who had played at our wedding – along with my aunt and uncle, lived.

Leeton is a relatively small town set in the agricultural belt that surrounds the Murrumbidgee River. The river itself provides essential irrigation for the huge farms that cover the landscape in this part of Australia, and the area is known for fruit farming, vineyards, and cattle rearing on a huge scale.

Having spent a few days with my relatives, it was finally time to head back to Sydney and start the long journey back to the UK. We said our goodbyes at the tiny airport that Leeton shares with the neighbouring town of Narranderra and, as our little turboprop plane climbed away, I couldn't help but wonder if I would ever be back in this part of the world and, if so, when that would be. After all, it was about as far as we could get to from Epsom and it had taken me twenty-nine years to get there for the first time. But like San Francisco, Hong Kong, Cedar Key, and the other wonderful places I have visited and enjoyed in my life, I made a mental note to return to Australia one day, hopefully sooner rather than later.

Once back home, we reflected on what an amazing time we had enjoyed in Australia and how fortunate we were to have been able to undertake such a trip. Given that I was born with a degenerative, chronic condition, it was particularly hard for me to assimilate how I was still able to do all of that, and the realisation of just how lucky I was to be able to see those things lodged at the forefront of my mind.

To put it into context, I was now twenty-nine years of age. So far, I was yet to spend a single night in hospital due to CF – and to be able to make such a claim is highly unusual for anyone with the condition at that stage of life. Many CF patients spend much of their childhood in and out of hospital, finding it hard to keep up with their schooling and having a 'normal' life. For them, the prospect of leaving home and furthering their education at college or university is simply not an option, although over recent years, as treatments have progressed, more people with CF are able to do so.

I might have spent a couple of weeks here and there taking IV antibiotics, (which can make you feel nauseous, tired, and lethargic) but that seemed to be a small price to pay for what I had achieved in my twenty-nine years of life.

Acutely aware of how fortunate I had been up until this point, it was hard not to counter my appreciation with fear that there might be a big shock waiting for me somewhere around the corner, and I often wondered how long it would be before I was finally admitted to hospital due to CF.

Being completely truthful, I didn't do as much as I could have to keep myself well when I was younger; I was simply fortunate, so I had a growing sense that something was about to happen. I had no idea what that might be or when it might take place, I simply knew that I had to carry on enjoying life because there would come a time when things would not be like this.

It's all very well getting on with your life *despite* having a chronic condition. But it is equally important to never take your eye off the ball because, one day, that ball might just hit you right in the face. And as I would soon discover, with chronic conditions like CF, when the ball hits you, it hurts – a lot.

HARDER TIMES

TWENTY-SIX

THE DAY THE WORLD CHANGED

Wednesday, August 15th, 2001 started like any other working day but it would end in tragedy. Little did I know when I woke that morning that one of the most significant events in my life would take place that day, and that I would end it bereft with grief, overwhelmed with despair, and feeling as though my whole world had been picked up, tossed about, and flung back down – shattered and un-mendable.

I had got up, got dressed, taken my normal CF medication, and had headed off from our house in Epsom to the town of Crawley, where I was now working as Commercial Manager for Virgin Sun. That week, Aisling was travelling for work and would be waking up that morning in Tenerife.

I had started back in Crawley in the spring of 2000 and simply loved my job; I was responsible for ensuring that our five aircraft were full on every flight they operated. With each aircraft flying two or three return flights a day, from either Gatwick or Manchester Airports, to Mediterranean holiday hotspots in the busiest months of the summer, I had an awful lot of seats to fill. But I enjoyed the challenge and got on well with the others in the closely-knit management team.

For the first time in a while, I felt really happy and settled. Aisling and I were married and had moved in to our lovely first home together in Epsom. In May 2001 we had been on our belated, yet epic, three-week honeymoon, and my health was generally good. However, just when things seemed to be going so well, CF resurrected its old habit of pulling the rug out from right under me.

Shortly after returning from our grand odyssey around Australia, everyone at work was called to the conference room to be told that for 'commercial' reasons our division was being sold off to another UK tour operator and that we would stop flying entirely under our own brand by October 2001. With this devastating news came the option of either transferring to the parent company Virgin Atlantic or to be made redundant and sent on my way with quite a tidy redundancy payoff in my pocket but, potentially, a gap on my CV.

For as long as I could, I kept my options open. I talked to people and explored what opportunities may be available to me, but I also privately explored what I might do if I opted to take the redundancy payoff.

This exploring took me around the UK and even as far as Singapore for twenty-four hours while I attended an interview for a commercial role at Singapore Airlines. How I hoped to manage my CF (or indeed my marriage) apparently never crossed my mind when I flew twelve hours around the world to spend forty-five minutes talking to some guy in an unremarkable office on the edge of Changi International Airport in Singapore.

Following this mad dash to Singapore and back, I returned to London and resumed winding down my airline's operation back in Crawley. However, there was one other option that I had been secretly investigating. I had, over the years, spent a lot of time dealing with lawyers of many flavours in my work and was particularly friendly with a couple who specialised in aviation law. I had become interested in the work that they did and, for a while, had fancied myself pursuing a legal career should an opportunity ever arise. I believed myself to have the basic academic ability to cut the mustard and I certainly had the interest and a reasonably sound experience base.

Up to this point, however, there had always been reasons *not* to take the plunge into a legal career – a steady job that I enjoyed, travel perks, a mortgage to pay, and so on. But with my job about to be snatched away from me and a tidy sum of cash offered as a replacement, such an opportunity now existed. My redundancy package would pay all the fees associated with spending the requisite two years at law school that I would need to complete before I could qualify as a solicitor.

So, after a lot of discussion with Aisling and a lot of soul searching, I decided that this would probably be the best and last chance I would get to change my career, particularly as I was getting close to thirty years of age and believed that I was running out of time to make such a life-changing switch.

My course would start in the first week of September, 2001 at the College of Law in Guildford, about thirty-five minutes' drive from Epsom. Having attended something that just about passed as a future entrant's interview, I was formally accepted onto the course and that was that; I decided to muddle through the last couple of months at the airline while simultaneously attending my course so that I could start that year.

By the June of 2001, everything seemed to be in place. Not even an invitation to fly back to Singapore for a second interview could tempt me away from my new direction. My mind was made up and there was nothing that could or would have altered my plans by this stage, right up until that particular Wednesday, three weeks before I was due to start at the College of Law, when my dad woke up and decided that he would go flying.

On this Wednesday afternoon, I had completed the daily ritual of heading into Crawley town centre to procure my lunchtime sandwiches and had settled back down at my desk for the afternoon's work. At about three o'clock, however, a police car pulled up outside the building. As our team's area overlooked the street outside, we all peered out, like nosy neighbours, to see what was happening.

Ironically, just the week previously, the police had been called to our office when a disgruntled Virgin Holidays customer had turned up to remonstrate with the Managing Director and the sight of this police car arriving led to some witty individual within our team remarking that another happy customer was obviously providing 'feedback' on their holiday to the MD upstairs.

After a few minutes with no obvious activity outside or anyone being hauled away by the scruff of the neck, we all settled back into our seats and resumed our work. And then I felt a tap on my shoulder. I turned around to find Michelle from our team standing behind my chair looking as white as a ghost, visibly distressed and with tears in her eyes. She asked if she could have a word with me and we walked around to a quieter area of the office.

Michelle told me that there were two police officers in the conference room and that they needed to speak to me urgently. She walked around with me to the doorway of the conference room and, as she opened the door, I saw the two female police officers in full uniform seated at the table with their hats removed and notebooks out.

It is hard to put into words the rush of thoughts and emotions that washed over me in just the few seconds it took to walk out of our work area and to the conference room. I recall desperately trying to remember anything I might have done that would warrant a visit from the police at my place of work. Perhaps I had committed some sort of traffic offence on my drive into work that morning or left Marks and Spencer's without paying for my sandwiches? The next few moments, however would reveal that my summons was not related to anything I had done; it was so much worse than that.

One of the officers invited me to sit down and asked me to confirm my name. She then asked me to confirm that I was, indeed, related to someone bearing my dad's name and with his home address. It was at this point that it suddenly, and with some force, hit me that something terrible must have happened.

The same officer then asked whether my dad flew a light aircraft from Cambridge Airport and whether I could confirm if he had been flying earlier that day. I told them that he did, indeed, fly from Cambridge but – having not spoken to him for a few days – I couldn't confirm whether he had been intending to fly that morning. I remember saying that, as it was a fine summer day, it was 'quite likely' he had decided to go up for a while because he often did at short notice when the weather was good.

Reeling off my answers, the reality of what might have happened began to dawn on me and a real sense of what I can only describe as suppressed panic began to consume me. As I joined the dots in the line of questioning, I knew that something awful must have happened. But it wasn't until I heard the words, "I'm afraid that I have to inform you..." that my worst fears became reality.

"I'm afraid I have to inform you that there was a light aircraft accident this morning in Suffolk and we believe your father was the pilot flying the aircraft. We are sorry to inform you that your father died in the accident."

Suddenly, I felt more alone than I had ever felt before and the sense of panic that had started to build overwhelmed me.

I felt hot, and sick, and shaky, and ill to my core. I sat there, short of breath, as my heart raced at a supersonic speed and with my head spinning. I tried to analyse what I had just been told, but there was no analysing to be done; my father had died and there was nothing I could do or say that would change that.

I wanted to argue with what I was being told, to find reasons as to why this could simply not be the case. I wanted to shout that there must have been some mistake and that it couldn't have been him flying that particular aircraft on that particular route. But knowing which aircraft he flew, where he liked to fly to, and that he always (like me) would fly with his licence and log book with him in case of such an event as this, I knew that there could be no doubt it was him involved.

Gathering up what little remained of my composure I tried to garner further information from the police officer as to what exactly had happened. I am not sure whether this is normal human behaviour but in what was quite possibly my darkest hour, I felt an overwhelming need to know every detail of the events that had befallen my dad.

Unfortunately, the police officers could offer little to satisfy me in this regard. It turned out that my dad's flight had been traced back to Cambridge Airport by Air Traffic Control and that it was Cambridgeshire police that had sought further details about the pilot involved. The desk manager of the flying club at the airport had informed the police that they were aware my dad had a son who worked at Virgin Atlantic and, through several phone calls, this had led to the police turning up at my workplace five or so hours following the accident.

It was 'with regret' I was told that the two officers before me could give no further details but suggested I ring Suffolk police for further information. One of them ripped out and handed me a page from their notebook with an Ipswich telephone number on it and the name of another police officer I could call. With that, and rather unceremoniously, they got up, offered me their condolences as they returned their hats to their heads, and left the room.

In those first few moments alone, I became acutely aware that what had just happened would affect the rest of my life. It truly felt that there had been a paradigm shift in everything. How different things already felt – they would never be the same again.

When the police left, Michelle entered the room and gave me a massive hug. Although I just wanted to break down, my emotions were overtaken by needing to know more and also by a sense of duty, realising that it would be up to me to pass this horrific news on to the rest of my family.

Michelle took me up to the Managing Director's office on the top floor of our building. She knew he was out for the day and had quickly arranged for me to use his office to make the necessary calls in private. The first thing I did upon settling into the leather chair at the MD's desk was send a text message to Aisling who (as far as I was aware) was still in meetings in Tenerife.

We had devised a rule (the reasons behind which were CF-related) that if we ever needed to get hold of each other urgently, we would send the other person a text message that would simply read 'SOS'. I dispatched the necessary text message and awaited her call. In the meantime, I dialled the number that the police officer had given me and asked to speak to the officer whose name appeared below the number on the rather scruffy bit of paper.

Having established contact, and having exchanged brief personal details to confirm my identity, I set about trying to establish what had transpired earlier that day. As it turned out, the police sergeant on the other end of the phone had been involved in the incident since the first calls to the police had been made about an aircraft in distress at around ten thirty that morning.

He informed me that he subsequently attended a location near to a disused former World War Two airfield in Suffolk owned by a local farmer. The farmer and his wife had heard an aircraft overhead with a spluttering engine, and the aircraft had then come down in a field on their farm.

Upon arriving at the scene, the officer had found the aircraft wreckage lying at the edge of the field, upright but heavily damaged and with my dad still at the controls. First aid was administered whilst still in the field location before my dad was airlifted by RAF rescue helicopter to Ipswich Hospital. He was pronounced dead a short time later.

It took a great deal to get through that phone conversation but I managed to establish the course of events, as far as anyone could tell me at this very early stage, and felt relieved that I was dealing with someone who'd had direct involvement in the incident.

I agreed with the police sergeant that I would need to take a bit of time to process what he had told me and that I would make contact with my sisters and my aunt who lived in Australia (my dad's sister) to let them know the news. I said I would call back later that day as arrangements needed to be made and formalities commenced – the most important being to identify my dad's body, which was now lying in the mortuary at Ipswich Hospital.

As I replaced the receiver on to its base, I was conscious of how increasingly hard it was to catch my breath. I had woken up feeling fine that day, but by mid-afternoon felt that I was having the last gasps of breath squeezed from my lungs as my heart raced like a runaway train heading at full pelt towards the buffers. I sat for a few moments just staring into space, noticing the peacefulness of the office in which I was sitting, and I recall questioning how such peace could prevail in circumstances of such utter horror and sadness. In those few moments alone, such a juxtaposition seemed utterly bizarre.

I was utterly distraught but I also felt an overwhelming sense of duty to get hold of my sisters and my aunt as soon as possible. The anger I felt at how this could happen to my dad was positioned in my head right alongside despair and sheer uselessness; no matter what I did at any point in the future, nothing would change what had happened or make it any better. My dad had died in the most horrible of circumstances and there was simply nothing I could do about it.

After a few moments, the stillness of the office was shattered by the piercing shriek of my mobile phone ringing. I looked down at the small screen to see that it was Aisling calling, responding to my SOS. As composed as I could, I told her what had happened.

Through streaming tears and trembling voices, we agreed that Aisling would immediately plan to return home that night, travelling from Tenerife via Madrid and getting back into Heathrow later that evening. I knew that the one person who would be able to make sense of any of this was Aisling and that it was her I needed by my side.

I hung up and tried to compose myself - but failed miserably.

The whole situation seemed so hopelessly impossible to bear and I felt so ill-equipped to deal with it. I knew I had to ring my sisters and let them know what had happened. I considered briefly how I would tell them and what I should say, even considering whether I should just say that something had happened to dad and ask them to ring me later. However, I soon realised just how ridiculous, not to mention utterly selfish that would be. Ridiculous too was the time I spent in trying to decide which sister to ring first, but my head was in complete freefall and my ability to think logically had all but escaped me.

Having completed the truly horrendous task of telling my sisters that dad had just died while they were both at their places of work, we agreed they would travel to mine and Aisling's house as soon as they could so that we could discuss our next steps. In the meantime, I would talk to the police again to find out what we needed to do and where we needed to be.

I subsequently agreed, upon speaking with the police sergeant, that we would attend Ipswich Hospital the following day to identify Dad's body.

It would be fair to say that, up until this point, neither me or my sisters had ever really had any exposure to death and this was, surely, the steepest and most emotional of learning curves. I also felt it was down to me to ensure my duties were carried out with as much dignity as I could muster, so that my dad would be proud of the way I conducted myself over those darkest of days.

Having spoken to my sisters and decided to defer calling my aunt until I got home, when it would be morning time in Australia, a quick call to my old friend Steve (who also lived in Epsom) ensured that I could escape the office. I was in no fit state to drive and Steve, the omnipresent stalwart that he was, duly collected me a short time later and took me home.

Having deposited me at my doorway and reassured himself that I was okay to be left alone, he then set off on the fifty-mile drive to Heathrow to be there when Aisling stepped off her flight from Madrid in a few hours' time.

I was at home, alone and afraid. The living room spun before me and my head felt muddled. I sat quietly for a while, trying to digest what had happened and I recall thinking to myself how difficult it was to comprehend it all. The room, its fittings, and its furniture were just as they were when I had left for work that morning, yet the whole world – in just a few short hours – had changed inconceivably.

By that evening, my two sisters, Aisling and I were all sat in that living room in shocked silence. Rounds of tea were consumed but no one felt like eating. I relayed again the information I had been given by the police, but it was apparent that there was still so much we didn't know.

Dad was an accomplished pilot and had been flying regularly over that summer. From the little I had learned so far, it sounded like there had been a technical issue with the aircraft that had resulted in him having to perform a forced landing. This is a manoeuvre you are taught during your training and which you are supposed to practise regularly, even when qualified, in case of an engine failure whilst airborne. We took out a map and looked to see where the disused airfield in Suffolk was located. It was directly on the track that would take you (as the crow flies) from Cambridge Airport to Southwold on the Suffolk coast. My dad would often bimble over this part of East Anglia as he loved visiting both Southwold and the neighbouring town of Aldeborough, and flying overhead offered a whole new perspective.

Before heading to bed that night, we agreed amongst us that we would all travel directly to Ipswich Hospital the following morning. I had never seen a dead human body in my life but, whilst initially reluctant to do so, knew that I had to see my dad one last time – to tell him I loved him and to kiss him goodbye.

TWENTY-SEVEN

ONE DAY, ONE SUMMER

Before we retired that night, my sister Louise opened a letter that my dad had left her – to be opened in the event of his death – and read it out loud. Apart from various financial details, there were instructions about funeral arrangements and what he wished for in terms of his ashes.

I couldn't believe that we were sitting there listening to those words. You always hope that such horrors won't happen to you. But it had happened and we were there, the four of us, drowning in shock and desperation.

As we sat there, tears rolled down our cheeks as happy memories of our dad were revisited. But the smiles we forced upon our faces were simply a facade, masking our overwhelming sense of loss and sadness. It was exactly twenty-five years from the very day when my dad had bundled us all into the family car and the following day onto that National Airlines plane at Heathrow to experience a new life in California, but now he was gone. And we were completely lost.

I slept very little that night. Grabbing snippets of sleep here and there, each time I woke, my brain revisited the events of the previous day like a stuck record. Did it really happen? Was Dad really dead?

We set off for Ipswich mid-morning and arrived at the hospital around lunchtime, to be met by the police sergeant I had spoken with the previous day. We were sat in a side room in the hospital mortuary, itself located in a wing of the main hospital building. The sergeant told us what he knew so far; that dad's plane had an engine problem and that he had made a distress radio call to air traffic. He had also told air traffic that as he was in the vicinity of a disused airfield, and that his intention was to attempt to land on what remained of the runway there.

He had passed very low over a farm on the periphery of the airfield but had come down short of the runway in an adjacent field. It appeared that he had either landed heavily or that he had hit the trees at the edge of that field and had come to rest in an upright position. Either way, the impact had been significant. The aircraft was badly damaged and my dad had probably died of injuries sustained during the impact.

Growing up, my Dad often told me that accidents may seem survivable but that it was the 'sudden stop' that would kill you. It was incredulous to think that this mantra had now come to pass.

I asked if we could visit the site of the accident and we were told that this should be possible but that the officer would have to make a couple of calls on his radio first to clear it. In the meantime, we returned to the business of formally identifying my dad's body for the police and the coroner's purposes. My sisters were still not sure whether they wanted to see Dad or not, so it was left to me to be the first in. Aisling offered to come with me and I agreed. Although this was the most awful and terrifying thing I had ever done, I needed to confirm in my own mind that *my* dad had actually died.

I was led to a doorway, which in turn led to a darkened room. The door closed behind us. I stood, clasping Aisling's hand tightly, with my dad laid out on a bed opposite us. He was under the crispest white sheet I had ever seen and, apart from a few cuts and bruises on his face, seemed remarkably unscathed. It was hard to fathom at that moment that he was dead. But there we were, the two of us together for what would be the last time.

I could not reach his hand as the sheet came to his upper torso, so I rested my hand on his shoulder and told him how sorry I was for what had happened. He felt cold but looked as though, at any moment, he would open his eyes, sit up, and tell me that there had been some awful error made and that in fact he had survived the accident after all. Yet, of course, he would not be opening his eyes again, not for me or for anyone else.

Only the week before, I had dashed up to Cambridge to visit him after completing a work-related meeting at Stansted Airport nearby. We had enjoyed a cup of tea together in his garden and had talked about our respective plans for the immediate future. As I left him that day, he had kissed me on my head like he always did and insisted that I go flying with him again soon. And now this would be our last goodbye.

I was twenty-eight years old, coincidentally about the same age as my dad was when he lost his father, but at that moment I felt like a little lost boy who just needed his father to give him a big hug, to show him his warm smile, and to tell him that everything would be okay.

After a short while, I returned to the waiting room to confirm that it was my dad lying in there (as if there had been any doubt). The police sergeant then gave us directions to the accident site from the hospital and told me that my dad's belongings – including his log book, pilots licence, and watch – had been recovered from the aircraft and taken to the police station in Beccles, Suffolk. We agreed that after visiting the site, Aisling and I would head to Beccles to collect his belongings. It was important to me that we regained possession of these items; I knew how valuable they were to my dad and I wanted them safely back in my care rather than locked in some drawer in a faceless police station.

My sisters decided that they would visit Dad separately, but I accompanied my younger sister Faith as she did not want to go alone. I will never forget how she cried out at the sight of him and how I had to support her as we approached his body.

It was the hardest day we had ever faced as a family and there was nothing that would or could make any of it easier. But we were together and, along with Aisling, would get through it… somehow.

Once we had said our own personal goodbyes to Dad, we headed from the hospital to the accident site. It was not easy to find (this being in the days before satellite navigation was commonplace) but with the help of one or two locals, and by identifying a red public telephone box on a lane leading to a farm, we were able to find it.

On seeing a police car at the side of the road and a few people wandering around in a field, we concluded that this must be the place. We got out of the car and headed to where the small group of individuals were congregated, to one side of the field where there was a tall hedgerow and some trees marking the field's boundary. As we approached the group, we were faced with the stark reality of the situation. There below the trees were the remains of my dad's aircraft. The wreckage of the plane was largely intact, although the front end (which had taken the force of the impact with the trees) was badly deformed. The door had been removed by the fire brigade the day before to extricate my dad from the aircraft, and the fuselage was sitting atop the wings which were folded upside-down underneath, the main undercarriage sitting vertically upright.

We were met by another police officer who had been tasked with escorting us around the wreckage. The Air Accident Investigation Branch (AAIB) investigators were already on site, having been there since the previous afternoon, and we were introduced to the lead investigator, who talked us through what he knew so far.

The aircraft had seemingly suffered a mechanical failure of the engine, which was evidenced by way of the heavy streak marks of oil strewn along the underside of the fuselage, as well as the distress call that my dad had made. The occupants of the farm at the top of the field (a husband and wife) had told the investigator that they heard my dad's aircraft making 'spluttering, rasping' noises as it flew low over their house and, although they did not witness the plane's final impact, they were the first on scene and had tried in vain to save his life. He was alive but unconscious when they reached the aircraft and the husband had helped ensure that my dad's airway was clear while his wife went to raise the alarm.

On hearing this I made a mental note to write to thank these people; witnessing such an event must have been deeply traumatic for them, yet they had done what they could to save my dad's life.

We were shown where one of the aircraft's main wheels had initially impacted the ground in the field, which was still full of pea plants waiting to be harvested. The investigator speculated that Dad had tried to lift the aircraft over the trees in order to avoid an impact, but the aircraft may well have stalled in the process due to a lack of airspeed. We were then shown where one of the wingtips had impacted the ground, leaving a metre-long gouge in the brown, sun-hardened surface.

The wreckage of the aircraft was like something from a film – a prop that had been dropped into this random field in Suffolk for a day's filming. The scene was surreal. With my head spinning from the emotion of it all, it was hard to take everything in. It was hard to rationalise that this was the place where my dad had lost his life and in such an awful fashion. I was standing in some random field on a random farm deep in the heart of rural Suffolk and *this* was the place where my dad had taken his last breaths.

My sisters, Aisling, and I laid flowers in the hedgerow just up from the aircraft and headed back to the car, thanking those remaining on site for their work. We agreed to keep in contact with the AAIB investigator as he carried out his work over the coming months.

I took one last look at the wreckage as we walked back past it, staring at it through my tired and teary eyes in sheer disbelief. Having been around small aircraft for a few years by this time, I knew how much fun flying them could be. And, although I had not flown this particular aircraft, I had flown others of the same type on several occasions. Yet, as I looked at the mangled, broken aircraft behind me, I felt nothing but anger.

Flying small planes, like many hobbies one can choose, carries risks and as a pilot you are trained to be aware of those risks and to mitigate them every time you take to the sky. However, you also consider how much fun you get from doing so and the exhilaration you feel when you are at two thousand feet above the countryside on a beautiful sunny day and have a view of perhaps 50 miles all around you. That exhilaration far outweighs the risks involved, which is why pilots like my dad, Aisling, and I continued with flying after achieving our PPLs. But on this day, in this place and with my head in turmoil, it was hard to see how I would ever set foot near a small aircraft again, let alone fly one myself.

The following few days were spent organising and arranging. Obituaries for the local newspaper as well as *The Times* were written and published, funeral arrangements were made, and I had the emotional job of retrieving my dad's car from outside the flying club at Cambridge airport. My aunt arrived in the UK from Australia along with my cousin Mark, and they were a great comfort to have around. My mum also flew over from her home in Florida so that she could offer her support as we faced the awful prospect of my dad's funeral.

Much time was spent talking about Dad and reminiscing about all the things he had achieved in his life, both the serious and professional and the bizarre, or even comical, scrapes that he often seemed to get caught up in. He had, only a year before, retired from working life, having spent the final stages of it as Chair of the UK Coordinating Committee for Cancer Research in London. Since retiring, he had been busy ticking items off his list of things he had always wanted to do. He had been to New Zealand, had walked the Machu Picchu trail in Peru, and had driven across the United States in a convertible Ford Mustang. Not one to sit still for too long in any area of his life, the next trip (a tour around Tuscany, Italy) was already planned and booked at the time of his accident.

Thankfully, the tasks we had to perform during those few days kept us all busy and, in a strange way, kept our minds off the sheer awfulness of what had happened. Dad's will was dealt with by his executor Robert (an old friend of my dad's who also happened to be a solicitor) whilst Louise contacted people in the cancer research world both in the UK and overseas to tell them the news and advise on funeral arrangements. We did what we could to make those days seem worthwhile but we were tired, in shock, and emotionally drained.

We muddled through as best as we all could until the day of the funeral, eight days after the accident, which also happened to be my aunt's birthday. In the lead up to the funeral itself, I tried to decide whether I should – or even *could* – do a speech of some kind. Although comfortable with giving speeches and presentations at work, my head was tormented with the thought of standing up in front of a couple of hundred people and talking about my dad. I was unsure what to say or how to say it. More importantly, though, I wasn't sure I would actually be able to speak or to get my words out in a meaningful order.

It was agreed that in the Order of Service booklets that Aisling had been busy preparing and having printed, there would simply be a section of the service entitled 'Tributes' and it was then open for me to speak or not speak depending on what I decided I could manage.

I battled with this 'should I/shouldn't I' dilemma until about forty-eight hours before the funeral. Aisling and I had taken ourselves off for a walk to clear our heads and we talked about what I was thinking. During our conversation, Aisling remarked that I had always been fairly adept at writing poetry. Whilst not being able to describe any poetry I had written as a work of art, I always seemed to have had a knack for producing little ditties in birthday cards to Aisling and others, and had done a couple of speeches in rhyme on occasion as well. I gave it some thought and decided that it was an excellent suggestion; reading a poem about my dad would convey my feelings to the assembled attendees and would allow me to simply stand up and read without getting too caught up in the emotion of it all.

So, that evening, having been toying with one or two ideas throughout that afternoon, I sat down at my dad's desk in his study where he had so often sat himself, with a blank piece of paper and a pencil. I wanted to write something that encapsulated all the feelings I had for him and how much I both admired and adored him. But I also wanted to write it as if it was a story being told by any boy about his father. In what seemed like no time at all I had written this:

<u>My Shining Light</u>

A boy looks at his father and wonder fills his eyes.

A shining light of everything, so great, so strong, so wise.

The boy sees in his father a hero every day,

A man so good at everything and nothing in his way.

The boy hears from his father words so true and right,

And thinks that no-one could ever doubt that shining light.

The boy talks to his father but never seems to say

The pride that he holds for him in every single way.

The boy dreams of his father, his mentor and his guide,

And his dreams will last forever, his father by his side.

This boy promises his father, that wherever he may be,

In my thoughts he will remain, and a part of him in me.

I sat back in my dad's leather desk chair and breathed deeply. I had written something I would be proud to read out the following day and also something that conveyed my feelings in full. It would leave those listening in no doubt as to what my dad had meant to me while he was alive and how much he would remain with me following his death.

TWENTY-EIGHT

LIFE WILL NEVER BE THE SAME

I still have the original scribblings of what became 'My Shining Light' at home, complete with words crossed out and notations for rearrangement. Upon reading the poem again, some eighteen years after it was first written, I was struck by how short it was. On the day I read it out to over two-hundred people at the funeral, it seemed to go on endlessly, yet to see it in its rather concise and 'to the point' final format, I was both pleased and surprised by how I had managed to convey all of what I wanted to say in six simple rhyming couplets.

The funeral lasted all of thirty minutes. A well-attended affair, with over two hundred people gathered to say goodbye to my dad. The congregation was made up of people from various aspects of Dad's life and was a strange mix of the past and present. Friends he had known for decades sat next to those he had worked with in London and Cambridge, whilst others from the local tennis club chatted in hushed voices with those from the flying club at Cambridge Airport. Jerry Brown from the village shop that I had worked in made a surprise appearance, along with others from our family's long and distant past.

The service itself was as beautiful and poignant as it could be, with my dad's coffin laid out at the front of the room just slightly offset from the centre. However, it also crystallised in me a genuine dislike for these funeral/cremation services. You hang around outside until the previous service has completed and the congregation has filed out of the front door. Meanwhile, once given the nod, you then all file into the same room from the back (seemingly just as the last lot have shut the front door behind them) and take your places in seats which are still warm. This whole process, whilst the staff and undertakers do their best to make it as respectful and dignified as possible, means you can't help but feel that you are in a production line of some sort. Whilst trying hard not to use the rather inappropriate 'sausage factory' analogy, a more apt and alternative description is hard to find.

Having attended several funerals of this type in the years since, including another in the very same room, I have decided – whilst still thinking that cremation is the way to go (quite literally, I suppose) – that this sort of funeral is most definitely not for me and I have said so in my will. Surely, there are better ways to say goodbye to someone? And I certainly know that thirty minutes of being ushered in, sat down, then ushered out again is not how I want to be sent on my way. With the benefit of hindsight, nor does it seem adequate for someone who had crammed as much into his life as my dad did.

During the service, Louise read out a short piece that she had written in tribute to my dad, of which I still have a copy. It reminded all those present how Dad had lived his life (sometimes relentlessly) in pursuit of the 'interesting, educational, and fun' and how he had instilled the importance of these values in his children. I still treasure that doctrine to this day, and life seems a lot more valuable when living it on this basis that Dad set out for us. With CF perhaps, it is even more important to have a sense of rules on how to live one's life – not because we are more precious or valuable than any other person, but because those with CF have a heightened sense of mortality and often seem more keen to 'get stuff done' in the time they have available to them.

As the opening bars of 'In Dreams' by Roy Orbison rang out after the all-too-brief service, it was finally time to leave Dad for the last time. My sisters, Aisling, and I stood by the coffin as everyone left, shaking the hands of those we knew and smiling politely through sad eyes at those we didn't until everyone was gone.

Aisling and I were last out of the room. I laid my hand on the coffin and left my copy of 'My Shining Light' on the top of it.

After a wake of sorts in my dad's back garden, lasting a couple of hours, the attendees drifted away to resume their lives and left us to try to put the shattered pieces of ours back together. I suppose holding the funeral and leading the formal goodbyes was supposed to bring us what people term in these soundbite-filled days as 'closure', but it brought me anything but.

The future looked strangely different. I was just twenty-nine years old, married less than a year, and the man who had been such an important part of my life was gone. There were so many things I needed to say to him, so many things left to talk about and to laugh over, and so many good times still to spend in each other's company. Without him, the future looked utterly hollow.

As we cleared up from the wake and sat quietly in the evening sun, I tried to draw some sense of consolation from the fact that Dad had died doing something he loved, but there really was none to be found.

———

In the weeks and months that followed, it took just about as much effort as I could muster to get back to any sort of normality, particularly as my imminent start at law school was bearing down on me. The three weeks following Dad's accident were the hardest I had ever had to face. Looking back, I don't know whether the start of two years at law school was a welcome distraction or whether it just added to my already-immense level of stress. Either way, I had enrolled and had paid the first instalment of fees, so there was no looking back.

The overriding factor that made this the case, however, was that I had told my dad of my plans just a week before his accident. I had been worrying about telling him for what felt like a lifetime; concerned about how he would react to the news of such a drastic move. I headed up to Cambridge after that meeting at Stansted and, as we sat in his garden that afternoon, oblivious to the fact that this would be the final time we would ever be in each other's company, he asked me what seemed like an endless stream of questions (as was his way). Having done my research well and being reasonably up to speed on the minutiae of what I was planning to do, I managed to bat away all his enquiries with confidence and aplomb.

Although he didn't say so on the day, I must have left him with some sense that I knew what I was doing as I heard at his wake – just a couple of short weeks later – from others that he had been impressed with me and my planning, and that he was very proud of what I was undertaking. Hearing that alone was enough to persuade me to proceed with my plans.

It would be wrong to suggest that the first year at the College of Law was anything but sheer hard work. Not only had I not studied for seven years and was now spending days very much feeling the fish out of water in a room with fifty bright young things, all fresh out of university, but I was also dealing with my dad's death and the various issues that his passing continued to throw at me.

Just six weeks after the accident, Aisling and I had our first wedding anniversary. Given everything we had just been through, we felt that we could use a short time away and decided to head back to Ireland to spend the weekend at Castle Leslie. Our intentions were good and we thought that it would be nice to 'return to scene of the crime' as we would jokingly put it. But our return to the place where we had enjoyed such a lovely time was tinged with sadness and was difficult to say the least. Where once the hallowed halls and reception rooms had been filled with love and laughter, they now seemed empty, soulless, and cold. Being back there on our own was very different and, with everything that we had just gone through, we found it hard to relax or enjoy ourselves.

As the months following the accident passed and 2001 became 2002, I knuckled down to some serious work at law school. The first year was spent studying for a qualification known in those days as the 'Postgraduate Diploma in Law' (PgDL), which was ostensibly the basics of a three-year Law degree crammed into just ten months of rapid-fire learning.

I found the frenetic pace hard to keep up with at times but muddled through as best as I could. My new routine was made up of mornings spent in lectures and tutorial sessions, followed by afternoons of follow-up work and whittling down the seemingly bottomless recommended reading lists for each of the nine modules I was studying. I hadn't worked this hard in years and just keeping up and making legible notes during lectures was a challenge.

After a year or so, the AAIB published their official report into my dad's accident. Having removed the aircraft wreckage from the scene and taken it to their facility in Farnborough in Hampshire, they could confidently state that the aircraft had come down due to mechanical failure of the engine, which they believed had been caused by a sudden and total loss of oil from the engine itself. Whilst their summations remained inconclusive as to the reasons for the loss of oil, the findings from their strip-down of the engine in the workshop had led them to make such a statement.

They also were of the belief that, as my dad had been attempting to land on the disused runway, the aircraft had stalled due to loss of airspeed. With the type of aircraft involved, once it suffers a stall there is a tendency for one of the wings to 'drop' suddenly and for the aircraft to enter a steep nose-down attitude. This is what the AAIB believe happened to my dad's plane, given the nature of the damage plus various marks found on the ground surrounding the wreckage.

At the inquest many months after the accident itself, the Coroner at Lowestoft Coroner's Court delivered the rather predictable ruling of 'Accidental Death'. With the court's duties discharged, the hearing had fulfilled its bureaucratic obligations to the letter, and we were sent on our way. Except that I wanted more; I needed someone to blame, someone to be held accountable for what had happened. It was not enough for me to simply be told that it was a terrible accident and that no-one was to blame. Surely, someone or something had to be the root cause of all we had been through?

With these feelings burning away slowly inside me, I took it upon myself to delve a little deeper. With the little knowledge of light aircraft performance and engines that I had acquired during my own PPL and subsequent flying, I knew that engines didn't just fail as if by magic or because the dark arts were at play. There had to be more to what had been revealed, and I saw it as something of a personal crusade, as well as the right thing to do for my dad, to investigate the matter a bit deeper.

Following the inquest, the AAIB investigator had invited Aisling and I to go down to Farnborough to talk through their investigation and to revisit the wreckage of the aircraft. I decided that this was an offer I really should accept. So, a few weeks following the inquest, Aisling and I – along with a senior aeronautical engineer who Aisling knew well and who we had invited along for some expert guidance – were sat in a conference room of the AAIB going over the evidence.

It was apparent to the lead investigator that the engine had seized due to a lack of oil within the cylinders, but they could not explain why the oil had exited the aircraft in the first place. There was evidence of metal fatigue or failure in parts of the cylinders, but this was inconclusive as to explaining why the oil had escaped so abruptly and spontaneously. We looked at photos the AAIB took, both at the accident site and of the wreckage, and looked at maps and other documents. We were then invited to head down to the hangar to see the wreckage.

This was a part of the day I had mixed feelings about; I wasn't sure whether seeing the remains of the plane in which my dad had lost his life would help my recovery process or if it would set it back once more. Having given this a great deal of thought, I had decided that I would see how I felt on the day.

As it was, there was no way that I was going to turn down the opportunity to see my dad's aircraft again and so, as a group, we entered a large brown hangar-like building with a small door at one end. Upon entering it, I was struck by how immense it was inside. Like some ghoulish aircraft museum, across the expansive floor space of the building in the gloom were parts of aeroplanes and helicopters, some largely intact and some barely recognisable as flying machines at all, laid out and segregated from each other by fluorescent ropes.

In amongst all this detritus were aircraft I recognised from recent accidents that had been in the news. There was a turboprop aircraft in British Airways colours that had come down in the Firth of Forth whilst on a night mail flight in poor weather. And there was the haunting sight of the burnt-out carcass of an executive jet that had overturned on take-off from Birmingham Airport a few months earlier, killing all five of the occupants inside. There was a palpable smell of burning in the air, too, despite the hangar being a draughty, open building; the acrid stench of death still lingering ominously in the air.

On the very far side of the building was the unmistakeable sight of the forward fuselage of the Pan American Airways (Pan Am) Boeing 747 (named 'Clipper Maid of the Seas') that had exploded over Lockerbie in 1986. Shuffling past it, I lost my spatial awareness for a second and bumped my head against a sharp protrusion of metal extending from the side of the fuselage. As I stepped back and looked up, this jagged slither of fuselage was peeled back like the lid on a tin of baked beans and turned out to be a piece of the aluminium skin surrounding the star-shaped blast hole where the bomb that had destroyed the aircraft mid-flight had detonated. Not only was this one of the most recognisable and notorious aircraft in the world, I had now just gashed my head against it.

Laid out in front of this infamous hulk of white and blue metal was my dad's aircraft. With the wings removed and its back broken, it looked more like a grotesque model than a real aircraft. Yet there it was, sitting forlornly in amongst other aircraft that had met equally tragic fates, waiting for the AAIB to complete their work before being sent off to be broken up unceremoniously at some scrap yard.

We looked closely at the engine parts that had been removed, but they offered little in the way of further explanation. Our engineer friend took some photos of his own and scribbled some notes in a notebook he had brought with him but kept his thoughts largely to himself for the time being; it was not until we spoke again a few days later that he divulged there was a particular part he was keen to investigate further but that he would not be able to until the AAIB had completed their work and the wreckage had been released back to the insurance company. We would then have to apply to have the part sent to us for further analysis.

His line of thinking was that the aircraft (which my dad rented from a syndicate group of owners) had undergone its major annual check some weeks before the accident and that the fatigue in the part that failed should have been evident at the time of inspection – had it been performed properly. This was speculation, of course, but was the glimmer of hope I needed to embark on finding a culprit for all this mess and to hold someone accountable.

Armed with this evidence, there was extra wind in my investigative sail and I set about laying the groundwork for when we may eventually take possession of the suspect part. I rang the company that manufactured the engine to enquire about the part that failed and whether they had any data pertaining to how many times it had failed inflight. I eventually got through to a nice chap who said he would investigate and call me back at the same time the following day.

True to his word, we did speak the following day but, untrue to his word, he had not carried out any investigating at all. What he had done was speak with his boss. In turn, his boss had spoken with this very large American company's very large legal department, who had told them – in no uncertain terms – not to have any further contact with me.

As my surprisingly helpful contact from the previous day pulled down the virtual shutters and turned off the lights, I was told that the company could not assist me any further but wished me well. Thus ended my all-too-brief relationship with the engine manufacturer, and my harsh introduction to the world of dealing with large litigation-averse corporations was complete.

Notwithstanding this early blow to my crusade for justice, I endeavoured to plough on. I made contact with the organisation that looked after the aircraft at its Cambridge Airport base who, by way of some sly questioning on my part, divulged who had been subcontracted out to overhaul the engine a few months before the accident. The subcontractors should (in my mind) have spotted the metal fatigue in this key part that appeared to have failed, so I now had my target and was resolute in making them accountable for what had happened.

I sought some advice as to how best to proceed and was told that the first thing to do was to get the offending part – or parts – analysed by a metallurgist. This would have to be someone who had access to specialist equipment and who could effectively x-ray the parts and provide an expert legal report that could be used in any litigation that may follow. After some further research, I was put in touch with such a person who, "Would be happy to help," and I was all set. At least, right up until the point this person advised that I would receive little change from ten thousand pounds for his work and that if further investigations were required (depending on what the x-ray showed) I could be looking at double that.

With that, my hopes of finding someone to hold accountable for my dad's accident were dashed. I did not have this kind of money and had no means of finding it any time soon. Whilst I didn't entirely give up on the idea of bringing legal action against the engine overhaul company, I simply didn't have the means to do so at the time. With the little legal knowledge I had acquired from my course by this stage, I knew that I had six years from the date of the overhaul in which to bring a claim. So, whilst financial constraints had forced me to park my crusade for the time being, I always intended to revisit it at some point in the future.

It would be fair to say that I have never got over the events surrounding my dad's death and I continue to struggle with an immense feeling of guilt over the whole matter. I try to convince myself that there was nothing I could have done to alter the events of that day, but such attempts are always overshadowed by thoughts of '*What if I hadn't suggested doing my pilots licence?*' back in 1996 or '*What if I had insisted to my dad that I wanted to do it alone?*'.

I will always feel an element of responsibility for what happened as it was ultimately me who started the chain of events that led to my dad flying what turned out to be a defective and unserviceable aircraft over Suffolk that afternoon. But I was not in the cockpit with him that day, nor did I ever train him on what to do in an emergency. He knew this for himself without any input from me. I always try to tell myself such thoughts are as futile as they are misconceived. Yet this never makes the events of that August morning back in 2001 any easier to live with.

I sometimes feel like I want to be angry. Of course, I was angry with the maintenance company and the owners of the aircraft for not ensuring it was safe to fly. But, just occasionally, I want to be angry with my dad too. I ask myself why he didn't put the aircraft down in the pea field or why he was so fixated on trying to position his stricken aircraft correctly to land at the disused airfield, potentially wasting valuable height and airspeed in the process, rather than picking any old field to land in? After all, the landscape in that area is ALL fields. But mulling over such questions brings no answers and provides little in the way of resolution.

There is an adage I have heard in aviation circles which says, "If your engine dies, the aircraft instantly becomes the property of the insurance company. Your sole job is to survive the forced landing." I don't know whether my dad heard anyone say this during the time that he had his PPL, but I wish with every breath in my body that he had.

Nonetheless, and despite how I felt and continue to feel so many years later, there is nothing I can do to bring him back. I miss him every day. I miss having him at the end of the phone to talk to and to seek advice from, and would have given anything to have had his guidance and no-nonsense approach through the obstacles I have faced in my life since I last saw him.

TWENTY-NINE
SPIRALLING

Throughout the events of 2001 and into 2002, it would be fair to say that CF was not my priority. I let stress get the better of me, was not eating or sleeping as well as I needed to, and probably even missed the odd medicine-taking and physio sessions here and there. Law school was pushing me hard and, with the shadow of Dad's accident still casting large over me, things started to slip health-wise. Eventually, I had little energy left to arrest that slide.

My dad's accident and the subsequent events were not the sole cause of the drastic decline in my health that was to follow, but it certainly proved to be the oxygen between the lit match and the puddle of petrol that was already sitting dormant within my body.

By the middle of 2002, I had lost a good deal of weight and my lung function was most definitely on a downward trend at each clinic appointment. Dr Bilton voiced her concerns and I vowed to eat more and exercise more, but these promises came and went with me falling back into bad habits as soon as anyone's back was turned. I experienced my first in-patient stays at Papworth in that time too, starting my long career of spending time within the confines of a hospital room – something I had always vowed I would never succumb to when I was younger (and possibly more foolish).

It wasn't until I started to wake up in the night drenched in sweat that it became clear there was something more going wrong than anyone had initially realised. What started with unexplained weight loss, steady but slow loss of lung function, and night sweats slowly progressed into spontaneous fevers during the day and bouts of 'the shakes' for no fathomable reason. I was popping paracetamol like sweets with worrying regularity to control my body temperature, but these relentless fevers became regular occurrences. Dr Bilton was by now seriously concerned. After some tests at Papworth, I was put on several different courses of IV antibiotics to try to get on top of whatever was going on but all had little or no effect.

By the autumn of 2002, I was also treated for a fungal infection known as aspergillus. Many CF patients will have come across this infection during their lifetime as it is prevalent in the environment in which we live. It thrives in bricks which are used to build new houses and, having moved into a newly built brick house some twelve months previously, this was thought to be the possible culprit for my rapid decline.

Dr Bilton tried different ways to get on top of what was going on, and I was in and out of Papworth on a regular basis, disrupting my studies and piling even more extra pressure on Aisling and I after what had been a very difficult few months. Towards the end of 2002, I had lost about twenty-five percent of my body weight. I could never have been described as 'well-built', but my clothes were now hanging off me and my lungs felt terrible. On the rating system that Aisling and I had initiated early on in our relationship, most days I was a 'one', with little prospect of reaching more than a 'two' any time soon.

It was at this point that mutterings of possible causes and the dreaded word 'transplant' started to be used in conversations at Papworth. But until anyone was sure what was going on and had a positive diagnosis of what was causing my speedy decline, there was a palpable reluctance amongst the doctors to do anything drastic that might cause further problems. By the end of 2002, I looked extremely ill and felt truly awful. I was attending Papworth as an inpatient with alarming frequency but little of what was being done was having any effect.

It really began to feel that I might be in trouble unless someone did something quickly. It had certainly been a difficult year and I had been stressed and tired for most of it, but I felt that there must be something else at work; something that neither I nor the medical team at Papworth had seen before.

I was scared and didn't know what to do. It felt like everyone we relied on was sitting us down and saying, "Don't panic," to our faces whilst behind the scenes they were flicking through every medical journal and textbook ever published, trying to find the answer to all of my issues which, by this stage, were piling up fast.

Everything came to a head during the night of 29th December 2002. Aisling and I had tried to enjoy a quiet Christmas at home and had invited our friend Steve over to spend the day with us. I was next due to visit Papworth sometime early in the new year but awoke in the early hours of that morning soaked in sweat and with a body temperature of 40.2 degrees. Shivering and shaking from head to toe, I felt exhausted and weak and, probably for the first time in my life, was ready to throw in the towel.

Aisling woke up and found me in this appalling state, and we talked about what we should do. I say 'talked' but this was one of the shortest conversations we had ever had; I simply looked at Aisling, noted the look of fear in her face, and said, "I think we need to go to Papworth – right now."

THIRTY

WHEN CF TRIED TO KILL ME

We drove through the night, arriving at Papworth sometime around four a.m. The hospital was quiet and dark, and the wards empty. Traditionally, the staff at Papworth worked hard in the lead up to Christmas to get as many inpatients as possible home for the holidays. Indeed, in those days, the CF Unit would shut down entirely over Christmas to make deployment of the reduced numbers of staff easier (and to save the hospital money by not having to heat and power a whole ward for just one, maybe two patients). Any CF patients still left would be transferred on to one of the general chest wards for the duration of the festive period until the CF Unit reopened after New Year.

We arrived on the Chest Medical Unit and I sat in a small waiting area adjacent to the lift while Aisling went off in search of nursing staff. At this point I was still shaking uncontrollably, was clammy to the touch, and just wanted to sleep, although I was scared to close my eyes in case I didn't ever reopen them.

A nurse came over and, upon seeing the state I was in, rushed off to bleep the on-call doctor. Soon, a junior doctor appeared and ran through the usual checks in order to assess my condition. My temperature was 40.8 degrees and was so high that the doctor sent for another digital thermometer in case the one he had was reading inaccurately. The alternative thermometer concurred with the first and the doctor listened to my chest through his stethoscope. By this stage, his initial jovial manner and polite conversation (despite having just been woken up) had vanished and he was now in full 'down to business' mode. As a few minutes passed by, he developed a rather poorly disguised level of concern and ordered the nurse to prepare a room for me on the ward while he went off to call his boss (Dr Bilton). I was taken along the corridor and shown, rather ominously, into Room Thirteen. I was told by the nurse to get undressed immediately because if my temperature rose any further, I would be at possible risk of cardiac arrest.

Room Thirteen was in the old part of the original hospital building with floor to ceiling glass doors on the external wall that looked out over the hospital grounds. As I removed my clothes, soaked from the perspiration I expelled during the car journey, the nurse flung open the glass doors, filling the room with icy cold air. Within a few minutes, I had a cannula in my arm and was given an injection of paracetamol in order to reduce my temperature as soon as possible. I was then hooked up to a litre bottle of IV saline fluid to try to get my body rehydrated.

Just half an hour after pulling up at the door, I was being cared for by numerous members of staff and the once-quiet ward was a bustle of activity. I tried to relax, Aisling reminding me that I was now in safe hands and was being looked after by people who knew what they were doing. I would probably have panicked if I'd had the energy but I was prostrate and weak, and my ability to reach anything resembling a state of panic had long since deserted me.

Over the following couple of hours, my temperature settled back a bit and, although it was high enough to continue causing concern, it had reduced to a slightly less dangerous level. By eight a.m., the day staff were drifting on to the ward to commence their shift and the hospital was once more waking from its sleep and springing into life, something which could certainly not be said about me.

I was offered breakfast but declined; I couldn't settle and the last thing I felt like doing was eating. The CF Registrar came to see me and stayed a while, asking questions and gathering information in preparation for when Dr Bilton would arrive on the ward shortly afterwards.

Before too long, Dr Bilton was in the room with Aisling and I and was already planning the counter-strike against whatever it was that was attacking me. It was soon apparent that this was possibly something even she hadn't seen before. Words like 'pneumonia' and 'pleurisy' were starting to be thrown around but without further testing, the medical team would be unable to make a positive diagnosis or formulate a structured care plan for me.

I took a great deal of comfort from simply being at Papworth and in the safe hands of the CF team. Yet I couldn't help but feel uneasy about the fact that the doctors didn't seem to know what was going on and that they were reluctant to start treating whatever it was that was doing this to me.

That first morning was taken up with blood tests, a chest x-ray, and a chest CT scan. Swabs were taken of my mouth and nose, samples of urine and sputum were sent off for urgent analysis by the laboratory, and some of my usual IV antibiotics were started.

Little did I know, upon admission that morning, that I would be hospitalised for many more days and that I would visit some dark places along the way; my illness upon admission represented just a snapshot of how I would feel as it progressed, and I had no idea how close I was about to come to losing my life.

Looking back now, so many years later, had I known what was in store for me during that admission, I may have given up there and then. Ironically, though, I remained in a state of ignorance. And being in this state saw me through those early few days on the ward.

New Year came and went, with New Year's Eve spent in Room Thirteen on the Chest Medical Unit with just a skeleton staff. It was the most miserable way to see in the new year, being hospitalised and with very little to celebrate or to look forward to. I felt so despondent, my prospects looked bleak, and 2003 was not looking like it would be the best of years. My usually optimistic attitude to life had deserted me and there were no 'Happy New Year' wishes exchanged that night.

Over the course of the first week, I underwent round-the-clock IV antibiotics and endless rounds of hourly observations where nursing staff came to check my temperature, blood pressure, and oxygen saturation levels. Things remained unstable and there was no sign of any improvement. Every other day, blood was taken for further lab tests, and one marker that would become a staple of the next few weeks was the CRP test. CRP stands for C-Reactive Protein and is a widely used quantitative measure of an acute-phase protein that rises in the blood whenever infection is present. CRP is used by clinicians to indicate the presence and intensity of inflammation in the body, normally – although not exclusively – caused by infection. The average person will have a CRP of less than ten. In those first few days on the ward, my CRP was somewhere north of four hundred and was proving resilient to the antibiotics that were being pumped into me.

After a week or so, and with little progress to show, the medical team decided to alter my regimen of IV antibiotics and give a revised combination a try. I was now in relatively uncharted territory, using antibiotics that I had not been prescribed before. With all such drugs come side-effects, and these side effects were wreaking havoc on my body. A constant sense of nausea prevailed over me and I was unable to keep any food, drink, or even water down. My temperature swings continued, with some drugs causing worse fluctuations than others. The most acute episodes would see my temperature soar and me, once again, start shivering uncontrollably (known as a temperature 'rigor') as I would feel impossibly cold. I was in a bad way.

I felt truly awful and far worse than I had ever experienced before. Doctors were monitoring me and my condition several times a day but the situation felt like it was spiralling downwards, and like I was being dragged down with it.

As the second week began, the veins in my arms, in which the IV cannulas were inserted, started to give up, simply through the sheer usage they were seeing. A more permanent solution was needed, and quickly. So, I had an IV line inserted into the main vein in my neck under sedation. As the veins in this area of the body are wider than those in the arms, they are generally able to withstand further and more intensive use.

A further concern for the medical team was that I was neither eating or drinking and my already-low weight was plummeting rapidly. After a discussion with the doctors, I very reluctantly agreed to have a feeding tube inserted through my abdomen straight into my stomach. This device, known as a PEG (or sometimes a 'button') would allow a high-calorie and highly nutritional liquid feed to be pumped directly into my stomach, thus avoiding the risk that anything I ate would be thrown straight back up.

I hated the idea of a PEG, as well as the need to go through a surgical procedure in theatre for the first time in my life to have it inserted. I also knew, however, that I had little choice but to go along with it; if I was to stand any chance of fighting this mystery infection, I needed to start putting on some weight and quickly.

With the IV line in my neck and the PEG inserted into my stomach, it felt like the fight back had commenced. My CRP was still sky-high and the temperature rigors were unrelenting, but I felt that I was slightly better equipped to deal with what the doctors wanted to throw at me. I was warned, though, that there would be no quick fix; the situation was grave and everyone, including me, knew it.

Whilst I knew I had to fight back, it was taking every ounce of energy I had just to survive. But I didn't let myself believe that fighting was futile, however much it felt like it was; as long as I could stay alive and put up with the unrelenting treatments, there was a chance for me to get through this. I decided very early on that, however grim things appeared, I owed it to Aisling and the team treating me to keep going. I also owed it to myself.

A small part of me knew that this might be the end, but as long as someone – anyone – had a glimmer of hope that I would survive, then I would hold on to that hope vicariously. After all, I had nothing else to hang on to.

Throughout all of this, Aisling stayed with me, sleeping on a fold out mattress on the floor of my room. Her being there offered a reassuring and comforting presence, whilst everything else appeared to be falling apart.

Very early on in January 2003, the staff who had been off over the holidays started to return to work. One of the first to come back was the Sister of the CF Unit that had been closed for Christmas. As soon as she got wind of me and my condition, she unilaterally took the decision to reopen the Unit immediately and for me to have one-to-one care straight away. With this decision made, the heating was restored to the CF Unit that morning and, by the evening, I was being moved along the corridor to Room Four.

Room Four was located right opposite the nurses' station and I was deliberately allocated that room in order to be near to the nursing staff at all times (in case my condition deteriorated rapidly). I realised this, and I was also very grateful to be back in the familiar surroundings of the CF Unit with people who knew me and who I trusted. I felt that if I was to survive and recover, then this was the right place for me to be.

For the first time in a couple of weeks, I started to feel ever so slightly more relaxed about what was happening to me, although I also knew that there was an awful long way to go yet. I was told that this would now be my home for however long I was to be hospitalised and that I was not allowed to enter or leave the room until they had a better understanding of what was happening to me. In particular, they needed to know whether I was a risk to other patients, or even to the staff.

After a few weeks of neck lines being changed weekly, the decision was taken that I needed a portacath inserted into my chest. A portacath is a small chamber made from titanium that sits just under the skin. It has a silicon dome on the top of it and an IV line that flows into a large vein close to the heart. In patients who require regular injections or IV medications (such as those with CF or various types of cancer), portacaths are a far more practical way of administering drugs; they are more resilient and are built to withstand more regular usage than the veins in someone's arm.

Although ports can become infected, blocked, or can simply stop working, they are commonly used. So again, however much I hated the idea, I agreed to the procedure because I knew it would make things slightly easier and that at least I would no longer need the neck line.

Over the following weeks, my intensive antibiotic treatment continued and I entered a frustrating cycle of reactions followed by a failure to respond to whatever drug was being tested. My doctors were keen to alternate the drugs around so that my infection would not become immune to any one combination. But after a few days of a new drug, and a small drop in my CRP, the rigors would start once more, and the CRP would creep back up. There was nothing during those early weeks that offered anything in the way of comfort or hope that we were getting on top of the infection, and my blood tests supported that. However, I knew that if I lost hope, even for one second, then I might as well have just given up and prepared to die. So, I hung on.

I wasn't ready to die. I was thirty years of age, had only been married for a couple of years, and felt that I had so much to live for. So, despite the gruelling treatment, the intense fatigue from not sleeping, and the ever-present nausea, sweats and shakes, I told myself that it would not always be like this; things would improve eventually and I would make it back home one day.

After the fourth week, however, it would be fair to say that I was struggling to keep hoping that things would resolve themselves and that I would survive this, whatever 'this' was. By this time, my medical team had ruled out all the 'usual' types of chest infections that affect those with CF, as well as many of the less common ones too. Tuberculosis, influenza, pneumonia, and pleurisy had all been equally discounted, leaving the doctors perplexed as to what the infection might be.

As the ideas started to dry up, Dr Bilton began to seek guidance from other CF centres, initially around the UK and Europe and then worldwide, casting her net as wide as possible in order to try and establish whether any of her colleagues had seen a patient with the same symptoms.

Aisling and I discussed my state endlessly and began to get disheartened. We were concerned that the people we were relying on to find the answer were struggling to do so, and that they seemed to be running out of options. We said this to Dr Bilton late one evening, and she suggested that we might go and visit a professor of CF who she knew from her previous hospital in Manchester.

After a couple of days of deliberating, and feeling as though we had little other option, Aisling and I decided to go and seek a second opinion – one that might at least provide us with hope that I might recover at some stage.

The necessary arrangements were made and, within a few days, Aisling and I were in our car heading up the M6 motorway to Wythenshawe Hospital on the south side of Manchester. Aisling opted to drive us rather than for us to travel by ambulance; we were on a private mission, seeking an additional medical opinion, so to use an ambulance for the day, and for the NHS to incur the cost, seemed frivolous even in my precarious state.

As soon as we arrived in Manchester, I was admitted on to the CF Unit at Wythenshawe Hospital and the next round of IVs were set up and pumped into me. After some further tests, and meeting some of the CF staff, we were shown into the professor's office for our consultation. Going in with high hopes was probably a mistake but, given the state of me, it was also unavoidable. The professor sat and listened as we discussed my history, my current condition, and my fears about what was going to happen next. We explained that we were struggling to remain positive as it had already been several weeks with no sign of an improvement, and that we were beginning to fear the worst.

After an intense session of me pouring my heart out, it was finally the professor's turn to speak.

He explained that the symptoms I was displaying had not been seen in the CF community before (certainly in the UK) and that the team at Papworth, along with others around the country, were perplexed by the resilience of the infection against the onslaught of antibiotics I was being prescribed. He told us that he could not really offer anything further in terms of suggested treatments, and that Dr Bilton was doing all she could to save me. He explained that there would be no quick fix and that I should have patience.

Neither of these were things that we had come to hear, but it was now obvious that there would be no magic potion to save me.

We left Manchester that afternoon, tired and dejected. We had harboured so much hope (somewhat misguidedly) that this trip would open the door to a miracle that would revive the possibility of my being okay. But we left with disappointment in our hearts and facing the very long drive back to Papworth and an even longer road that might lead to any sort of recovery.

THIRTY-ONE

DARKEST HOURS

It was probably around six weeks before my CRP came under a level that anyone could be 'happy' with or before any real improvement in my condition was observed. Aisling continued to sleep on the floor in my room. The days passed by, the daily routine becoming increasingly monotonous. Bloods were taken first thing and sent off to the lab, and the day would then be spent hooked up to my IV pump with regular doses of paracetamol administered to try and keep my temperature under control. The rigors were so vicious during those few weeks that no one seemed to know whether it was the infection causing them, a reaction to the incredibly toxic antibiotics being used to treat the infection, or a combination of both.

The drugs being administered continued to be switched around every week or so, with doses tweaked in attempts to improve their effectiveness. I was also hooked up to another pump for eight hours in the evening to administer the enteral feed into my stomach, and physiotherapists visited twice, sometimes three times, a day to try to get my lungs cleared and to get them working harder.

Any person without CF would find this daily pattern arduous, and I wrestled with it constantly. I found it virtually impossible to keep up with; not only was it physically hard but the monotony of it was mentally draining.

Noting my struggles with the whole situation, the ward staff summoned the assistance of the hospital's clinical psychologist to come and spend some time with me. I had nothing to lose by speaking to this person and, although I was put off by the stigma that seeing a psychologist might bring, I reluctantly agreed. After all, how was I in any sort of position to contest?

It would not be an understatement to say that my one and only session with the psychologist did not go well. This lady, with her awkward demeanour, seemed fixated on the fact that I was likely to die and that, while I waited to do so, I might consider taking up a hobby like crochet or watercolour painting to pass my final hours and days on the planet. After an hour (that felt like a lifetime) in which I just got more and more angry, firstly with this woman and secondly with my whole situation, she left the room with a strangely upbeat spring in her step as if to say, "My work here is done." On coming back into the room and noting just how angry and upset I was, Aisling quickly informed the ward staff that I wasn't to be visited by the psychologist again. Things were hard enough, without her 'help'.

After about seven weeks came the first sign that there might be an alteration in my direction of travel. The doctors were so concerned that my immune system was not fighting the infection (whatever it was) in the way that they expected that they began to consider why that might be.

The conclusion they came to was that perhaps my immune system was *unable* to fight the infection due to being compromised in some way. Dr Bilton's desperate fishing expedition had thrown up that some HIV patients in the USA had displayed similar symptoms because their damaged immune systems were unable to fight infection. Consequently, it was put to me one afternoon that I may have somehow contracted HIV and that I needed to consent to an immediate blood test.

After some counselling from one of the nurses, I agreed to the test and the blood was taken on a Friday morning. In those days the test results took three days to come back, so Aisling and I spent the weekend locked away in my room, desperately trying to talk and think about something other than my HIV result.

It was one of the most difficult times in my life and that Saturday and Sunday dragged horrendously. Nurses came and went but the CF Unit was relatively quiet and we were left largely to ourselves. We shed a lot of tears that weekend and barely slept. We tried to tell ourselves that at least if it was HIV it would explain an awful lot and an appropriate treatment plan could be put in place. But it remained incredibly difficult to focus on the potential positives of the situation.

2003 was still very early days in terms of treatments for HIV, with effective and licensed antiretroviral medicines still in their infancy. Whilst hoping for a negative result, we couldn't help but worry about what a positive result might bring. By the time Monday finally came, my nerves were ripping me apart and my stomach was in knots.

Waiting for your A-level results, doing your driving test, and playing the drums in front of two thousand people, even if all three were to happen on the same day, would have nothing on the way I felt that morning.

On Monday afternoon, there was a knock at the door of the room and the CF registrar entered. She entered and pulled up a chair. As she opened my ward notes, I struggled for breath and my heart raced; in the next few seconds my life may change for ever.

"It's come back as negative" the registrar said with an expressionless face. "You don't have HIV." In a pure release of stress and emotion, both Aisling and I failed to hold back our tears. We hugged; after weeks of little progress laced with bad news, this was the first glimmer of hope that we had to cling to. The result did not tell us what was wrong with me, nor did it provide a solution. We were no further forward in real terms, but at least we were no further backwards either.

Over the following couple of weeks, nothing really changed. My raging temperatures continued, and the nursing staff could regularly be found rubbing ice cold flannels over my body to try to reduce my temperature. On more than one occasion, when the rigors hit, I was made to stand out in the snow (yes, snow) on the balcony outside my room in order to achieve a similar result. Believe me, if I was shivering before I went out onto the balcony, I was trembling from head to toe by the time I was allowed back inside again. Although this method did reduce my temperature, it did nothing in terms of preventing me catching a head cold. The lesser of the two evils, though, at that point, I suppose.

Two events during would prove to be milestones during my time at Papworth. On 1st February 2003, in the late afternoon, I had turned on the small television in my room to try to distract myself from the nausea and tremors I had been experiencing all that morning. I became aware very quickly that something big was happening because the BBC were showing a newsflash of something terrible occurring over in the United States.

The NASA space shuttle *Columbia*, the very one I had seen launch with my dad back in February 1996 in Florida, as well as the one I had seen launch on the television back at school in 1981, had been due to land back at the Kennedy Space Centre that afternoon. But as the pictures being looped on the television screen showed repeatedly, it looked very much like the shuttle – as it descended over Texas at six times the speed of sound –had disintegrated. Multiple streams of white smoke and flashes appeared on the screen. This was *Columbia*'s 28th mission (the one I had watched launch in 1996 was its 19th) and it had seemingly ended in disaster, with the loss of both the shuttle and its entire crew of eight. Whether it was through sheer tiredness, the side effects of all the medication I was taking, or simply feeling emotionally drained anyway, what happened to *Columbia* upset me greatly. The loss of 'my' shuttle, the one I had got such a thrill from watching both as a small boy on television and 'in person' as an adult, felt devastating.

Witnessing *Columbia*'s launch back in 1996 had come at the end of a very special time for my dad and I, and this terrible accident brought all of those happy memories flooding back, just when I was at my most vulnerable. I missed him so much and needed his support and guidance more than ever.

A little bit of something inside me died that afternoon as I watched, in silent disbelief, the horrific scenes unfolding over the clear blue skies of Texas.

The second event that left a scar on my memory was when I felt that all was lost and came very close to giving up. Aisling had been dashing back to our home in Surrey to check on the house for the odd day here and there and to touch base with her work, who were continuing to pay her in her absence. Therefore, I had been spending a bit more time on my own. On this day, our friend Steve had come up from his home in Epsom to spend the morning with me.

I found his visit hard. I struggled to hold a conversation through my shortness of breath and fought to stay awake for much of the time. I felt jealous hearing about Steve's antics out in the 'real world' whilst I had been confined to four walls, away from home and from everything I had enjoyed for so long. After just about managing to keep going for a bit, I told Steve that I really didn't feel well and that perhaps it was time for him to leave so that I could rest. I felt guilty asking him to go, knowing that he had spent a couple of hours driving up to see me and faced the same journey back home, but I was in no fit state to continue conversing with him. Steve was kind and polite, as he always was, and accepted with grace that it was time for him to leave. As he departed, he told me to, "Hang in there," and that he would be back to visit again very soon. I asked him to look after Aisling for me and to make sure that she was okay, and he confirmed that he would. On his way out, I asked Steve if he would get one of the nurses to pop in and check on me as I was highly agitated and shaking like a leaf through yet another soaring temperature.

The nurse swiftly came, pushed some IV paracetamol through my portacath, and suggested I settle down, turn the lights off, and try to rest. She was visibly worried about me, though, and scuttled off (unknown to me) to call Aisling and ask her to return to Papworth as soon as possible. As Steve headed back to his life, his job, and his home – far away from Papworth – my heart sank. I was in a state of utter despair; I was losing the fight and I had little energy or desire left to continue the struggle.

Looking back, knowing that I even had those thoughts makes me feel terribly guilty. But, just for that short while, that one afternoon, I was overcome with a sense that all was lost, that what hope I had held on to for so long was gone, and that my demise was inevitable.

I put a song from one of my favourite bands on the CD player in the room and set it to repeat. I pulled the bedsheet up to cover my body, closed my eyes, and cried myself to sleep. Whilst I did not know whether I would wake up again or not, I had reached the stage where I no longer cared – I just wanted my nightmare to be over. The pain and the struggle had become too much. I needed it all to stop.

As my eyes closed, I took one last look around the room, shrouded by the gloom emitted by just the night light above my bed, and thought about everything and everyone that I loved and cared about.

I thought about Aisling and our wonderful wedding. I thought about the good times we had shared and wondered how it could have possibly all come to this. I considered the life we would have had, the places we might have gone to, and the children we may have had. I thought about my dad and wished that he was with me, making things better like he always seemed to when I was growing up.

Yet there were no more answers to be found, no solutions and no magic pills that would make this situation right anymore. I was certain it was the end of the line for me; I had reached rock bottom. It was my time to go. With my eyes closed and with my mind overflowing with despair, I drifted slowly off to sleep, giving in to the notion that I may not wake again.

A few hours later, I was stirred from my deep sleep by a noise in the room. I opened my eyes to see Aisling standing next to my bed. She had driven up from Epsom and had just arrived on the CF Unit. The overwhelming relief I felt, knowing that she was back with me and that I had actually woken up, was huge. We hugged and I held on to her like never before.

I had just been to the lowest place it is possible to go to and it had (almost) scared the life out of me. But I was still alive, still in that room, and still breathing – with everyone doing whatever they could to keep me that way.

I have always believed in fate – to a degree – and I suddenly realised that, because I had woken from that deep sleep, this was not the end; somehow, I would get better. Looking at Aisling, I knew I had to keep fighting and that I owed it to us both to do so.

This was a defining moment, a milestone for me to use in order to take a new direction and start fighting back. More than nothing else, the events of that day made me realise that, while I was still able to breathe, there was everything to live for. Hope was not lost, simply hard to find.

Whilst Aisling had been at home, she had been sitting up long into the night trawling the internet (still in its infancy and referred to back then as 'the worldwide web') for anything that might shed a light on what was going on. During her searches, she had come across an article in a medical journal written some months earlier. It related to a sample of CF patients in the United States, presenting with symptoms not dissimilar to mine, and how they were being treated. While we had no idea at this stage of the significance of this article, it was to prove the key to unlocking the door, not only to what was happening to me but to issues affecting many others with CF. That article would go on to impact the CF community *worldwide*, an impact that continues to be benefitted from even to this day.

The doctor who had written the article was based at one of the largest CF treatment centres in the United States, at a hospital in Denver, Colorado. They had seen an increasing amount of CF patients with the same bacteria growing in their lungs, causing symptoms such as high temperatures, weight loss, and chest tightness. These bacteria proved to be hard to treat with one, two, and even three IV antibiotics used in combination. In many of the cases, the team in Denver had started using up to four different antibiotics in series (one after the other) around the clock in order to get on top of the bacteria, which had now been classed as a 'non-tuberculosis mycobacterium' infection (or 'NTM')[1].

The article suggested the antibiotics that the bacteria had appeared to respond to and stated that the research results should be used if other CF patients around the world presented which symptoms that were proving resistant to more conventional drugs.

I didn't read the article when Aisling showed it to me. I understood from talking it through with her that it was largely full of medical jargon and that it was hard to understand whether its findings were relevant to me or not. But Aisling said that she would show it to Dr Bilton the following day to get a rather more expert opinion on its relevance to me and my situation.

With that, we left all thoughts of the article there. We had no idea, however, what would transpire over the coming days. Unknown to me, Aisling slipped the article under Dr Bilton's office door later that night in the hope that its contents would be digested by someone with far greater medical wherewithal than us. We didn't want to put too much importance on its contents for fear of our hopes being dashed. But we were also fearful not to, as there seemed to be no other answers to be had.

It would be a couple of days before we had any feedback on the article but when it came, it was if everything had suddenly changed. Dr Bilton had not only read it but had spoken to her counterpart in Denver, the author of the article itself. Between them, they had concurred – with cautious optimism – that I may well have contracted NTM as it would explain both my symptoms and my infection's resistance to all the antibiotics that had been used on me up until this point.

Not only had they concurred on a possible diagnosis, they had also formulated an action plan consisting of four different IV antibiotics, plus regular injections of a substance known as interferon gamma (IFG), three times a week. Interferons are found in the blood and make up key components of the body's immune system. If a patient is lacking in certain interferons, the body's immune system is compromised and therefore incapable of fighting infection.

Dr Bilton explained that the antibiotics they were going to give me were 'bottom-drawer' drugs, meaning they were not the usual 'go-to' antibiotics used to fight infection but more specialised drugs. They were rarely used in the combination that Denver used, but they had seen success with it when fighting NTM in CF patients. Within twenty-four hours, my whole medication regimen was changed and I was slowly introduced to the new drugs and the thrice weekly injections of IFG. With everybody's hopes resting on the experience of the doctors in Denver, my fight back against NTM commenced.

It was quite a few days before we saw any first glimmer of hope with my new treatment plan. Over the course of the next week or so, my temperature began to slowly settle and my CRP, which had been stuck in the hundreds for several weeks, started to head downwards. The drugs continued to make me feel sick and gave me excruciating headaches, and I still had the shakes on and off after they were administered, but these were merely side-effects and I was told that if I could put up with them, then time would soon tell whether we were heading down the right path.

It was easy to tell that everyone involved in my care had collectively crossed their fingers, toes, and everything else they had in the hope that things would turn around for me.[2] And over the next two weeks there was a clear improvement in my condition. My CRP continued to fall, I started to eat a bit more, sleep a bit more, and was more coherent and lucid during the times I was awake. The treatment schedule was relentless, however, and I remained confined to my room until a positive diagnosis was confirmed by the Pathology Department.

Lab tests eventually came back confirming that I was suffering from the same strain of NTM that had been seen in the patients in the United States. And there it was – I had just become the first CF patient in the UK to be diagnosed with an NTM-related lung infection. This revelation brought to a close weeks of being hospitalised with an undiagnosed condition and also a much longer period in which the NTM had been taking a firm hold of my wellbeing, slowly strangling it to within touching distance of its very limits.

Having a positive diagnosis seemed to give all the staff new hope. Although I was told to expect a long and difficult recovery period, likely to stretch into months rather than just weeks, the early signs indicated that I might have just turned a corner and be over the worst. Again, with very cautious optimism, Aisling and I allowed ourselves to start believing that I might recover and that we could start thinking about having a future together after all.

In just a couple of weeks, I had gone from being at death's door to having genuine hope and optimism that a viable treatment plan was underway. After eight weeks of uncertainty, doubts, and despair, the light at the end of the tunnel finally came into view. Although, with what Aisling and I had just been through, it was hard to believe that this was anything other than the next oncoming train hurtling towards us.

THIRTY-TWO

TURNING THE CORNER

Over the course of the next six weeks, things generally stayed on an upwards trajectory. A slight hiccup in my treatment was the development of tinnitus (ringing in the ears). I initially put this down to being tired but, after a few days of doing my best to ignore it, I eventually mentioned it to the medical team.

It turned out that tinnitus and partial hearing loss is a regular side-effect of one of the antibiotics I was being given and, unless things were changed, full hearing loss was the likely result. The doctors quickly decided to change this drug for another within the same family of antibiotics, hoping that their effect on the infection would be much the same. I still have tinnitus to this day, some nineteen years on, and it is unlikely to ever resolve itself. I was offered counselling so that I could deal with it, and even pain management classes so that it's effect could be mitigated but I declined to take up these offers. After what I had been through, a bit of ringing in the ears seemed to be a small price to pay for my life being saved, even if it did mean I would struggle to hear a conversation in a noisy environment for the rest of my life.

I quickly learned to put up with the ringing and only notice it these days if I stop to think about it or if someone asks me about it. Drugs can do so much good, but they also often come with a cost. Tinnitus was the permanent price I had to pay for surviving what had been the most scary and difficult period of my life. But I was happy to pay it, and would have paid a lot more to have this fresh chance that finally, after having suffered for so many weeks, had seemed attainable.

The next six weeks or so were very different from the first eight I spent at Papworth; I was allowed out of my room and was actively encouraged to go for regular walks around the hospital grounds. In a sentimental nod to the very reason why the hospital had been set up by Doctor Varrier-Jones back in its early days, the staff were keen for me to get as much fresh air and sunlight as possible, having been confined to Room Four since early January.

It was now early March 2003. The days were warming up, daffodils were in bloom, and the blossom was starting to appear on the trees. The long, dark winter started to fade into the background to be replaced by spring's sense of newness and optimism. With the arrival of spring, and with a renewed sense of hope, I too started to feel alive again.

As the weeks passed by, the doctors started to talk about plans for getting me home. The fact that we had been through such an ordeal together had rendered the medical team reluctant to just let me walk out and carry on with life as if nothing had happened. My discharge from Papworth was to be a staged process. It would start with a few hours off the ward here and there followed by weekend leave, when I would be released on a Friday to return to the hospital late on Sunday evening.

My intensive treatment regime would be scaled back slightly to allow me to administer my IV medications myself whilst at home and then ramped back up on my return to hospital. Initially, Aisling and I would venture off the ward and head out for lunch somewhere local or for a stroll around the streets of Cambridge. I initially found these trips difficult and would often be keen to cut them short and head back to Papworth early. After the events of the previous few weeks, being away from the place and having freedom was an unsettling experience, and one that I struggled with from the outset.

Similarly, the first couple of weekends at home were strange affairs. I was, of course, back in familiar surroundings and yet I had not been at home for about ten weeks by this point. It just felt odd, and the feeling I had the most trouble coming to terms with was that, for the time I was at home, there was no safety net. There was no red button to push, no one to call if I needed help, and no doctors or nurses to come running if something went wrong. Similarly, there was no structure to anything; I could just do as I pleased. I was freed from the routine of daily life in hospital. My days were no longer structured around the next mealtime, drugs round, or session with my physiotherapists. And I felt lost. In those past ten weeks, I had travelled so far from who I really was and I was tormented by how low I had sunk.

The time back on the wards during those later weeks became more manageable. Those were the days when the risk of cross-infection between CF patients was not fully understood, when they could mingle and socialise unfettered from the segregation that now sadly keeps the CF community apart and unable to meet in person.

To illustrate this, there was a patient's dedicated kitchen on the CF Unit containing a communal seating area. This area would double up as a de-facto social club for those on the ward at any given time, and offered a space outside of one's room to meet others and spend a while thinking or talking about anything else other than CF and how unwell it was making you feel.

Although it sounds utterly inconceivable to anyone I mention it to nowadays, there was also a pool table in the wider part of the corridor offering an alternative venue for CF patients to mingle, chatter, and (as it now turns out) to cross-infect each other. I spent many hours in these venues, allowing me just a short time away from the confines of my room and to meet others with CF.

During that time I made two very good friends (Sammie and Ross) with whom I remain close some seventeen years later. Sammie, back then in her early twenties and a young mother, has recently just turned forty and held a big party in order to celebrate the auspicious milestone she believed she would never see. Sammie keeps herself well and, thankfully, is a long way off having conversations about lung transplants just yet. Ross, on the other hand, had a double lung transplant several years ago, having undergone a liver transplant some years before that. Although Ross suffered from a range of complications following his lung transplant, he is now fighting fit, working full time, and enjoys international travel as much as he can. I formed a particularly strong bond with Ross and Sammie, and they remain two of my closest friends to this day.

Others I got to know during those few weeks have not been so fortunate and have succumbed to CF in the years since we met. During the time I was resident at Papworth, there were also some very sombre days when the awful news spread that one of our fellow CF patients had not made it through the night. On such days, a real sense of darkness descended over the ward and most of us would confine ourselves to our rooms, unable or unwilling to leave in case it showed an element of disrespect to the person who had died or to their family, who often continued to mill around the ward hours after the event itself, in a state of shock

Such days were few and far between but, when they did come along, they hit hard. The death of a fellow patient or friend was sad and terrifying in equal measure, reminding us all of what we were up against and reminding everyone else of what those with CF have to deal with on a daily basis.

During the long days of March 2003, when I was starting to recover and feel a little more like socialising with the other patients, I spent a lot of time with Ross. We had all-day pool matches, breaking only for lunch, IVs, naps, or physio sessions. Whether due to the high doses of medication we were on or the giddiness induced by weeks of incarceration, Ross and I were prone to lark about a bit.

We would make up games for our own entertainment and to while away the long, tedious hours. Such larks included trying to fire bungs off the end of syringes and out over our balconies, the owner of the furthest-fired bung being crowned the winner. We also held eating challenges to see who could drink the most hot chocolate in the space of five minutes or who could eat two, or more, ready meals the fastest. (Bear in mind that these were NHS ready meals and were not the most appetising food available – finishing one was hard enough, even when you weren't being timed.)

We decided, however, that our pranks had gone too far on the day we devised the '*Who can mix and administer their own IV antibiotics the quickest?*' challenge. Realising that rapid infusion of such nasty drugs could cause at best anaphylactic shock and at worst cardiac arrest, we reconsidered this challenge on the basis that we were supposed to be at Papworth to get better, not to make ourselves worse. (I won, by the way.)

One day, Ross also managed to persuade one of his visitors to smuggle on to the ward a bottle of Jack Daniels (his favourite tipple) plus some cans of coke, and we spent numerous evenings in each other's rooms, chatting and laughing while enjoying a little nightcap of this contraband, using the NHS's finest plastic beakers for glasses. Our regular get-togethers with our new best friend Jack certainly took the gloom off being in hospital and took my mind off what I had been through since the start of that year.

One night, one of the other patient's parents brought in a Karaoke machine and the whole ward spent a few happy hours crooning (badly) away to popular hits of the 80s and 90s in one of the spare day rooms on the ward that, for one night only, had been converted into a *de facto* CF social club (under a degree of resigned indignation from the nursing staff on duty that evening).

There is nothing quite like being in a room with a load of other people who, just like you, have CF to deal with daily and who just want to have a bit of fun and enjoy some escapism for a few hours. The evening certainly offered that, and the memories of that night – from my fellow patients shrieking out the chorus to Bon Jovi's hit 'Livin' on a Prayer' to the image of Ross swigging from a coke can laced with his smuggled-in Jack Daniels – have stayed with me for the past seventeen years.

In the room that night, some of us were more ill than others. Many who attended have since lost their lives to the cruelty of CF. Yet, congeniality and the ability to smile in the face of adversity is something I noted in all the attendees that evening, the memory of which has never left me. The laughs, joviality, and all-round good humour of the evening will always remind me that, no matter how bad things seem, there is usually a laugh or a smile to be found, somehow.

As March passed by, my lung function improved and my weight increased. I was far from 'back to normal' and still had a long way to go, with possibly months – if not years – of treatment ahead of me for the NTM infection. My doctors were not sure whether the NTM would just fade away altogether over time or if it would sit in the base of my lungs with the ever-present risk of it flaring up in the future. Too little was known about the behaviour of NTM bacteria at that time, and the approach that was to be taken was very much on a 'suck it and see' basis.

Towards the end of March, discussions were held and plans were made for me to be discharged at some point in the next two weeks or so, but only on the proviso that there were no other complications along the way. It was easy to tell that the medical staff were wrestling with their enthusiasm to get me home once and for all and their nervousness at doing so. Whilst they did not want me to be leaving the ward on a so-called 'hospital at home' basis (where I would spend my days carrying on the arduous treatment regime I had faced for the past three months instead of relaxing or recuperating), a compromise had to be found.

This compromise came in the form of oral antibiotics, which enabled the IV variety to be switched to their tablet counterparts. With oral antibiotics, my NTM treatment could continue but I would not be restricted by IVs. They did, however, come with the caveat that at the very first sign of absolutely *anything* being amiss I was to return to Papworth immediately to restart the IV medication.

Given the amount of time I had spent on the CF Unit that year so far (one hundred percent of it), I would have agreed to anything at that point in order to be allowed to return home. And so, the plan was set; I would spend the next week slowly switching to the oral variety of antibiotics and, barring any further hiccups, would finally be going home.

This prospect filled my heart with hope. It was the start of April, the cold winter was over, and the summer lay ahead. A long road of recovery and getting my strength back beckoned. I had cheated death and, although the future remained somewhat uncertain, my sense of optimism was renewed and my hopes for the future were kickstarted.

Perhaps Aisling and I could now, after all, consider what kind of life we were going to have, the places we might visit, and the idea of starting a family. It was the strangest of feelings; to have come from the very depths of despair to a new dawn full of promise and expectation, but with a deep sense of caution still present. But, since the start of the year, we had been though a living hell and we were desperate to cling onto our revitalised sense of optimism.

On Wednesday 9th April 2003, a multi-disciplinary team (MDT) meeting to discuss my case took place. I stayed in my room throughout, reluctant to start packing up my stuff for the risk of tempting fate, yet my mind was already racing out the door, down the road, and heading for home.

I sat quietly on the bed, contemplating everything that had happened over the past fourteen weeks. The television chattered away in the background. US armed forces had just liberated Baghdad (the capital city of Iraq), Saddam Hussain had fled into hiding and the war in Iraq was over. My glance flitted between the green grassy field beyond the balcony (the same balcony where I had stood in my underwear a couple of months earlier) and the sight of US troops dismantling a bronze statue of the former leader of Iraq, in the middle of a roundabout, with the assistance of a tank and some chains.

I waited patiently for the final verdict on my fate, knowing from bitter experience that CF has a habit of spoiling everything just as my hopes were lifted.

At around three p.m., there was a knock on my door and in flooded what seemed like a cast of thousands – medical staff of every discipline, from doctors to nurses and physios to pharmacists, all seemingly just there to witness the verdict being delivered to me. In short, it was just as I had hoped; I would be going home that day, on a whole bucketload of pills and potions, and with the requirement to return every Wednesday to clinic so that I could be kept an eye on. I was asked whether I was happy to agree to being discharged on this basis, and I could barely speak. After one hundred and one days of being hospitalised, I was going home and something that had seemed impossible just a few weeks previously was finally a reality.

I was aware that there was still a distance to travel on my NTM journey, but this was a massive leap forward and an opportunity I was not going to let pass me by. I signed the necessary paperwork and the pharmacist rushed off to start preparing the drugs I would need to take home. I telephoned Aisling, whose sense of utter relief was palpable over the telephone line, as if all the stress she had endured over the previous few months melted away as we spoke. She immediately left Epsom to come and collect me.

And, with that, my time on the CF Unit ended. I knew I would be back there, possibly even in the very same room, in the future. There was a palpable sense of inevitability about this. But I was not troubled by the prospect. After all, it seemed like there couldn't possibly be anything worse for CF to throw at me than what I had just been through.

I left that day with a sense that if I could survive the past fourteen weeks, I could get through anything. I was weak, tired, and mentally drained, but I had a future. A prospect that had looked so remote a few weeks ago was now *real* and tangible.

Aisling arrived and, with the aid of a wheelchair that she commandeered from along the corridor, we loaded my belongings into the car and returned to the ward for our final goodbyes. I would be back there in clinic in only a matter of days, yet the enormity of that afternoon cannot be understated.

I had battled so hard against NTM and had escaped with my life. Others had come and gone from the CF Unit during that time, some of whom had recovered whilst others had lost their struggles against this awful disease. For whatever reason, whether it be fate, divine intervention, medical expertise, or simply having a positive mental attitude (depending on your disposition), I was to be one of the lucky ones this time. CF had tried to squeeze the last breaths out of my body, but I had managed to fend it off. Nothing could ever cause me to forget this, and I left knowing that I owed it to myself, as well as everyone who had stood by my side and battled so hard to save me, to make the very most of my second chance.

Since the events of 2003, that particular period of my life has often been cited by Aisling and I as our lowest point and our darkest hour. So much has happened since then, but that episode will never be forgotten both for me, as the patient, and for Aisling as the person who worked so hard to make sure we had a life together, despite everything that CF could throw at us. Without her, we might never have discovered the article about NTM. Without her, I almost certainly would not be here now, writing this book that you are now reading.

During that time, I had become the UK's leading case for treating NTM in CF patients and had unwittingly instilled Papworth as one of the world's leading CF centres for dealing with them. Indeed, the hospital's work in this field continues and its expertise and research into NTM is renowned worldwide even to this very day.

Despite what I went through, I have gained a huge amount of solace from the idea that through my experience, and the knowledge gained by those treating me, awareness of NTM infections has increased enormously, benefitting many hundreds of CF patients in the years since. Drug therapies have been developed and refined, medical expertise has been shared, and NTM – although far more common these days than back in 2003 – is more diagnosable and *treatable*.

Sadly, whilst the prevalence of NTM, along with other bugs, has led to greater knowledge of the risk of cross-infection between CF patients, it has also ultimately led to CF patients being segregated wherever they might come into contact. This makes living with CF a much lonelier existence, but it is a vital step in ensuring that as many people with CF as possible get their own second chances, just as I did.

As for the Papworth CF social club, karaoke evenings, and pool competitions – they are nowadays confined to CF folklore. Those who are still alive to remember such times do so with fondness. Yet, to those who have only ever known being confined to their rooms whilst on CF units, 'meeting' others with CF only through online chat rooms and social media, such silly stories seem unbelievable; totally alien from a life today with CF.

During those one hundred and one days at the start of 2003, I went from being as far down as I could possibly go to having another chance at life and making some of the best friends I could ever wish for; friends who know what it is like to live with CF, whose partners watch them suffer on a regular basis, and who spend their life battling this wretched disease. A disease that, in all likeliness, will eventually take those they love away from them. One cannot underestimate the importance of having partners and friends like these in one's life.

For those with CF and those around them, life cannot be relied upon. We will not always have it and must always try to enjoy it. Because one day, and possibly when we least expect it, it could all be gone.

THIRTY-THREE
ANOTHER CHANCE

Looking back, it is hard to encapsulate the mixed feelings I had upon leaving hospital. Of course, I was elated to be home, away from my tiny room and the monotonous routine of daily life on a hospital ward. My relief was made up of two equal parts: one being the comforting warmth of just being back in a familiar environment where you can finally do your own thing and be yourself; the second being the elation that stemmed from the knowledge I had just been through hell, cheated death, and had lived to tell the tale. I would often sit, sometimes for what would seem like hours, contemplating what Aisling and I had been through, as if in a state of post-traumatic shock. Although I am no psychologist, I am sure that PTSD is what my diagnosis would have been had I been assessed by a mental health professional during those initial few weeks at home. It was certainly a bitter-sweet period and one that I still have very mixed feelings about, even now.

Notwithstanding this quagmire of emotions, however, nothing could surpass the pure joy of being back home with Aisling, being able to sleep in my own bed, and being able to eat what I liked when I liked. The ability to do these things was truly liberating. After four months of hospital food, believe me, there is nothing quite like the knowledge that if you wake in the night (as I often do), you can go downstairs and make a three course meal consisting of anything you can find that's edible. I bathed in this apparent luxury of culinary freedom, and I needed to. After such a long time in hospital, my weight was the lowest it had ever been and my body mass index was nowhere close to the 'acceptable' range.

Upon discharge, I was under orders to follow a supercharged version of the CF self-care triple whammy. I had basically been told to eat as much as I could, to exercise as much as I could, but also (in direct conflict with the previous item) to rest and recuperate as much as I could. It was made abundantly clear to me by the medical team at Papworth that, although I had made good strides of recovery as an inpatient, the real hard work started once I got home. I was tired and weak. But doing nothing and languishing was not going to save me, and was certainly not going to get me on the fast track back to full strength.

I had been given numerous drugs to nebulise, swallow in tablet form, and inject, as well as overnight feeding to make me look less like a skeleton. If I wanted to return to living a normal life, or at least the life I had been living before NTM, I had to muster up some energy, pull myself together, and do everything I was supposed to do. I had been offered the priceless opportunity of another chance of life. But, to take advantage of that chance, I had to put the work in and not expect a return to the good times to happen as if by magic.

In those initial few weeks, I fought hard to fend off feelings of institutionalisation from my time in hospital. Aisling was back at work and I was spending the days at home alone. I had gone from four months on a noisy, busy hospital ward – where there were always people around to help me – to being on my own in a quiet house, and I found this situation disconcerting.

This was probably due to the underlying sense of fear that I felt. I had been through so many ups and downs during my time in hospital – fourteen weeks of hoping for an improvement in my condition whilst facing setback after setback – and it seemed that any time there had been a glimmer of hope it was snatched away again by some rogue blood result or temperature spike. This overriding sense of vulnerability was hard to shake off, and I continued to do battle with it once I was discharged. In my mind, I had been allowed to return home – the best thing to have happened to me in a very long time. So, surely, with such a huge rise must come a big fall?

That's what CF does to the mind… "Never count your winnings whilst you are still at the table," as the old saying goes.

I continued to see the CF team at Papworth on a weekly basis. Each Wednesday, I would drive one hundred miles to Papworth, spending the few hours I had there undergoing breathing tests, talking to the dieticians and physiotherapists about how I was getting on at home, and seeing Dr Bilton each time.

Slowly but surely, over the course of the following few months, my weight started to come up and my lung function began to improve. It wasn't until during the summer of 2003, though, that Dr Bilton was assured enough by these continuous improvements to declare that, in her opinion, we had beaten NTM 'for now'. However, she was also keen to point out that my body had been compromised by what happened and that the need for close monitoring would continue going forward. See what I mean about any positives being closely followed by a downer?!

At home, I continued to feel fragile for some considerable time and took nothing for granted. It wasn't until the June of 2003 that Aisling and I did something to dispel these feelings of vulnerability and institutionalisation once and for all – we went on holiday.

Having discussed our plans with the CF team, and having paid an obscene amount of money for travel insurance, we set off for a week in the Algarve, Portugal. We flew to Faro Airport, courtesy of the airline that Aisling worked for at the time, and stayed in one of the high-rise, mass-market hotels that are scattered along the coastline close to the main resort town of Vilamoura.

Along with our suitcase of clothes, some reading material, and suntan lotion, we had a whole 'wheelie-bag' full of medication for me. During the first few months following my discharge I was taking IV antibiotics every few weeks to fend off any return of NTM, and it just so happened that I was on the IVs when we decided to go on holiday. Rather than cancel the whole trip and miss out entirely, a real sense of 'we can do this' took over and that, combined with the absolute desperate need that we both felt to get away for a short time, was enough to get us to go through with it.

Despite anticipating it being difficult, we had a truly wonderful time on that trip; we spent our days in the sunshine either by the hotel pool or down on the beach, constantly reminding ourselves and each other how lucky we were to be doing this after all we had been through.

This lounging around in the sunshine was only disrupted by the need for me to skip back to our room and administer my IV drugs after lunch. Whilst I had decided not to worry about sitting around the pool with my shirt off, revealing my portacath, dressing, and the long tube hanging down from it, to all who cared to look, drawing up medication with syringes and needles and shooting up poolside where small children were playing seemed a step too far.

I still look back at the photos of that holiday and feel proud that I was confident enough to bare all (if you will) in a public space. I can only conclude that near-death experiences can help to crystallise a feeling of 'I don't give a toss what people think' inside one's mind.

That week in Portugal really was a turning point in my recovery; I was starting to feel better both mentally and physically, and the change of scenery had shown me that I could start to get back to something approaching normality. Over that summer, I continued to build up my strength and NTM seemed to slowly fade into the background.

My days alone at home after returning from hospital gave me a lot of time to think, and I made a positive decision to turn my attention to the future and to always look ahead rather than backwards.

CF is hard work in that respect; I have found it all too easy over the years to worry about what might happen and to fear things that I either have no control over or don't know enough about to form an opinion over. Particularly after my recent run-in with NTM, I found I was constantly wondering what would happen next and whether I would be so lucky the next time around.

Unfortunately, with progressive and degenerative diseases such as CF, there will *always* be a next time around. That is one of the harsh realities of the disease. As sure as night follows day, there is no such thing as an easy path with CF, but that path can be navigated better if your attitude towards it is right.

If NTM had taught me anything, it was to never take anything for granted and to not delay doing the things you want to do because you never know what CF will throw at you next. Like I have said before, when you get hit by a curved ball thrown by CF, it can hurt a great deal. It can also leave you battered, wounded and, sugar-coating aside, it might just leave you dead.

Now, more than ever, I was determined to get on with my life and to do anything I wanted to, within the constraints that CF imposed on me. I wasn't going to jet off into space any time soon or become a deep-sea diver, but I began to harvest a real feeling of wanting to do things that I had never done and to not let CF or NTM stop me. More so than ever before, I was ready to stick two fingers up at CF, smile, and say, "I am going to live my life in the way I choose *despite* you rather than because of you." This mantra seemed appropriate at the time and has stuck with me ever since. I still believe that having these words lodged firmly at the forefront of my brain has got me to where I am today and has allowed me to do all that I have done over the years.

So, in consultation with Dr Bilton at Papworth, I decided that I would aim to resume my second year at law school at the start 2004. I had dropped out of my course at the beginning of 2003, so restarting it in the January meant that I was effectively re-joining the course exactly where I had left off, albeit one year later and with a different cohort of students. Once this decision was made and had been successfully negotiated with the College of Law in Guildford, my immediate plans were safely cemented into place, and I set about ensuring I made the most of my remaining convalescence.

Aisling and I decided that, having safely negotiated our way to Portugal in the June of that year, we would (and should) venture further afield for our third anniversary at the end of September. Having sat down and gone through a list of places we had always wanted to visit, we finally decided to spend the two weeks surrounding our anniversary on the tropical island of Mauritius in the Indian Ocean. There were particularly attractive deals on offer to Mauritius at that time and, with my newly found sense of 'come on, why not?' within me, we booked the flights.

The thought of a twelve-hour flight didn't put me off in the slightest, nor did the idea of being so far from home (and by that, I suppose, I mean from Papworth should anything go wrong). I was brimming over with my renewed desire to travel and was ready to spread my wings once again.

Our trip to Mauritius was amazing and the fortnight was over all too soon. We saw only limited parts of the island as we spent most of our time in our perfectly manicured resort, on the pristine private beach or by one of the beautiful swimming pools. With no IVs or port lines to worry about by this time, it felt like we were on a *proper* holiday and that we were finally over the ordeal that NTM had put us through.

Towards the end of 2003, I was starting to look forward to resuming my studies at law school, although I was slightly intimidated by the prospect too. Starting at the College of Law in 2001 had been difficult after so many years away from studying (and with the added stress of my dad's accident just three weeks previously), and I envisaged that this new start would be equally so. But I decided that if I could make it through from January 2004 to the end of the course in June of the same year, I would be happy enough.

Fortuitously, 2003 was a World Cup year for rugby union (being held in Australia) and England had been tipped to do well. I therefore spent my days revising my law subjects whilst catching up with the latest action from the tournament on television, following the participating home nations' progress during the group stages. It wasn't until England were to play Wales in the quarterfinals, however, that things really hotted up. After a thrilling game, in which Wales led at half-time, England ended up the victor. They won with twenty-eight points to Wales' seventeen, and this was on 9th November 2003. England had progressed to the semi-finals and things were beginning to get interesting.

They got far more interesting later that same evening when Steve popped over for a beer and a catch up; he just happened to be due some leave in the coming days and wasn't sure where to go. He still worked for Virgin Atlantic, so could get staff travel tickets anywhere in the world for next-to-nothing yet didn't fancy heading anywhere on his own for too long.

It just so happened that I had been on the internet that day and, purely out of interest, had discovered that tickets for the World Cup semi-final (in which England would be playing France) were still available and on sale, albeit at the rather exorbitant rate of four hundred pounds. The match was scheduled for 16th November, just a week away.

Like a light bulb turning on over our heads simultaneously, within less than a minute we had decided to head to Australia, tour around for a bit, and then attend the semi-final, which was being held in Stadium Australia in Sydney (the stadium built for the 2000 Olympics). By the end of that evening, it was all sorted; we would be spending the next couple of weeks in Australia.

By the following evening, Steve had organised the air tickets and I had severely dented my credit card by purchasing the rugby tickets online. And a mere two evenings after that, Steve and I were sitting in the Virgin Atlantic Clubhouse lounge at Heathrow Airport, enjoying a beer or two whilst waiting to board our flight.

We spent the few days leading up to the match in and around Sydney and, although we had both been to the city before, also spent a couple of days on the tourist trail, visiting the sights and enjoying the warm days of early summer in the Southern Hemisphere. We were staying in the eclectic Sydney suburb of Glebe with a friend and old Virgin Atlantic colleague Mark, who had bizarrely decided that the beautiful harbourside city of Sydney offered something more than the 1960's metropolis of Crawley, West Sussex.

Whilst Mark went to work at his day job at Qantas, Steve and I walked the length and width of the city, along the coastal pathways to secluded beaches and outlying suburbs such as Manly (where the England rugby team just happened to be staying). We relaxed and people-watched whilst enjoying ice-cold lagers at some of the bars lining Bondi beach. And all of this was just seven months on from when I left Papworth. The realisation that I was sitting drinking beer on one of the most famous beaches in the world, in the sunshine, on the other side of the planet seemed almost surreal.

I felt extremely lucky, particularly to be sharing this experience with Steve, one of my closest friends. Steve knew exactly what Aisling and I had been through over the previous couple of years and, although the words were left unsaid, I am sure he understood what was going on in my mind.

Following the Semi-Final match against France (which England won) we headed to Tasmania for a few days before returning to Sydney. However, having exhausted every avenue available to us, we were unable to procure tickets for the Final against the host nation, Australia. So, we decided to take a ninety-minute flight from Sydney to Leeton in New South Wales where my aunt, uncle, and cousins lived (including Mark, who had performed at mine and Aisling's wedding). There, we watched the game at the town's community centre on a big screen, with Steve and I the only ones wearing white rather than the obligatory gold and green colours of the favourites (England won, by the way… just saying).

A few days later, I was back at home with Aisling in Epsom. With the year quickly heading towards its conclusion, it was hard to come to terms with what had happened over the last twelve months. The year had started with me being gravely ill and at the lowest I've ever been – both physically and mentally. Conversely, it had ended with me travelling to the other side of the world and experiencing a 'once-in-a-lifetime' opportunity with one of my best friends. And now, I was looking forward to restarting, against all the odds, my studies at law school the following January.

It had been a truly remarkable rollercoaster of a year, both for Aisling and I; we had been through the nightmare of near-fatal illness and the idyllic high of sitting of a Mauritian beach. The dichotomy of this contrast in fortunes was not lost on us and has never been since; to this day, in all that we do, the spectre of 2003 looms large and is often cited by Aisling and I as our lowest point.

Despite that, or perhaps because of it, I headed towards 2004 with a real determination to put NTM behind me and to get back to 'normal' as quickly as possible. I saw restarting law school as the best way to achieve this, and so for me, for my dad, and for me and Aisling's future, 2003 finally closed with me gripping onto a sense of real optimism that there was so much more to come in my life.

ONWARDS AND UPWARDS

THIRTY-FOUR
BACK TO BUSINESS

As 2003 slipped into history and 2004 began, Aisling continued to work for her airline at Gatwick and I duly restarted my course in Guildford. Being a year later, the forty people I now shared the lecture rooms with were new to me, so I didn't especially engage with my new cohort. Instead, I got my head down, worked hard, and tried to survive the final exams at the end of June 2004.

Once my two years at law school were up, I then had to complete what is known as a 'Training Contract'. This is two years of on-the-job training with either a law firm or an organisation that would have a big internal legal department that could meet all the training criteria set by the Law Society. Only upon the successful completion of a training contract would I be fully qualified and able to call myself a solicitor.

Both demand and competition for training contracts is high, and multiple applications are often required in order to successfully land one. Experiences with training contracts can vary enormously, and as a law student I heard and read numerous horror stories of how trainees spent two years making the tea, photocopying, and filing (no, seriously) instead of meeting clients and doing actual legal work on cases (under supervision, of course).

Larger firms seemed to offer training contracts with better salaries alongside greater experience, and so this was where I focussed my attention when sending out applications. I thought (perhaps somewhat arrogantly) that with age and my commercial experience, I would be snapped up in an instant by a law firm in London offering silly money in return for my services for the two years. How misguided I was.

Alongside my final six months of studying, I spent every spare moment completing application forms or sending off my CV to a whole host of different law firms. From January 2004 to Easter of that year, I sent off over fifty applications only to receive very near that number in rejections. Others simply didn't bother responding, saving some money on stamps by stating on their application forms:

If you have not heard from us within four weeks of your application, you have been unsuccessful.

In any event, by Easter 2004, with my early arrogance firmly wiped away, it was taking a good deal of effort not to be completely demoralised by my lack of progress in securing a training spot for the next two years.

Eventually, I decided that nepotism might be the best way forward and contacted an old friend who had worked in the legal department at Virgin Atlantic. He had completed a training contract some years earlier with a law firm in the City of London that specialised in aviation law. I was aware that he was still in contact with partners at the firm, so wrote to him to ask who I should contact in order to apply for a training contract with them. He duly responded telling me to write directly to the Managing Partner (whom he knew well) and I did just that.

To my amazement, within a week or so I had been for an interview and a little while later an offer of employment dropped through our letter box. I was ecstatic – not only had I secured a dream training contract in aviation law but the job was in London (a relatively easy commute from our home in Epsom). Plus, the salary was good too. The only downside was that, as I was applying very late in the day, my starting date would have to be in the September of 2005 rather than 2004. This did not both me in the slightest, however, and I set about finding something to do in the intervening year.

After a few emails and phone calls to local law firms, I was offered a position as a paralegal with a medium-sized firm in Kingston-upon-Thames. Being a paralegal can also be a life of mixed fortunes and it is not unusual for them to be treated even worse than trainees in the same firm. So rather than being the one tasked with the photocopying and tea making, the paralegal's role in many law offices is to turn the photocopier on or to stock up the tea bags in the kitchen and ensure there is fresh milk in the fridge so that the trainee can make the tea.

Nonetheless, I was grateful for the offer and it seemed like this would give me some valuable experience before my training contract started. Although the salary was not great, it was at least something and, after two years at law school, my healthy redundancy payment from Virgin Sun was largely gone. I accepted the offer and, with that, the next three years of my life were secured and my route to becoming a fully qualified solicitor was mapped out. I just had to complete and pass my final law exams without any further health-based hiccups, which I managed successfully in June 2004.

By the end of my time at law school, I was completely exhausted with studying and was ready to return to working life. And as it turned out, I had rather an enjoyable year at the law firm in Kingston; I was identified by one of the partners as having a little extra 'something' and so was permitted to work on proper cases within the Civil Litigation department, under the supervision of one of their junior solicitors.

I was also farmed out to Kingston Borough Council one day per week to man their Trading Standards legal helpline – a guaranteed hoot with all kinds of nutters ringing in for, frankly, ridiculous reasons. One of my favourites was the guy who had owned a washing machine for ten years and, although it had been out of warranty for nine of those years, couldn't understand why he could not take it back to the shop for a full refund when it broke down. There was also the lady who had bought a tube of a well-known hair removal cream from a market stall and who had applied this cream to various parts of her body in healthy-sized dollops. The cream had caused severe rashes over the applied areas (the exact details of which I was, thankfully, spared). I asked her to confirm to me the instructions on the tube, but she promptly responded that she couldn't as it was all in Greek. Upon further enquiry by the Trading Standards team, it transpired that the cream had been illegally imported into Britain from Greece where (putting it delicately) people's body hair tends to be darker and thicker than their Northern European counterparts. As such, the chemicals in the cream needed to be stronger in order for it to perform its function adequately. Unable to read the instructions, this particular lady had applied what she considered to be a decent UK-sized helping onto certain intimate areas, and was consequently left unable sit down for too long in one position.

Every shift I had on the Trading Standards hotline I would take calls like this. I would also spend a hugely unproductive amount of each shift talking to lonely old folk who clearly just wanted someone to chat to. Some callers wanted to sue everyone they knew for something-or-other that had happened twenty years previously whilst others wanted to bring legal action against huge Asian electrical corporations because they had bought a television that was either too small, too big, or not the right shape for their living room. I have to say I did enjoy manning the hotline for all the local weirdos, although I now know where my reduced levels of patience and tolerance may have first developed.

Upon completing my year as a paralegal in Kingston, I was ready to start my new life as a trainee solicitor. During the summer, just prior to me starting, the aviation law firm in London was swallowed up by a multinational firm also based in the city. For me, this meant a slightly shorter walk from London Bridge station each morning, a higher training salary, and more departments in which I could chose to spend my four six-month training seats. So, rather than starting as the sole trainee for the firm I had applied to, on 8th September 2005 I found myself in a room *of twenty* trainees, all fresh-faced and ready to start their two years of photocopying and tea making.

Reaching this point was a major milestone for me. My four months of NTM treatment at Papworth had taken their toll on me – both mentally and physically – and for the a great deal of time afterwards I felt very vulnerable, fearing a return of this thing that had tried so hard to end my life and to take me away from Aisling.

Slowly, however, I noticed these feelings change into something more positive. I had not received any advice from anyone about having a 'positive mental attitude', seen any psychologists, or been given therapy of any kind, yet I was somehow able to conjure up a more productive, forward-facing approach to life. I had been able to restore the ambitions and aspirations that I held prior to NTM, and I put this down to Aisling's support and love, my dad's attitude to life, and an overriding sense that I was not yet 'done'.

In time, I began to realise the importance of using this reprieve to maximise what I did with my life. I really began to think about my hopes, aspirations, and where I wanted to be in two, five, perhaps even ten years. I didn't sit down one day and write a 'bucket list' of things I wanted to achieve. I did, however, sit and consider what I wanted from life, what would make me happy, and what would make me look back and feel proud that I had made the most of the extra time fate had afforded me.

When living with CF (and other serious, progressive conditions like it), you can guarantee that it will almost certainly kill you in the end. I say *almost certainly* because you run as great a risk as everyone else of being knocked down by a bus, catching a fatal tropical disease from a public toilet, or being bored to death when your Spotify account inexplicably locks itself into playing Simply Red's greatest hits on repeat.

Whilst the old adage about 'living every day as if it is your last' is wheeled out all too often for it to sound like anybody actually means it, there is a hint of virtue in its sentiment.

I have never been scared of death or of dying, but I do fear the weight of regret I might feel if I knew that my time was just about up and if I had not used the time I did have wisely enough.

I do not advocate living in endless pessimism, always expecting the worst and watching the proverbial sword of Damocles floating precariously over one's head. What I do advocate is living for the future and allowing hope to prevail. Hope is such an important concept and simply cannot be underestimated for those with chronic conditions like CF. Looking backwards, living in the past, and dwelling on what might have been are all idle sentiments; unproductive and ultimately unrewarding.

Increasingly since 2003, I have worked hard to use my time productively and to make life as fulfilling as I can. CF has not allowed me to do everything I have wanted to, but I do see this quest as something of a debt that I owe to all those with CF who died before getting the chance to achieve their dreams.

Probably the best example I can give of spending my time doing what I enjoy is travelling; travel represents one aspect of my life that I have enjoyed ever since my family and I first departed the UK for San Francisco in 1976. It is also one thing that both Aisling and I enjoyed before we met and continue to enjoy together.

After my recovery from NTM, our mutual desire to explore more of the world really took off. Our travels have taken us throughout Europe, Northern and Southern Africa, the Middle East, North America, Indian Ocean islands, the Far East, Australia, and New Zealand. To date, I have visited just over forty countries across four continents and fully intend to add to this tally in the future – not bad for someone who was not expected to live into double figures when they were born!

If I hadn't decided to go on the transplant list, I would have added to this total. But once placed on the waiting list for a double lung transplant at Harefield, I was informed that I must remain within the UK and within reasonable proximity of the hospital itself so that I am able to be there quickly should my time come.

Whilst this was one of the main disappointments I felt when being placed on the list, it is a necessary evil and one I have to live with for as long as my wait lasts. If I am lucky enough to have a successful transplant, I will be able to reap the rewards and enjoy unfettered travel rights in the future.

I hope to visit so many more places. Perhaps in my lifetime, space tourism will be the next big thing, although I am not sure that my limited travel budget would stretch to the type of trip currently being planned by companies like Virgin Galactic and Blue Origin. Maybe though, just maybe…

During those terrible days (and nights) when I was battling NTM at Papworth, I would read travel books and leaf through travel magazines; it gave me something to hope for. I would lie there, as the fevers shook me to my core and nausea gripped my entire body, promising myself that if I was given a second chance at life, I would do it full justice. Being placed on the transplant waiting list reminded me of the thoughts and hopes I had back then, but I know now that when the time finally comes – when CF finally beats me, and my body is finally ready to give up and turn the lights out – I can look back on my life with a smile.

THIRTY-FIVE

MANAGING A CAREER WITH CF MANAGING ME

From as far back as I can remember, I never saw CF as a hindrance to doing what I wanted to do. This included my working life. As long as I could manage my health and keep the ravages of the condition as a sideshow to whatever else was or is going on in my life, I felt able to do as much as the next person. I never stopped to consider that CF might, in time, dictate a course in my life other than that I planned for myself; I was fortunate to have been well enough to complete my schooling and university careers with very little absence and, although CF had caught up with me during my two years at law school, somehow I had returned to complete my studies.

I had decided on a new career path in law and by 2005 all that stood between me and being a fully-fledged, fully qualified solicitor was a two-year training contract.

It was the beginning of September 2005. I had spent the summer finishing up my paralegal job in Kingston-upon-Thames and preparing for the next two years, knowing that they would be hard work and would take a lot out of me physically. I would be commuting from Epsom to London every day, arriving into London Bridge station and then having a fifteen-minute brisk walk across the River Thames into the financial and legal heart of the capital.

On the morning of Monday 8th September 2005, with shoes polished, suit brushed, and shirt pressed, I set off on the first of the many journeys I would take to London over the next twenty-four months as a trainee solicitor.

With my first seat to be in aviation transactional law, I was taken off to meet Jim, the first supervising partner of my training contract and an 'old-school' lawyer of the brace-wearing, pinstripe suite brigade. Jim initially came across as quite brash and dismissive. On my first day, rather than give me any real work to do, he sent me off to the nearest post office to renew the car tax on one of his several cars. With the horror stories I had heard about being a trainee in a large city law firm ringing in my ears, I dutifully set off on my errand, keen to impress.

However, after a few weeks of getting to know each other and of Jim beginning to learn that I may be more than just a fresh face out of law school, he took me under his wing and I began to learn a lot about the legal complexities of buying and leasing commercial aircraft. I sat in Jim's office with him and listened to him on the phone to clients and others, picking up tips along the way.

The work was interesting and varied, and Jim soon revealed himself to be quite a character and an affable sort of chap. He enjoyed hearing about my days working for Virgin Atlantic, Airbus, and EasyJet and I enjoyed hearing of his time in the RAF and the many tales he would tell of japes in the officers' mess at RAF Cranwell where he had learned to fly.

Jim was partial to the odd pint at lunchtime and would always disappear at around midday for a couple of hours. In fact, on a fairly regular basis, he would sigh, sit back in his chair, and say, "Well, we're not doing anything here that we can't be doing down the pub." And, with that, I would be instructed to gather up whatever documents we were working on and decamp to the pub to continue over a 'nice glass of beer'.

Over time, this alternative working venue adopted a codename to ensure its ongoing anonymity. As the pub in question was called The Three Lords, Jim and I were often found holding curiously spontaneous meetings in 'Meeting Room 3L'. However, whilst Jim had a staggering ability to drinking several pints at lunchtime and then work long into the evening, I most certainly did not and I was often forced to ring Aisling, having been down the pub all afternoon with no discernible intake of food to speak of, to ask her to pick me up from the station as I was in no fit state to make my own way home.

I ended up on very good terms with Jim and he eventually trusted me enough to allow me to take his place on a very important telephone call. An airline in India for whom we acted was just about to take delivery of the first in an order of thirty new aircraft from Boeing in the USA, so I (representing the airline) was tasked by Jim to join a conference call with about twelve other lawyers from various companies across the USA, Ireland, India, and the UK to finalise the acceptance of the first aircraft.

After about two hours, sometime towards midnight, I was called upon to make my little speech that would bring matters to a celebratory close. At the appropriate moment in the call, I confirmed to all parties that the various documents and licences were in order, the financials had been agreed and completed, and that the final instalment of funds allowing the airline to take delivery of the aircraft (about twenty million US dollars) had just been wired to Boeing's bank account.

Following a short delay whilst Boeing confirmed that the funds were indeed in their account (yes, this is really how it works), their sales representative confirmed that our client had 'just bought themselves an aeroplane'. With the customary whooping and clapping from the various other attendees on the call, the deal was finally complete and the aircraft was now the property of the airline in India. The keys of the aircraft were officially handed to the airline's CEO (yes, this also happens, although the keys are just symbolic and don't actually start up the aircraft) who was sitting in a conference room at Boeing's headquarters in Seattle and I could finally hang up and head home to bed.

This was a momentous moment for me and one that I enjoyed immensely. Although it had been nerve-wracking, I was proud that I had been part of a deal that would see our client with a whole new fleet of planes in just two years' time. For the rest of my time as a trainee solicitor, I had a photo of that particular aircraft next to my desk, partly to inspire me but also to remind me that being a trainee may not always be about making tea, doing the photocopying, and renewing the boss's car tax.

Despite Jim's good nature, those first six months working in London were hard. The hours were long and the pace of work quick. The time spent at The Three Lords really did nothing to promote my good health, either, and commuting twice a day on a train full of people coughing and sneezing around me was just asking for trouble. Nonetheless, I escaped from catching anything too nasty, although I did have to keep going back to Papworth for regular courses of IV antibiotics that I would take to work with me and administer in the toilets during lunchtime.

Jim was unaware of my condition and I had decided (as I had so many times before in my life) that I would keep things to myself until I had felt that he really needed to know. Upon reaching the office each morning, I would immediately disappear into the toilets and have a quick physio session, clearing my lungs and getting ready for the long day ahead. Occasionally, when a tickly cough would get the better of me, Jim would ask if I was okay or exclaim that I, "Really should give up the twenty-a-day habit." He would also offer me these strange little cough sweets – curious black nuggets of something that had a strong menthol flavour and that Jim swore by. Despite knowing that they would do nothing to help my predicament, I would always graciously accept one and carry on working, hoping that – just by chance – the coughing would subside, which it normally would (eventually).

After six months with Jim, it was supposed to be time to move on within the organisation. However, it seemed that somehow I had made myself 'indispensable' to his team (his team consisting of just Jim and myself). So, he pulled strings, attended meetings, and made phone calls, the result of which was that I would remain under his guardianship for the following six months too.

In order to avoid contravening any of the training guidelines laid down by the Solicitors Regulation Authority (whereby a trainee solicitor is supposed to spend each of the four six-month training seats in a different area of law), Jim arranged for me to go on secondment to the Finance and Leasing Association near Holborn. This was to be for three days a week, leaving the remaining two for me to work back with Jim in his office. Whilst falling just within the letter of the rules (although probably falling outside the spirit of them) everyone involved seemed happy, so I started the next six months shuttling between the different parts of London where my two jobs were now based.

However, as is the life of a trainee solicitor, on the days that I was at the FLA Jim would often call me up and request my presence in his office that evening to work on some 'really important' piece of work or other. Towards the end of that second training seat, I was a regular on the Number Nine bus route that runs between Aldwych and the Tower of London, shuttling between my two jobs on an increasingly frequent basis. "Not bad for a person with a chronic condition," I would tell myself, whilst blatantly ignoring any harm that such endeavours might have been doing to me. Still, I was enjoying myself, enjoying the work and, in my eyes, I was sticking two fingers up to CF and all that it involves.

After a further six months of this double life – part-time trainee solicitor and part-time legal advisor at the FLA – it was time for the SRA rules to kick in and put an end to it all. For my third training seat, Jim finally had to let me go and go and experience another area of law in another part of the firm.

After a year of commuting by train and walking a couple of miles each day on top of that, it was time for me to step back, to consider my options, and to listen to what my body was telling me. I was tired and the need for IV antibiotics was becoming more frequent. The life of a commuter was also taking its toll on my lungs. It was now September 2006 and I knew that something had to give before my body did. So, I opted out of the London rat-race and decided to apply to transfer to the firm's Dorking office for my following training seat, working in the Commercial Litigation Department. Although I would still be travelling to my new workplace by train, the journey time was shorter and there was less of a walk once off the train at Dorking. This seemed like the sensible way to see through the forthcoming dark, wet, and cold winter months.

My time in Dorking was spent on a range of different cases, all of which were interesting in their own way but were not really what I wanted from my legal career. After all, I had set out to be an aviation lawyer, and the only proximity I had to anything with wings during my time in Dorking was to the passenger jets that would circle over the office as they made their final approach to land at the nearby London Gatwick Airport.

At the end of the six months, and having survived another winter of commuting, it was time to get back to London for my final training seat. Still harbouring ambitions to become an aviation lawyer upon qualification, I took up my final seat in the Aviation Litigation department. I worked on many cases during that time, involving everything from large commercial airliners (accidents and disputes), small aircraft, and helicopters to regulatory and licensing issues. The work was varied, interesting, right up my street, and I initially considered this to be the department into which I would like to qualify come the summer.

However, it was not to be and – for just about the first time in my life – CF started to dictate the course that I had to follow.

During that last six months of my training, I found commuting into London very hard work. Looking back, I don't recall whether there was a definitive single trigger for this change, but my lungs continued to grumble and complain and, despite it being the warmer spring and summer months of the year, my chest was really not where it should be or, indeed, where I wanted it to be.

While Aisling knew that I was doing exactly what I had dreamed of doing for years, she could see the toll it was taking on me and my body, and would often voice her concerns about how much of an impact this vehement pursuit of my chosen career was having on my health and wellbeing. By the end of each day, I was exhausted and the last thing I wanted to do was to haul myself back to London Bridge station for the slow, unpleasantly crowded train back to Reigate in Surrey where Aisling and I now lived.

The days seemed harder to get through, my health was taking a hit, and I started to wondered whether as a person with CF, having recently survived a prolonged battle with NTM and heading quickly towards my mid-thirties, commuting and long days in the centre of a polluted city like London was really the sensible way forward.

After a lot of soul searching, and many hours of discussions with Aisling, I finally started to come to terms with the fact that my body was telling me enough was enough. I had worked hard to get to where I wanted to be but there was little doubt (however much I hated the concept) that this lifestyle was unsustainable and would do me real harm if I persisted with it.

I was doing IVs far more often than I was happy with, and I was in and out of Papworth more and more regularly for two-week stints here and there.

In the end, I had to decide whether to follow my head or my heart. And whilst my heart screamed as loudly as it could that working in aviation law was all I had ever wanted to do, my head (as well as my lungs) were drowning out those pleas and telling me that if things didn't change, I wouldn't have a legal career left to worry about in any event. It was time for some cruel, hard, decision making and, although I hated the fact that CF was telling me which way to turn next, it simply could not be ignored.

During my last few weeks within the Aviation Litigation department, I shocked everyone by informing the training department of Human Resources that I wished to return to Dorking and to the Commercial Litigation department to continue my career when I qualified that summer. The partners in the Aviation Litigation group were stunned. I also surprised Jim, who had clearly always hoped that I would return to his fold and who had even held a slot open for me.

It was therefore with a very heavy heart that I signed the papers requesting my transfer back to the Dorking office come September 2006 and, for a few days, I hated CF and everything about it. I was frustrated and angry, but it was finally time for me to realise that I was not immortal and that, despite what I had believed up until this point, I couldn't simply *will* CF to simmer away quietly in the background.

CF is real. It is unfair and unkind, and it does not let those affected by it simply live their lives in parallel to it. At some point in the lives of everyone who has CF, these two realities cross paths and, from that point on, the future takes on a different perspective. I had reached this point and, as much as I hated it, felt that my hands were tied. CF had decided my future for me. But as Aisling would remind me, despite this disappointment, I had set out largely what I had hoped to achieve – I had completed all the hurdles to become a qualified solicitor and a new career lay before me. Rather than disappointment or frustration, I told myself I should be proud of my accomplishment and thankful to have reached this point despite CF and what it had thrown at me.

THIRTY-SIX

BUYING MYSELF TIME

Despite my resolve to never let my life be guided by CF, I had finally had to capitulate. Reality was bearing down on me and I knew I had to make way for it. For so long I had felt invincible, yet NTM had turned that sense of invincibility into a vulnerability I didn't recognise. Unfortunately, this was to become a recurring theme as I headed towards forty years of age; my life's journey bringing me to the almost inevitable destination of a double lung transplant.

In the September of 2007, after a couple of weeks off when Aisling and I headed to the west coast of Florida on holiday, I was officially enrolled by the Law Society and was now a fully paid-up member on the roll of solicitors of England and Wales. Aisling and I attended a qualification and enrolment ceremony in the wood-panelled rooms of the Law Society in London, where my cohort and I were told that our main purpose was to help people and relieve their tension when faced with stressful situations. This was obviously to dispel any misconceptions we may have held (along with the rest of the population) that lawyers' primary goal is to relieve people of their money. Aisling and I followed the ceremony with a posh lunch at an expensive restaurant to celebrate my qualification and, at last, I felt that five years of effort had been worth it.

I settled back into the Commercial Litigation department at Dorking with ease. I threw myself into work and developed a nice routine, not working too late and leaving enough time in the day to look after myself. I had bought a nice BMW to get me comfortably to and from our home in Reigate every day, avoiding the need to travel by slow, uncomfortable, and unreliable trains. Things all seemed to have fallen largely into place.

The NTM episode of 2003 seemed like a distant memory and, for the first time in a long time, I felt that things were back under my control. However, like before, it is in these moments when it is all too easy to become complacent. And, like it did before, CF chose to pull the rug from under me.

It was a cold morning in early January 2008. I had just set off from home and was driving along Reigate High Street about a mile from the house when I had to pull the car over. I had felt a little under the weather when I woke that day and my chest had felt odd. I had an unusual twinge in my chest, one that I had never experienced before. After giving it little thought, however, I had duly carried on, got ready for work, and set off in the car.

After a couple of minutes driving, I knew something just wasn't right. What started off as a twinge had become a sharp pain in one side of my chest, making it very difficult and very unsafe to continue driving. I felt clammy and hot and, for the first time since NTM, knew that something was wrong. I sat in the car, pulse racing, gathering my thoughts.

It was hard not to panic, fearing the worst and struggling with the pain both at the same time. I sat there watching the rain roll down the windscreen. I knew I had to compose myself, to take control of the situation and resolve it as best as I could. But I wasn't sure whether to ring an ambulance or make my own way home. I thought I could probably manage to get back to the house if I calmed down and took it carefully. Plus, with a truly remarkable (and equally misguided) level of 'stiff upper-lip' Britishness, I didn't wish to tie up an ambulance or its crew for the best part of an hour or to cause a spectacle on the High Street.

I called Aisling to tell her that I was not feeling well and that I was returning to base. She said that she would meet me back at the house and I limped home slowly in the car, working hard on keeping my composure the whole way. The journey would have lasted five minutes at the most, but when you know that something has gone very wrong with your body that five minutes can easily feel like five hours.

Once Aisling and I were home, we held our own little triage assessment of what might be going on. Was I in pain? Yes. Was I short of breath? Yes. Was the fact I was in a state of mild-to-medium panic causing my shortness of breath? Probably. Did I need to go to the local Accident and Emergency department? Almost certainly. So, after a quick cup of tea to calm our nerves, we set off for East Surrey Hospital just a few miles away.

Being a relatively quiet time of the morning in the middle of the week, thankfully our wait in A&E was short. Like many with CF, I knew far more about CF and the treatment of it than the junior doctor working the cubicles in A&E that morning. Despite having not experienced this combination of symptoms before, I already had a pretty good idea of what was happening. But, as always in these situations, decided I would rather a qualified medical professional tell me what they think before I impart my own opinion.

After a rapidly organised X-ray, however, my fears were confirmed; my right lung had become detached from the chest wall and had deflated at the top, medically known as a *pneumothorax* but more commonly known as a 'collapsed lung'. Such occurrences are annoyingly common in those with CF and other chronic lung conditions. The outer fringes of the lungs become damaged by either infection or bacteria and the lung is no longer able to adhere itself to the chest wall, thus detaching itself and deflating to a lesser or greater degree. Upon further discussion, and after a few phone calls from the junior doctor to the CF team at Papworth, it was decided that I would transfer straight to Papworth by ambulance to be sorted out there. Aisling was to follow in my car so that she could get back to Surrey under her own steam later that day.

Following a long and uncomfortable transfer on the two-hour journey to Papworth, I breathed an albeit shallow sigh of relief as the vehicle pulled in through those familiar hospital gates. I had faith that the CF team would be able to put me back together and this, along with a strange way of coming *home,* was enough to settle me down for the first time that day. As the ambulance crew unloaded me and we headed indoors, I knew I would be okay.

I spent my first few days at Papworth waiting for my lung to reattach itself, which apparently is what is 'supposed' to happen in the case of smaller collapses such as the one I'd had. When it became clear that this was going to be problematic, I had my first ever chest drain fitted (a small tube inserted through the skin and into the cavity where trapped air was sitting between the lung and the chest wall). This was attached at the other end to what can only really be described as a 'bucket' into which any trapped air and fluid can escape.

Having gone through the rather uncomfortable process of having the chest drain fitted, I hung all my hopes on it resolving the pneumothorax. Once again, however, my hopes were dashed. After five days, it was decided that the only way this would be resolved was via surgery.

That evening, I had a visit from a very nice surgeon who talked me through the procedure. I would be put under a general anaesthetic and, whilst under, the surgeon aimed to (as he put it), "Stick the lung back on to the chest wall with the aid of some surgical glue." Although this sounded like a Heath Robinson, amateurish sort of approach to what I considered to be a serious situation, I had to place my rapidly decreasing trust in this chap. Thankfully, he sold a good story and conveyed a sense that he knew what he was doing and he breezed out of the room with a cheery, "See you in theatre in the morning."

I had been in the theatres at Papworth before, for the fitting of my portacath and the feeding PEG during the 2003 NTM episode. This was, however, the first time that I would undergo a large surgical procedure and, although it was to be done via laparoscopic ('keyhole') surgery, I felt incredibly daunted by the prospect.

I slept very little that night and when the nurse came into my room the following morning to get me ready to be taken to theatre, I remember saying, "I just hope the surgeon slept better than I did."

Back on the ward some hours later, I had been patched up and, apart from three incision points in my right-hand side and some drowsiness from the general anaesthetic, I was no worse for wear. I was relieved that it was over and, in a moment of misplaced wishful thinking, hoped that I would not have to go through anything like it again.

How foolish of me to think this would be the worst that CF would throw at me in the coming months and years!

Four months later, at the start of May 2008 and with my birthday just days away, I was at work one day when suddenly I felt very unwell. However, unlike back in January when I had no idea as to what was going on within my chest, this time I knew exactly what had happened. I was hot, breathless, and just wanted to go to sleep. But, for reasons that to this day I have not been able to reconcile, I carried on with attending a departmental lunch at a restaurant in Dorking town centre before returning to the office and finally throwing the towel in.

I knew that my lung (the same one) had collapsed again and that I needed to get to hospital as quickly as possible. However, and again for reasons which still elude me, I drove home to Reigate and met Aisling at the house.

A few minutes later, we were pulling up outside the A&E Department at East Surrey Hospital once more and hoping that I would be seen quickly, arriving as I was with a self-imposed diagnosis. Once more, an X-ray confirmed what I had expected; my right lung had again collapsed, but this time the collapse was more severe. With a real sense of disappointment and frustration, as well as the discomfort of carrying around a deflated lung, I resigned myself to a further few days at Papworth whilst this latest setback was dealt with.

Given that it was only two days from my 36th birthday, I also was resigned to knowing that my birthday would be spent at Papworth, in discomfort and seemingly with little to smile about.

This time, I required full-on surgery with a large, curving incision across the right side of my back so that my lung could be stitched back into place and held firmly against the chest wall. If the previous episode had been frightening, it was nothing compared to this. As I was briefed by the surgeon, there was talk of prolonged recovery periods, epidurals (for pain relief following the operation), and the possible need for numerous chest drains following the procedure.

Rather than being reassured in any way, as I said goodbye to Aisling outside the theatre doors, I quite literally shook like a leaf in pure fear of what was to come. It is all very well for medical staff to tell you that it will, "All be okay," and that, "You're in safe hands," but there is always a part of you that thinks, "Yes, but what if it's not okay?"

As I sat on the bed before being wheeled into theatre, a team of people busied themselves around me in what appeared to be a well-organised and choreographed attack. They were inserting cannulas into my arms and drawing markings on my back with marker pens. "I just hope that they are not drawing or writing anything rude about me," I quipped as I tried to lighten the very dark mood that had come over me. After a fifteen-minute kerfuffle where various people tried and failed to insert the epidural (a pain-killing injection) into the correct spot in my lower spine, the idea was abandoned entirely. I was flustered and stressed but as the first portion of the general anaesthetic was pushed through the IV line into my arm, I finally felt my body relax. As the room started to spin, I was quickly off to sleep once more.

I awoke with Aisling by my bedside. I felt terrible. I was sore all over. I was dehydrated and was in a lot of pain. I was hooked up to a machine that would administer pain relief on-demand through one of the remaining IV lines in my right arm. Known as Patient Controller Analgesia (PCA), upon pressing a small button on a handheld trigger device, a small dose of morphine is administered directly into the bloodstream to numb the pain causing the trouble. If it doesn't, you simply push the button again, although the device will only allow you to push a certain number of times in order to avoid an overdose (or, worse still, addiction).

Unfortunately, morphine has nasty habit of stopping the body's waterworks from functioning properly and so, alongside the IV lines and the two chest drains I had inserted into my side, I also had a catheter inserted to help prevent the build-up of urine in my bladder. In summary, I was lying there with multiple tubes and devices connected to me, in a lot of pain, feeling really rather sorry for myself.

It would be days before I would manage to get out of the bed again, to go to the toilet properly, or to have a proper wash. As the days had gone on, having become increasingly dirty (and probably smelly), the sense of needing to have a wash had become overwhelming. So, when the moment finally came and Aisling helped me to have a sit-down shower, the feeling of being at least semi-clean was divine.

After a couple of weeks, I was discharged once more to continue my recovery at home. I took a further two weeks off work and tried my best to take things slowly (although I have always found this very difficult to achieve, regardless of the circumstances that I find myself in).

Whilst I had been at Papworth, Aisling had been having several conversations with my boss at work and had been forced to disclose my condition and what CF meant to me on a daily and ongoing basis. My boss had responded positively and had told Aisling that the firm would do whatever was necessary to make things manageable for me from a CF point of view.

Firms are, of course, required by law to make what are known as 'reasonable adjustments' for employees with a health condition or disability, but it was nice to have this confirmed to us, relieving the stress we had been feeling after how much time off I had been forced to take during 2008.

I was back at my desk by the start of June of that year and, with the long summer ahead of me and a surgically restored right lung, was able to settle back in and carry on. The warmer months passed by with few further CF-related problems and my health seemed to pick up. A real milestone that summer was that NTM had now been absent from my sputum samples for over two years. So, the Papworth team decided that, although I should keep up with the Interferon Gamma immune system injections that I had been administering since 2003, the rest of the anti-NTM medication could now be discontinued. After five long years of multiple oral antibiotics, it was finally time to wave goodbye to them and settle back down to a more 'routine' regimen of drugs.

I welcomed this news with a real sense of relief, and Aisling and I marked this major milestone with a small celebratory meal out. Could it be real? Was the whole episode finally over? Was I NTM-free at last?

With my treatment for NTM seemingly behind me, Aisling and I took the decision to restart our flying hobby. It had been seven years since my dad's accident and, although the horror of that event will never leave me, following much soul-searching we decided to give aviating another go.

It seemed a shame that we had lost seven years of flying after what had happened to my dad, but by July 2008 the time felt right and we were both ready to take to the air once again. Having taken this decision, we dug out our logbooks, brushed the dust off our licences, and within days had enrolled at our local flying club based at Redhill Aerodrome in Surrey to renew our licences.

A few days later, I found myself in a two-seat Cessna training aircraft, identical to the ones I had learned to fly in all those years before in Florida, running through vaguely familiar checklists with an instructor. Within moments, I would be airborne once again, enjoying the feeling of the ground dropping away beneath me and heading into the bright blue summer skies above the Surrey countryside. With a huge smile on my face and the excitement tying my stomach in knots, I pushed the throttle forward, released the brakes, and my little aircraft shot down the grass runway and leapt into the air.

Within a few weeks, we were both signed off once more to act as the commander of single-engine piston aircraft, although I now had the additional stipulation on my licence that I could only fly with another qualified pilot on board in case I should collapse at the controls.

Over the next few months, Aisling and flew together when our weekends, budget, and of course the weather would allow. We initially hired the club's aircraft from Redhill and would fly to various other airfields in the south of England for an afternoon out and a cup of tea. This type of flying in the USA is termed the 'five hundred dollar hamburger' as this is the total amount you end up spending to fly for an hour and have a burger at some airport cafe before returning back home.

Flying had become more costly during our seven-year hiatus and we only had the financial means to take such trips once or twice a month. It soon became clear to Aisling and I that spending a small fortune on hiring a club aircraft for the afternoon was unsustainable, so we eventually decided to purchase a share in an aircraft in order to reduce the overall cost. After searching for a while, we found a one-sixth share in a four seat Cessna based at Biggin Hill Airport in Kent. Although about thirty-five minutes from our home in Reigate, Biggin Hill was a much bigger airfield with greater activity and some more interesting flying experiences to be had.

Often, we would find ourselves waiting to line up on the huge 1,820-metre-long asphalt runway behind a landing business jet or being told by air traffic control to circle the airfield whilst a pair of spitfires took off. Our aircraft was old, but in good condition and flew nicely. Aisling and I spent many Saturday and Sunday afternoons dotting around the countryside in that plane, taking in the views and reminding ourselves how lucky we were to be doing this once more, given all that we had been through since we had last flown.

The remainder of 2008 passed largely without incident health-wise and it really felt that perhaps I was back on top of CF once more. Although I would never have CF fully under my control like I had in the past, at least I could be thankful that I was NTM free, my overall health seemed good, and there was almost no chance of my right lung collapsing again any time soon!

As summer transitioned into the autumn and winter of 2008/9, I did my best to avoid the coughs and colds going around the office and kept as well as I could. Apart from the occasional two-week course of IV antibiotics, I managed to stay out of trouble and away from Papworth. I knuckled down at work, engrossing myself once again in a career that I was continuing to find both interesting and stimulating.

But in March 2009 I found myself an inpatient once more. Having completed yet another two-week course of IVs with little appreciable effect, I was admitted to the CF ward for additional antibiotics, including some of the NTM ones just in case the bacteria was starting to show its face again. Thankfully, my lungs responded, and I was discharged two weeks later to go and get on with my life.

Whilst I worked long days, I made sure that I took some time out at lunchtime to walk around Dorking town centre and get some exercise and fresh air. Being confined to an office for nine hours straight with no exposure to natural light doesn't do anybody any good, and for those with CF moving around and filling your lungs with 'real' (i.e. not reconditioned) air is paramount. So, unless something really needed completing, I would religiously down tools at about twelve thirty and head out for a forty-five-minute stroll around the lanes of the old town, making sure I took full advantage of the hill on which the High Street is located for additional aerobic exercise.

One aspect of working in Dorking that I particularly enjoyed was that my firm had connected with a local school as part of its outreach programme to provide reading assistants. Perceived as a way for the firm to give something back to the local community, the younger members of staff were encouraged to give up one of their lunch hours each week and head off to the school to listen to the children as they learned to read. I thought this was a wholesome thing to do (not giving a moment's consideration to the fact that entering a school full of cold-ridden, snotty-nosed kids with less hygiene awareness than a soggy sock was simply asking for trouble) and signed up to volunteer my services.

On my first day 'on duty' at the school, the session started well. The first few kids through the door were well mannered and reasonably competent at reading their books of choice. It wasn't until one child, who for the purposes of this story I will call Sam, wandered in. Sam seemed a nice enough lad yet rather quiet and shy.

Sam's reading was not quite of the standard of his classmates and I recall him sitting down nervously and opening his book with a palpable sense of trepidation – as if something was going to leap from the pages and bite him. Facing what must have seemed like a terrifying sea of words before him, Sam just stared at the page and after a few moments started crying. As an external assistant, I had been provided with no real guidance about how to deal with such scenarios. I was used to trying to get to the bottom of legal problems and formulating arguments either for or against a particular set of events. And I had absolutely no idea how to handle a child who I didn't know sitting and crying in front of me.

Whilst just wanting to put the book to one side, stop what we were doing and just give Sam a hug and some reassurance, the one thing that all of us reading assistants had been told was to never, ever touch the children in any way whatsoever.

Although I had passed the required child protection checks and protocols before even entering the school for the first time, this rule was of the 'utmost importance' and we were told it should be at the 'forefront of our minds at all times'. I therefore gave Sam as much verbal reassurance as I could muster, and we eventually picked up the book and carried on. I say 'carried on' but the first word on the first page would prove to be the stumbling block.

That first line, as in all good children's books, began with 'Once upon a time'. Sam looked at the word 'once' then looked at me with a very blank expression on his face. Having seriously misjudged how difficult certain words must appear when written down, I set about explaining to Sam (using phonics) how the word 'once' actually works.

I asked him to tell me the phoneme (phonic sound) for the letter 'o', which he did, pronouncing the 'o' in question as in the word 'orange'. Whilst I gave Sam due praise for getting this right, I then had to explain that in this instance – thanks to the complexity of the English language – the 'o' in 'once' was pronounced the same way as the letter 'w' in 'window'. Sam looked at me with utter puzzlement on his face. However, undeterred by this tricky start, we pressed on. Thankfully, he knew the phoneme for the letter 'n' too, so we proceeded swiftly. But then came the letter 'c'.

Whilst Sam stated with a deep sense of pride that he was sure the letter 'c' was pronounced as in 'cat', he was visibly crestfallen when I explained, although in most cases he was right, the 'c' in 'once' was actually pronounced in the same way as 's' for 'snake'. Once more, Sam just stared blankly at me, and I could just begin to see a hint of doubt washing across the poor kid's face.

By the time we reached 'e' which was not pronounced like the 'e' in 'elephant' but was, in fact, totally silent, Sam looked like he was going to cry again; our first very word was made up of an 'o' that is pronounced like a 'w', a 'c' that is pronounced like an 's', and an 'e' that you don't need to pronounce at all.

Goodness knows what Sam must have made of it all but, as he sat there alternating his gaze from my face to the words in his book, his internal monologue must have been along the lines of, "Blimey, this guy's even worse at this than I am!"

After this debacle over the very first word in the book, leaving poor Sam in a state of complete confusion and with my integrity shattered, his time with me was up. He closed his book, dried his eyes, wiped his snotty nose on the sleeve of his school jumper, and headed back into his classroom. As he left, he glanced just briefly back in my direction as if to say, "You're a prat."

Should Sam ever come to write a book about his life in the future, I will take some consolation from the fact that he will at least know how to spell the word 'once', as in: *I once met a solicitor called Luke. He was an idiot.*

It wasn't until the end of April 2009 that I found myself on the CF unit once more, and this time I felt that I was really struggling. After the ubiquitous X-rays and CT scans of my lungs, I was formally diagnosed with pneumonia and put on a load more IV antibiotics, along with various other medications and treatments, to help assist my breathing and make it less laboured. Over time, my temperature settled and my breathing eased, yet for the second year in a row I spent my birthday on the CF ward at Papworth, a long way from Aisling and from home, missing out on a nice night out that Aisling had arranged for us and blaming CF for ruining my birthday celebrations once again.

It was during this admission that CF would, again, play a fundamental part in mapping my future. One afternoon, after the CF team's ward round was complete, one of the CF consultants popped back in, "For a quick chat." I got on well with all members of the CF team at Papworth, but I got a sense very early on that this was not a social call. The discussion was not terribly long or particularly in depth, but the gist of it knocked me back so far that I struggled to get over the shock of it in the few days that followed.

The doctor, as nicely and in as friendly a way as she could, enquired as to how much I was working during an average week and whether I found my job hard, enjoyable, or stressful. I answered all of her questions truthfully but started to wonder where her line of enquiry was heading.

It soon became apparent that the doctor was building up to something and, as the conversation progressed, the purpose of this 'quick chat' became obvious; given that my CF history over the past year or so had been what could best be described as 'chequered', the team's recommendation was that I gave real consideration to reducing my workload. This would, they said, allow more time for me to rest and look after myself.

I was floored by their suggestion. They wanted me to cut down my working hours to allow more time for the management of my CF. I was angry and, despite it being with my best interests at heart, I wanted to reject the idea; it was too early and I was too young to be considering such a drastic change at this point in my career. Yet again, my misguided sense of invincibility did its best to hoodwink me. But over the following few days, and with a heavy heart, it became obvious to me that I was struggling.

I was juggling CF, my life, and my career. And it was not working.

My health was declining and my head was telling me (exactly how my dad would have been if he was still alive) that now was the time to step back, accept my own mortality, and reduce my hours.

Yet again, I felt that I had arm-wrestled CF and lost. But I realised that without following my doctors' advice, further complications would become more and more common and, before long, I would be facing the possibility of a transplant square in the face. It was therefore with a sense of deep despair that, on my return to work, I handed in a formal request to reduce my hours from five to four days a week. My request was accepted and, with disappointment but a sense of reluctant resignation, from that point onwards I was no longer a full-time employee of the firm. CF had taken over and was shoving me down a path that was not of my choosing.

After that, everything felt different. Everyone in the office knew that I had taken a lot of time off in the past few months and that I was now only in the office from Monday to Thursday, although they almost certainly did not know why. By this stage, I didn't really object to people knowing about my CF (I had become simply too tired to worry about such things). What I was not so comfortable with was the concept of others knowing my private business.

As you might have discovered by now, I have never been the sort of person to brandish my condition around like some sort of badge of honour, nor have I wanted to be treated any differently from anyone else. Yet things were changing; my whole life was changing. CF was managing me instead of me managing it, and I was being forced to come to terms with that shift.

Whilst the situation was not of my choosing, the way in which I dealt with it *was*. So, this was the real challenge that I now had on my hands.

Those who knew about my CF at work, the head of my department and the partners for whom I worked, were relatively sympathetic and accommodating, firing the occasional, "How are you feeling?" or, "Is everything okay?" at me from time to time. But I felt that I had started on some form of 'slippery slope', and dealing with the mental repercussions of this was hard. As was trying to get on with a normal working life in an environment where, ultimately, I felt that no one was really terribly interested in me or CF as long as the work got done.

As that year concluded and 2010 began, I was very aware that I was struggling both mentally as well as physically. I was finding it harder and harder to keep up with all of the balls I was attempting to juggle. I was constantly tired and by each afternoon at work I was exhausted.

On such days, had someone said that there was a dark room in the basement where I could go and lie down for a quick forty winks, I would have been down there like a shot. A lot of the time, it was hard to concentrate and completely focus on what I was doing. Additionally, by the middle of the afternoon, my chest would feel ropey and extra physio was required to get me through to the end of the day. Sometimes, I would head down to the basement car park and sit in my car, patting my chest to clear my lungs before heading back up to finish the day's work.

Whilst I was fully aware that this was not ideal, I saw little alternative but to get on with it. I began to dread the days when I would have to go to client meetings or to court in London because I knew they took so much out of me. For the first time in my working life, I had an increasing awareness that CF was really starting to get the better of me. This filled me with a real sense of despair and frustration in equal measure, and yet it really felt like there was little I could do about it. There as almost an inevitability as to what might happen next. But I pressed on regardless, causing probably irreparable damage to my body and my mind in the process.

Aisling continued to support me in every way she could, but I think we both knew that simply reducing my hours was not enough. She would often ring me at work to check in on me and make sure that I was okay, but it was becoming apparent that her concerns for how long I could keep this all up were building - quickly.

The inevitable conclusion to this decline in my health was that, at some time in the not too distant future, I may well need to admit that I was no longer able to hold down my job and carry it out to a satisfactory degree. I knew I was struggling, but the hardest thing for anyone with a chronic condition to face up to is that the condition itself is worsening and that it is imposing limits that were not there before.

The awareness of declining health is heart-breaking, and the reality is hard to face up to. However long I had known that CF would catch up with me does not make the day it does any easier.

By the autumn of 2010, things had come to a head. My chest starting to play up again was causing me to take further time off work. The sucker punch came in September of that year – I was attending Papworth for a routine appointment on a regular Friday afternoon when I was asked by a clinic nurse to take myself away from the main waiting area and sit in a side room down the corridor. This was unusual and the gravity of the situation was enhanced by the fact that the nurse was wearing a face mask and gown over her uniform – something I had never seen in clinic before.

With everything I had been through over the preceding years, I immediately knew something was up. I kept my composure as best as I could while I waited for the consultant to appear and convey the bad news. When it came, although I had been warned that it could happen, I was devastated.

The consultant came in, also gowned and masked, and simply said, "I'm sorry to have to tell you that the lab has detected NTM growing in your sputum. We need to restart treatment as soon as possible."

To say that these words destroyed me would be a gross understatement. I had hoped that such a day would never come. Yet, there I was, seven years after having beaten off the bacteria that tried to kill me, facing the spectre of it once more. A rigorous month of nasty, toxic IV antibiotics that, although treating the NTM, make you feel so desperately unwell, lay ahead of me and it was agreed that this treatment would start as soon as a bed became available on the CF Unit.

Whilst I worked hard to keep my composure in the presence of others, as soon as I reached my car I fell apart. More through frustration than fear, I cried my heart out, hitting the steering wheel and dashboard as hard as I could in a state of sheer desperation. I was so angry with CF and all that it had thrown at me over the years and I just wanted it all to stop.

Over time, I had noticed that others with CF who I had come to know never appeared to feel sorry for themselves. I had always tried hard to follow suit, and believed this attitude was what got me as far as I had managed to go in life and in my career. All that said, however, now more than ever, I just needed someone to give me a reassuring hug and to tell me that things would be okay.

I rang Aisling and told her the news. With her reassuring voice and loving tone, as ever, she knew the right thing to say. "We have beaten this once darling and we will do so again."

I spent the following month on the CF Unit at Papworth once more, although not in one of the main patient bedrooms. This time, I was in a room just outside of the unit itself because NTM had, by this stage, become more prevalent in the CF community. Cross-infection between CF patients was also better understood and being taken far more seriously. Despite feeling something of an outsider, the care I received was as outstanding as ever. Over the next five weeks, I endured round the clock antibiotic IVs, spending most of my waking hours with my head hovering precariously over a sick bowl as the toxicity of the drugs took effect.

Aisling and I spent our tenth wedding anniversary on the ward at Papworth with me hooked up to a drip-stand and unable to leave the building. Thankfully, one of the nurses had taken pity on my predicament and bought me an anniversary card for me to give to her when she arrived that evening. And, whilst being hospitalised on such a milestone was a prospect that neither of us had wished for or expected, we dealt with it with as much resolve as we could muster – all while, deep down, wishing that things could have been different.

After those five weeks, I was discharged and sent home to continue the regimen of oral antibiotics that I had come off some two years previously. In the years since 2003, when I had been the first CF patient in the UK diagnosed with NTM, the community's understanding of the bacteria had improved immensely and antibiotic treatment for it had been developed. It was therefore something of a consolation to realise that CF patients all around the world (including myself) were now able to benefit more quickly from appropriate NTM treatment regimens, and that this was due largely to what I had endured.

But however hard I tried to pick myself up after this latest setback, I no longer felt the same as I had about many aspects of my life. This included my career; I knew in myself that drastic action was needed to arrest my decline and stabilise matters so that Aisling and I could have a future worth living together. I saw little virtue in working myself to the bone for someone else if it rendered me unfit to enjoy my own private life and married life with Aisling.

During that chat with the consultant at Papworth, when it was suggested that I switch to part-time hours, it had also been mentioned that I could consider retiring at forty and taking on a more relaxed, less stressful lifestyle. But by late

2010, I already knew that the game was up and that I may not even make my fortieth birthday given the way things were going.

I felt, deep down, like I was finished. I could no longer continue working at the expense of what remained of my health.

Given how difficult I had found it in the past to take so much time off and then to reduce my working hours, the decision staring me in the face was surprisingly easy. I could continue to work and risk everything or stop and preserve what I had left in my tank in order to have some sort of future. When put in such black and white terms, there really was no choice to be made. So, as I penned my letter of resignation, both my heart and my head were telling me that this was the right thing to do.

Not for one moment have I ever regretted writing that letter and, looking back, I now consider it to be anything *but* giving in to CF. Quite the opposite – it was a brave, strong decision that ultimately may have let me reach where I am now – nine years on and still going.

Within a couple of weeks and following a sequence of meetings with my boss and the partners for whom I worked, my leaving date was formally agreed by all parties.

I left the firm on 6th December 2010 with little fanfare. A few colleagues stopped in to say goodbye on their way out of the door that evening, but word had obviously got around that I was not leaving through choice or to move on to bigger and better things.

None of this bothered me, however, as I knew that leaving was probably one of the best decisions I had ever taken. I was finally giving CF the respect and consideration it deserved and, in doing so, was buying myself valuable extra time. And with some major events about to unfold in the months ahead, that time (which would turn out to be amazing and life-changing) was just about to start.

THIRTY-SEVEN

"YOU WILL NEVER HAVE CHILDREN"

I had always wanted to have children and to be a father. Being around children gave me a sense of being young again and reminded me of my childhood, unencumbered by the shackles of the chronic disease that blighted my life in later years. As if I needed an excuse (those who know me best might say), being near kids also gives me an excuse to act in manner somewhat younger than my actual years. Having children is something that Aisling and I very much wished for. Yet, as with so many other aspects of a life with CF, there is a difference between what you might want and what you can possibly have. To that end, having children, no matter how much we longed for them, was never going to be straightforward.

Throughout my adolescence, no one (as far as my memory serves me) had ever mentioned that CF adults can face fertility issues when trying to conceive and that – certainly in CF males – without medical intervention, the chances of a successful natural conception is rare if not impossible. With such an important piece of my CF education missing, I entered my relationship with Aisling blissfully unaware that there were potentially going to be difficulties on this front.

Looking back, it seems incredulous that not one person, not the medical professionals I sat in front of or, indeed, my own parents, deemed fertility issues news-worthy enough to talk about. *No one* saw fit to enlighten me about an affliction that I would almost certainly have to face at some point during my life. Yet, this was the reality of the situation.

Whether those who were in a position to know better found it too hard to address this issue, were relying on others to pass on the message, or simply thought that I would have enough to deal with growing up without the stress this particular nugget of information might cause, I'll never know. What I do know is that when I finally became aware of the harsh truths about the difficulties in reproduction for CF adults, it hit me very hard indeed.

As you know, it was some time into mine and Aisling's relationship before I came clean about having CF. After my revelation, and no doubt driven by my track record of being less than transparent with her, Aisling began her own research into the realities of life with CF and, to this end, she borrowed a book from the local library that laid out the specifics in stark, monochrome reality. It would be this book that would hurl the grenade of fertility issues into our relationship.

The author's 'no holds barred, here it is' approach was probably written for people just like me who had, up until the point of reading it, wandered through their CF life, living contentedly with the horrifically misguided belief that, despite everything else that CF could throw at them, at least there were to be no worries in '*that department*'. But it was certainly not easy material to digest.

As Aisling ran though the highlights she had gleaned from reading this manual of doom, in a Brighton pub one evening in 1998, this was the one item on the list of challenges we might face that stuck in my head and troubled me more than any other. Despite all the caveats that the book had presented, ranging from the ever-hopeful 'in some cases CF adult males will be able to conceive naturally' all the way to the rather finite 'there are always other options open to CF couples wanting to start a family, such as adoption', in my mind there was little room for doubt; for Aisling and I, having children would be very, very difficult.

In those days, when fertility intervention techniques were less developed than they are now, and certainly less successful, digesting the cold contents of the chapter on fertility left me with my fatherhood bubble well and truly burst. Whilst I had always hoped that, one day, I would be 'Dad' to a little person of my very own, I was left feeling bereft, despondent, and deflated. Aisling on the other hand, seemed to face this next challenge on our journey together as just another hurdle to overcome, and was resolute that we would become parents, by some means, if that was what we both decided we wanted.

In the days that followed, I tried to tell myself that perhaps there had been some sort of mistake, that the book was horribly out of date or simply just out of touch. The truth of the matter, however, was that, no matter how much I tried to sugar-coat it, the message I took away was that 'as a CF adult male, face up to it mate, you will never have children'.

Without drilling too far into the medical nitty-gritty of fertility in adults with CF, and turning this chapter into some sort of horrific medical paper, it would be fair to say that either fate or bad fortune (I'll let you decide) means that adults with CF will face difficulties when trying to conceive.

For women with CF, their fallopian tubes may be blocked by mucus or the natural production of eggs may be disrupted though illness or the use of medication. CF females are also, generally speaking, smaller in frame than non-CF females, enhancing the health risks that pregnancy and childbearing can bring. In males, abnormalities in our plumbing system mean that sperm may either not be able to find its way into the outside world by the normal means of navigation enjoyed by non-CF males or may not even be produced at all. Either way, for me to have any chance of fulfilling my dream of having children, there would be a very long and particularly arduous path to travel.

By now, and at this point in my life, I had become more accustomed to adversity and to the concept that things were generally more difficult than they would have been if I had been born without CF. Through these experiences, however, I had become more resilient, battle-hardened, and determined; if I was to achieve my dreams of fatherhood, then this would simply be another hurdle to overcome rather than an obstacle to stop me in my tracks.

Aisling had always been as keen as I was to start a family, so we decided early on that, when the time was right, we would explore all the options available to us. The years following the NTM saga of 2003 were spent getting myself as well as possible. After all, it would not be fair on either Aisling or I to bring someone else into the world unless I was fully capable of doing my bit and of enjoying fatherhood to the extent that I always hoped I would.

The optimism that we shared of one day becoming parents was, though, constantly overshadowed by feelings of guilt and conflict. I would spend hours considering the notion of whether it was *fair* to bring a child into the world who would have a parent with CF and who may possibly lose that parent early on in their life. Was it *fair* to blight that child's life with the dark shadow of CF hanging over the whole family and with having a parent in and out of hospital on a frequent basis?

However much I turned these issues over in my head, there was never a right (or wrong) answer to be found. All I knew was that, although Aisling and I would be *able* to live our lives without becoming parents, we owed it to ourselves to at least explore the options and to try our best to make our dreams reality.

We had taken the first steps in this new journey back in early 2009 when we decided to investigate exactly how the land lay in terms my physiology. Whilst many men would baulk at the very suggestion of their ability to reproduce (and, in the eyes of many, their 'masculinity') being brought into question, let alone examined in microscopic detail, I had no such qualms. I knew that if there was to be any chance of having children, then I needed to set my male pride to one side and leave my dignity at the door. This was to be an invasive, undignified, and possibly degrading process, but one that simply couldn't be avoided if I had any hope of, one day, being called 'Daddy'.

Receiving the results of a fertility test was never going to be a barrel of laughs, particularly for someone who had a predisposition for difficulties in this particular arena. As it was, and following analysis of a sperm sample I'd provided, I was sitting in my car outside an office block, waiting for Aisling to finish work, when I received the call from my GP. She explained with as much empathy as she could muster that, although my sperm count was low, the good news was that there were live sperm traceable in my sample, which meant that fatherhood remained a possibility, albeit a remote one.

She went on to explain that seeking the guidance of a reproduction expert would be the best way forward and that she could refer me accordingly. Around the same time, Aisling had undergone genetic screening via a simple blood test to ensure that she was not a carrier of the CF gene. You may recall that for two people who are both carriers of the defective CF gene, there is a one in four chance of having a child with CF. Whilst screening was only advanced enough to screen for the top twenty-or-so most common defective CF genes, this would give us as much reassurance as we could get that any future children we might have would not be born with CF.

When Aisling's results came back, she was found to be clear from any of those defective genes. So, armed with this knowledge, the information we had about my fertility, and the referral to a fertility specialist, the stage was set for us to start exploring whether we really could ever hope to have children of our own.

(I should state that had Aisling been found to be a carrier of a defective CF gene, this may not necessarily have prevented us from proceeding to the next stage. But no one would wish to conceive a child with a serious lifelong and life changing illness, and such a finding would have made the decision to progress much, much harder.)

Now, I have always been a keen supporter of the NHS and hate the very idea of scarce health service resources being used (or abused) for frivolous purposes. Some would argue that spending millions of pounds every year helping couples to conceive is not a fruitful use of resources when, just to take two examples, so many people are suffering from and dying of cancer and increasing numbers of the population are being struck in their later years with incurable dementia. The very concept of taking up valuable NHS time and money just because Aisling and I fancied becoming parents seemed, on the one hand, entirely selfish. But this was guidance that we really needed in order to be able to make an informed decision about how, and if, we could move forward.

As it turned out, after just one meeting with a fertility specialist at a particularly uninviting and dilapidated Crawley Hospital, much of the decision-making process was quickly taken out of our hands. The specialist we met wasted no time in making it very clear to us that because of my condition (yes, you did read that correctly), and although IVF treatment may be successful for us, it would not be available to us under existing local health funding guidelines.

After that, we were ignominiously shown out of the door with little in the way of empathy or emotion as the specialist moved swiftly along to the next couple amongst the growing number of people in the waiting room, all harbouring their own hopes and dreams of parenthood (and also for NHS assistance to achieve this). Even a glancing, "Good luck," would have been nice, but instead we were left feeling abandoned and alone, as if the whole of the NHS (which for so long had been on our side) had suddenly turned against us.

Following this point-blank rejection for NHS fertility treatment, we were on our own, and so started a long period of searching for fertility centres that may be able to help us. After what felt like months of scouring the success tables of different centres (generally given in percentage terms of live births in proportion to IVF cycles undertaken), we settled on one in the heart of London, run by a fertility specialist who was internationally renowned for his expertise. We had seen him being interviewed on television several times and knew that his services wouldn't come cheap. But after a great deal of soul searching, and the construction of several – very complex – budgeting spreadsheets, we decided to proceed and to engage his services.

Taking this decision meant that we were resigning ourselves to placing all of our eggs (another pun) into one basket and, effectively, gambling a significant sum of money in the hope of reaching our objective. There were no guarantees that we would end the process with anything other than a huge hole in our savings, yet Aisling and I both agreed that it was a price worth paying and a bet worth taking if we were ever to have a family of our own.

The first steps of this process were to have sperm surgically extracted from myself and placed into storage, which would later be used to fertilise eggs extracted from Aisling. This procedure is known as ICSI (Intracytoplasmic Sperm Injection) and is now the most common form of IVF for those with CF who wish to conceive children naturally.

This process, putting it simply, involves a very large needle and (in my personal experience) not nearly enough sedation. You get the picture. As we left the clinic that day, with me walking like I had just completed a six-month pony trekking expedition, the first real first steps to becoming parents had been taken and we were on our way and we tried to focus on the immense joy that a successful outcome might bring.

Over the next few weeks, it was Aisling who endured the real hardship and emotional turmoil that the IVF process imposes, with me assuming the role of bystander; a mere passenger in the whole scheme. Aisling was the one who endured daily blood tests, hormone injections, scans, and various other tests in order that her eggs could be extracted and fertilised by embryologists in the lab some time later. All of this lasted several weeks, with Aisling travelling by train into London every day so that the clinic could keep an eye on proceedings.

Milestones came and went, and eventually the day came when the fertilised egg (which had been 'harvested' by this stage and had become a viable embryo) was implanted by the world-famous embryologist himself, who also happened to be the medical director and owner of the clinic. This was Sunday 13th June 2010, which was coincidentally Father's Day that year. We were both conscious of this fact as we spent our morning at the clinic in London, although we tried not to dwell on it too much. After all, wouldn't it be just perfect to conceive our first (and quite possibly our only) child on such a day? We couldn't possibly be that lucky.

After embryo implantation, it was ten days before we found ourselves back in London. We had done everything we could to avoid mulling things over during the intervening time, yet it was hard to keep such thoughts at bay. On the following Wednesday, we were back at the clinic early for Aisling's blood to be taken and we were then sent away to wait for the results, which would show whether Aisling was pregnant. Whilst we could have done this ourselves with a home testing kit from a pharmacy, we decided to leave this crucial part of the process to the experts. After all, the blood test would provide a far more reliable result than a home testing kit would, and at such an important stage we didn't want to leave any room for error, ambiguity, or doubt. The process had been an emotional whirlwind so far and, if it were to end that day, the result had to be certain so that we could take stock and move on.

After a meandering walk down Bond Street and past the high-end jewellery shops of Mayfair, we stopped for a cup of tea before making our way to Green Park. It was a nice sunny morning and, after the anxiety of the past few weeks, it was just nice to sit on the dry warm grass, to chat, and to contemplate life for a while. We sat in our own little bubble as the world dashed past us, awaiting the call that might just change our lives forever. The tension was almost nauseating, yet there seemed little that we could do to make it any easier.

The call finally came at around eleven thirty that morning. Aisling had the phone on speaker so that we could hear the result at the same time. Having verified Aisling's full name, date of birth, and clinic number, the doctor (with genuine excitement in her voice) said, "Congratulations, you are pregnant..."

After quietly agreeing to return to the clinic and talk through the next steps, Aisling hung up, turned to me, and we simply sat there, hugging and crying, oblivious to anyone or anything going on around us. Our heads were spinning and I completely and unashamedly let my emotions get the better of me. I knew that we had an awfully long way to go and that the next few weeks were fraught with risks, but we had passed the first milestone and we were elated. For the first time, we allowed ourselves to believe that maybe, just maybe, we would become parents after all.

Aisling's pregnancy was not an easy one and certainly had its ups and downs, with all the associated stress that such fluctuations bring. Like most other over-enthusiastic couples expecting their first child, as the weeks passed by, we read up on what was happening at each stage of the pregnancy.

We also diligently attended our weekly antenatal classes, meeting five other couples all in the same boat as us. One interesting difference, however, was that everyone else in our cohort knew the sex of their soon-to-be-born baby and we were the only couple in the group who had opted otherwise. We were certainly not the type of couple to parade around exclaiming that we, "Wanted a surprise," when our baby was born. After all, it is only ever going to be a boy or a girl and would only be a genuine 'surprise' if it came out as a puppy.

But, for us, the decision not to find out the sex of our baby was mainly because we were just so *thankful* to be expecting a baby at all. To be having a baby, defying the odds of CF and then the equally stacked odds of the IVF process, was more than enough for us and more than we could have ever hoped for. Whether we had a boy or a girl was incidental, and the *penchant* for 'reveal parties' in the modern world simply makes me cringe with despair. But each to their own, I suppose.

Our baby was due 9th March 2011. This was a date that was etched into our brains from very early on, through the twelve-week scan and the twenty-week scan, and into the final trimester. As the weeks rolled by, we prepared the spare room at home for our pending arrival and filled it with neutrally coloured clothing and accessories (mostly white), given our self-imposed, non-partisan approach to the sex of our baby.

We went and had a 3D scan of the baby whilst they were still 'in utero', a process that proved to be trickier than first envisaged; rather than posing diligently for its photo-call and providing us with lovely images of its face, the baby made everything as difficult as possible for our sonographer by determinedly sucking its thumb throughout, thereby obscuring much of its face with its own fist. These must be the most expensive photos of a fist anyone has ever paid for. Consequently, whilst Aisling and I could have spent hours arguing who the baby looked more like, we were saved from this particular discussion. After all, we had much more important matters to debate, like whose intense stubbornness the baby had inherited.

On the night of the 7th March 2011, Aisling and I had been for a drive and had sat at the top of Reigate Hill in Surrey close to our home. This was a place that we often came to in order to clear our heads, talk about things, or simply just to sit, enjoy the view, and mull over life's nuances. We knew that the baby's arrival was imminent and, after eleven years of marriage and a further three together, the time of it being just the two of us was in its final days. Little did we know as we sat looking across the South Downs towards Sussex and beyond, that we were in fact experiencing our final *hours* of being a 'couple' rather than a 'family'.

THIRTY-EIGHT
AGAINST ALL ODDS

We had not been home long from our little sojourn to Reigate Hill when Aisling fell ill and ran off to throw up in the bathroom. After composing herself, she still looked distinctly unwell, so we telephoned the maternity unit at our local hospital for advice. On speaking with one of the midwives on duty, we were advised not to panic but to make our way into the hospital as soon as possible. The hospital was only ten minutes' drive away and so, upon grabbing Aisling's hospital bag and with me throwing a few things together, we were on our way.

We arrived on the ward at around seven thirty p.m. and so commenced the longest, and possibly one of the most traumatic, nights of our life.

It was quickly confirmed that Aisling was in labour and she was monitored for the first few hours as the spacing of the contractions reduced and her dilation increased. We were looked after by a wonderful midwife by the name of Fiona who had clearly been doing her job for years. Each time she entered the room, she popped by with a spring in her step and a smile on her face. In fact, one of the very first things she said to us that evening, upon noting the expressions of nervous anxiety spread across our faces, was that for as long as she remained smiling, we could smile too.

As the hours wore on, and as midnight passed, progress was slow, and I tried to relax as much as possible. It would be fair to state that my emotions were a heady mix of excitement and apprehension in equal measure; my optimism just slightly overshadowed by a sense of foreboding at what the next few hours might bring. Fiona did her best to relax us, and Aisling performed her tasks with amazing composure and with her usual 'let's get down to business' approach.

I did as much as I could, remembering all that we had been taught in our antenatal classes, and tried my best to maintain a reassuring and relaxed demeanour. I knew that my heart rate was galloping with increased speed with each hour that came and went, but I also knew that for the sake of Aisling and our baby I had to do my very best to appear calm and composed throughout this frankly terrifying ordeal. I was used to being the patient, to having people caring for me and rushing around doing things for my benefit, and this was the first time I had really seen Aisling vulnerable and in pain. It was this sight that nearly brought me to breaking point. I was familiar with being the one in need of assistance, in pain and in fear, but I struggled to see someone I loved so much in a similar position.

By around five a.m., Fiona was starting to get ever so slightly concerned as to why the baby had not yet appeared, and the delivery process had seemingly stalled. By five thirty a.m. the on-call obstetrician had arrived to see how things were going (or not). After a few minutes of prodding and poking, she decided that our baby was slightly twisted and that it would be unable to make its way out unassisted. Aisling and I were told that intervention was probably going to be required, meaning that either a ventouse delivery (which involves a suction cup being placed over the baby's head and gently pulled so that the baby is eased down the birth canal) and/or a forceps delivery was going to be necessary.

Having learned about these types of delivery interventions during our antenatal classes, we were aware of what was involved and how they would be performed. What we were not expecting, however, was when Fiona explained that this hospital liked performing these procedures in theatre just in case they were unsuccessful, leaving a caesarean section as the only remaining option. I was now concerned that what had started off as a 'normal' labour had become one that would end in an operating theatre. Having had experience of being in theatres myself, this was not somewhere I had hoped that I would see my child born. But my apprehension was nothing compared to the horrors of what would happen in the next couple of hours.

A short time later, with Aisling prepped and me changed into scrubs, Fiona escorted the two of us into the theatre itself, where the obstetrician and various other medical staff were gathered around the periphery awaiting our arrival. Once in and settled, the team started their choreographed and well-rehearsed drills of preparing the room and the equipment in case a caesarean became necessary. Aisling was given some additional light sedation and connected to various monitors whilst I sat quietly holding her hand, a mere spectator to the proceedings being played out around me.

With all hands on deck and the theatre ready, the obstetrician approached with ventouse in her hand and got to work. It was by now about six forty-five a.m., almost twelve hours since our arrival at the hospital the evening before. Having quickly determined that the ventouse was not going to be successful in extracting the baby, the obstetrician moved swiftly on to the forceps. After a couple of minutes of twisting and tugging with what looked like little more than a set of barbecue tongs, everything changed and the atmosphere in the room suddenly took on a completely different feel.

An alarm on one of the monitors started beeping in the background and Fiona alerted the obstetrician that the baby's heart rate was dropping rapidly. Aisling looked at me for reassurance and I just squeezed her hand tightly. A second alarm sounded and, by this stage, Fiona's ever-present smile had vanished. As she maneuverered herself for a better position, she exclaimed that there was a prolapsed cord and that they needed to get the baby out as quickly as possible.

A prolapsed cord is when the umbilical cord attaching the baby to the mother is compromised and is no longer able to supply oxygen and blood to the baby. In our case, the twisting of the baby had allowed the cord to slip down between the birth canal wall and our baby's head and was effectively starting to starve them of oxygen.

A quick-thinking Fiona managed to hold the cord between her fingers long enough to allow it to continue pulsating with blood as the anaesthetist and surgical team swiftly moved in. Fiona declared that this was now an emergency and asked for various doctors to be bleeped immediately to attend theatre. What had started as a calm, slow burning labour had now become what's termed a 'crash caesarean'. This is one level up from an emergency caesarean and is defined as where 'the life of the baby and/or the mother is in grave danger'. Of course, I was not aware of the specifics of this terminology at the time, but I could tell things were going very wrong, very quickly.

Although there remained a sense of underlying professionalism in the room, with people going about their jobs in a wholly proper manner, there was also a feeling that the tide had turned against us and that, unless someone managed to turn it back very rapidly, things were not going to end well.

Aisling looked at me, clearly scared by the goings-on, and asked me what was happening. I could barely speak myself, so just smiled as best as I could whilst explaining that there was 'a problem' with the cord but that Fiona was in control and that the baby would be there shortly. Inside, though, I was in pieces; my whole world was disintegrating before my very eyes. I struggled to hold it together and just squeezed Aisling's hand tightly, as though her life depended on it, which at that moment, I thought it might just do.

After a few more seconds, in which a screen was positioned between me and Aisling and what was happening further down the bed, a large incision was made across Aisling's abdomen. More and more medical staff hurried through side doors into the theatre, filling the space. But Aisling and I could do nothing other than just be as close to each other as we could.

Eventually, the baby was extracted and rushed away to the far side of the room where an infant resuscitation table was already hooked up and ready to be put into action. I immediately noticed that the baby was not crying, and I knew that Aisling had too. Once again, she asked me what was happening, and I told her that the baby was out and that they were just giving it some oxygen and cleaning it up.

I could see over the barrier screening Aisling's lower body that two midwives were looking after our baby, one rubbing it vigorously with a towel whilst the other stood alongside holding a tiny oxygen mask at the end of a tube. I put my head to Aisling's and we cried together. My mind was racing. For a fleeting moment, I was furious. How could we go through so much only to lose the baby *now*? At the last moment. Surely, that wasn't possible?

The theatre was now deathly quiet, as the surgical team started to piece Aisling back together and the midwives continued to work on the baby. Resisting thoughts of how unfair life would be should our baby not survive, I told myself to simply be thankful that Aisling had. I was still gripping her hand when this train of thought was abruptly splintered apart by the cry of a small baby from the far corner of the room. Mine and Aisling's silent tears suddenly became a flood as one of the theatre nurses, smiling from ear to ear, quietly said, "Don't worry, he's going to be okay."

All I could do at that moment was put my head down in sheer relief, but Aisling was still alert enough to ask, "Are you sure it's a *he*?"

Aisling had maintained throughout her pregnancy that she had had a feeling the baby was going to be a girl. But when the nurse had hurriedly dashed back to reconfirm his position on such matters, he returned to inform us that, yes, we definitely had a little boy.

For a second, the world stopped spinning. The reality of what had just happened overwhelmed us – we were parents, at last. Aisling and I kissed and she closed her eyes, physically and emotionally exhausted.

It was now seven twenty-three a.m., almost exactly twelve hours since we had walked through the doors downstairs. At last, and flying in the face of all the odds, we were parents. And what an amazing and mind-spinning feeling it was. A few minutes later, after our baby had been weighed, he was finally presented to us, cleaned up and wrapped in a fluffy white towel. Fully aware that this was a moment I would never forget, when the nurse handed him to me, I simply looked at him, smiled at him, and kissed his tiny blood-stained head. Then I whispered to him the first thing that came into my head: "I am so pleased you're here. We are going to have such fun."

One issue we had explored in the days and weeks leading up to the birth of our son was the prospect of having stem cells from the umbilical cord extracted, frozen, and stored. This was at a time when stem cell research had really taken off and the commercial side of the process was a burgeoning industry. Companies in the field were publicising that scientists were now successfully repairing or replacing damaged cells in people with health conditions and were either reversing the progression of these illnesses or preventing them altogether.

Around thirty major conditions had been identified that could be treated or prevented through stem cell transplants and, although CF was not one of those on the list, there were many others that were.

Maybe it was our somewhat enhanced knowledge of congenital conditions (through CF) that led us down this path, but Aisling and I decided very early on that it was something we would like to pursue if possible. We discussed it at one of our antenatal appointments at the hospital in the weeks before the birth, which led to a long and protracted correspondence with the head of midwifery services. Eventually, the healthcare trust agreed. Seemingly, our request was something they had never been asked to consider in all the many thousands of births performed at the hospital so far.

In this respect we were trailblazers of sorts. At least this were how we were described, but to us it seemed remarkably obvious. After all, if you could do anything that may prevent your child developing or suffering from a serious health condition at some point in their life, then surely as parents it is your responsibility to do so. At least, that was the view we took.

Although our son's actual birth had been traumatic and was problematic, the extraction of the cord blood (performed by a private phlebotomist engaged by the stem cell firm we had contracted) all went smoothly. In fact, this was the one element of the whole birthing experience that had caused the most uproar through its organisation yet, ironically, turned out to be the most hassle-free. To this day, our son's umbilical cord blood is stored in a giant freezer somewhere in the English countryside, ever ready should the need arise.

After a few hours of being back on the ward, I left Aisling to sleep and headed back home for some rest myself, having been up for about twenty-eight hours by this point. When I got in, I called my mum (a former midwife herself) to firstly tell her that she was a grandmother but secondly to tell her the full horrors of what we had just been through. When she explained how horrific cord prolapses can be and how they don't tend to end well, I lost it once more. The tiredness and the emotion of the previous night completely overwhelmed me, and I let it all out to my mum on the end of the phone. Despite all the difficult times I had experienced in my life, some related to CF and some not, this was one of the hardest things I had ever been through. I knew that it would take some time to get over and, although I told myself repeatedly that it all ended well and that Aisling and our baby were both alive and well, the trauma of thinking I might lose them had taken the shine off what should have been one of the happiest days of my life.

After a couple of hours of disturbed sleep, followed by the usual routine of nebulisers, physiotherapy, and chest clearance (CF never gives you a break, even if you have just become a father for the first time) I rang Aisling to see how she was getting on. She explained that our son's temperature had spiked, his heart rate and oxygen saturation levels had fallen, and that the staff had whisked him off to the special care baby unit (SCBU) for monitoring, leaving Aisling alone on the postnatal ward, surrounded by new mothers who were all cooing over and feeding their newborn babies.

My heart immediately sank again as I gathered my things to head straight back to the hospital. By the time I had arrived, Aisling had been moved to a side room of her own, the nursing staff having taken pity on her for being the only mother without her baby and given her some space away from the constant soundtrack of crying infants.

Upon my arrival, Aisling led me down the corridor and to the SCBU where our son was in an incubator, being warmed up and sleeping cosily. He was already yellow in appearance; the traumatic nature of his arrival having induced jaundice, which we were told would subside in a few days' time. Compared to the other babies in the room, most of whom were premature and looked tiny in their incubators, our baby was huge and barely fitted into his.

After a couple of days in the SCBU, Aisling and our son were moved to a special four-bed room just off the postnatal ward, where Aisling was the only patient and had one-to-one care from a dedicated nurse throughout her five days in there. Our son enjoyed regular tanning sessions under a special UV light to reduce his jaundice and he began to stabilise. He was with his mother and had round-the-clock care and attention, and a week after arriving into the world, albeit with a bump and a scrape, he was well enough to be sent home to start his life as the newest member of our little family.

THIRTY-NINE

NEW ARRIVALS AND GREAT ADVENTURES

Over the next few days, a small and steady stream of visitors called at the house to see Aisling and to welcome our son into the world. Steve was the first through the door, with a card for us and a Fisher Price jungle activity playmat for our son, a gift which he would enjoy daily in the months to come and which we still have somewhere.

The whole ordeal of the birth had been as traumatising as it sounds and had left deep emotional scars on both Aisling and me, as well as the physical scars left on Aisling. The emotional scars would be the ones to take far longer to heal and, unknown to us at the time, would be opened again soon. In the meantime, however, we settled into life as a new family with all the sleepless nights and stress that having a baby involves. But we were happy and relieved; we had once more been through the toughest of times and, although battle-scarred and damaged, we were alive and so was our son.

The summer months of 2011 were some of the nicest I could remember for a long time. Aisling was at home (having taken a year of maternity leave) and we spent our days enjoying both the weather and our new baby. We took him to Northern Ireland for his Christening, which was performed by Father Martin, the same priest that had married Aisling and I some eleven years previously. By the end of that year, we were making plans to do something wonderful with our new son early on in 2012. We wanted to use the time that Aisling had off from work to do something amazing and memorable, plus 2012 would be the year that we both reached our fortieth birthdays and we were keen to mark the milestone with some fanfare.

We had always talked about touring around New Zealand in a campervan. So, on 16th January 2012 (some five years to the day before I would officially go on the transplant list), we set off from London's Heathrow Airport to Hong Kong. From there, we would travel to Auckland, New Zealand to start a four-week motorhome road trip around the North and South Islands, before heading across to Australia to spend three weeks visiting my aunt and uncle in New South Wales. We would then stay in Perth with my friend Helen and her husband. I had met Helen back at EasyJet in 1998 when she worked for me in the Flight Operations department. She had emigrated a couple of years previously and I had always said that we would meet up if Aisling and I ever found ourselves back in Australia.

The whole of that seven-week trip was simply amazing and I would recommend exploring New Zealand by such means of transport to anyone. Whilst some thought we were mad to be heading away for so long with a relatively new baby, and to be cooped up in a small campervan to boot, we saw the opportunity as a challenge and one that would be fun to accomplish. Besides, as our son was unable to walk at this point, he was neither going to take up much space or wander off anywhere on his own.

On our arrival in New Zealand, we spent the first week in and around Auckland, hiring a car and visiting the Coromandel Peninsular for a few days before returning to Auckland for a flight down to Christchurch on the South Island, where we would pick up our campervan.

The only hiccup of this whole trip occurred during the ninety-minute flight from Auckland to Christchurch and was one which severely dented our confidence. It was only a short flight, but it would be one of the most dramatic experiences during my forty years of having CF.

As the aircraft reached its cruising altitude, I settled back to look out of the window whilst Aisling cradled our son in her arms as he slept. The next thing I was aware of was that I woke, hot and sweaty and unable to focus on anything or anyone. I was disorientated and confused. I quickly alerted Aisling that something was wrong and that I didn't feel well at all. She tried to give me some water, but I was unable to hold the cup steady to drink from. She then tried to get me to take my jumper off to cool me down, but I was unable to coordinate myself to manage even this simple task.

Disorientated yet fully aware that I was in a real state, my first thought was that I was suffering from hypoxia (a condition induced when there is a lack of oxygen in the brain, preventing it to function properly). Aisling and I had first learned the intricacies of hypoxia when completing our PPLs and were aware of the symptoms to look out for – confusion and disorientation being at the very top of this list. Aisling took the quick decision that I needed supplementary oxygen, fast, and alerted the cabin crew immediately. Within a few moments, they were back with a small oxygen cylinder and a face mask and I started taking long deep breaths. We were alone in a foreign country, far from home, with a young baby – now was not the time to get ill. Besides, we still had six weeks of the trip ahead of us.

The cabin crew alerted the captain about my condition and he (although we were only to find out upon landing) consequently requested an expedited descent and a priority landing into Christchurch. He had also radioed ahead for the emergency services to meet us on arrival. The remainder of the flight felt like an eternity as we descended through the levels and made our approach into Christchurch Airport.

Having taken some oxygen and some water (albeit spilling a good deal of it down my front in the process), my condition settled somewhat and by the time the aircraft touched down and taxied to its stand, I was more aware of what was going on. Although the airport fire service came onto the aircraft to assist me, I was by this stage able to get out of my seat and walk down the aircraft steps unaided, reducing the fire service staff to assisting Aisling with our hand baggage as she carried our son off the aircraft.

We were then escorted to the airport's medical room for me to be assessed by ambulance staff. This was now nearly an hour after the first symptoms had set in, and I was feeling much better and able to converse relatively coherently with the paramedics. We ran through the standard set of questions regarding my medical history whilst routine observations were carried out.

My oxygen saturation levels were back to normal and my temperature was in the acceptable range. In fact, it was clearly quite hard for the ambulance staff to find anything wrong with me at all and, after monitoring me for a while, they declared that they were happy for us to go on our way on the strict proviso that we headed immediately to hospital should any of my symptoms return in the coming days. They were even nice enough to take us in their ambulance round to the campervan hire company on the far side of the airport. However, after the scare we'd just had (which we eventually put down to tiredness and dehydration caused by a long hot coastal walk the previous day), we decided to scrub our plan to drive a couple of hours up the coast and, instead, stay at a campsite on the outskirts of Christchurch for the next twenty-four hours, just to make sure I was fully recovered.

If this whole experience was scary for me, it must have been terrifying for Aisling who, following this episode, had both me and the baby to worry about for the rest of the trip. After all, we had several more flights to endure before we made our way back to the safe haven of our home in the UK.

Thankfully, the remainder of the trip was uneventful from a CF point of view and was wonderful in every other way. We took our new son to the cities of Melbourne and Perth and introduced him to my relatives in New South Wales and to Helen in Perth. We went up Fox Glacier by helicopter in New Zealand, landed on top of the glacial ice sheet itself, and introduced him to snow.

We drove along the Great South Road in the state of Victoria in Australia, visited the famous coastal landmark known as the 'Twelve Apostles', and took a ferry to the stunningly beautiful Rottnest Island off the coast of Western Australia, abeam the gleaming white sand and azure seas of Scarborough Beach just north of Perth.

At the beginning of March 2012, we landed back in the UK. Our son was approaching his first birthday and the first signs of spring were starting to show. As Aisling and I approached our fortieth birthdays, life was good and things started to return to normal. I say 'normal' but, of course, life was now very different.

Although Aisling returned to work after her year of maternity leave ended, I was no longer working in the traditional sense. My new full-time career as a 'stay-at-home' dad (whilst simultaneously doing my best to keep myself well) took up all of my time and was far harder and more demanding than any day of work in any office that I had experienced. Although, in fact, I spent my fortieth birthday as an inpatient at Papworth hooked up to yet more IV antibiotics, and the milestone itself passed by largely unmarked, this didn't particularly bother me. It was the third birthday in the previous five years that I had spent in hospital and, by now, I was making a habit of it – habitually wrecking the wonderful plans that Aisling had made on almost an annual basis. At least I was consistent, I would often argue in a pitiful attempt at a defence.

Before our son was born, Aisling and I would have been grateful just to have the opportunity to be parents to one child. So, when we sat down at the start of 2013 to talk about the possibility of going through the whole IVF process again, it felt greedy and frivolous, as if we were not already happy with 'our lot'. After all, we had our son. We had defied all the odds to have him, and it was highly unlikely that we would be that lucky a second time. Above all else, though, we had been through hell (Aisling in particular) during his arrival. Surely, we didn't want to put ourselves through all that again?

The contradiction to this all, however, is that we did not wish our son to be an only child. We wanted him to a have a sibling to play with, to talk to, and yes, perhaps in later years, to bicker and fall out with on a regular basis. We decided that all of this was worth another shot, and so the whole merry-go-round of

IVF started again from the beginning, although this time I was spared the big needle treatment as there was still sperm left in storage from my previous extraction (much to my sheer relief).

By the late summer of 2013, Aisling had once more exceeded expectations and was pregnant. Again, the pregnancy was not without its issues, but things progressed more smoothly than the first time around. At least they did, right up until a couple of months before the due date towards the end of April 2014. At one of our regular antenatal attendances, we brought up the circumstances surrounding our son's traumatic delivery – a conversation which we both struggled to complete without becoming emotional. It was clear to the doctor that we had suffered mentally as a result of everything that had happened around our son's birth and that we still had emotions that had not been properly addressed. He referred us to a midwife counsellor and suggested that we attend a 'birthing choices' clinic to discuss whether we plough on and aim for a natural birth or whether we opt for an elective caesarean early on.

Over the next few weeks, we attended both and, although the counselling was useful up to a point, it still didn't really deal with the underlying tension remaining from our previous birthing experience. With about two weeks until Aisling's due date, we attended the antenatal clinic one last time to decide upon our options. However, no sooner had we entered the room – we hadn't even taken our seats – than the doctor quickly stated that, although we had attended the birthing choices clinic, there was no longer a choice for us to make.

Given what had happened last time around, the hospital had decided that the only option on offer to us (at this hospital at least) was an elective Caesarean. As some sort of weird consolation prize, however, we could name the date on which we wanted to have this performed. Noting the list of dates being presented to us and also noting that the long Easter weekend stood in between us and our second child, we opted for the first day after the Easter break – Tuesday 22nd April 2014. We had the whole of that week to choose from but as Aisling's birthday also happened to be later that week, we opted for the first available slot in the hope that we would be home with our new baby before her birthday. In hindsight, this was rather optimistic and misguided given what had happened previously. But this was the day we chose, and so the timetable was set for the birth of our second child.

On the morning of 22nd April, we set off early, dropped our son at his nursery, and headed off on the short drive to the hospital. The whole experience was as different as it could possibly have been to the first time around; everything was organised and planned out, and there was no sign of chaos anywhere. Aisling was prepared for theatre and I gowned up once more in scrubs.

We had a lovely chat with a very nice anaesthetist who talked us through the procedure step-by-step and reassured us constantly that it was routine, that they did it all the time, and that nothing was going to go wrong. Whether he had been tipped off by someone as to what we had been through with our son we didn't know, but his calm voice and relaxed demeanour certainly made the whole process far more manageable.

As Aisling was wheeled into theatre and I tagged along behind, things could not have felt more different to last time. The staff busied themselves with their assigned tasks and, as the procedure started, I told myself to try and enjoy the experience. With our son, the ability to do this had been cruelly taken away from us but now we had a chance to experience something different. So, I took a few deep breaths, squeezed Aisling's hand, and we allowed ourselves a brief smile to each other as the main event got underway.

It was ten sixteen in the morning by the time we entered the theatre. At ten forty-eight a.m., our second child was lifted out of Aisling's tummy and taken to be cleaned up and weighed. Unlike last time, the sound of our baby crying was almost immediate, and Aisling and I hugged, kissed, and smiled. It was all over, and Aisling had done it. We were now a family of four, and it suddenly felt like life was complete. The only thing left was to discover whether our son, who had just turned three years of age, had a little brother or sister to dote over and play with. As the midwife handed the baby over to me, she asked us whether we had already chosen a name. She looked rather taken aback when we explained that, unlike most other couples, we didn't know the gender of our baby. With that, and with a huge smile on her face, she quickly removed the towel surrounding our new baby (she clearly didn't get to do this much anymore) and revealed that we had a little girl to add to our family.

And so, it was done. We had a daughter and, along with our son, our family was complete. As with our son, we had arranged to have our daughter's umbilical cord blood extracted and taken away for storage and this proceeded smoothly just as expected. Later that day, I picked up our son from his nursery and took him to the hospital to meet his new sister. Despite his young years, he was compassionate and loving from the outset and was genuinely excited to be a big brother. "I don't suppose they will always get on as well as this," Aisling and I said to each other, almost in unison.

Life changed again for Aisling and I, perhaps not to as great a degree as when our son was first born but the paradigm shift from just one little person to feed, look after, and keep safe to two was significant enough. Aisling took another year off work and we had another twelve months to enjoy as a family. In the same way that we had marked our son's arrival by heading off to Australia and New Zealand for seven weeks, we were keen to take a similar trip now that there were four of us. So, in the October of 2014, we headed off for six weeks driving up the eastern coastline of the United States.

We started this latest trip in Tampa, Florida, where we stayed for a week before heading off in a rental car to see just how far we could drive northwards. Our route initially took us across Florida to the Kennedy Space Centre for a day's visit, where we got to see the space shuttle Atlantis which had only just been put on display following its retirement in 2011 and which was the last space shuttle into orbit in the July of that year. The following day, we visited the area around Ormond Beach to the north and the airport itself, where I had learned to fly in 1996 with my dad and where Aisling had done likewise a year later. It was strange being back there after all those years; so much had happened since we were last there. Without my dad, though, the place seemed lonely and soulless, perhaps simply because of the passing of time but also due to the good times I had enjoyed with him so long ago. We lingered for a bit but saw little virtue in hanging around too long as it was bringing on feelings of melancholy for both of us.

From Florida, we drove just short of one thousand miles on the Interstate 95 highway, passing through Georgia, North and South Carolina, Virginia, and finally Maryland. Along the way, we visited enchanting southern cities such as Savannah and Charleston, and stayed on the coast in Hilton Head and on the Outer Banks, a long archipelago of islands off the North Carolina Coast. We visited Kill Devil Hill (close to the small North Carolina town of Kitty Hawk), virtually a Mecca for any aviation enthusiast of any kind. This was the exact spot where the Wright Brothers, two bicycle manufacturers from Dayton, Ohio, had constructed their Wright Flyer and where, in December 1903, Orville Wright became the first person to successfully fly a heavier-than-air, powered aircraft.

Our journey reached its end in Manchester, Maryland, where we stayed with some very good friends for a few days before starting the journey back southwards towards Florida, taking a more inland route back via Washington D.C.

By the time we made it back to Florida, we had two weeks of our trip left to visit the idyllic beach cities of St Petersburg, Clearwater, and Sarasota and to take some time to relax. It was still late summer, and the weather remained hot enough to spend our days lounging on the beach with the children or taking day trips to places of interest around the area. Our experience in New Zealand and Australia had taught us some valuable tips about traveling with small children and, despite now having two with us, the trip was truly memorable for so many reasons. By the time we returned home, it felt like we had evened the score; we had now done something amazing to mark the arrival of both children and had many fond memories to look back and reflect on in the years to come.

With time marching ever onwards, and having won big twice on one of life's most difficult and deeply intimate personal gambles, it was highly unlikely that we would decide to put ourselves through it again, however rich the reward. We would both have liked more children, but time and luck were both now firmly against us.

It would be disingenuous to say that my condition was not a factor in our decision; looking after one child had been hard on me and had seen me in and out of hospital on a frequent basis. Looking after *two* very young children was going to take every ounce of energy I had, and there was only so much my faltering body could take.

I relished the chance to start the whole process over again with my daughter but the reality was that, despite the joy of having these two little people in my life, it would take its toll on me and CF would do all in its power to take the opportunity to get the upper hand.

I wasn't getting any younger, my health was unstable, and I was now at a stage in my life and with my condition whereby CF could easily throw something at me that could beat me. Now, more than ever, was the time to do all I could to ensure I looked after myself and these two very small and very precious additions to our family. I told myself very early on that in order to be able to look after the children, I had to look after myself, fulfilling a promise that I made to Aisling before we even started the IVF process the first time around.

Having children and being a father changed me enormously, enriching my outlook and hopes for the future. On the morning of our wedding day, I was struck by the fact that, from that point on, it was no longer just 'me' but 'us' and that I was now part of a team. Similarly, the responsibility of being a parent was substantial and I have never – not for one second – under-valued that responsibility or taken it for granted.

Becoming a father strengthened my resolve against CF and reignited my desire to do all I could to stay one step ahead of the condition. I was now an integral part of something bigger and, for my family to exist and to thrive, I had to stick around.

This was a pure example of symbiosis, whereby my family needed me as much as I needed my family. In the years since becoming a father, I have often wondered what my dad would have thought about the job I was doing as a father and what he might have said. I can hear his voice in mine when I talk to our children, and I often tell them about what he was like and what he would have thought of them. My dad would have loved to have been a grandfather I am sure, and I am also sure that the children would have made him as proud as they make us every single day.

Over the years since my children were born, I have been thankful for the time I have managed to spend with them in their younger years watching them grow and develop. I fully appreciate that many fathers do not get to enjoy anything close to the time that I have had to spend with our children and, although it may sound odd to some, I am incredibly grateful for it.

I am proud to say that I am a 'stay-at-home' dad, ignoring the stigma that society may bring to bear on such a role (even in the 21st century) and, although it has had its ups and downs, I wouldn't change it for the world; I get to share my life, and spend most of my time, with two little people made up of a part of me and a part of Aisling, which for so long I never thought would happen. And, despite them living with the same shadow of CF hanging over them as it does me, I am determined that their lives should not be hindered by it. I want them to wring as much out of life as they can.

I once read that 'being a good father is the most important job a man can ever have' and I would find it impossible to disagree with this statement. Since I was forced to stop working just before our son was born, I have seen it as my main role in life to be as good a husband and father as I can possibly be. This is partly, I suppose, because I have always believed in having a purpose in life; having something to get up for and try my very best for each day. But it is also because I hold a wish that should anything happen to me (and I say that knowing, of course, that it eventually will), my children will be able to look back on me and my life and know that I did all I could for them, despite having this horrid illness that would so often distract my attention and occupy me elsewhere.

My wish is that they will look at me as much of a role model as I did to my Dad (and continue to do so, despite his absence). Above all though, and whilst I am still able, my wish is to make sure that their lives are as interesting, educational, and fun as they can possible be – just like my dad did for me.

In the same way that the above mantra inspired me and continues to remind me to do my best with each and every day that I am given, I also once read a line that a father had written to his children that strikes a chord with me more than any other. This line reads:

My job as a father is not to make your lives easy but to make them interesting.

In our family, where not a day goes by without CF getting, at best, a mention or, at worst, putting me in hospital and taking me away from those I love most, life will never be easy. But in the same vein, it will always remain interesting. That is one thing CF *can* guarantee.

REFLECTIONS

FORTY

WHAT HAVING CF HAS TAUGHT ME ABOUT HAVING CF

CF is a horrible, cruel and selfish disease. It hurts people and their families, and spoils short-term plans and long-term ambitions without conscience. Moreover, as much as it affects your physical health and condition, over time I have discovered that it is an attack on your mental wellbeing too. There is no let-up to this onslaught. It is a two-pronged pincer movement of an assault that never leaves you alone, day or night, every day of the week and every week of every year. You never get a break from it. It is always there, casting a shadow over everything you do and all that you wish for.

Despite this, however, I have also learned that finding a mechanism to accept all of this for what it is, is the only way to navigate your way through a life with CF – not necessarily unscathed, but perhaps somewhat more intact. Whilst some may find it hard to develop a coping mechanism, to others it may come more readily. Either way, it remains my belief that accepting CF and finding a way to live with it, rather than forever fighting against it, is the best approach. Accepting CF will allow you to live a life outside of it and to avoid having your existence entirely consumed by it.

As discussed in a very early chapter of this book, life with CF is a never-ending string of challenges. Those challenges take many forms; they originate from many different sources and each one takes a great deal of effort to cope with and to overcome, so that life can move on. Just when you think you have beaten a challenge, there is always another waiting in the road to stumble over. This isn't me being melodramatic or attention-seeking, it is simply how it is. And perhaps this is why it's hard for those with CF to celebrate even the smallest of successes, when the next thing to come and get you is normally lurking just around the next corner.

Other peoples' perception of me and my condition has always fascinated me; when I was younger, I feared being treated differently or, worse still, being pitied or mocked. This remains true even today, although I am somewhat more battle-hardened than I once was. Largely, the opinion of others is something I am indifferent towards. But, even on days when I have been doing all right and have my CF under some semblance of control, daily life has a nasty habit of throwing up little reminders that I am different and that I have so much more to deal with than most.

Going all the way back to my school days, I was determined to be just like everyone else. The odd occasion when I was tripped up by CF would devastate me and severely set back my confidence. I therefore started to develop something of an exoskeleton to protect myself from the harsh words or behaviours of others, whether they be drawn out of malice or simply ignorance.

As anyone with CF will tell you, when a coughing fit starts it is hard to do much about it, let alone to bring it to a swift conclusion. In fact, the opposite is true in my experience. When you are in a quiet place – a classroom, a courtroom, or a meeting with others around you –the worst thing you can do is try and stop coughing; this only makes it worse. If anything, the aim is to try to refocus the mind on something completely unrelated in the hope that the less you think about coughing, the less likely you are to do it. This doesn't always work, in which case you must simply sit there, embarrassed and flustered, hoping that the ground will swallow you up and put you out of your (and everyone else's) misery.

On the fairly regular occasions at school when I coughed in class, I would be sent out to go and get a drink of water. I used to take this very personally and saw it as some form of personal insult, verging on victimisation, towards me. Looking back now, I realise that this was the only tool the teacher of the day had in order to remove a distraction from their classroom, if only temporarily. Being a largely compliant child, I would always follow such requests, knowing full well that drinking a glass of water (or even ten gallons of the stuff) was not going to solve the problem. I found these events embarrassing as they singled me out from my peers and made me look different at a time when I was striving to look 'normal' and to fit in. Once despatched from the classroom, I would sit in the corridor or loiter in the boys' toilets for a while, pondering whether I should worry about the way I felt whilst simultaneously praying for the coughing to stop.

Over the years, I became used to this ritual and it fazed me less and less. That was up until one day in an A-Level geography class when one of my coughing fits kicked off. My teacher, an older lady with a low tolerance threshold for disruption, decided that the best way to deal with me was with to 'tut' under her breath every time I had to cough. These tuts became louder during the lesson and were eventually joined by either a roll of her eyes or a sigh, followed by a pause as she spoke. As you can probably imagine, none of these actions helped to quell my need to cough and as she got increasingly worked up about the whole situation, so did I. Things came to a head when the teacher finally lost control of her frustration, saying to the whole class, "We will now look at glacial formations in mountain areas, IF LUKE WILL LET US," while glaring at me with eyes like daggers as she spoke the final five words of this statement. Up to this point, I had mostly got away without being bullied at school by the other kids too much, and so I was somewhat unprepared for being bullied by a teacher.

I excused myself (using the 'maybe I should go and get some water' routine as an excuse) and disappeared out of the classroom door. As I left, I could feel the heat rushing to my cheeks as I blushed with the embarrassment of it all and quickly headed off down the corridor. I didn't know what to do about what had happened and have to admit I blamed myself for the situation arising. After all, had I been transparent with the staff at school about having CF, it is likely (or so I would like to think) that none of this would have happened. The events of that day scarred me so much that I can recall the exact words used and the way I felt, so vividly I'm able to write them down some thirty years later.

That was the first real time in my life when I was made to feel *awkward* and embarrassed about having CF. No one, regardless of their illness or disability, should be made to feel that way about something they have no control over, and yet it continues to happen to me (as I am sure it does to many others) on a tragically frequent basis.

The times when people give me 'dirty' looks, roll their eyes, or tut when I cough (in all manner of places) is quite astounding. I have had people move away from me on trains and buses, and I have even had one woman on a commuter train into London sit opposite me with a handkerchief over her mouth and nose whilst glaring at me. I have had a person behind me in a supermarket queue shout out, "Eugh," as I gave out a particularly chesty cough one day, and I have had another person wipe down the keyboard of an ATM I had just been using, despite having coughed into my elbow whilst at the machine. I have become accustomed to people who find it almost amusing to say, "You really should see a doctor about that cough," when I inadvertently cough in their presence, and if I had a pound for every time someone had said to me, "Cough it up, it could be a gold watch," I could probably afford to buy myself a gold watch.

Over the years, such comments have come to affect me less and I would like to think that I am ready to retaliate should such events happen in the future. I don't mean in an aggressive way. But I am more prepared these days to retort with an appropriately measured and intelligent response, hopefully making the perpetrator more aware of their own ignorance rather than of any physical condition I may have.

CF brings experiences such as these with disappointing frequency. Sometimes they hurt and sometimes I just laugh them off. The way I deal with such events depends largely on how I am feeling physically (or mentally) at the moment of impact, or how I may feel about having CF at that time. Whilst I might be able to better ignore such occurrences as I have grown older, there are other elements of having CF that I have found much harder to reconcile.

One of the earliest questions that would trouble me as a youngster (as I am sure it does everyone who is affected by chronic illness or some form of physical disability) is the 'why me?' concept. Why did CF choose me rather than my sister, or one of my friends, or anyone else at my school?

I would spend days pondering this, wasting energy searching for answers that were never to be found. It would be terribly easy for me, even now, to sit around and dwell on this question. But a day came – somewhere during my teenage years – when I realised that this approach was futile and a total waste of time. Not only that, but to sit around moping and feeling sorry for oneself does not change anything; it only serves to make things seem worse than they possibly are.

One day, as I sat at home revising for some school exam or other, I was half listening to the radio when the programme being broadcast caught my attention. What I heard that day changed my life forever; the radio host was interviewing a lady who had recently been diagnosed with terminal cancer. She was not long married and had two young children, and the thing that struck me most about this woman was the composure and humility she showed as she spoke. She talked about the sadness she felt at the prospect of not seeing her children grow up, go to university, or get married and have children of their own. She also talked about how she was angrier about the opportunities she felt she had wasted or let pass her by, than with the cancer that was going to kill her in the next few months.

However, the most remarkable thing about this lady was her apparent ability to accept what was happening to her and the consequences it would have on her husband and her family. She explained to the host that she had decided the only way to deal with the 'why me?' question was to counteract it with the alternative: 'why not me?' After all, cancer is always going to target *somebody*, and she had decided that she was just as likely to get it as anyone else.

She seemed somehow *content* with the grave situation she found herself in and, rather than spend her last precious months wondering why this cruel thing was happening to her and not someone else, she had made the conscious decision to accept the status quo for what it was, to get on, and to make the most of the time she had left.

I was initially stunned by her approach, but as I thought about it and about what she had said, it dawned on me that she was entirely right. Through adopting this approach, she had made peace with her predicament and her illness, leaving her with time and energy to invest in something wholly more productive. I was blown away by this lady and by her positivity in the face of adversity. From that day on, I have never forgotten her or the words she spoke; listening to her on the radio that day changed my whole outlook on having CF. Ultimately, she was so inspiring that I decided I wanted to be just like her.

And so, from that point onwards I have adopted a 'why not me?' approach to having CF and have put far more effort into getting on with my life than dwelling on regrets and thoughts about what might have been.

Living with CF is tough. My days are governed by routines and regimes, and the monotony of all this can be tedious in the extreme. Even 'good' days will involve multiple rounds of physio, dozens of tablets, nebulisers, and relentless coughing and shortness of breath. The not-so-good days involve adding tiredness, wheeziness, a lack of appetite, lethargy, and chest pain into this already challenging mix.

As you will have deduced by now, a life with CF is far from easy and certainly takes its toll on you, your family, and others around you. Thankfully, this is far more recognised than it once was, and CF centres do what they can to provide psychological support to their patients, realising that caring for the mind is every bit as important as looking after the rest of the body.

I have found through my own experience that the mental challenges that CF presents can be overpowering if one allows them to be and should never be ignored, regardless of whether the day is a 'good' or a not-so-good one. On the tough days, it is easy to be consumed by feelings of dread, expecting the worst, and the 'why me?' conundrum. On the good days, I spend my time trying to let that little voice in my head tell me that things aren't so bad really and that it could be so much worse. I ask it to shout louder and to overrule the opposing voice, which is whispering to me that my next bad day is just around the corner and that these good times can never last.

I guess the message I am trying to convey is that a life with CF can be stressful beyond measure, over and above the physical strains it imposes. Those with the condition have so much more to deal with than simply worrying about whether they left the gas on, posted that birthday card to Aunty Mabel, or what they fancy for dinner (although we worry about these types of things as well, of course). As if having knackered lungs and numerous other physical afflictions aren't enough of a challenge, CF presents a whole extra level of mental complexities to deal with.

One thing that has troubled me throughout my life is when people with CF are referred to as 'sufferers'. I have never used this term and have always had an issue with it. Not only does it convey a sense of vulnerability or weakness but, in my view, gives an impression of someone who has acquiesced to the substandard set of cards that life has dealt them and has become, to some degree, subordinate to CF.

Those I know and have known with CF (and I include myself in this) do not consider themselves as *sufferers*. When you live with something like CF as part of your everyday life, you develop coping mechanisms to deal with what it throws at you and you work your way through it. Rather than being subordinate to CF, people I have known with the condition are some of the strongest, most determined, and resolute people I have ever met. When faced with adversity, these people rise to meet the challenge head on. They have an uncanny ability to laugh about having CF and to make self-deprecating jokes about themselves and their condition with ease. During my time at Papworth in 2003, my ward-mate Ross would regularly stand outside my room and sing me his own rendition of 'The Drugs Don't Work' by The Verve through the door. Even in those dark times, I smiled each time Ross chose to serenade me, but I suppose it was just our way of dealing with what was going on.

Most people I know with CF seem to have an amazing ability to display almost superhuman levels of pragmatism, stoicism, and optimism in equal measure. Whether this forms part of coping with the condition or develops naturally because of having it, I don't know. What I can say is that being able to draw upon such characteristics makes dealing with CF more manageable, although I wouldn't go as far as to say 'easier'.

Whilst some choose to embrace having CF, others find this harder to achieve. I don't advocate for either approach; I am fully aware that everyone's CF journey is different and everyone's way of dealing with it must be as unique as their own fingerprint. I am also aware that it is important for everyone with CF to find their own mechanisms for facing up to the regular challenges, pitfalls, and disappointments that it undoubtedly brings.

I have found my own way over the years, although it has not come naturally. Receiving bad news never really gets any easier, no matter how often it happens, but how one deals with receiving that bad news is the key to your way out the other side. I chose very early on to embrace CF and to work *with* it rather than against it. I don't see CF as my enemy; I have simply never considered this to be a healthy or fruitful approach.

It annoys me how often the words 'sufferer' or, even worse, 'victim' are used to describe those with CF. I must also stop myself from wincing when the words *struggle*, *battle*, or *fight* are deployed. Having had CF for forty-eight years now, I have never referred to myself having to *fight* it or talked about my *struggle* with the condition. I just don't see my relationship with CF in that way.

A long time ago, I decided that as CF was never going to go away, I might as well work with it rather than against it. I felt it was better to stand up to CF and acknowledge its presence than to let it lead me down dark alleys, to dark places, where bad situations can seem worse than they actually are and where one can so easily lose the ability to find the way back out.

This might be hard for people to understand. But CF is part of me, so it was always going to be imperative for me to find a way of co-existing with it – as if it were an awkward roommate with annoying habits and personal hygiene issues. Had I not adopted such an approach, I have always feared that CF would take over and that I might slowly start to fade away.

I am a great believer in positive thinking and have always tried to concentrate on what I *can* do, rather than dwelling on what CF has prevented me from doing. After all, and in the great scheme of things, no one will remember me for what I couldn't do; they will remember me for what I did, who I was, and what I achieved. In terms of legacy, surely that is the more important and, certainly, the more positive of the two approaches available?

Living with CF throws up, as in life generally, all manner of situations and scenarios. These can range anywhere on a scale from life threatening and gravely serious at one end to light-hearted and amusing at the other. But while me and my CF friends joke with one another when one of us faces a setback, as if to say, "Guess what has happened to me now?", things can often take on a more sinister tone.

With CF, it is inevitable that there will always be another "Guess what has happened to me now?" moment, but as long as I remember that, and expect it, then when it happens, at least I am better prepared for it – if only slightly.

FORTY-ONE
THE RESILIENCE OF HOPE

From time to time, I have to stop myself from getting mentally bogged down by thinking about those with CF who have not been as fortunate as I have, as well as those who have died from the disease (people I have known and those I have not).

Those qualified in such matters might diagnose me as having what is colloquially known as 'survivor's guilt'. And I suppose this is probably linked to the 'why me?' predicament – why have I made it to forty-eight years old and many others haven't?

This question has the potential to trouble me greatly. But the antidote I have found, when such thoughts threaten to consume me, is to remind myself to make as much of my life as I can, to achieve as much as I can, and to be as content as I can be. After all, I still have my life. So, to do otherwise would be an insult to those with CF who have lost theirs. I owe it to them, as much as I owe it to myself, to enjoy my life for all its good points whilst doing my best to ignore the bad.

A similar dichotomy arises with the concepts of luck and of being lucky. So many people have used the word 'unlucky' in reference either to me or to having CF. So much so, that the real meaning of these words has become eroded to the extent where they no longer mean very much. From the outset, people consider it *unlucky* that I have CF. If you examine the odds of being born with CF, then I accept that it is of course against the 'normal' odds. But is it 'unlucky' to be born with the condition and am I unlucky to have it? It strikes me that people who don't have CF have far stronger opinions of what constitutes luck than I do.

Do I consider myself unlucky to have CF? No, I don't.

Do I consider it unlucky to have nearly died from NTM or, alternatively, lucky to have recovered from it? It is an impossible question to answer.

Many people with CF who I've spoken to about this concept make the same point: being born with CF is all I have ever known. With CF, you know that there will be ups and downs, difficult times, and dark days. That big black CF cloud hangs over you day in and day out, and there is no escaping it. It would certainly be easy to brand oneself 'unlucky' and to adopt a pessimistic world view based on such an assumption. Yet, rather than being unlucky, I consider myself extremely *lucky* to have done as much as I have and to have had the opportunities I have had.

Though there are experiences that have been out of my reach because of CF (I will never be an astronaut or go deep sea diving), I have been fortunate enough to experience many things that others would only dream of. I have been married for twenty years, I have two fantastic children, and I live a relatively comfortable life. I have my eyesight, my hearing, my ability to get up and walk around, and (arguably) most of my marbles. Compared to so many people, I am incredibly lucky. So, it seems ridiculous to consider myself unlucky just for having CF.

I used to find it irritating when people called me 'unlucky'. But now, when people say things like, "You are unlucky to need a lung transplant," or, "Poor you for having to spend time in hospital," – however well-meaning such comments might be – I simply force myself to smile politely and take a very deep breath (or at least the deepest breath I can muster).

There are people with far worse illnesses and afflictions than CF. There are those who cannot wash or dress themselves or leave the house. There are people, such as the lady I listened to on the radio, who are diagnosed with something that will end their life much, much sooner than they ever imagined. And there are people living with dementia, who physically live on but whose memories have long since departed.

Thinking of these people makes me realise how *lucky* I really am.

To me, luck is a subjective matter. Those with seemingly nothing to worry about in their lives will, by their very nature, consider those who they perceive to have less than them as unlucky. But I am lucky to have reached forty-eight years of age when so many others with CF will not reach half that number of years. I am lucky to be able to remember all that has happened to me and to be able to write it all down for others to share. And I was lucky to be well enough to be placed on the lung transplant waiting list in the hope of being given a whole new chance in life. With a condition such as CF, ironically, it can be the situations that others may see as unlucky or unfortunate that present some of the best things we could ever hope for.

That last sentence introduces the concept I consider to be the most important in a person's mental health toolkit; having hope is *vital* in order to cope with life in general, not just a life affected by CF (or any chronic illness or disease for that matter).

Everyone hopes that in their lifetime they will enjoy good health, be happy, and win the lottery. They hope that their children will excel at school, be polite and kind, and that they might actually enjoy eating vegetables. Yet, for those with CF, having hope on a much higher level than this is vital in order to navigate the choppy waters presented by the condition and to steer a course toward the next safe harbour.

Such higher levels of hope are induced by the fear of what might happen – the fear of getting ill, of spending long periods in hospital and, of course, the ever-present fear of death. Hope acts as a counterbalance to such fears and stands as a levelling force against them. Hope is the mind's way of restoring order and it provides a mental suit of armour to use in defence against the adversities that CF throws up.

I have used hope throughout my time with CF. Even in the worst of times, alone at night, ill and in a hospital bed, concentrating on thoughts of positivity and of great expectations are what pulled me through, and saw me out the other side, time and time again. The only moment I truly lost sight of this was in 2003, during my time with NTM. Although I am not proud of doing so, it serves to remind me how scary things can be when that feeling fades away.

My experience has shown me that hope is resilient. When life is going well, hope encourages you to dream of bigger and better things. When your route ahead appears dark and fraught with obstacles, hope provides a flicker of light to show you the way forward. If anything, during my toughest moments with CF, my hope for a better time is even stronger. In those times, what I wish for feels remote and intangible, and having such thoughts seems fanciful or even decadent. Yet, without hope, hopelessness can quickly take over. And that is a very grave place to be.

Once hopelessness sets in, dreams you may have had for your future fade into the background and are replaced by darkness and despair. Apart from that one occasion in 2003, no matter how bad things have been, I have normally been able to retain just the briefest glimmer of hope that things will improve and that better days lay ahead. And after all, a glimmer is all you need; like the embers of a dying fire, unless completely extinguished, there is always a chance that they will spark up again. And if they do, a whole new inferno might just rage into being.

I have talked a lot about not wanting to be treated any differently from anyone else, to be pitied, or to be patronised. The way people treat me or act towards me can sometimes induce thoughts or feelings that are not conducive to the way I view myself as a person with CF.

I am certainly not special and would hate to be treated so. I simply have an illness. I am a complete person, despite this illness, and have feelings and emotions just like everyone else. There is not a piece of me missing, so I do not need to be treated any differently just because some may consider that there is. All I want is for people to respect me for the person that I am rather than the person they may perceive me to be. I know I am not like others, but ultimately none of us are the same.

Regardless of our backgrounds, state of health, or experiences, we all want to be loved, to be happy, and to enjoy our lives. Just because I have CF doesn't mean I don't wish for these things just like anyone else. I want as much from my life as anyone else and, although I know that such things may sometimes be harder to achieve, this only serves to make me more determined.

You can't change what life throws at you, but you can choose how to deal with it. I have always done my best to tackle my setbacks with CF with as much composure and as level a head as I can muster, although at times this has been very hard to do. Living with CF is never going to be easy. So, finding the right balance between the condition itself and living your life is vital in order to negotiate your way safely through.

I am no expert on such matters, but I do know the methods and approaches that have worked for me. My secret to happiness (if I can put it like that) has always been to accept things for what they are and not what they might have been or how I would wish them to be. I will always have CF. It is never going to go away. So, I remain focussed on what I can do rather than what I can't, and CF just comes along as my passenger.

People who really love me and care about me don't care about my CF and, although it would be disingenuous to say it that it doesn't come up in conversation with those people, to them I am just another person getting on with their life.

If having CF has taught me anything at all about having CF, then it would be that it should not rule your life. Nor should it ruin it either.

Just as that lady said on the radio so many years ago – energy is precious, so invest it wisely by enjoying the good parts of life rather than wasting it by dwelling on the bad. After all, you never know when that life might be gone.

FORTY-TWO
LIFE ON THE LIST

"Prepare for the worst but hope for the best." This was one of the first things that Aisling and I were told as we sat down with Tim, a specialist transplant nurse at Harefield Hospital near Uxbridge, west of London, in early December 2016. Harefield, like Papworth, is a major cardio-thoracic specialist hospital and one of the UK's leadings transplant centres for heart and lungs. It is, ironically, just a few miles away from Ashford Hospital (also in Middlesex) where I had been born some forty-four years previously.

This phrase was to become a recurring theme; a mantra which would govern everything I did for the next few weeks, and which we would be reminded of regularly over the months that lay ahead. Christmas was around the corner and the children were already bursting with excitement. Yet there we were, sitting in front of someone explaining in unpalatable detail a medical procedure that could quite possibly kill me.

After being accepted on to the transplant waiting list at Harefield, I had been invited down to spend the day there for a full briefing on what I was really letting myself in for. Naturally, I had asked Aisling to accompany me. After all, this affected her as much as it did me. A briefing like this is given to all those who are about to give consent to going on the waiting list, so that they go into the process fully informed.

A few days previously, I had been on the phone to my consultant at Harefield discussing how the decision to put me on the list had come about (and if I am being honest, for the lawyer in me to explore whether there were any loopholes I could use to my benefit in order to get myself out of this). We talked a lot about the fact that I needed to go on the list now because, with my current rate of decline, I may not have a huge amount of time left during which I would still be considered well enough to be placed on the list at all.

The overriding sense that this chat left me with was that this could well be now or never; if I wanted any sort of chance at a longer life, this was probably it. During this conversation, the consultant explained incredibly frankly that a double lung transplant is fraught with danger and that there was a one in ten chance he would kill me by putting me through the operation.

When unwell, your defences are stripped back and you become more fragile to receiving such news. Although he was simply stating facts, the consultant might as well have said that there was a *ten* out of ten chance he was going to kill me; I felt sick to my stomach. Nonetheless, and regardless of how I felt, I knew that my time was starting to run out and that even agreeing to go on the list gave no guarantee that I would get as far as the operating table. This was a 'take-it-or-leave-it' scenario and, however hard it was to accept, I knew it.

The briefing with Tim was a major step. Over the course of about four hours, he explained everything in enormous detail, stopping regularly so that we could ask questions and explore things in greater depth. Both Aisling and I have always wanted to be fully appraised on anything and everything to do with my care and have never shied away from the nitty-gritty, however hard it may have been to swallow. You can believe me when I say that the time we spent with Tim that day was, in fact, wall-to-wall nitty-gritty.

If I was to try and sum up that day with Tim, I'd say it was ten minutes of, "Think of all the good that a transplant could bring you," followed by literally hours of all the things that could go wrong. The latter half of the session was like happy hour at the pub coming to an abrupt halt and quickly turning into 'miserable hour', where drinks are one for the price of two and Celine Dion records blare out of the jukebox on a loop. What started off as an upbeat chat, full of hope and excitement for the future, very quickly turned into one that left us scared stiff and in tears. Tim did his very best to make everything more digestible but given the subject matter, his wriggle room was very limited.

We were told that my body would try to reject the new organs from the get-go, hence the need to take immunosuppressant drugs for the rest of my life. We then talked about how these drugs can affect the body – from a greater risk of contracting certain forms of cancer to the development of diabetes, liver and kidney damage, and other horrible outcomes.

We were told that during the operation the body can go into spontaneous cardiac arrest or respiratory arrest and what these terms meant. We were then led through all the things that can go wrong immediately following the operation, including the most common pitfalls that kill patients during the first thirty days. The last part of the talk was to discuss what I needed to do in order to be ready to go on the list. I was told that I should make sure my will was updated, to put a Lasting Power of Attorney in place in case something adverse happened during the operation that left me mentally incapacitated, and to write a 'Letter of Wishes' pertaining to my end of life care in case I was rendered incapable of stating my wishes in person (due to being in a coma, for example).

I was made to sign various consent forms and given a list showing the classes of potential donors. I was asked to tick anyone I would be unwilling to accept new lungs from but, as I mentioned very early on in this book, I signed the big box at the bottom of the sheet that basically stated I would accept 'anything from anyone'.

By mid-afternoon Aisling and I were emotionally shattered, and the NHS must almost have run out of boxes of tissues. I had been warned beforehand by someone who had gone through a lung transplant some years previously that briefing day would be tough, but I had no idea it was going to be *that* tough. As Aisling and I left the hospital that day, although more enlightened about the next stage of my journey, we were tired, drained, and almost shell-shocked from what we had just been through.

The harsh reality of the situation was that things were going to get worse before they had any chance of getting better. We were told by Tim that following the briefing I could go 'live' on the list as soon as I was ready. All I had to do was to give him a call and he would push the necessary buttons. It was three weeks before Christmas, and I had just been given a to-do list unlike any other constructed around that time of year. Rather than featuring tasks like wrapping presents, buying the turkey, or writing to Santa, I was looking at a dazzling array of tasks to complete in the event of my death. How jolly festive.

I set myself the target of four weeks to complete these tasks, notwithstanding the fact that Christmas landed right in the middle of this time. I worked on what I could in terms of the administrative tasks but left by far the most difficult one to almost last.

I needed to write final letters to Aisling and each of the children to be opened only in the event of my death. I had not particularly intended to leave this until last, but simply did not know what to say or how to say it. So many times, I sat down to start writing something but just could not do it. In the end, I decided that I would focus all my efforts into writing the letters *after* the holidays.

Two weeks before Christmas and continuing our tour of healthcare professionals who were poised to scare or upset us, we had a chat with a palliative care consultant at Papworth Hospital. We had sought her advice about how we should deal with all that was going on, both in ourselves but also how we should approach the children. It is all very well saying that Daddy may be getting new lungs, but it's another thing entirely informing them that the operation to give Daddy his new lungs might just kill him. We had our own ideas about how to do this but sought corroboration to ensure we did it right.

The consultant was lovely with us – compassionate and calming. She offered advice on how to tell the children and gave us a book to read about it. She also told us that it was important not to sugar-coat the situation (it was important they understood the gravity of what was going on) and to use normal terminology through our dealings with them so that they felt they were fully included in the process. This advice flew in the face how we usually handled CF with the children at home. For example, rather than using the word 'drugs' in everyday parlance, we always used the term 'special medicine' when referring to my tablets, IVs, or anything else I took to keep CF at bay. This was mainly because we realised very early on that there could be serious repercussions if one of the children went to school and announced to everyone that their daddy 'takes loads of drugs' or that he 'loves taking drugs as they make him feel better' and so on...

Our chat with the palliative care consultant was useful and gave us some ideas about how we should address the situation with the children. But despite this, it did not make me feel any better about what was going on or what I was dragging Aisling and the children into by going on the list. As a father, it is my job to make things better and to fix things, but in this situation I could do neither.

I was wracked with guilt alongside utter despair. But as someone at Harefield told me, it was important to remember that I was going onto the list *because* of Aisling and the children; to volunteer to put myself through all of this was one of the most selfless acts I could ever choose. I should, therefore, try to be proud of it rather than beating myself up about it.

Christmas itself was tough that year. Very tough. Although Aisling and I did our best to give the children a wonderful time and keep everything as normal as possible, things were far from it. I held it all together until a couple of days after Christmas when it all boiled over and the stress of what was happening became too much for me. I had spent that morning in a dark mood, barking at the children and Aisling with a scatter-gun approach. No one was safe. By mid-afternoon I had upset everyone so much that I felt (however misguided it might have been) that Aisling and the kids would be better off without me around for a few hours.

I set off in the car and drove. I travelled all over the county that afternoon and evening, stopping here and there to try to get myself together, but each time failing. By late that night, with the children long since in bed, I headed back home. On that final drive back to the house, I had a moment which, although I wouldn't describe it as an epiphany, was when I finally managed to calm my nerves, settle my brain, and let reason take over.

I told myself that this journey was going to be tough, but I had been through worse and there were so many better times to be had on the other side of transplant. Therefore, I should channel what energy I had into making the most of the time I was waiting on the list and to think about things that we could all do after it was all over, whenever that may be. We were all going into this together and we would come out on the other side together too.

As January 2017 began, Aisling returned to work and the children to school. I had just a few days remaining of my self-imposed deadline to complete the pre-transplant 'misery' task list and then to make the phone call to Harefield that would change everything forever. By this stage, I had checked that my will was up to date, had written my Letter of Wishes about my care, and had applied for the Power of Attorney for Aisling to manage my affairs in case I was no longer able to. There were two tasks left. The first was to pack a 'grab-bag' full of essentials, which would then follow me around everywhere for however long I was on the list (night clothes, slippers, washing items, socks, spare clothes, etc.). The second, and last, was to write my letters to Aisling and the children.

I had delayed this seemingly impossible task until I could not avoid it any longer. So, one day during the first week of January 2017, I woke up, saw Aisling and the children off, and then just sat down and did it.

I had been drafting the wording for the letters in my head during the previous few nights and on that day it finally all came to me. Whilst the thought of writing those letters was one of the hardest things I had ever had to do, on this particular day it seemed like the time was right. Within a couple of hours, all three letters were written, printed, and folded carefully into envelopes, only to be reopened again should the worst happen.

On the morning of January 16th, 2017, the Lasting Power of Attorney arrived back in the post, all signed and approved. This was the final piece of the jigsaw. I was ready.

I felt sick with nerves, anxious, and upset. I had a lie down for a bit, hoping a rest would help me calm down. When I woke, and still sitting on my bed, I lifted the phone and dialled the number for Tim at Harefield. After a brief discussion and a final run through of the to-do list, Tim advised that he was now able to place me on the official waiting list for a double lung transplant. And so, it was done. With a gracious, "Good luck," from Tim, and a lump in my throat the size of a bus, I hung up. I took a deep breath (or as deep as my worn out, damaged, and scarred lungs would permit me) and still sitting, contemplated what lay ahead.

The first few months on the list were very much spent finding a new 'normal' for us all. We started to delete certain events from the calendar that we knew we would no longer be able to do, we became paranoid about ensuring that if we were out we both had fully charged phones, and that the 'grab-bag' was always in the boot of the car. I was fastidious about telling Harefield if we went anywhere that might extend our journey time to the hospital and we always kept ourselves abreast of who might be available to look after the children at any given moment should the phone ring from Harefield. I became mildly obsessed about keeping the car at least half full of fuel as, if the call came in the middle of the night, we did not want to be taking up valuable minutes by driving around looking for a petrol station that might be open.

One afternoon, we were at a local garden centre when upon realising that neither of us had mobile phone coverage, we piled the children swiftly back into the car and left immediately to drive to a location that had reasonable reception.

Those early days consisted of a heady cocktail of emotions, from anxiety to excitement, despair, and anger. It would only be the course of time that would alleviate these feelings – time itself being the only drug that numbed the pain caused by such wildly varying emotions.

During my time on the list, I was required to attend Harefield every six months and to speak with one of the transplant specialist nurses every three. In addition to this, I was under very strict instructions to advise Harefield if my health deteriorated in any way; even the slightest cough or cold may render me out of contention for a transplant, so it was vital I kept the hospital in the loop about how I was feeling.

After three months or so on the list, I was at Harefield for routine checks when the hospital's clinical psychologist popped by to see me. On being asked how I was doing, I responded that I had just passed the one-hundred-day mark of waiting but that I was holding up okay. With a stern tone in her voice, she told me to stop counting the days immediately. Whilst I had initially seen this counting as useful, she quickly advised that doing so was the best way to induce feelings of hopelessness as time went by and that it would only lead me to dark places. I agreed that I would stop, although – being the sort of person that I am – I knew that I would always be conscious of how long I had been waiting, regardless of whether I counted the actual days or otherwise.

As weeks on the list became months, life settled into a routine that felt uneasy but bearable. Don't get me wrong – every time the house phone rang my heart would stop and Aisling and I would exchange just the briefest of glances. I would look down at the receiver, note that it was not the area code 01895 calling (the Harefield code) and would give a brief shake of my head in Aisling's direction, letting her heart resume beating. As the wait went on, the house phone ringing never got easier to cope with; indeed, the later in the day it rang, the more stress-inducing it was.

In the summer of 2017, knowing that we were constricted in our choice of holiday destinations and had to stay within the UK, we decided to head to Cornwall for a couple of weeks, renting an apartment overlooking Falmouth harbour. The weather was tolerable but was far from being a 'scorcher', so we spent much of the time in the apartment itself or using picnic blankets as makeshift rain shelters on the beach or at the local municipal pool.

Whilst it was nice for a change of scenery, and for us to spend some time away from our normal routine, we were still living under the cloud of me being on the list. We may have given ourselves some breathing space by going away, but we had also made our journey to Harefield about four times longer than normal should the call come whilst we were there.

Towards the end of that first year on the waiting list, however, our early anxieties settled and something of a Dunkirk spirit set in. Whilst feelings of 'this is not so bad' or 'why was I ever worried?' might have remained wishful thinking, it would be fair to say that I began to feel less uptight about the whole situation. As autumn came and went, we looked forward to Christmas once more and to what 2018 might bring. However, a serious chest condition would play a major part in how our first Christmas with me on the waiting list would play out, although this time it was not me who would be the one affected.

FORTY-THREE

A FALSE ALARM

For several years, our friend Steve had been fighting an increasingly persistent cough and a wheeze that for an awfully long time went unexplained and undiagnosed. One of the last times I had visited Steve, we had been walking along Epsom High Street after lunch when he asked me if we could slow down a bit. In his own humorous, self-deprecating style he quickly followed this up with, "Things must be bad if I'm asking you to slow down!"

I don't think back then, that either of us could have predicted what was to follow for Steve.

By mid-2015 he had been formally diagnosed as having idiopathic pulmonary fibrosis (a progressive and incurable condition that leads to scarring of the lungs, loss of lung function and, without a lung transplant, premature death). It took Steve so long to receive this diagnosis that by the time he did so and had subsequently been (with a huge dose of irony) referred to the very same team of transplant doctors at Harefield that I was seeing, his health had deteriorated too much and he was not considered suitable for transplant; he simply would not survive the operation.

Hearing this from Steve almost broke my heart. Why should I get the chance of new lungs and not him? Why did I deserve a second chance but he didn't? I felt like a fraud. I was full of guilt and felt like, in some way, I had cheated Steve. Out of the two of us, his need was now greater than mine, but he would not get the golden opportunity that I had been given. It just felt wrong and I felt terrible about it.

Things reached a head for Steve at the end of 2017, just as I approached the first anniversary of going on the transplant waiting list. Steve and I had been exchanging text messages, and he had explained that he was on supplementary oxygen around the clock and was having carers come in daily to feed and wash him. Aisling and I were shocked and upset; our friend had gone from being a jovial person who would do anything for anyone to someone who was dependent on others. And the fact that it had happened in such a short space of time was tragic.

After speaking with Steve's daughter (who confirmed that his condition was grave and that he was in a very bad way), we decided to go down and visit him that same evening. We told him by text that we were coming, although as normal he responded saying he was 'fine' and not for us to waste our time and energy driving two hours on a Friday night to see him.

Having left the children at home with a hastily arranged babysitter, we headed down to Surrey. Steve had arranged for the last nurse of the day to leave the front door key under the doormat so that we could let ourselves in. We entered his living room and found him in a hospital style bed, with an oxygen machine alongside and various other medical devices and paraphernalia surrounding him. Steve himself looked awful, barely recognisable from how he had been the last time we saw him. I commented to Aisling, on our way home later that night, that he looked like a little old man who was playing the part of Steve; his speech and mannerisms were ones we recognised but the man sitting in this hospital bed, in a room where we had shared so many chats, laughs, and beers over the years, was completely different from the person we remembered.

Steve, always a proud man, gave us an insight into his rapid decline over the previous few months and divulged that he had been in and out of Epsom hospital a few times during that period. He was frank and honest, seemed aware of his vulnerability and predicament, but did his best to put a brave face on what clearly was a very serious situation.

As we drove back home that night, Aisling and I vowed to go back and see Steve the following week and to keep more in touch with him than we had done in the months previously. About eight days later, though, Steve stopped replying to my messages. Again, we contacted his daughter for an update. It transpired that a carer had found Steve in a semi-conscious state the day before and that he had been rushed to hospital by ambulance.

We dropped everything the next day (a Saturday) and dashed down to Epsom with the children. The two of them were used to seeing me in a hospital bed and knew Steve, so we had no reservations in taking them with us. At the hospital, we each took it in turns to spend some time with him, although he was struggling to hold anything resembling a conversation at all by this stage.

As visiting time ended, Aisling went into the room to say goodbye, followed by me. I said that when he felt better he must come up and stay with us for a while, and that we would come down to collect him. In that moment, we both knew this was never going to happen, but it was nice to pretend it would.

As I got to my feet, I gave Steve a hug. Unsure of what to say, I simply repeated a phrase that someone had said to me once: "Keep fighting the fight." When I let him go, we smiled at each other and I tried not to look back as I left the room.

It seemed almost unfathomable that after all the years of Steve asking me how I felt and how my chest was, it was now him that was struggling to stay alive because of a chronic condition killing his lungs. This was a week before Christmas, with fairy lights and decorations dotted around the ward. Yet there seemed to be so little for anyone to celebrate.

Steve was discharged a few days later and taken back home. His daughter visited him on Christmas Eve to cook him a meal and she let us know how he was. She said he seemed, "Better in himself and pleased to be home." That consoled us and we hoped that he might somehow rally and start to pull things around. We went to bed that night more hopeful that we may see Steve again in the next few days, a bit brighter and more like the man we knew and loved.

At nine thirty on Christmas morning, the house phone rang. Aisling and I shot glances at each other (as we now did habitually whenever the phone rang, expecting it to be Harefield). However, it was Steve's son. Steve's nurse had let herself into his house early that morning to find Steve unresponsive and with no vital signs of life. At some point during the night, as Christmas Day dawned, Steve (one of our best friends for twenty-three years and who had done so much for us) had died.

In the same way that a life with CF has a habit of pulling the rug from under you just when things are going well, it equally has a habit of kicking you when you are already down. Steve's passing was a major blow just at a time when I was already feeling emotionally vulnerable. To lose one of my best friends to a disease so similar to mine shook me to the core.

I had always assumed, perhaps conceitedly, that it would be Steve visiting me in hospital (as he had done previously) when I was ill and that it would have been him supporting Aisling and the children should anything happen to me. I was in turmoil. I was full of regret that I had not been to see him more frequently and felt selfish that we had not done more for him. I simply could not believe that he would be no longer there for the occasional chat (albeit by way of text messages), to exchange the same old jokes with, and to reminisce on the happier times we had shared. At a time when I was already all at sea with what I was going though, Steve's passing had cast me even further from the shore with no coastline in sight.

As 2017 became 2018, cries of, "Happy New Year!" seemed hollow and meaningless. I was approaching my first anniversary on the list with not one call from Harefield, and Steve's funeral was on the horizon. Things seemed bleak, and there was no light to be found at the end of the tunnel we found ourselves firmly lodged in.

On the morning of Wednesday 4th January 2018, however, things took a dramatic turn. It was almost a year since I'd gone on the transplant waiting list and we were at home, with Aisling and the children yet to return to work and nursery respectively. Aisling was working downstairs and I was up making our bed when at eleven eighteen a.m., the house phone went. I jumped (as usual) but quickly managed to dispatch my fears as I had done many times previously. However, as I looked at the small LCD screen on the phone, I felt myself go cold and started to shake. The number displayed on the screen started with 01895. I sat down and tentatively answered.

A nurse called Jane asked me to confirm my full name and date of birth for her. Following this and with my head swirling, Jane spoke the words, "We think we might have found a pair of lungs for you. How are you fixed to make your way into Harefield as soon as possible?"

I felt sick. My hands were trembling. I replied that we could be on the road in an hour and would be at Harefield within three. Jane asked us to keep in touch should that estimate change and hung up. I drew a few breaths, attempted to calm myself and headed downstairs to find Aisling. I found her on her mobile phone to work but I indicated that she needed to hang up as quickly as possible, which she did (presumably noting the ashen, panicked look on my face).

I explained what had just happened and that we needed to get going. Unlike me, who had already by this point started to fall apart, Aisling held it together and got everything organised. We told the children what was happening before they were ushered off to our neighbours next door to await further news. Whilst I was subdued and quiet, they rode the waves of excitement and exclaimed how happy they were. We tried to manage their expectations by repeatedly telling them that the transplant may well not happen, but they were not to be told.

I did my best to hold my emotions at bay but as they skipped out of the front door, waving and giggling in hopeful anticipation, I lost composure and burst into tears. For the first time since I made that call and went onto the waiting list, I was genuinely terrified.

We got in the car and headed off on the one-hundred-mile journey to Harefield. I called Jane back once we were on the motorway to reconfirm our estimated time of arrival and then settled into the drive. I spent most of that ninety minutes in quiet contemplation and didn't speak much. Memories, thoughts, and hopes were washing over me like the waves on a seafront in stormy weather. I was trying desperately to keep calm and concentrate on the events at hand. I wanted to say so much to Aisling but couldn't find the words; knowing that this could be the last few hours we might have together made telling her how I felt all the more important yet all the more difficult.

Upon arriving at Harefield we were shown to a room and told to wait. The nurse asked me how I was feeling. "Nervous," I replied, seriously underplaying the turmoil raging in my stomach. "Nervous excited or nervous frightened?" was his response. "A bit of both I suppose," was mine.

Soon afterwards, Jane appeared to explain the process once more and to check me over. Blood was taken, all vital indications monitored and recorded, and I was asked how I was feeling, whether I had any coughs or colds, or if I had been sick in the past forty-eight hours. I replied that I was feeling okay and that I knew of no reason why the transplant could not go ahead. Jane explained that she was in regular contact with the transplant team who, as we spoke, were with the donor waiting for brain death to be declared and for the lungs to be assessed. Ironically, Papworth and Harefield work collaboratively on such matters, each providing a surgical team on rotation to be despatched at a moment's notice across southern England to assess potentially viable transplant organs. On this particular day, although I was sitting in the confines of a hospital room at Harefield, ironically it was doctors from Papworth who would be giving the verdict on whether things would proceed (or otherwise).

I was told to shower (using special pre-surgery, anti-bacterial shower lotion supplied by the hospital) and to change into a surgical gown. I signed various consent forms and was visited by the anaesthetist who would shortly be putting me to sleep for the transplant operation. The hours slipped away like seconds. We waited and Jane delivered regular updates on the progress being made with the organs. "All is looking good at this stage," she would report, knowing as well as we did that everything could stop at any moment.

After about four hours of waiting, the donor lungs had been extracted and were being assessed before being flown to Harefield. We understood that the donor was in a part of the country that had been fogbound that morning. There had, therefore, been a delay in getting the organs despatched as the aircraft being used to transfer the lungs to Harefield was unable to land at its destination.

Having explained all this, Jane left the room stating that she would be back in a few minutes with the first dose of anti-rejection drugs to be taken prior to the operation starting.

Reality was hitting home by this stage and it felt like things were really happening. We had been told of people who had waited many years for a transplant and had endured multiple false alarms during that time. I had also been told of someone who waited just four hours on the list for a new heart up at Papworth. I had been on the waiting list for fifty weeks and had received no false alarms during that time. Was everything about to change? Was the wait over?

It was about half an hour later when Jane finally returned, empty handed. We looked at her and she sighed. "I am really sorry to have to tell you that the team have decided the lungs aren't viable. I'm afraid they are not going to proceed." I don't know how to even start to describing the emotional rollercoaster that those last few hours represented. Going from fear, to excitement, to being terrified, to feeling utterly let down in the space of just a few short hours was mental torture.

Jane explained why things had happened the way they did and did her best to console us. "At least you have had a call now, so you know it could happen and that you are still on our radar." But, inside, I was destroyed. As Jane left Aisling and I alone, I let my emotions explode and burst into floods of tears. I was angry, upset, and disappointed. It was a strange paradox to be in – wanting something so much yet being so fearful of it too. After a while, I got dressed and we left the hospital – exhausted and broken – for the long drive home.

The next day, Jane rang to ask how I was feeling. How could I even contemplate answering such a question? I didn't know how I felt; I had no idea. I did my best to put a brave face on things and to tell her some lies about looking forward to the next time and that it was business as usual – yet it was anything but. I was broken inside, I did not know how to even start reconciling what had just happened and had no idea how I could go through all that again, should I even be lucky enough to get another call.

FORTY-FOUR
THE WAIT GOES ON
(AND ON...)

January 16th 2018 came and went, largely unmarked. This day represented exactly one year since I had made that call to Tim to put me on the waiting list. The wait so far had been tough, but with Steve's funeral just around the corner, and with the seemingly never-ending road on the list stretching out in front of me, this was no time to celebrate.

2018 seemed to pass much quicker than 2017, yet the waiting never got any easier and life continued in a state of suspended animation as the months rolled by. No further calls came from Harefield but, despite the silence, we remained ever hopeful that my day would come.

By the summer of 2018, however, the tension had started to build within me and, as a naturally impatient person at the best of times, my frustration started to increase. By June, I had reached the point where I knew that something had to give. I needed to find a way of letting go; I was holding on so tight each day that unless I found some form of relief, further waiting was going to become intolerable.

I decided that what we all needed, as a family, was a holiday – a complete break from everything, so that we could enjoy our time together unencumbered by Harefield, Papworth, the waiting list and, as much as was possible, CF itself.

Harefield had always said that they would consider granting suspensions from the list for good reason and, following a short email exchange with the transplant team, I had secured fifteen days off the list to pull myself together and to prepare myself for returning to it afterwards, hopefully with a renewed sense of hope and enthusiasm.

Following a short chat with Aisling, and having quickly decided that another fortnight in the rain-drenched UK was not going to cut it, I booked for the four of us to go on a package holiday to Zakynthos, a medium-sized Greek Island located in the Aegean Sea. Aisling's parents would join us for the middle week, allowing Aisling and I to spend a bit of time together away from the children and just the two of us. I was advised by Papworth that my lung function was so low by this stage that I would need supplementary oxygen on the fight there and back, so I set about arranging it. Although I had never travelled with oxygen on a commercial aircraft before (other than that infamous incident on that Auckland to Christchurch flight) I put any thoughts of being embarrassed or of it being a hassle aside and got on with it as best as I could.

Those two weeks in the sunshine served as a real tonic to what was going on back home and were an antidote to all the stress that had been building inside me. We had a wonderful time away and made many happy memories. The children were in their element on the beach, building sandcastles and splashing in and out of the waves, and for just those few days the whole idea of a lung transplant seemed a distant, bad dream.

By September 2018, however, the honeymoon period induced by our fantastic family holiday had faded and the hiatus from my feelings of gloom had long since come to an end. As time passed by, the increasing pressure began to take its toll and the situation only became more stressful as time went by. I was aware that worrying about the length of my wait, and thinking about what might not happen, was unhelpful and was making me feel worse. But I battled to find a way of dealing with the pressure in a logical, rational manner.

I requested to speak once more with the psychologist at Harefield in order to explore ways of dealing with the frustration I was feeling. We talked about coping mechanisms and strategies, about positive thinking and making plans for the future. One subject I mentioned was that for many years I had considered writing a book about living with CF. As we talked this over, new plans and ideas formed in my mind and I started to feel something inside me that I had not felt in a long time – a sense of purpose and of having something constructive with which to occupy my time. After bouncing a few ideas around between us, I boldly stated that in the next few days all those thoughts and dreams of writing something down about my life with CF would come to pass and that I would attempt to turn those thoughts into reality. "Don't write it for anyone but yourself," I was told, and that is the approach I have tried to take.

I saw that day how writing could be a form of therapy, to help give me focus and to keep my mind active whilst the wait for new lungs continued. Although, starting out, I didn't know whether I would ever get to finish the job, somehow that wasn't relevant. The writing process itself would be my purpose, so whether I ever reached the finish line didn't really matter.

The following day, I took out an old red jotter that I'd had kicking around for a year or so and started making a few notes, which quickly turned into a skeleton chapter plan, which then became a flood of ideas that, despite going as fast as possible, I still couldn't seem to write down fast enough.

As I worked away at my writing, the remainder of 2018 flew by. Some days, the ideas just threw themselves onto the keyboard and on to my screen. Other days, nothing would come, and I realised that I needed to step away. But writing had restored my hope, I felt driven by the writing process itself and by the thought that the children might be left with a better idea of me as a person should the call for the transplant never come or if it did and didn't end the way we all hoped.

I didn't consider what I was writing to be my 'legacy' and it was certainly not some sort of misguided vanity project. It was just my way of finding a use for the time I had available until the day when my luck might just cash in and the all-important call would come.

Christmas 2018 was a more manageable experience than the previous two. In 2016, I had been preparing to go on the list and Christmas 2017 was the day Steve passed away. So, I approached Christmas 2018 with much more hope and optimism; firstly, that the call would come and secondly that I was working toward something which would stand as a true and worthwhile testament to my time on the waiting list.

Preparing their lists for Father Christmas that December, my son displayed as much maturity and forethought as you could ever expect from a seven-year-old boy. As he showed me his list, my eyes were immediately drawn to the item placed right at the top, above the Lego, and the microscope set, and all the other items his dreams were made of. Sitting right in the number one spot, above any other request, he'd written:

A new set of lungs for Daddy.

As Christmas drew near, I think we all hoped that Father Christmas would fulfil his task and, in the very near future, deliver up the necessary goods.

At the start of 2019, almost two full years after going on the list, I was throwing all the energy I had into writing. I was still attending the CF clinic at Papworth every four weeks and was in regular contact with Harefield as the schedule of calls or visits dictated. On the second anniversary of that momentous call to officially go on the transplant list, I decided I needed to take myself away for the day, to get some air, and to take stock of where I was. Twenty-four months had passed and sitting on the bed with the phone in my hand now seemed so long ago.

Once Aisling had left for work and the children for school, I headed to the Suffolk coast, to the seaside and port town of Felixstowe. This was a place we had come to know quite well since moving to East Anglia from Surrey back in 2015, and we had spent many happy summer days as a family playing on the beach, eating ice creams, and basking in the warm summer sun.

On Wednesday 16th January 2019, however, Felixstowe sea front was a far cry from those gorgeous summer days lodged in my memory. Desolate and cold, the leaden sky ominously shrouding the town, it felt as though I was the only one there. I took a photo of the promenade that day to show the others; where just a few months previously it had been thronged with people laughing and enjoying the fine weather, it was now windswept and deserted. As I sat on a bench along the seafront, it felt like I was the only person on the planet, let alone just in this little corner of Suffolk.

As the drizzle turned to rain, I sought refuge in a beachfront cafe and sat in quiet reflection with my cup of steaming tea, thinking about the previous twenty-four months. Despite the weather and the seemingly endless gloom prevailing over the town that day, I felt reinvigorated by my time there. I left feeling more optimistic about the future and looking forward to the day in just a few months' time when I would be back on that beach, in the sunshine, with Aisling and the children. I hoped with all my heart that I would be lucky enough to be there once again, bathing in the sound of the children's laughter and shrieks of excitement that, despite all that was happening in their young lives, always seemed unshakeable.

Following my optimism of that day, however, the whole situation soon started to feel increasingly intangible. Hope that I might survive the time waiting for suitable lungs to be found was beginning to fade. To the outside world, I did my best to keep a positive outlook on matters, to stay objective and to 'hope for the best' just as Tim had advised from the outset. Yet with each week that passed, and with no further calls from Harefield, my spirits would drop a little further and the ray of hope that I clung on to so desperately would shine just a little darker.

I was dejected and was becoming demoralised with the whole process. I needed to find a way how *not* to feel like this. But with my hospital attendances becoming increasingly frequent and my reliance on IV antibiotics growing as the months passed by, there seemed to be little to be optimistic about by this stage. I was truly struggling to find my way out of the emotional black-hole I was sinking into and my stoicism and resolve to stay hopeful had long since deserted me.

I decided that another chat with the psychologist at Harefield may be useful; I was struggling to find a mechanism to help me keep pessimistic thoughts at bay and didn't want to end up anywhere near the slippery slope of despair that I had evaded for so long. So, she called and we talked through what I was feeling. Whilst the psychologist's words were sometimes hard to swallow, I knew they made sense and that ultimately I had little choice but to accept them.

One phrase that really stuck with me was when I was told, "You think being on the list is tough, you wait until the recovery." Now, whether she intended it or not, these few words struck a chord with me on various levels, despite them sounding rather negative in tone. Firstly, they gave me a renewed hope that, despite how I felt, this stage would end at some point and that a recovery period could still happen. Secondly, they helped me to see that, however difficult things seemed, there may well be tougher times ahead, so I should view being on the list as 'the calm before the storm' and enjoy it for what it was. Lastly, she helped me to see that being on the list is *supposed* to be tough (how could it not be?) and that I should simply try to remember this fact and move on.

She also reminded me that I was now entering the phase (based on averages) when a call was most likely. Tim had told us back in December 2016 to expect a wait of twenty-four to thirty-six months and we had just passed the twenty-four-month mark. Rather than being upset about how long it had been so far, I should be excited that I was now in the time frame when a call was most likely to come. After our talk ended, I hung up feeling ever so slightly revitalised, with renewed energy for the next part of my wait, and with hopeful expectation safely restored–at least for the time being.

The other thing the psychologist told me was that I was entering a crucial stage of my wait, so it was vital to focus on my overall fitness. I was reminded that your fitness level when you go into the transplant operation has a huge impact on how you recover from it and how long it takes to make that recovery. I decided that I needed to do more in this regard and engaged Terri, a personal trainer that Aisling knew, to come to our house once a week for an hour of intense exercise. Whilst I might refer to it as 'intense exercise', it was more just a case of Terri shouting at me over loud pumping dance music for an hour, while I did my best to stay standing and to comply with her instructions without collapsing. Stops for breath were frequent, with occasional sit downs and large gulps of cold water to help me get to the end of the session. I never felt that great after these sessions, but I tried to focus on the fact that it was supposedly doing me 'good' and that I needed to just shut up and get on with it.

As winter became spring in late February 2019, I looked ahead towards the summer, which would be my third on the waiting list. I have always loved this time of year, when the evenings stay light a little later, daffodils start appearing in the garden, and that there is a palpable sense in the air that the long dark winter is drawing to a close. Everyone with CF would probably say the same about winter; it is our nemesis – the time of year when coughs and colds are rife in the community, when influenza sees more and more people hospitalised each year (despite a widely publicised vaccination programme), and when living with CF under such circumstances means running the gauntlet daily. Nonetheless, with the spring approaching, I felt like things would improve and that the extra vitamin D from the lighter, longer days would certainly help my mood.

On 25th February 2019, I was startled awake by the house phone. It was three twenty-three a.m. At this time of the day/night, a phone call is never going to be good news or someone simply ringing for a chat. So, as I picked up the receiver, I almost knew that the code on the LCD screen would be 01895. When I visually confirmed that it was, I felt no emotion. Once more, thirteen months after the last call, Harefield wanted us to get there as soon as possible because a suitable pair of lungs had come up.

Once again, we got ourselves together, got the neighbours up to come and look after the children, and set off for Harefield. By four thirty a.m., we were heading away from the house and by six a.m. we were at the hospital. I recall feeling different to when we received the previous call; I was less nervous than before, probably because I had been through one false alarm already. I also remember being much more aware of the odds of the transplant actually going ahead being just forty percent. On the drive there, I didn't let myself feel excited at all, almost as if I was telling myself that within a few hours I would be back at home with a second false alarm under my belt.

I now knew what to expect when we arrived at the hospital and we went through the motions once more, signing forms, having blood taken, and being prepped for theatre. Once again, Aisling and I sat quietly together, occasionally chatting but also sitting largely in the quiet as the transplant team conveyed messages to the nurse looking after me as to their progress.

In a much shorter time than in January 2018, we were told quite swiftly that the lungs were not suitable and that there would be no transplant for me that day. Once again, we were told that we could leave when we were ready to and I was asked whether I needed a little time off the list to recover from the events of that morning. I declined to take such a break. I needed to stay live on the list, now more than ever. Although the wait might go on, I had to go on with it. I had paid my fare and boarded the bus back in January 2017. I was not yet at my destination, so to disembark prematurely seemed entirely against everything that we had been through up until this point.

We were back home by that lunchtime and collected the children from the school bus later that afternoon. Once again, their innocence as to the gravity of what I was facing was alarming and yet, somehow, entertaining and heart-warming beyond measure. As they stepped off the bus with expectant smiles on their faces, they said (almost in unison), "So did you get your new lungs Daddy?"

Unlike after the first false alarm, when I had been inconsolably upset, this time I was angry – very angry. I felt like kicking the walls, punching the doors, and shouting every obscenity I could possibly think of at the top of my voice. I did manage to keep a lid on things (just), but once again I began to let despondency take the place that optimism had just vacated.

February became March, which became April in quick succession. Time seemed to be flying past faster than ever and the stopwatch tracking my time on the waiting list was clocking up days at an astonishing rate. By April 2019, I had been waiting for twenty-seven months, with two false alarms behind me and no end in sight. It was becoming harder and harder to pretend that I was feeling *okay* or to tell myself that things would seem better tomorrow. I arranged another call with the Harefield psychologist to discuss my state of mind, and we agreed to speak on the morning of 30th April 2019, a Tuesday.

On Wednesday 24th April, Aisling and I headed out for dinner in Cambridge to celebrate her birthday. We had a fantastic evening at one of the best restaurants in the country, at ease in each other's company and managing to put aside all thoughts of transplants, Harefield, and CF for a just a few short but enjoyable hours. We splashed out on a taxi home, so that we could both enjoy a nice bottle of wine during the meal, and the restaurant provided the refuge we needed from the stormy seas that seemed to be surrounding us. Looking back now at the selfies we took that evening, we both look relaxed and happy, carefree and untroubled. But we could never have known what was lying in store for us just a matter of days after those photos were taken.

On 30th April 2019, I had my scheduled chat with the psychologist at Harefield by phone. I think she could sense the levels of tension in my voice, as she sounded more concerned about my welfare than she had previously. We went through everything once more and she did her best to focus my attention on things in my control rather than those which were not. She commented that it was my birthday in a couple of days and asked if I had any special plans. She asked how the writing was going and if I was enjoying it, even commenting on a more positive turn in my voice as I updated her on my progress. But I think she knew that, after all this time, and with no end to the wait in sight, I was beginning to find the whole situation overwhelming and the hopes for my big chance to come were starting to get lost in the fog that was rolling relentlessly over me.

At three twenty-three a.m. on Wednesday 1st May 2019, the home phone rang. I was having an unusually deep sleep that night. It was two days before my forty-seventh birthday, and I was looking forward to spending the extended bank holiday weekend with Aisling and the children. I recall feeling particularly annoyed that, once again, Harefield had shown the audacity to wake Aisling and I up at some hugely unsocial hour, to ask us to get out of bed, get in the car, and drive one hundred miles to the hospital. Like our previous encounters, I fully expected to be back home by lunchtime, feeling disappointed and even more dejected (if that was even possible by this stage).

However, things felt different this time – very different. The nurse on the other end of the phone asked how soon we could get to Harefield (which we had not been asked on either of the two previous occasions) and told us that the potential donor lungs were already en route to the hospital, having passed all of the preliminary testing stages.

By four thirty a.m., we were heading down the M11 in the darkness, quiet and tense. My mind raced through things I had not done or had left unfinished. I was only part way through writing this book and I recall feeling somehow cheated that I may not get to finish what I had started. As we pulled up at Harefield, dawn had broken and the sky had started to get light. We parked the car and, holding hands tightly, headed for the main entrance.

Was this my time? Would it turn out to be 'third time lucky'? Would this day be the day I finally got my new lungs? Only the next few hours would tell us that...

ALMOST REACHING THE END (AGAIN...)

FORTY-FIVE
AND THEN IT HAPPENED

As we sat in my allocated room up on the ward, awaiting my fate, things felt more streamlined than they had before and were clearly moving forward quickly. It was Tim looking after us that morning, the specialist transplant nurse who had talked us through the whole process back in December 2016. He bustled in and out, checking I was feeling okay and that I was still happy to go ahead with the operation should the lungs be deemed acceptable by the surgical team. Nervously, I confirmed I was.

Tim advised that the lungs had been tested and approved whilst still inside the donor, that they had already arrived at Harefield, and that they were now downstairs being tested again. He told me that everything was looking good and, although the process could be halted at any time, that I would know swiftly if the transplant was to go ahead. On being told this, I felt sick but tried my best to compose myself. The lead surgeon who would be in theatre that day appeared and ran through his checklist with me, confirming that it was my signature on the consent form and that I understood the risks of the operation. I confirmed that I did, and he duly hurried off to finalise preparations down in theatre.

Once more, I took off my clothes, showered, and changed into the surgical gown and gorgeous surgical stockings that would prevent any deep vein thrombosis (blood clots) from developing during or after the procedure. I had blood taken, along with swabs of my throat, nose, armpits, and groin for any signs of infection. And then we waited.

Whilst a part of me felt like this would, yet again, be a false alarm, another part felt like it might just happen this time. Everyone who rushed in and out seemed to have much more of a sense of purpose than before; almost verging on a mild sense of urgency. I don't know whether Aisling noticed the difference, but it certainly did start to feel as though this could really be my time.

I did my best to hold it all together, every couple of minutes just taking some deep breaths to reduce my heart rate. I have had a lot of things in my life, but a panic attack is thankfully not one of them. However, if I was to have one, then that was likely to be the moment and so I tried my best to stay calm.

Aisling and I talked in hushed tones, with her sitting alongside me on the bed. I ran through where I had stored everything back at home; my will, the instructions for all the bank accounts, my digital passwords, the letters for her and the children, and so forth. We made small talk just to pass the time but my mind raced away, thinking about a million different things all at once.

That moment, when you don't know whether you will still be alive in a few hours, is utterly surreal. I was telling myself it would all work out and that everything would be okay, but I knew there was a one in ten chance it might not be; I might – right at that moment – be going through the last few minutes of my life, in that room, with the person I loved the most. There are no words I can write to describe that feeling, and it is as awful and as sad as it sounds. I held Aisling's hand tightly and we hugged, desperately hoping that this would not be the end of everything, or of us.

Jane, the transplant specialist nurse, entered the room (Tim having now gone off duty) with some papers and some tablets for me to take. I knew as soon as she appeared what she was about to say. She told us that the lead surgeon had deemed the lungs to be viable and that we were heading down to theatre.

I took the anti-rejection tablets she had brought in with her, sipping just enough water to get them down but ensuring that my stomach remained empty ready for the operation. A porter duly arrived and, about two hours after walking through the door at Harefield, we headed out of the room, down the corridor, and towards the lift. Within minutes we were in the small waiting area of the theatre suite downstairs, segregated from the main corridor and just outside of the theatres themselves.

Both Jane and Aisling stood alongside me as the lead anaesthetist appeared and double checked that something terrible hadn't happened to me in the last hour and that I was still fit and ready to proceed. I confirmed that I was and she said she would be back in a moment, and that now would be a good time to say goodbye to Aisling. Jane left the room too, leaving Aisling and I alone for a few moments.

In the months leading up to that moment, I had always told myself that I must be brave at this point; I didn't want what was potentially our last moments together to be tainted with Aisling seeing just how scared I really was. I did my best to keep calm. But can you imagine keeping calm knowing that this may be the last time you ever see the person who has been with you through everything over the past twenty-plus years, the mother of your children, and your best friend?

Aisling did her best to tell me that it would all work out and that she would be there when I woke up. Through my tears I forced a smile, whilst squeezing her hand tightly as if to silently say, "Take me away from all of this. Let's just go home."

Aisling handed me the greetings card that I had brought with me – a Father's Day card from the previous year from her and the children. On the front was a black and white photo of the three of them with smiling faces and shining eyes. It was beautiful and when I first saw it, I knew exactly what I would use it for.

Throughout my time on the transplant waiting list, I had always said to Aisling that my one wish should I die was to not die alone. We had talked about this and, ever since, I had kept this card in the grab bag ready to come to Harefield with us. Aisling was not allowed to come into theatre with me, so I had decided that the next best thing would be to have this photo with me instead. This way, at least when I was taken into theatre, the three of them would be with me. I was adamant that I did not want to spend my last few moments, should this all go horribly wrong, looking at a room full of strangers. I wanted my family's faces to be the last ones that I saw.

Jane came back in and saw the card. She told me that it might not be allowed into theatre as it was not sterile. However, presumably noticing the crestfallen look on my already anguished faced, she managed to rustle up a clear envelope from somewhere, which apparently the surgeons were happy with, and I was left with my treasured photo, clinging onto it as if it were life itself.

Jane asked whether I wanted to keep wearing my wedding ring or pass it to Aisling for safekeeping. With previous surgery, I had always opted to keep it on but to have it wrapped in surgical tape and so I did again this time. Whilst I briefly considered handed it over to Aisling, I was keen to keep it on my finger; the thought of me not wearing it should something awful happen in theatre was simply too much to bear.

Aisling and I hugged one last time and kissed. We whispered that we loved one another and as the porters released the brakes of my trolley bed and pushed me through the double doors towards the theatre, I looked back at Aisling through my tired and scared eyes and simply said, "I'll see you very soon."

Once through the double doors, I was taken into a side room just outside the main theatre. More lines were inserted into my arms and more sensors placed on my upper body. I was asked to reconfirm my name and date of birth, and to go over any allergies I had to any specific medication. As people rushed about me, busy carrying out their assigned tasks, I did my best to relax. I answered their questions quietly and politely as machines hummed and beeped faintly in the background. By this point, and having been up since the early hours of the morning, I was exhausted and could not stop yawning. I wanted to sit up and look around, watch the proceedings as they unfolded around me with idle curiosity, yet I was too tired. Instead I just lay back and tried to breathe deeply.

In those last few moments, apart from thinking about Aisling, who had been left outside alone and afraid, my mind wandered through so many subjects. Most of all, though, I thought of Aisling having to return to the ward to gather up my things – as I would be taken straight from theatre to the Intensive Therapy Unit (ITU) – and head off to find somewhere quiet to wait for news.

She had been told that the transplant could take between eight and ten hours, depending on how easy it was to remove my right lung (the one that had been surgically fixed back to my chest wall back in 2008) and I felt awful that she would have to wait all that time by herself. I thought a lot about the children, who would be getting up and getting ready for school with our wonderfully kind neighbours doing their utmost to reassure them. I told myself that, in terms of having everything ready for this moment, I had prepared as well as I could have. All I could do in these last minutes really was to just hope for the best.

I also spent these remaining minutes reviewing the past twenty-six months, in which I had waited for this moment with both excitement and trepidation in equal measure. After all the frustration that had built up over those months, I could not come to terms with the fact that my transplant was finally happening. Even at this late stage, I expected someone to burst through the door and say there had been some terrible mistake and that we were not going ahead after all. But that never happened. I was informed that theatre was ready for me and that everything was in place. An oxygen mask was placed over my nose and mouth and I was instructed to breathe deeply whilst someone syringed a milky white liquid into the IV line in my right arm.

I looked down at my trembling hands, holding my Father's Day card in its clear plastic envelope. Aisling and the children looked back at me, smiling as if, for the final time, to reassure me that everything really *would* be okay.

The lights of the room got brighter and brighter and it started to swirl. I felt hot and weak and, although I fought the urge for as long as I could, my eyes were just too heavy to hold open. Within seconds, they finally closed, and I was gone.

FORTY-SIX

A BIT OF A BLUR

It was six whole days before I regained any sense of being awake or any awareness of where I was or what had happened to me.

During the time I was asleep, a great deal happened to me. My forty-seventh birthday came and went. More significantly, though, two days following the transplant (almost forty-seven years to the day after it had first started) I came very close to losing my life. Much of what follows is from Aisling's account of what took place during those first and very turbulent few days. I find listening to her version of events harrowing and still struggle with the thought of what she must have gone through during that time.

The transplant operation lasted about ten hours. Aisling was allowed into ITU (Intensive Therapy Unit) later that evening to visit me for the first time. Before being allowed in, she was spoken to by the surgeon who had led the operation. He told her that, although the transplant itself had gone well, for unknown reasons (which would later be put down to "irregular vascular architecture" in my upper torso), my upper body and my head in particular had swelled massively during the operation. He was unsure how this had happened, but suspected that multiple blood clots had formed in the major veins in my upper chest, which may have restricted the blood supply to my head.

The surgeon explained that my head remained enlarged and that my face was a deep purple colour. When Aisling asked him directly whether I might have suffered brain damage as a result of the swelling, he told her that this was 'probable'. He also told her that the next twenty-four hours were crucial in terms of whether I survived and that I was in a 'very precarious state'.

Before she left my side that night, she noticed that my wedding ring was still on my finger and that, given the severity of the swelling, she had voiced her concerns to the nurses that it may need cutting off to save my finger. The following morning, when Aisling was allowed back into ITU, she was handed my wedding ring by one of the nurses who had been looking after me that night. Miraculously, they had managed to remove the ring intact and Aisling placed it on her own finger for safekeeping. It would be many, many months before I was able to wear my ring once more.

Over the next few days, Aisling stayed with me as much as the staff on ITU would allow. The visiting hours on ITU were very restricted and at times Aisling had to fight hard to be able to stay with me, despite my delicate condition. Each time she left, Aisling had no idea whether she would ever see me alive again. To go through all this, largely on her own, must have been absolutely horrific for her. I shudder even now to think about the sights she saw in ITU, and the thoughts she must have had during those first few terrible days. The guilt I still feel about not being able to support her (although I was indeed there) still haunts me; we have always supported each other through hard times and yet for this there was simply nothing I could do to help her. All I could do was try and survive.

Over the course of that first week, my condition deteriorated and the swelling in my head spread to my whole body. I collected an awful lot of fluid in my torso, arms, and legs (known medically as 'oedema'), probably due to the damage to my vascular and/or lymphatic system resulting from the operation. I say 'an awful lot of fluid' and this equated to around twelve kilograms of the stuff spread all around my body, giving me a similar appearance to the character from the Michelin Tyres advertisements. Also, during that time, my blood pressure dropped to critically low levels, my newly installed lungs refused to inflate properly and my kidneys failed, making me reliant on a dialysis machine.

After six days of being kept in a medically induced coma and having regular CT scans to check my brain for early signs of damage, the decision was taken to start trying to bring me round and to see how bad the suspected brain damage might be. As the drugs keeping me asleep were slowly withdrawn, I began to regain consciousness. Almost a week after arriving at Harefield, I woke up, my artificial ventilation was withdrawn, and I started breathing on my own again, albeit with someone else's lungs inside me.

My recollection of those few hours of coming around are scant at best, still swimming as I was in the sea of painkilling drugs that were coursing through my veins at that point. So, all I can do is give you a rundown of those early few days as best as I can remember them.

My first recollection is of hearing beeps and buzzers, and of feeling awfully uncomfortable. I could hear someone talking to me. At first, I struggled to respond, not because I didn't want to but because I simply could not be bothered – I just wanted to sleep. I was aware of this person asking me my name. Eventually, I quietly responded, "Luke." I was then asked whether I knew where I was. "Harefield," I responded. Lastly, I was asked if I knew what had happened to me. "Transplant," was all I could muster. I thought at the time that they were just trying to wake me up. I certainly had no idea that the staff were checking to see whether I had suffered any brain damage as a result of what had happened. I asked where Aisling was, and they promised that she would be back later.

I had absolutely no idea whether it was day or night, that I had been asleep for six days, or where in the hospital I was. What I did know was that I was alive and awake (sort of) and that the transplant had taken place. I felt so tired and weak, probably the worst that I have ever felt my entire life (and believe me, I have had some pretty bad hangovers in my time).

At some point later, having been passing in and out of sleep, I became aware of someone holding my hand. I opened my eyes to see Aisling standing at the side of my bed, smiling. I wanted to smile back but it was hard. I was aware of being hooked up to various machines, with tubes and wires sticking out from all parts of me, and I was unable to move.

I asked Aisling what day it was, and she told me it was Tuesday. I recall being surprised by this as we had arrived on a Wednesday, so how could it *possibly* be Tuesday? Aisling confirmed that it was Tuesday of the following week, that I had been asleep for six days, and that I had missed my birthday. She also informed me that the transplant had gone well and that the surgeons had told her the donor lungs were 'beautiful'. They had experienced a little difficulty with removing the lung that they thought would potentially be problematic (the one that had collapsed years earlier), but everything had generally gone well. Initially, I was relieved. But then Aisling explained that there had been some 'complications' during and immediately after surgery, that there were still some issues the doctors were sorting out, but that I was not to worry about them for now. My focus was to relax, rest, and sleep as much as I could in order to let the healing process get underway.

The bad dreams during those first days of being semi-conscious were horrendous. I can still vividly remember the one in which I was told by the nurse that unless I gave my teeth a proper clean, they would all start to fall out. Upon asking the nurse if this conversation really had taken place, she swiftly dashed off to summon backup. Shortly after, the psychologist appeared (the lady I had met a few times whilst on the waiting list). I told her of my concerns about my teeth and she reassured me that there was nothing wrong. She offered to find me a toothbrush and toothpaste, so that I could clean them if that would make me feel any better. I told her there was one in my grab bag and she rifled around until she found it. She also found a nurse to help me and afterwards, still feeling like death but now with minty fresh breath, I felt ever so slightly reassured.

I had always held expectations (which were completely misguided, as it happens) that immediately after the transplant, I would sit up, take a deep breath, and marvel at how fantastic my new lungs were. It was not like that at all; in those first few hours after waking up, I recall feeling that I couldn't breathe too well. Whether it was the drugs making me feel uneasy or whether I was simply panicking a bit, I kept calling the nurses over to check everything, telling them that I felt like I couldn't breathe. Their response was the same each time, that my new lungs were working well, my oxygen saturations were fine, and that I just needed to relax and rest. This was probably well intentioned, but it did little to calm my racing and slightly panicking mind.

However, after four days since coming around , my new lungs *did* try to give up on me – obviously being slightly homesick and objecting to their new surroundings. On day ten, I went into respiratory arrest (where the lungs stop working and breathing either stops entirely or isn't effective enough to enable oxygenation to take place, which again can result in brain damage). I was put back into a medically induced sleep and was intubated once more (a tube being thrust into my mouth and down my trachea for support with ventilation).

I was on a ventilator for a further two days until I once more woke up, more alert this time and being checked over by various members of the medical team. I was conscious that there were other patients near me and of what was happening around me but felt little urge to engage with any of it. I was only interested in Aisling being there and when she was not, wondering when she would next be back.

In those few days, I lived a very strange existence. It was almost as if I was looking through a window of opaque glass at myself and all that was going on around me. I was having numerous nightmares and was finding it hard to tell whether I was awake or asleep for much of the time. I was aware of the times when Aisling was with me, but I have little recollection of the times she wasn't.

After a few days, a physiotherapist called Andy arrived. I had been warned many months beforehand that the physios were brutal (in the nicest possible way) and would arrive shortly after I came around to get me mobilised and to start using my new lungs. Andy's first objective was to get me sitting up on the edge of the bed, which I was to achieve with the aid of a device that you hold on to whilst it pulls you up under pneumatic power. After three miserable attempts at this, it was quite apparent to both Andy and I that it was way too early to expect me to accomplish this seemingly simple task. Once the towel had well and truly been thrown in for the day, Andy told me to rest and that he would be back tomorrow for another go. I was frustrated. "Why can I not even sit up?" I asked myself. It seemed like I was being asked to climb Everest, and it took many attempts in those first few days to achieve this ostensibly straightforward task.

After fourteen days in ITU, I was moved to my own side room on the High Dependency Unit (HDU) with one-to-one care. I wasn't entirely sure why this was and put it down to just being what happened once you were a few days post-transplant. The day (or night) I was moved, I don't really remember much. But I do remember that, some time just before I woke up in an entirely different setting to the one that I had got used to, a nurse who had been on shift in ITU came along and, without saying a word to me, picked up the greetings cards that were on my bedside table, gathered them in a pile, and unceremoniously dropped them into a nearby bin.

You must understand that I was barely conscious at this point, it was dark, and I was drugged up to the eyeballs. Yet I recall lying there, watching this happen, and wondering why someone would do such a thing. These were birthday cards from my wife and children, plus get-well cards from other well-wishers; they were not rubbish.

When I awoke in my new room, I mentioned what had happened to Aisling and, having had a quick scout around and through my belongings, she confirmed that she could not find the cards anywhere. She mentioned it to the nurse in charge of looking after me that day, but the nurse responded that I had been brought to the new room without any cards and that, in any event, the rubbish bins on ITU would have been emptied by that stage.

Despite the perplexing disappearance of my greetings cards, I thought I had been given my own personal side room – away from the lights, buzzers, and general disorder of the ITU – for my comfort and so that I could get some proper rest. However, the reality was a great deal more serious than that.

Following the transplant, I had been given a huge amount of IV antibiotics. With these, I was *supposed* to take *further* antibiotics to cover me in case of Clostridium difficile making an unwelcome return, a bacterial infection of the digestive system that I had been affected by a couple of times in the past at Papworth. However, no such coverage had been given by the medical staff treating me. So, I spent the next few days and nights with uncontrollable and deeply unpleasant diarrhoea (as if I didn't have enough to contend with). I was moved to an individual room for isolation purposes, so as not to infect other critically ill patients with this bug that has a rather nasty habit of finishing off already compromised patients with relative ease. Although I still had one-to-one care from the nursing staff, and a window, I was very much confined to my bed and in an awful lot of pain and discomfort.

It was in this room that the hallucinations really started. When I first woke there, I was aware that I had been moved but did not know where to. I convinced myself that I had been moved out of ITU, out of Harefield Hospital entirely, and had been relocated to a room above the local library in Harefield village! As I lay there with this drug-induced misconception, I was aware of people coming and going in and out of the room whilst visiting the library. There was an elderly couple, who had sat down near me and were eating their sandwiches, and a young mother who came in with a child in a pushchair. When I woke to find Aisling beside me, I asked her why they had moved me to a room at the library to which Aisling tried to reassure me that they hadn't. I followed this up by saying that, if that was the case and that I was still in the hospital, why was there a decorator standing next to me, roller in hand, repainting the ceiling? With a long sigh (I can only imagine), Aisling did her best to reassure me that none of this was real and that it was just the medication playing tricks on me.

Aisling asked me what else I might have seen that had unsettled me. I told her that I could remember being in ITU, and the sound of a violin being played. I vividly remembered at one point seeing a concert violinist in full black-tie, complete with tails, roaming around playing familiar tunes from the musicals intermingled with more classical numbers. Following what Aisling had said about hallucinations, I had told myself that this was just another one of them. "Oh no," Aisling told me, "that did actually happen!" She explained that every Tuesday there is a guy who visits the hospital. An orchestral musician by night, he comes into hospitals during the day and plays his violin to cheer up patients and their visitors. This seemed completely bizarre, but she reassured me it was true. As if things were not confusing enough, the line between what was real and what wasn't now seemed even more blurred!

My week or so on the HDU was slow and hard. The days and nights merged into one everlasting period of drifting in and out of sleep. When awake, I was never sure whether I actually was awake, and the nights were long and difficult, with a regular flow of bad dreams and me waking myself up by shouting and swearing. There was one night when my nurse washed her hair in the little sink in the room five times (in the 'real world' she was obviously just washing her hands) and another when I was in a trench on some battlefield or other, in the cold, the dark, and the wet, with bombs and bullets raining down on me. This was intermingled with the reality of me constantly being woken up for my bed to be changed as the Clostridium difficile had got the better of me once again. All in all, a deeply disturbing and very unsettling experience.

Whilst in this room, the physio Andy continued to make his daily visit and to try to get me to sit up. I managed this once or twice but the concept of standing up out of bed and moving anywhere seemed like a distant dream and completely unrealistic. Each day, Andy would arrive with renewed hope and an infectious degree of optimism and yet would leave just a few minutes later with both of our hopes dashed once more.

One event that *did* occur, on the second or third day in the HDU, was when Aisling was with me one afternoon. A cleaner came in and handed me a pile of cards, asking whether they were mine. We couldn't believe it. Somehow, this guy had found the cards in the bin back in the ITU, had fished them out, and had then tracked me down to another part of the building to hand deliver them back to me. I was as delighted as Aisling was relieved. During those dark times, this lovely man had shown us that there was still real goodness out there, even if it may have been hard to see at times.

Several days into my stay on the HDU, Aisling decided that the time was right for the children to visit me. We had agreed that Aisling would have to decide when the appropriate time was as I wasn't mentally capable of making such a decision. Children were not allowed to visit on the ITU in any event, so this was the first real opportunity that we'd had to bring the children in.

Additionally, after all this time, they were eager to see me. It was now about two weeks since the transplant operation and, although things were still far from ideal, I was feeling and looking a bit better than I had been. A very kind nurse looking after me that day offered to wash my hair and shave me (for the first time in nearly three weeks) and I gratefully agreed. Anything I can do to make myself look a bit more presentable, and slightly more 'normal' for the children, I thought to myself.

I remember the children entering the room. My son walked in cautiously and quietly, with my daughter hiding somewhere between him and Aisling. He approached the bed and held my hand, visibly shocked by my appearance. There was his dad, wired up to various devices, pumps and a dialysis machine, lying helpless, and with a feeding tube sticking out of his nose. It would be fair to say that I was not exactly looking my best and I am sure I was quite a sight to behold, certainly a scary one for an eight-year-old. He asked me if I was okay and whether I needed anything, to which I responded in my croaky voice that I was and that no, I didn't. My daughter, however, was very scared and would not approach the bed at all. Aisling lifted her up and brought her over, but she could barely bring herself to look at me. I reached out my hand to reassure her and my son said, "He's still just Daddy but he looks a bit different." But for a five-year old, seeing me like that must have been truly shocking. Thankfully, though, and with luck, it's a sight that she will have been too young to remember in years to come.

After they had stayed for a few minutes, Aisling took them back outside to where her parents were waiting. Aisling then returned and reassured me that they would be fine. I had found the experience quite emotional and traumatic; I felt bad that I could not have made it any easier for them. Yet we were where we were, and there was never going to be a right time. But despite all the medical care I was receiving at that time, seeing my two children in the same room as me and hearing their young voices back with me was all the medicine I needed to pull me through

FORTY-SEVEN

GREAT STRIDES THROUGH TINY STEPS

Just over three weeks following the transplant, and with the Clostridium difficile back under a degree of control, I was moved out of my room on the HDU and down to the post-transplant ward. My recovery was well underway, but it didn't feel like it to me. I'd heard about others who had lung transplants and were up on the exercise bike a couple of days after their operation. After nearly two weeks, I couldn't even get out of my bed unassisted, let along walk across the room to get to the exercise bike that was sitting forlornly in the corner.

My various chest drains were withdrawn one by one, IV lines were removed, and eventually I was freed from the pieces of medical equipment that had been keeping me alive. This felt like a milestone, if there was one to be reached.

The daily visits from the medical staff continued, checking my progress and changing things that were not going quite the way they wanted. I developed fluid on the lungs, which required a further chest drain in the side of my chest. This was done under just a local anaesthetic, and seemingly by a doctor who displayed little pride in her work and even less in the way of bedside manner.

I like to think that with all that I have gone through over the years and being no stranger to being prodded, poked, jabbed and stabbed, I have developed a relatively high tolerance to pain. However, this chest drain was inserted with all the finesse of a ham-fisted gorilla and Aisling, sitting way down the corridor in the waiting area, heard my shout of pain as the doctor twisted and pushed the drain into place. When it was withdrawn some three days later, the transplant registrar who did the honours was so surprised by the twist in the drain tube that he bleeped a colleague to attend, just to double check that no further damage had been caused by its withdrawal.

On the post-transplant ward, my daily visits from Andy the physio continued. Now that I was free from the HDU, he was more determined than ever that I would be walking again within days. This seemed heartless at the time, but looking back I am so grateful that he took this attitude.

Over the course of the next few days, Andy started with getting me to sit up, followed by making me sit on the side of the bed and then stand on the floor, firstly assisted and then on my own (although this was only for a few seconds before my legs gave way). With this achieved, we moved on to taking slow, steady steps across the room, with me holding on to Andy in sheer terror. In the days ahead, he had me leaving my room and heading along the corridor, aiming to get a bit further each time. Again, this was firstly achieved by me hanging off Andy. After that, we moved on to me slowly and awkwardly holding on to a walking frame while Andy followed close behind with a wheelchair for when my legs crumpled and I needed a break.

It took days to get anywhere close to the point of the corridor where the lift and stairs were located, and we set ourselves this goal for the end of the third week. By Friday of that week, we were only halfway there. So, Andy left for the weekend telling me to do my best to 'keep up the good work' and that on Monday we would pick up where we left off.

By this time, I was rather despondent. Not only could I not put one foot effectively in front of another, the mere *thought* of walking unassisted scared me to death. I was completely perplexed as to why this was the case. They had operated on my chest, right? So, then why I had completely lost the ability to walk? How could it be that I had walked perfectly happily from the age of about one, yet here I was at forty-seven years old, totally incapable of doing just that.

Whilst others tried to reassure me, told me this was to be expected, and that I was finding it hard because my legs were full of excess fluid and therefore very heavy, it troubled me greatly and was the source of deep frustration.

That weekend, though, I miraculously turned a corner. My old friend Ross (of Papworth Hospital fame), who had undergone a double lung transplant himself in 2015, had been through similar times and was no stranger to such difficulties. He arrived on Saturday morning, obviously having already decided that he was going to get me walking during the time he was with me – even if it killed me, or him, or quite possibly both of us.

We worked on standing up and getting moving. He slung my arm around his shoulders, and we walked up and down the corridor for what seemed like hours but was significantly less than that. We broke for lunch, where he wheeled me over to the hospital cafeteria for lunch, and then wheeled me back for more walking. Upon his departure that day, I seemed to have regained much of my lost confidence and had a new sense of determination to impress Andy when he reappeared on the Monday.

Whilst my days on the post-transplant ward were taken up with regular drugs rounds and observation checks, me drifting in and out of sleep, and Aisling – and occasionally the children – visiting, the nights were endless. I was on my own and the bad dreams were relentless. I was in a lot of discomfort and the noise and lights from the ward outside my room never diminished. I would stare for hours at the cards from my children that were now pinned to the board opposite my bed, and just wished I could go home. I felt rough and looked even rougher. Aisling had taken photos of me at various points of my recovery up until this point, although I still haven't been able to bring myself to look at them, even now.

Lying there at night, with the minutes passing slowly away as if they were hours, my mind would take me to places I didn't want to be, and feelings of helplessness and frustration started to creep in. Whilst I tried my best to cling on to the strong sense of hope that I have always sworn by, in the darkness of my room and with each minute that passed, those hopes would come in to question. And it wasn't until I talked to the hospital psychologist that things began to change for me.

On her next attendance, when I asked her how long most lung transplant patients spent in hospital before being discharged, she informed me that for Harefield this was six to eight weeks but that, "Everyone's transplant journey is different." She also told me that with everything I had been through, I should expect my stay to be *at least* that long.

On the day I heard this, I was three weeks and five days post-transplant. I had already had enough and just wanted to go home for a hot bath, a proper meal, and a nice sleep in my own bed. I asked her what kind of things I would need to do before I could be considered for discharge. I was informed the main things were to be able to mobilise myself unaided and to manage my own medications. I had started to move towards achieving these goals but remained a long way off. Upon her leaving my room, however, I became determined not to settle for being 'average' and that I would be out long before six to eight weeks had passed.

On Andy's next visit the following Monday, I told him that not only would we be walking as far as the lift and stairs, but that we would be trying to head up the stairs as well. He appeared somewhat surprised my new-found sense of resolve and ambition. Sure enough, though, we got to the foot of the stairs and I confirmed that I was ready to give them a go. The stairs to the first floor consisted of three separate flights of about seven steps, with a small landing after each. To Andy's amazement, and through sheer gritted teeth and determination, after several minutes of heavy breathing and very regular stops for breath, I made it to the first floor. I could not believe it. Ascending that stairway had seemed like climbing the highest of mountains, and just a week or so before I hadn't even been able to put one foot in front of the other. Yet I had made it, and by doing so had cleared a major hurdle to getting signed off by Andy as being ready for discharge. Over the following few days, we worked on these stairs more and more until, eventually, I was able to go up and down them three times (albeit taking an age to do so).

From the start of my fourth week in hospital, my eyes were firmly fixed on getting home, so much so that almost every waking hour was consumed by such thoughts. I worked hard at getting to grips with the myriad of drugs I had to take and, although my swollen hands and fat sausage-like fingers would not let me push the various types of tablets and capsules out of their blister packs so that I could take them, I would tell the nurse on the drugs round (working to a pre-written checklist) what I required and they would dispense them for me into a little paper cup. I was told that as I would have Aisling at home to assist, knowing what I needed to take was enough to be signed off for discharge.

The other thing I managed to do that week was to finally find a male nurse who had a spare hour (an extremely rare beast in the modern NHS). The nurse probably regretted coming into my room that morning and, after telling me he would be looking after me that day, asking if there was anything I needed.

A cup of tea or a biscuit is no doubt the normal response to such a question, so dragging me to the shower and hosing me down was probably the last thing he expected to be doing later that morning. I had not had a proper wash or shower for over four weeks by this stage and had been telling staff for about two of those weeks how much better I would feel if I could just have a shower. It was apparent that everyone was either too busy, or too distracted with other patients although there also seemed to be a tendency for staff to find spurious reasons as to why I couldn't be showered – "it's too soon after your operation", "it's not permitted", "not until you are deemed safe" and so on.

Anyway, this lovely male nurse was my saviour that day and, true to his word, returned to spend almost an hour helping me achieve my goal to be clean. I still have the photo on my phone that I sent to Aisling that lunchtime of me clean shaven, showered, and with clean, fluffy hair once more. It was one of the best feelings I had experienced in those four weeks, although I was starting from a very low basis, admittedly.

As the fourth week passed, it became apparent that the doctors were starting to consider whether I was fit enough to be discharged. I was asked for my opinion on the subject. With what was probably a hopelessly misconceived level of arrogance, fuelled by a desire to be anywhere but in that hospital, I confirmed that I would be ready to go by the end of that week. Plans were therefore put in place and, for the first time, I felt that I might actually get out of there.

Just three obstacles remained. Firstly, I had to have one final chest CT scan to ensure that there was no further fluid building up in the lungs. Secondly, Andy had to run through a list of exercises with me to ensure that I could keep my new lungs clear but that, whilst exercising them, I did not overexert them. Lastly, I had to have a long briefing from the specialist transplant sister about the do's and don'ts of a new life with donor organs.

The chest CT was fine, showed that all was well and that everything remained clear following the butchery that had taken place with the last chest drain. Andy ran through his exercises with me and briefed me on ways I could mobilise myself and exercise my new lungs. We talked a lot about breathing exercises. He explained that all my life, my lungs had trained my brain into believing that I was only capable of short, shallow breaths. Having new lungs, he explained, meant that my brain had to be completely wiped of this information and re-trained to take much longer, deeper breaths. This would take time, he said, and would not be an easy thing to overturn. But we went through breathing exercises that would help to achieve this and he suggested apps that I could download to assist with breathing techniques. I was walking now, although still very tentatively and anxiously, but I knew that if I got home, I would at least be able to get around the house (however long it may take) and, most importantly, between my bed and the toilet.

My chat with the transplant sister was delayed from Wednesday to Thursday as she had other commitments that day and Aisling was also unable to be there at the allocated time. She had been driving between our home and Harefield (about one hundred miles each way) every day for the past four weeks and driving on the M25 daily had really taken its toll. Nonetheless, at lunchtime on the Thursday of my fourth week on the post-transplant ward, the three of us sat down and ran through a pro-forma that the sister had brought with her.

This 'get home' checklist included going through my numerous medications – the dosages, the times to take them, and what to do if I either ran out of them or missed a dose. We also discussed attending clinic going forward; my attendances would be twice weekly to start with then weekly for three months, fortnightly between the three and six months mark, then monthly between six and twelve months post-transplant. This was going to be a hard schedule to keep to given that we were not exactly just around the corner but we were told that it was essential; the first twelve months post-transplant are the riskiest time of all and the team wanted to keep a close eye for the first sign of any trouble.

We talked about organ rejection, the types of rejection, and the first signs of each type. I was given a handheld device to monitor my lung function with each day and was also told to check my temperature and weight each morning (a fever or rapid weight increase can be the first signs of organ rejection).

We ran through guidelines about diet and the foods that I could no longer eat. Sadly, some of my favourite foods were now off limits due to either being deemed 'high risk' or because they would interfere with the anti-rejection medication I was now taking. Items I had previously enjoyed, like blue cheese, smoked salmon, grapefruit, pâté, runny boiled eggs, and rare-cooked steak were all now off limits.

Our discussion meandered its way through a multitude of other subjects too, such as alcohol consumption, the risk of having pets, driving (not permitted until twelve weeks after transplant), returning to work, travel and holidays, care in the sun (transplant patients are one hundred times more likely to develop skin cancer due to their anti-rejection medication), and oral health.

We talked for about ninety minutes and there was a lot of information to take in. Luckily, a lot of it was common sense and I was told that as long as I was sensible and careful, then I would be doing as much as I could to protect myself from further hospitalisation. Things could still go wrong, and the sister told me I should almost expect them to, but it was up to me and only me to look after myself as best as I could from this point on. Checklists were ticked off and papers were signed. And, with that, I was told I could *finally* go home.

All that remained was to overcome the types of hurdles that discharge day always throws up. Anyone well-versed with hospital stays will tell you that discharge day from hospital is one of the most frustrating experiences you can ever endure. Whilst you may wake bright and early, full of expectation and raring for the off, those who are in control of events seem to be working to a completely different timetable to you. Drugs need to be delivered from pharmacy, your observations need to be taken (seemingly a million times) and signed off by a doctor who appears to be more of an imaginary, Wizard of Oz, type character than a real person. And a discharge letter must be drafted from scratch, giving a blow-by-blow account of the past however-many weeks of your life under their charge. As you can probably tell from my tone, I hate discharge days passionately and, however many of these debacles I have been through in my life, they never seem to be managed any more efficiently or get any easier to tolerate.

By mid-afternoon on Friday 31st May 2019, just as I was starting to give up hope that I might be in my own bed that evening, a doctor appeared at the door, discharge letter in hand. Following a brief exchange, she wished me well, told me that she would see me in clinic the following Monday and that I was free to leave.

Exactly four weeks and two days after entering the hospital with old, infected, and worn-out lungs, I was heading back out of that same building with shiny new ones. And with them, a whole new world of possibility lay before me.

I knew I had been through a hard time and that the immediate future was not going to be easy, but I was willing to give it a go. After staggering across the hospital car park and clambering unceremoniously into the passenger seat of our car, with Aisling following closely behind with my stuff, I sat back and for the first time since the house phone rang at three twenty-three on the morning of the transplant, I allowed myself to feel ever-so-slightly relaxed.

———

It would be wrong to say that my first week at home went well. It did not. Aisling had to shower and change me, do everything for me, and watch me not sleeping and becoming increasingly unsettled. I was exhausted. I felt as though my pain was not under control and simply did not know what to do with myself. After a week of struggling through all this, we decided that I need to go back into Harefield for a few days to get myself slightly more straightened out. Reluctantly, and with a heavy heart, I did this and looking back I am thankful that I did. Those additional few days helped to iron out a few more creases physically and gave me time to consider how life would *really* be at home. I had hoped to go home and be out cutting the lawn, going for long family walks, and generally enjoying myself. But this was not going to be the case any time soon and I had to come to terms with that fact – quickly.

After a further week as an inpatient, I was again released into Aisling's care at home. The second time around, I was much more aware of how different life would be for the next few months. And I knew I had to adapt to it in order for my body to start healing.

Those five weeks following the transplant were tougher than I had ever expected for so many different reasons, and they had left me battered and scarred, both mentally and physically. But I finally had new lungs. After 865 days or 20,040 hours of waiting, my chance of a transplant had finally come. I had made it through the perilous and lengthy operation. I had survived.

I had waited for so long and hoped so much for this moment and now it had come to pass. The biggest thing that would ever happen to me in my lifetime was finally over. The road of recovery was long and stretched far into the distance. All I could do now was ride the bumps and keep focussed on my destination – a new and brighter future with new lungs and with my beautiful family.

WHERE DO I GO FROM HERE?

FORTY-EIGHT

THE LANDSCAPE CHANGES

It really is the strangest feeling: after waiting for almost two and a half years for something, two and a half years in which that something consumed and tarnished every waking hour of every single day, it is no longer with me.

Not having it there leaves an enormous void, a wide-open space laid out before me and waiting in anticipation for me to fill it with something else.

Looking out over a lush grassy meadow, deserted yet bathed in warm sunshine. A tropical beach with no-one there but me to enjoy the waves that are quietly lapping the shoreline and the warm summer breeze that gently rustles through the branches of the palm trees. This is how I see the life I have ahead of me.

Where once my mind was full of disturbance, noise, and chaos, that disruption has now fallen away. It has been replaced by something more serene. But this serenity has taken a great deal to come to terms with; I am staring at the blank canvas that is inviting me to fill it with a whole new way of life. Less than a year ago, this is something which seemed utterly intangible.

It has now been several months since the dramatic and life changing events of May 2019. It would be wrong to say that my recovery has been straightforward and free of obstacles. It hasn't. In fact, the past few months have seen me back at Harefield Hospital more times than I care to count, as the transplant team have carefully managed one post-operative issue after another. The psychologist was correct when she told me that the immediate aftermath of the transplant would be tougher than the lead up to it. Yet, here I am, undeterred by everything that has happened and still as determined as ever to make the very most of the most wonderful gift anyone could have ever given me; the chance of a new life with new lungs.

It has taken many months for all the swelling to settle down and for my arms and legs to return to their normal size. In fact, to illustrate this, I have only just managed to start wearing my wedding ring again. Thankfully, it was somehow miraculously removed (with some haste, I should imagine) after I began swelling up during the transplant operation.

I have been left with a constricted airway into one of the new lungs, which is going to require a stent to maintain the opening and to allow me to fully benefit from having the new lungs. This is more of a nuisance than anything, is nothing that the medics haven't seen before, and is certainly very treatable.

Perhaps more significant than the constricted airway, I have also just been diagnosed with diabetes. You will recall that those with CF are prone to developing diabetes (at least one in every three CF patients will develop diabetes at some point in their lifetime). With CF, the pancreas suffers damage from the build-up of mucus in the body and its ability to produce insulin is compromised. The type of diabetes that CF patients develop lies somewhere between Type 1 and Type 2, the former being the type normally managed by insulin injections. My diabetes appears to be leaning more towards Type 1, so I recently started round-the-clock blood glucose monitoring and an injection of insulin before every meal.

Diabetes is a well-known and well-documented side effect of the immuno-suppressant medication that I started to take following the transplant. In fact, four out of five patients who are prescribed these anti-rejection drugs will develop diabetes during the first year following their transplant. When adding these two contributing factors together, it was almost inevitable that I would develop the condition at some point. Towards the end of 2019, I had started to feel 'not right' and was failing to gain weight, despite my chest feeling better than ever and me eating more than ever before. But a couple of weeks of pricking my finger with a small device confirmed the suspicions of my medical team and insulin treatment was commenced.

To many people, receiving a positive diagnosis as an insulin-dependent diabetic would be devastating and I can fully understand that sentiment. Having been on the receiving end of bad news more than once in my life, I know just how hard it is to accept things are going to be different and that your life is going to undergo a seismic change. That said, the news that I had developed diabetes myself was met with little more than a shrug of my shoulders and a wry smile.

I have been asked recently how I feel about it, as if I have been cheated or conned somehow. I have even been asked, "How does it feel to have bad lungs replaced by diabetes?" Whilst I do my best to answer such questions with a decent sprinkling of humour, in a lifetime spent dealing with one medical complication or another, this is just another hurdle to be overcome. After all, as I keep boasting to people, "It's really no big deal – I've still got the new lungs."

My greatest concern now is the risk of my body rejecting the new lungs. The risk of this is highest during the first year following the transplant and, as I write this, I am still well within that window. The body can reject new organs for any number of medical reasons but when you stop and think about it, it feels almost a 'given' that this would be the case. The human body is an amazing and complex machine. If you so much as cut your finger, it springs into action to fight any infection that may ensue and goes into healing mode to mend the skin as quickly as possible. Liken that to taking a part (or parts) of the body out and replacing them with similar, but also very different, parts from someone else entirely and you begin to get the picture. I now take anti-rejection medication twice daily to suppress my immune system, so that it doesn't see the new lungs as either an infection or some form of 'alien invasion' and begin attacking itself, rejecting the lungs entirely.

There have been people who have had a lung transplant but whose body has rejected those lungs, forcing them to undergo a second transplant with a further pair of donor lungs. Whilst such events are rare, it can and does happen. I have known people who have died from rejection and others who have had no issues in this regard. I can only hope that I fall into the latter of these two categories.

I do my best to not dwell too much on this issue. After all, I have only just got these new lungs and I want to enjoy them not worry about them. I feel that I have done my time worrying about my lungs, at least for a while. I take my anti-rejection drugs religiously, twice a day, at set times. I check my temperature, weight, and lung function on a little hand-held device each morning for the first signs of anything heading on a downward trend and have the Harefield Transplant team on speed-dial should anything appear abnormal or irregular.

It would be very easy to spend my day being consumed with fear over the risk of rejection. But I have been there and done that. I have just spent the last three years of my life worrying about something that didn't happen. So, for now, I need to take a mental break, not just for myself but for those around me.

I found the early months post-transplant especially difficult. Not just from a physical point of view but from a mental one too. My mood swings were severe and would come along without warning. I was angry for much of the time, frustrated by my apparent lack of progress. People would tell me that I was doing incredibly well but, however much I could do, it never seemed enough. I could not seem to grasp the scale of what I had been though or comprehend that it takes the body time to mend following such a traumatic event. In my own impossibly impatient style, I wanted to be climbing mountains or running marathons straight away. The ability to even contemplate why such feats were not yet possible eluded me.

My apparent lack of progress annoyed me to the extent that I couldn't sleep, couldn't settle, and became quite irritable around the house. I would scare the children with my short fuse and bad temper, and I am convinced that Aisling must have given serious consideration to the idea that Harefield might have performed a personality transplant at the same time they gave me new lungs. In hindsight, the huge cocktail of medication I was taking, combined with major sleep deprivation and possibly some degree of post-traumatic stress, would have played a huge part in tearing my confidence, my optimism, and my patience to shreds, just when I needed them most.

Going through a period in life when everything is on hold, your nerves are constantly on edge. And being in a state of high alert for such a long time would wreak havoc with anyone's mind. Like a huge balloon that has been continuously filled with ever increasing amounts of air, when it finally bursts there is an *enormous* bang. Although you expected the balloon to burst, and knew the bang was coming, it still makes you jump when it does.

It would be easy now, a few months down the line, to almost brush off the stress that I experienced during the time I was on the list. It would be easy for me to understate the 'weight of the wait' as I have described it to others. But I know deep down that it had an enormous effect on me as a person and that it will take time to heal those wounds. The physical scars from the transplant may be starting to fade on my body, but I suspect the emotional scars will take a great deal longer to do so.

I don't seek to use any of this as an excuse, you understand, and I wish to take this opportunity to apologise to Aisling and the children for my adverse behaviour towards them over those first few months. They were hoping to get their daddy and husband back, new and improved with a shiny pair of lungs and a refreshed outlook on life. But what they actually got was probably worse than what they had before the transplant.

During that time, I felt as though I was slowing tearing our family life apart bit by bit and things inevitably came to a head. I did another of my disappearing acts for a few hours one evening, to find some space to breathe and to give myself a good talking to. I reminded myself that I had everything I had ever wanted in my hands yet (for reasons totally unknown to me) I was squeezing the life out of it all. I was fast running out of time and out of chances to put things right. My whole outlook had to change, and I had to start making those changes immediately.

After some discussion with Aisling, we concluded that after all that had gone on, not only in recent weeks but over the past two and a half years, I just needed to learn how to relax once again. I looked for ways of doing this and, having considered many options, in the end the answer was relatively simple: I would seek to spend more of my time working harder at doing nothing.

To those who don't know me, this may seem like an oxymoron, but I have always struggled with the concept of doing nothing. And that struggle only intensified after the transplant. So, I signed up for a new Spotify account on my phone and compiled a playlist of around one hundred and fifty tracks spanning a range of genres but all with one thing in common; each piece of music on that playlist reminded me of a happy time in my life or a treasured memory of something or someone. Listening to these songs and other pieces of music would sometimes make me emotional, when my state was delicate and I was physically and emotionally exhausted, but they helped me to relax, helped me to unwind and, on many evenings, helped me drift off to sleep.

This reminded me never to underestimate the power of music, particularly that which stirs up thoughts of happier times and familiar faces, in order to settle a troubled mind. With the soundtrack of my life being played out over the top, those first few months suddenly seemed easier to cope with. This was the real medicine I needed in order to soothe the turbulence within me, to calm me down, and to carry me through to the better times I am now enjoying. Some of the music that featured on that list can be found in Appendix Two of this book (in case you might be interested).

FORTY-NINE
MORE TOMORROWS

I still feel as though I have cheated the system in some way. I feel in many respects like a bit of a fraud; the transplant was the most significant thing to happen in my life, yet I largely slept through it and the horrors that it presented. It was Aisling who lived and breathed every horrific moment of it and is still picking up the pieces even now. In so many respects, I feel like I was simply a passenger along for the ride and that it was Aisling who was sat in the front seat watching the car crash unfold before her. I will never appreciate the trauma she must have gone through, particularly during those first two weeks following the transplant operation. I will never be able to compensate her in any way for what she endured during that time, and the feelings of guilt I have over those events will never leave. So, I have to hope that the fact I survived and pulled through those toughest of times will be enough for her somehow; it is all I have to offer but it is also everything because it means we have a future.

As I reflect on what has happened over the past few months, I am very conscious that I must not languish or simply rest on my laurels. This is no time to be driving whilst looking constantly in the rear-view mirror. Questions like, "What do I do now?' and, "Where do I go from here?" are looming large before me and cannot be ignored. I feel as if I have a heightened sense of duty to take this opportunity and march full steam ahead. This is not the end of anything, but the start of something new, exciting, and fresh. And while I rest and recover, it is important to remind myself of that.

I think about how things are versus how they might have been – in an alternative version of reality, I could very easily have been really struggling by now with the lungs I was given. I could even be dead. I have a long way to go on my road to recovery, I am aware of that, but I take an enormous amount of solace from just being on that road, travelling forward. And, regardless of how many potholes I may hit on the journey, I am determined to get there.

I find it useful to stop and reflect on things; there is so much to process, so much to come to terms with, and so much to reconcile, pack away, and bring out again in the future to discuss at a time when feelings and emotions may not be so raw. For the moment, the transplant has left something of a void in my life, although this is not necessarily a bad thing. The time I would have spent dwelling over 'what might be' and 'what happens if...' is largely mine again. The mental capacity to contemplate better times and the good things to come has been handed back to me, although somehow, I feel uneasy with it all and not sure exactly what to do with it.

I feel a palpable sense of guilt. Apart from feeling guilty over what Aisling had to go through during the transplant and the weeks following, I also feel guilty that someone has died in the process of me getting new lungs. I keep reminding myself that they did not die just so that I might have the chance to live – the donor died and as a result of their (and their family's) generosity I was able to receive their lungs and, along with them, a new chance in life. The distinction is slight but important and I know I must do my best to keep everything that has happened in perspective.

One way of dealing with my post-transplant guilt was to write to the donor's family. This is something you are briefed on both before and after transplant – Harefield handed me a little leaflet on the topic when I was finally discharged following the operation. For months afterwards, I was simply not ready to do this. The events of May 2019 were too raw and, like the letters that I had to draft to my family before I went on the list in January 2017, the thought of even trying to accomplish this was just too difficult.

Questions like, "How would you even go about thanking someone for such a gift?" and, "Can just saying 'thank you' ever be enough?" turned over and over in my mind. It is simply not normal to owe such a massive debt to someone you have never met and will never meet. And in any event, does writing something down to send to their loved ones 'mean' anything? What does it achieve?

I have always tried to teach my children that, regardless of what the situation is, it is always important to do the right thing. You don't need to be told what that might be, and whether it is appreciated or acknowledged by a recipient is irrelevant. I knew for many weeks that writing a letter to my donor's family was not only the right thing to do but that I needed to do it for myself. What it would achieve was some sense of closure; a sense of drawing a line in the sand and finding a datum point from which to move on.

In early December 2019, I finally sat down and wrote that letter. Like those I wrote to my family before going on the list, the actual writing of it was easier than I'd envisaged, and I hope it came across as heartfelt and personal. As a transplant recipient, you are not automatically told anything about your donor. Given this, I wasn't even sure that there was a family to write to, but that was no reason for me not to *at least* try to reach out.

The words 'thank you' could never even begin to cover my limitless gratitude towards my donor, nor do they come close to matching the value of the gift I received from that person, whomever he or she is. But I wrote my letter knowing that their family was just about to head into the holiday season without their loved one for the very first time, possibly leaving an empty chair around the Christmas dinner table that year and forever more.

Having been through terrible grief in my own life caused by a catastrophic event, I was full of sympathy for their situation and could imagine the struggles they may have been through since the death of their loved one, and my donor, some seven months previously. I explained that I had a wife and two young children, who would now have their husband and father with them for many more years to come. I talked about how unwell I was leading up to the transplant and how difficult life had become beforehand. I explained what receiving new lungs meant to me and my family, and what I planned to do now that I had them. I promised the donor's family that I would look after the lungs and would use them to their full potential. After all, I had been given another chance in life – one that the donor would never have. Signing off, I promised that I would always endeavour to make the donor proud of me and of what I achieve while carrying part of them with me.

I handed this letter to the transplant team at Harefield a few days later, who then forward it to a central coordinating office that handles such matters. Whilst the donor family can choose to write back if they so wish, at the time of writing, they have not done so. That is not important, though. I certainly don't expect anything back and I'm not sure whether I even want or need a response. That was not the point of me writing; what I needed to do was say thank you in the best way that I could, with carefully chosen words and a huge degree of sentiment. And I feel that, as much as I am ever going to be able to, I have achieved that.

I tell myself that the mix of feelings I have experienced over the past few months, and that I continue to experience, will settle with time. A whole new chapter is starting in my life, yet because of the medical complications I have had (and to a small degree am still experiencing) any feelings of euphoria and of being able to move mountains are suspended for now.

I still sometimes find myself asking why I got lucky that day rather than someone else and whether I cheated someone else out of lungs they may have needed more than I did. I feel sad that Steve never got the opportunity to be in the position that I am now in and, in a way, I feel a bit of a fraud. Did I really do enough to deserve these new lungs? Was I really sick enough to need them? Notwithstanding all of this, though, and however difficult it is to accept at times, I have them. So, what is important now is to appreciate the golden opportunity that they present to me – what might just be the ultimate in second chances.

I am acutely aware that I have been handed the largest slice of good fortune by receiving the transplant. The sheer weight of this opportunity bears down on me and is something I am constantly conscious of. The tardiness of my recovery frustrates me intensely and I have struggled to find a new 'normal' so far. But it will come. There will come a day when all these feelings will dissipate, leaving blue skies and a clear path. I wonder if I will return to work one day. I enjoy work but have been away from it so long that I wonder whether I would be able to fit back in, certainly to what I did before. After all, I have been through so much that almost everything else seems trivial in comparison. To go back to spending my days concerned with whether Company A has paid Company B for goods or services and, if not, advising them what to do about it, seems quite ridiculous in the grand scheme of things. It feels like everything has moved on since then; life has moved on and there are so many more things that really matter. Everything else is, at best, slightly inconvenient or, at the opposite end of the spectrum, totally irrelevant.

All that said, plans for the future are important. I have my responsibilities as a husband and father to honour, which I will continue to do to the best of my ability. I owe it to my family, to my donor, and to myself, to keep well, to do all that I am asked to do from a medical standpoint, and to look after my new lungs. The transplant has been simply amazing for so many reasons, but it is something I would not wish on anyone and nor would I want to go through it again. Receiving a transplant should be a once in a lifetime event. And I certainly hope that it will be for me.

So, what comes next?

Early on in my time on the transplant waiting list, I told the children that once a year had passed following my transplant, Mummy and I would take them anywhere they wanted to go in the world. Transplant patients are restricted from flying for twelve months post-transplant due to the heightened risk of becoming unwell or of organ rejection whilst overseas. Commercial aircraft, with their air conditioning, are particularly bad for passing illnesses between passengers and, as transplant patients have compromised immune systems, it is best to let things settle for a year before venturing up into the sky in a metal tube full of people coughing and sneezing all over you.

My son's answer was brief and straight to the point: Australia. He has long held a dream (possibly from having watched far too many David Attenborough documentaries) to snorkel on the Great Barrier Reef, to visit the rainforests, and to see the amazing Australian wildlife in their own habitat. I reminded him that he might also wish to visit members of his own family that live there there too!

My daughter's response, perhaps due to her being five years old, was far simpler (and thankfully far less expensive). After careful consideration, clearly weighing up her options, she delivered her verdict: Wales. "At least we can just drive to the Norfolk coast for the day and tell her we are in Wales," I said to Aisling. I am hoping that my daughter learns to broaden her horizons and develops more of a sense of wanderlust in forthcoming years, just as Aisling and I did as we grew up. But, for now, Wales it is.

This year also marks mine and Aisling's twentieth wedding anniversary (yes, that does say twenty and is not a typographical error). Just being alive twenty years after we married is something of a miracle, perhaps as miraculous as Aisling standing by me through everything that has happened in that time. On our wedding day in September 2000, I don't think that either of us, or anyone at our wedding, would have dared to consider that we might reach this point, yet here we are. For all that those twenty years have thrown at us, the good as well as the not-so-good, we remain as close as we always were and have so much to live for and to look forward to. The future will not always be plain sailing, and nothing is assured, but the outlook is brighter now than it has been in a very long time.

One thing that I truly hope to take up again is flying. This pursuit was the one thing I could always count on to take me completely away from anything at all to do with CF. There is so much to think about and to concentrate on, as well as the thrill of flying yourself in a small aircraft, that there simply isn't the mental capacity left to consider anything else. Flying provided me with a sense of escapism unlike anything else I have done, and the sights and experiences I had while up in the air were opportunities I could only have dreamed about once upon a time.

I have also recently become a governor at my children's school. Partly to give something back – to repay society in some small way for all that it has given me – but also to occupy my mind whilst I ponder what to do next with my life.

The pressure to make sure I do something with this new life is sometimes hard to handle. But thoughts of hope, optimism, and brighter skies abound. I hold dear a real and renewed sense of making the most of my time. I will never take this for granted, although complacency may set in over time. When I went on the list, my hope was to survive long enough to get the new lungs. Now, my hope is to make everyone proud, to be a good person, and to always ensure that I do the right thing. Given everything I have put the people I love the most through, I owe them that at the very least.

In recent months, I have been called 'amazing', an 'inspiration', and someone very close to Aisling and I has ventured so far as to call me a 'hero'. I have accepted such praise with a sheepish smile and the good grace with which it was intended, and yet I find such terms very hard to accept. In my view, such descriptions apply to anyone who lives their life with CF, regardless of their age, gender, background, or whether they have had a transplant or otherwise. Every single person in the CF patient community is a hero to me.

So, where do I go from here? The answer is simple: forwards. Filling the blank landscape that stretches out before me with new hopes, new wishes, and new experiences. Never forgetting what has gone before, but not letting it consume me either.

As long as the good times of the future outweigh the bad times of the past, then I will be happy.

FIFTY
AN ENDING WITH A NEW BEGINNING

It has just gone five p.m. on Friday 1st May 2020. It is exactly one year to the day that I had my transplant and two days before my 48th birthday. I am once again sitting on my bed at home. I am once again on my own, and the house is quiet. In a rare moment, I allow myself to stop, *really* stop, and reflect on the magnitude of what I have been through in the past twelve months. My mind spins through the maelstrom of thoughts, experiences, and emotions I have endured; not only during that time but throughout my life.

I have talked in previous chapters about my decline and the events that led me to needing a lung transplant. I have taken you through the journey that saw me prepare to be placed on the list, the seemingly endless time I spent on that list, and how I feel having had the transplant and come out the other side. It doesn't feel, however, like everything has come full circle, at least not yet.

Things are not like they were and I am not the same person I was; everything is different and I feel different both physically and mentally. It is too early, and the transplant is too recent, for me to have a true sense how life has changed. But deep down inside, I know it has and there is a little piece of me that wants to be excited for the future and to scream this from the rooftops.

I still have CF and all that a life with it entails. That particular cloud will always be there. But with my shiny new lungs, a renewed sense of hope, and so much optimism for a future I doubted I would ever have, I can head onwards and upwards. That CF cloud has filled my sky forever, but it really does feel like I have finally found a silver lining. The cloud may remain, but behind it hangs a bright blue sky filled with light.

As you know, I was always conscious of being the same but different. For years, I saw this as a bad thing and tried to disguise my CF. I was embarrassed, scared of being singled out, and I certainly never wanted to be treated any differently or to garner anyone's sympathy.

Now, such sentiments seem to be completely misguided and, should I have my time all over again, I would probably approach the whole CF 'thing' very differently. Rather than hiding it away, I now feel able to tell everyone about it, even those who may not want to listen. I am proud to have made it through the transplant and to discuss this accomplishment.

I have CF and I have had a lung transplant. But consider everything you have learned about me, all that I have experienced and achieved – I have done this with a chronic condition that was supposed to kill me before I reached double figures, which proves that life can be incredible. It can drag you so far down that it is hard to know which way is up. But it can also take you to places you considered far beyond your reach. Had I not been the same but different, I may have never experienced such extremes; seeing things at their very worst makes the good times seem not just good, but truly amazing. Now, I am proud of who I am and I am proud to be different. My life with CF, for all that it might have taken away, has given me that at least.

I am, like most, the sort of person who will always have dreams about what I would like to achieve in my life. It would also not be inaccurate to state that I have always been rather *compulsive*, identifying something I might like to do and making sure I achieve it in reasonably short order. I'm unsure whether having CF made me like this, but it certainly contributed to it; living with CF has meant living with the prospect that I could become very ill very rapidly and that I may not live long enough to tick items off my 'wish list'. This is part of the reason I have always *hated* the concept of 'bucket lists' – because they imply that one has an infinite amount of time available in which to complete one's list.

However, had the younger me been forced to write a list of what he would like to achieve in his life, I should imagine such it may have read as follows (in no particular order):

1. Go snorkelling on the Great Barrier Reef, Australia.
2. Learn to fly and obtain a Private Pilot's Licence.
3. Be at the launch of a space shuttle.
4. Go on a seaplane in the Maldives.
5. Tour New Zealand in a camper van.

6. Fly in a vintage Tiger Moth.
7. Own a classic Mini Cooper.
8. Climb Sydney Harbour Bridge.
9. Climb to the top of the Statue of Liberty, New York, USA.
10. Own a share in a light aircraft.
11. Attend university and successfully complete a degree.
12. Enjoy careers working full-time for a major international airline and as a lawyer.
13. Travel extensively worldwide, visiting numerous countries across North America, Europe, Asia, Australasia, Africa, and the Indian Ocean.
14. Take a helicopter up a mountain and land on a glacier.
15. Visit at least one of the top three beaches in the world (Whitehaven Beach, Queensland, Australia).
16. Live in a foreign country (USA, France).
17. Go gliding over the mountains of South Island, New Zealand.
18. Get married.
19. Have children.
20. Write a book and have it published.

Previously, the thought of writing such a list never entered my head. The irony, however, is that I have accomplished every item on the list above and hope to do so much more in the future. The list, however fanciful and improbable it may have seemed had I written it thirty years ago, has all been achieved. But nor should this list be considered exhaustive or complete; I remain fixedly determined that it will be added to in the years to come, in whatever time I am afforded by CF.

Reflecting on the things I have done, I am content with what I have managed against a backdrop of fighting infections, taking silly amounts of medication, and undertaking daily physio routines. Given the long-term prospects of a person born with CF way back in 1972, and the life I was *supposed* to lead, just to reach an age where I could contemplate such things was hugely against the odds. Thankfully, though, and with the love, assistance, and support of so many others throughout my life to date, my dreams became reality and those odds have been defied, time and time again.

I suppose the message I am trying to convey – and which I have tried to convey throughout this book – is the importance of remaining positive and hopeful, of using time wisely, and of doing everything you want to do *now* not later. CF has certainly taught me that living for today is crucial, because one day tomorrow won't come. I am deeply aware of the fragility of time, something I doubt I would have had without having lived with CF. I chose a long time ago to jump onboard life with all that I have for the fear of getting left behind. The above list is testament to that choice. To simply make the best of here and now is all I can do, as I don't know what the future may hold.

You may be reaching the end of this book with the conclusion that I have not had a good life. CF is cruel and relentless and, admittedly, life with it has been tough. I also lost my dad far too young and have spent almost half of my life without him. I still miss him every day and I think of him constantly. I always consider how he might have dealt with the things I have been through and how he would have helped me in such times. Aisling and I mention him a lot to the children and joke with them about the things he might have said or done in certain situations. He is everywhere in our lives, even though he is gone, but I like it that way.

I also lost one of my closest friends to a cruel disease not dissimilar to CF. Steve was in a very similar position to me, with his lungs failing and in urgent need of a transplant. Yet he was deemed too ill to be listed, and his subsequent death was extremely hard for me to accept. Steve was one of life's good guys and did not deserve to end his as he did.

But, despite the bad times, there have been wonderful times too.

To have been married for twenty years this year means everything to me. Aisling entered our marriage with little understanding of what living with someone who has CF might bring. It has certainly not been easy for her and she has my utmost admiration.

To have reached such a milestone in our lives says as much about her endurance and resilience as it does about my determination to do her proud and not let her down. Furthermore, in my view, anyone who has a partner with CF deserves at least a medal (if not a huge cash reward) in recognition of their dedication. Whilst I always knew what a life with it can entail, Aisling chose to stick around, to provide endless support and love at the trickiest of times, and to keep her head while everyone around us were losing theirs. She rode the CF rollercoaster alongside me, forever knowing that the ride may stop at any time, showing bravery and a degree of selflessness that is *really* inspirational.

CF has also come a long way since my diagnosis back in 1972. Treatments have been revolutionised and medication is not even comparable. Life with CF remains tough, but as new medications are developed and made available to patients, hopes are raised that CF will be so much more manageable, and therefore more tolerable, in the future. Perhaps even one day, with the plethora of discoveries that genetic science is throwing up on an almost weekly basis, CF will be cured. No more would parents have to receive the devastating news that their child has CF. No more would those with CF have to dwell on life expectancy figures and what may lie ahead. Wouldn't that be wonderful?

In the meantime, and until science makes this fantasy a reality, we rely on the scientific and pharmaceutical advancements that are being made. And on the generosity of those who offer up their organs for transplant upon their death, prolonging our lives so that we might fulfil whatever it is that we wish to achieve. Knowing such people still exist gives hope to all with CF that, should they near the end of their journey, a whole new one might start just around the next bend.

If you are reading this as a person with CF, or you know a person with the condition, the message I wish to leave you with, almost over any other, is not to see the diagnosis as a negative thing. It is not a curse or, worse than that, a death sentence. CF is a condition that will influence your life and how you live it, but not something that should overshadow all you do or everything you might want to do. I would encourage anyone affected by CF it to see it as a springboard – a catalyst, if you will – to feel even more determined to do all you want to do, and to live the life you want to live.

Through exploiting this mentality, I have achieved so much more than others who perhaps just take life for granted, content in their own complacency and with little to motivate or drive them on. It is this approach that allows me to say I have truly lived my life in the best way I could, achieved more than I wanted to achieve, and that I have filled the time between my birth and ultimately the end of my life (whenever it comes) with as much as I possibly could.

Always believe you can do it, even if you think you might not be able to. Don't believe those who say no when your head and your heart say yes, and never concede in the hard times that CF will put you through. When you come out the other side, you will feel stronger, fitter, and more capable of living the life you want to lead, and not the life that CF wants you to lead.

I feel now that I can head to the future with cautious optimism. I know that, despite the transplant, things can and will still go wrong. This is the reality of CF. But I am not scared of dying; death comes to us all in the end. Our lives are just a moment in time, yet they are *our* moments and it is what we do with them that counts.

If anything, what scares me is the thought of leaving things undone, unseen, or yet to experience. The thought that I may not see my children grow up and have children of their own breaks my heart. Thoughts of not seeing them get married or graduate from university, and of not knowing what they might become, are almost too much to bear. I find it better not to dwell on such matters, as they can only cause upset and regret. My time and energy are better invested in returning to full health, to be the person I have always hoped to be, and to make my donor, as well as my family, proud of me and what I achieved during my own particular 'moment'.

Sitting here on the end of my bed, and as this brief time for reflection draws to a close, I allow myself to feel pleased with what I have done in my life so far, and with how I have faced up to the difficult times and the challenges I have endured with CF. But feeling satisfied does not come easily to me, and I always tend to steer away from reflecting too much, not enjoying the awkwardness that shining the spotlight upon myself brings. Despite this, I try to remind myself that I should be proud of how I have overcome these difficult times; notwithstanding unwavering help and support from my wife and others, it has been me (with my positive outlook and a deeply engrained sense of determination), along with a decent measure of good fortune, that has brought me to this point.

As my reflection of the past turns into contemplation of the future, I let optimism and hope prevail once more. I feel the palpable sense of an ending. Yet I also feel like a new dawn has broken and that bigger and better times are surely to follow.

And as I sit alone in this quiet house, I allow myself to smile, if only for the briefest of moments. At times, life with CF may not offer up much to smile about. But I am still here, still alive, and still able to tell my story. For me, this is enough and it is more than I ever expected to have. During the more difficult periods in my life, to have the chance to share a bright new future with my loving, supportive wife and two wonderful children is more than I could have ever wished for.

One day, inevitably, it will all come to an end and my life with CF will be over.

Having CF may have taken me on a different life journey to most, yet it has made me who I am, has taught me so much about myself and how to face up to adversity, and has shaped me into the person that I am today.

Whilst I cannot say that having endured a life with CF will ever sit comfortably with me, nor am I bitter about it either. CF has been with me and has been a part of me for as long as I have been alive and living with CF is all I have ever known. I have always lived with the awareness that CF is likely to beat me in the end, by one method or another. But knowing this has given me a great deal of time to process the status quo, to rationalise it and to accept it for what it is.

The reality of a life (and a death) with CF can be cruel and hits harder some days than others. It is relentless. It never goes away, it never leaves, and I am all too conscious of the fact that it will be with me to the end, turning the screw until it finally takes over and beats me. On that day, CF will claim another victory. I will be simply one more person who has lived with the condition, persisted doggedly through their life with it, and who has ultimately been forced to submit to the ravages that it imposes on both the body and the mind.

Until I reach that point, and for as long as my body allows, I will continue making memories and squeezing as much out of my life as I can. Until my body is exhausted and my brain is tired, I will continue to strive for a better existence, never losing hope and always wanting more. Until my journey is over, there will always be more to do, places to go, and experiences to enjoy.

No matter what, I will always strive to do the right thing for my family and will never let go, give in, or submit to whatever obstacles come my way. No matter what happens from this point on, I will look on my life as a work in progress, a project which remains unfinished and unresolved. For as long as I am able to, I will keep fighting the fight, dreaming big, and living life in the best way that I possibly can. Until I have given all I have to give, until I have achieved all that I want to achieve, and I can finally feel that I have fulfilled my purpose, I will go on.

It has always been my hope that those who know me best will remember me and my journey with a smile; I would prefer them to forget about me rather than to remember me with tears. Despite everything, I have enjoyed my life and have taken so much more from it than I could have possibly hoped for.

So, as I gather myself, take a deep breath and leave the bedroom to rejoin my family, it strikes me that being the same but different has not been such a bad thing after all. And despite having lived with CF, I know there is so much more to come – because just now, and after everything I have survived, it feels as though I am going to live forever.

I'll see you on the beach...

AND FINALLY...

I have often wondered what would happen if CF entered the room and sat down in front of me. What I would think, how would I feel and how might I react? If I were given a single, hypothetical chance to get everything off my chest (pun fully intended) what is it that I would really want to say to CF?

There would have been a time some years ago when I would have been furious with CF and would have been grateful to be in the same room as it; to have the opportunity to vent my anger and frustration, and to lash out with the aim of overwhelming CF with all the venomous feelings I bore inside me. My life has repeatedly wandered through the good times only to be caught out by the bad. I used to want to blame CF for everything that went wrong.

This is, however, no longer the case. CF is not to blame for everything and cannot be held accountable for all that has happened to me. Sometimes CF only serves up the pitfalls and it is how I have chosen to deal with them that has dictated whether I have sunk or swam in response. On some occasions, I have coped well and found a way of navigating through the difficulties, whilst at other times I have tripped and fallen, to flounder lost and broken in the very place where I fell. Yet time and experience has taught me a lot about CF. I know that it is completely okay not to be okay about what might be happening to me; that there is always someone to reach out to for emotional support. Being angry is ultimately futile. It has never helped me to feel better about CF or how I am. Yet being aware of this reminds me to seek out better ways of dealing with the difficulties that a life with CF brings, and to that end, having such an awareness serves its purpose.

I would inform CF that I see it as entirely part of me and my existence. It has always been with me and always will be. I do not see it as the enemy, nor do I hate it for what it has done to me or put me through. By being respectful of CF and the risks and limitations it imposes, I remain alive. In all I do, CF merely comes along for the ride. Having CF there is a constant reminder to look after myself, to live life productively and above all to enjoy it for all that it offers me (although these are rules that everyone should follow, whether they have CF or not). I don't hate CF, yet we are not exactly the best of friends either. CF has made me who I am, and I would like to think a better person for it.

I imagine we would talk about the specifics of what CF has put me through. Why did things happen the way they did, and why did CF choose to inflict them upon me in the way that it did. Were those events tests of some sort; CF checking how robust my resilience is or was it just CF having its fun? Was I supposed to get through those events alive or not? Did I outwit CF and survive its evil plans to get rid of me or have I just postposed the inevitable and that it will be CF left with the last laugh?

I would ensure that CF knew that it wasn't invincible, and although it may enjoy making people's lives difficult, its grip over them only makes them stronger and heightens their resolve to find a way to overcome CF and its horrible armoury of symptoms, effects and complications. I would also remind it that there are scientists working day and night to find a cure for CF. That one day, CF's day will have been and gone and it will have taken its final curtain call. No longer will people fear it, be subordinate to it or vulnerable to its ravages. Humankind and science will meet the challenges that CF presents and eventually confine it to medical history. For thousands of people that day can't come soon enough. It can play its silly games now, but the end for CF is looming larger now than it ever has done before.

As the conversation dies and as I rise from my seat to leave, I would simply tell CF the following. It may well be that one day CF will overcome me, get the better of me and end my life. I am very aware of that fact yet do not fear it. Whilst CF may well view my demise as a victory for itself, such a victory will be hollow and will lack any true substance. There will be no cause for CF to celebrate or to seek accolades for such a victory. I would remind CF that things were always likely to end this way between us.

Yet as my parting shot, I would tell CF that despite everything it has done to me, put me and those I love through, and however much it has affected both my life and how I have lived it, none of that will matter in the end. With all that I have been able to do, the places that I have been, the experiences that I have had and with all the love that I have been shown by those closest to me, its victory will ultimately be meaningless – as I have already won.

THANK YOU

Thank you for reading 'Coughing It All Up'. I hope you enjoyed reading the book as much as I enjoyed writing it. If you did, please consider leaving a review on Amazon or Goodreads.

APPENDIX ONE – MY LIFE WITH CF IN NUMBERS

876,000 tablets taken

35,040 physiotherapy sessions

20,040 hours on the transplant waiting list (835 days, or 119 weeks and 2 days)

18,520 nebuliser sessions

820 blood samples taken

188 weeks spent in hospital (or 1,316 days)

120 chest x-rays

32 abdominal ultrasound scans

40 CT scans

50 Electro-cardiograms (ECGs)

30 bronchoscopies

4 birthdays spent in hospital

3 cases of NTM

3 holidays cancelled due to CF

2 collapsed lungs (pneumothorax)

2 PEG insertions

2 Portacaths

2 cases of double pneumonia

2 music concerts missed due to CF

1 medical incident on a passenger plane

1 New Year's Eve spent in hospital

1 double lung transplant

But 17,660 days alive – and still counting…

APPENDIX TWO – PLAYLIST OF A REMARKABLE LIFE DESPITE CYSTIC FIBROSIS

Throughout my life I have always enjoyed a variety of music, whether it be through my love for drumming, being part of a choir, playing the guitar and piano (albeit badly), or simply listening to a range of music spanning many genres. I have relied on music to get me through my hardest times - in hospital as well as out, but also to celebrate the best times of my life, as well as everything in between.

The following twenty-two songs not only give you a flavour of my eclectic taste in popular music, but their lyrics resonate with me on a personal level and they also loosely follow the chronology of this book in terms of their respective release dates. I have many other favourite pieces of music, and this list is by no means exhaustive, but these twenty-two songs vaguely fulfil the criteria above.

If you have a moment and feel so inclined, I would invite you to search for the lyrics to each of the songs on the internet, the poignancy and relevance of which should become clear as you read them. Regrettably, copyright law prevents me from reproducing them to any extent here.

Should you wish to listen to the playlist (either in its entirety or just selected songs), you can do so via Spotify, the link for which is included in the 'Useful Links' section of this book, or by entering 'Coughing It All Up' in the Spotify search tool. Should you not have access to Spotify, you can also find them on YouTube or in many cases, the corresponding music video can be found on Vevo.

It Can Never be the Same (The Cure)

If there was a single band that I would say was my favourite of all time, it would have to be The Cure. From my formative teenage years until present day, they have been recording new music and with it, providing single-handedly the soundtrack to my life. I spent my early working years in Crawley, West Sussex where the band first formed back in the late 1970s. I have seen them play live on several occasions. I even passed the lead singer (Robert Smith) in the foyer of the hospital where both of my children were born.

This song, first performed on the band's North American tour of 2016, is a song of sadness and regret, reflecting on missed opportunities when something (or someone) you love is no longer there. I listened to this song a great deal towards the end of that year, as my health fell away and as I underwent the testing required to be entered onto the lung transplant waiting list. The lyrics are impossibly sad, trying to tell oneself that things will be all right although knowing that they won't be, and knowing that things have seismically changed forever.

Linger (The Cranberries)

This song, originally released in 1993 and then again in 1994, reminds me of my final year at university. It was often the last song played of the night at Student Union discos and party nights as a wind-down song at 1.55am as the night drew to a close. The beautiful opening melody and the almost ethereal strains of Delores O' Riordan's voice still makes the hairs on the back of my neck stand up when I hear the song now. The song is about hoping for something to be reliable, dependable, and unfailing; and yet feeling terribly let down and disappointed when you find out that it is not. Truly a metaphor for a life with CF.

The First Picture of You (The Lotus Eaters)

One of the earliest pop records of the 1980's that I remember really enjoying whenever it came on the radio. Formed in Liverpool in 1982, this was the band's biggest selling single when released in July 1983 and for me became the sound of that summer. When I hear the opening bars even now, my mind returns to those long hot days of an English summer, being eleven years of age, and not having a care in the world - despite having CF hanging over me and the potential effects it would have on my future self.

She Sells Sanctuary (The Cult)

One of my favourite rock anthems of all. Just the sound of Billy Duffy playing the notes of that first unmistakeable guitar riff still gives me goose bumps. This is a song that needs to be played loud, so that the crashing guitars and thumping drumbeat penetrate your whole body and leave you exhausted by the end, as if you have just gone twelve rounds with the world heavyweight champion, almost relieved that it is all over.

This song takes me back to my early drumming days at school when my first band would play (in all likeliness) a very poor cover version of it. If played loud and fast, and with everyone generally in time and in tune with everyone else in the band, it had the ability to make us feel like kings and ready to take on the world. Rock legends we were not but legends in our own lunchtime - well, possibly.

Crash (The Primitives)

Probably the shortest piece of music on this list but one of the catchiest with its memorable chorus hook. This song blasts in from almost nowhere, takes you on a rollercoaster ride of two verses and two choruses and then disappears, leaving you feeling somehow short-changed and wanting more. From the opening bars, this song with its rock/post-punk/pop fusion, is two minutes and eighteen seconds of musical delight mixed with simple lyrics sung by the lead female singer with the improbable nomenclature, Tracy Tracy.

This song is the one that my university band 'The Confession' would end our set with at every gig we played. Always guaranteed to get the crowd dancing and jostling for floor space at the end of a long, hard evening of drinking, we would play out the final bars over and over, ending with a big crashing finish that no-one ever seemed to want to end. If any song I ever played made me want to emulate my ultimate drum hero (Animal from 'The Muppets'), this is that song.

Are You Ready to Fly? (Rozalla)

Perhaps ever-so-slightly cheesy but still one of my favourites from the early 1990s dance scene. This song is held firmly in my mind from my days at Virgin Atlantic Airways.

This song featured as the soundtrack for a corporate VHS video I would show whenever doing presentations about the airline to external audiences on my travels around the world. The video itself was a 5-minute visual spectacle of all the glossy and sexy parts of the company, intermingled with some absolutely stunning air-to-air footage of Virgin Atlantic aircraft flying through clouds, over mountains and across oceans (although this may have simply been the English Channel, located just a few miles south of Gatwick Airport in Sussex).

Either way, showing that video always filled me with a sense of corporate pride and reminded me how lucky I was to have landed my dream job with my dream company. And to answer the question posed by the song title - yes, I was born ready. And no - I don't still have a copy of the video (sadly).

Vapour Trail (Ride)

A song that takes me back to my time at Aston University, finding my feet and living alone with CF for the first time before heading off to Crawley and starting my working life. The aviation reference of the title also fits well with the contents of *The Early Years.*

Melodically beautiful and with lyrics that remain as fresh today as the day they were first written in 1991, this song conjures up images of crisp blue skies streaked with brilliant white lines created by jet aircraft at high altitude.

A fantastically gorgeous love song which ends with the jangly guitars falling away to be replaced by a string section taking the final bow before finally fading out. Ride as a band were leaders in the 'shoe-gazing' era of the late 80s and early 90s, slightly before the heady days of the Madchester music scene took over. Anyone for 'pills, thrills and bellyaches'? (and if you understand that last reference, you were probably born before 1980).

Friday, I'm In Love (The Cure)

Another song from my favourite band, Friday I'm in love is probably the closet the band has come in their forty-plus years of recording to releasing what could be described as a 'pop' record. Glistening with The Cure's enigmatic guitar sound and an easily memorised lyric, the track when released as a single in 1992 reached number six in the UK singles chart and is almost certainly one of the most widely recognisable songs of the band's extensive back catalogue.

When Aisling and I first got together in 1997, I would compile mix tapes (of course – isn't that what everyone did back then?) which we would play in the car and sing along to at weekends. From memory, this was the first song on the first compilation tape I made for her. This was also one of the very few songs that I could at one time play in full on the guitar (although I wouldn't dare try that now).

Dance, Girl, Dance (Cinerama)

When living in Toulouse, rather than invest in a television and immerse myself in the intricacies of the French language, I would listen to the BBC World Service on a long wave transistor radio. Once a week, the legendary DJ John Peel would spend an hour playing records from up and coming recording artists that he chose to 'champion' the cause for. One of those bands was Cinerama, whose lead singer and main song writer David Gedge had formed the band in 1998 as a side project from his day job fronting The Wedding Present, a band who enjoyed some success during my years at university.

Combining classic pop sounds with full orchestral arrangements made for a unique late 1990s sound, also utilised by other artists around at the time including The Divine Comedy (featuring the charismatic composer/song-writer Neil Hannon) and My Life Story.

Baby, Can I Hold You? (Tracy Chapman)

Although released some years earlier, and despite Irish 'boy' band Boyzone doing their best to ruin it with their own version in 1997, this song was the song that Aisling and I had our first dance to at our wedding reception in September 2000.

Tracy Chapman's eponymous debut album (on which this song features) was played a lot in my house as a teenager and brings back so many happy memories from my very first day of married life with Aisling.

In Dreams (Roy Orbison)

Roy Orbison was one of my Dad's favourite artists, and as children we would often be subjected to Roy's greatest hits booming from the cassette player in the family car with my Dad crooning over the top. Given our age, we had little comprehension as to the appeal of Roy's songs and even less awareness that we were listening to arguably some of the finest love songs ever written.

At my Dad's funeral in 2001, this was the last of three pieces of music that were played to the congregation as they filed out and it still brings a lump to my throat when I hear it now. The lyrics describe how the mind reminds you of people and places forever gone but never forgotten and as such seemed entirely apt in the circumstances, as well as being one of my Dad's favourite tracks from 'The Big O'.

I Had a Time (Embrace)

This band, originating from Yorkshire close to where my Dad was born and grew up, rank in my top three all-time bands. Aisling and I have seen them play live eight times over the years, I have a signed copy of one of their albums and even have one of drummer Mike Heaton's drumsticks (thrown into the audience at the conclusion of one of those gigs) treasured away in my desk drawer at home.

There are so many songs by Embrace that I could have chosen to feature on this list although this remains both one of my favourites and one of the most poignant. This was the song that I put on repeat that day in Papworth in 2003 when I was ready to give up and let CF and NTM defeat me. Aisling couldn't be with me that afternoon, and if I were to die alone, this was the last thing I wanted to hear.

As you will have gathered if you have read this book, this turned out not to be the last thing I would hear, yet it still stands as a reminder of that horrible day when I felt like I was finally beaten. Although I still love this song, with its powerful lyrics of wishing for things that could have been but also being grateful for what you have been fortunate enough to enjoy, I still find it hard to listen to, even now many years later.

All the Small Things (Blink 182)

A song that is so simple in its construction yet whose chorus hook is hard to get out of your head once it is in. I am a fan of the pop/punk genre, and of the bands to come out of the Southern Californian scene in the mid-Nineties, Blink 182 remain my favourite and continue to record new material today, albeit with a slightly rearranged line-up.

One of my other drum heroes, Travis Barker, takes centre stage on many of the band's tracks, with simply breath-taking displays of drum skills that I could only ever dream of possessing. Also, if you feel inclined, I invite you to view the video for this song on YouTube - a humorous, tongue-firmly-in-cheek take on 'boy bands' of the time, served with the usual wry Blink wit and a hefty dose of sarcasm.

I have never seen Blink 182 play live, although I have tried. In 2013, Aisling and I were due to see them play at Wembley Arena in London although the gig was cancelled that same afternoon due to singer/bass guitarist Mark Hoppus losing his voice. Played regularly on car journeys, Blink songs are some of my children's favourites (although I must be selective in my choices as some song titles or lyrics are most certainly not age-appropriate).

Somewhere Only We Know (Keane)

Keane are high up on my list of favourite bands, ever since their debut album 'Hopes and Fears' was released in 2004. In fact, the version of that album that we have at home concludes with a bonus track – a live version of the band's song 'Bedshaped' which was recorded live at the Brixton Academy on 18th November 2004, a show that Aisling and I actually attended.

This song reminds me of the years that Aisling and I spent together before our children came along, living in our first home in Epsom and although by that time, my ongoing struggles with CF were well underway, we always seemed to find a way to look on the bright side of life and to get through. Sitting down and talking through our situation and what we can do about it has certainly helped us through time and time again.

That said, this song is inherently sad – reflective and rather melancholy in its tone. The song's lyrics are a reminiscence if you will; a search for 'simple things' and longing to return to the times before life got complicated and an attempt or a desire to bring everything back to basics.

The lyrics also remind the listener to have something to cling on to in times of adversity, whatever that 'something' may be. When one might be feeling old and tired (feelings that I have felt regularly throughout my adult life with CF), the vocal line reminds us the importance of having 'something to rely on' and having 'somewhere to begin'.

In a life fast becoming complicated with the various nuances of CF, this song resonated with me back when it was released in 2004, but also remains a beautifully heartfelt piece of music that I still enjoy immensely when I listen to it now.

Lippy Kids (Elbow)

Possibly best known for their festival friendly, rabble-rousing anthem 'Beautiful Day', Elbow released their fifth album 'Build a Rocket, Boys' the week that my son was born in 2011. In fact, it was Steve who bought us a copy of this CD as a musical memento of this most significant of events in our lives.

The song tells of endless summer days as a teenager spent hanging around, being out of the house for hours and falling in love. Whilst my early teenage years were not entirely as romantic as this, I will always remember this song being released the week my first child was born, and the immense pride I felt having overcome the odds to have finally become a father myself.

Chasing Rainbows (Shed Seven)

Another song that falls outside of strict chronological ordering (having been released in late 1996) but I still enjoy listening to today. Shed Seven from York were another band that were big in the 'Britpop' music scene of the late 90s, along with other representatives of the genre Embrace and of course Oasis, featured elsewhere on this list.

This song also featured on one of the many mixtapes that I made for Aisling when we first started seeing each other in 1997 and reminds me of that period in my life when everything seemed to be going my way before CF would firmly take over.

Set against a backdrop of a delightfully alluring tune, the lyrics talk of doing all one can to hide one's secrets from everyone and to have dreams that although impossible to achieve, remain important to cling to, nonetheless – all themes discussed somewhere within this book.

Still Waiting (Tom Chaplin)

In 2017, the band Keane (who feature elsewhere on this playlist) were on hiatus and their lead singer Tom Chaplin recorded a solo album entitled 'The Wave' on which this song was featured and which remains my favourite track on that album, with the possible exception of 'Quicksand'.

2017 marked the first year of me being on the transplant waiting list and Aisling and I went to see Tom and his band play live at the Cambridge Corn Exchange in the May of that year. 'Still Waiting' sums up my predicament during that time perfectly. The lyrics talk of being hopelessly lost, yet still clinging desperately on to the hope that things will not always be like this and that something will come along to change the status quo. I couldn't have put how I felt at that time any better myself - so thanks, Tom.

One More Light (Linkin Park)

I was always on the periphery of being a fully-fledged Linkin Park fan, enjoying some of their songs whilst not caring very much for others. Tracks like '*Numb*', '*What I've done*' and '*In the end*' are particular favourites, although this song is streets ahead of any other from the band. Upon the death of lead singer Chester Bennington in 2017, this song was given huge amounts of airplay and I first heard it around the time I had been on the transplant waiting list for several months and was feeling lost, scared and angry.

The lyrics are tear-jerkingly sad, about losing someone you love and feeling angry about it, wanting for it not to be real and vowing to never forget that person although over time, others might. The song encapsulated my fears that should I not survive the transplant operation, that I might just fade in people's memories over time and eventually be forgotten.

The song also took on even more personal sentiment for me at the end of 2017, when one of my best friends (Steve) died of a chronic lung disease. As if things were not hard enough for my family and I at that time, Steve's death seemed to multiply everything ten times over.

Whenever I hear this song, the memories of all the good times in my life play out in my mind, making me want to both smile and cry at the same time.

Eighteen (Pale Waves)

In the summer of 2019 whist at home starting my long hard road to recovery after my transplant, I tuned in (as I try to most years) to the BBC's coverage of the Glastonbury Music Festival.

As the television flickered to life, Pale Waves, an exciting new indie-pop band from Manchester took to the stage and performed an energetic set based on their newly released debut album, 'My Mind Makes Noises'. The set culminated with this song, which became the song of that summer for me, as well as of my post-transplant recovery.

We still play this song regularly at home and in the car, and Aisling has a fantastic video on her phone of me playing the drums along to it, whilst my daughter (who was five at the time) is singing and dancing along frenetically in the foreground. Happy memories, albeit from a very difficult time for us all.

All That's Left is Love (Angels and Airwaves)

Released in April 2020, as I completed the first draft of this book and started to think about what might come next, as well as shielding myself from a global health pandemic, the lyric of this song encapsulates everything I feel about all that I have been through with CF over the years.

Recorded by Angels and Airwaves, a band started by Tom de Longe following his departure from Blink 182 (who feature earlier on this list), it is as though this song was written specifically to accompany this book. Like 'Coughing It All Up', this song is about reflecting on your life, never losing hope in dark times, looking ahead through optimistic eyes to the future and knowing that better times are just beginning. Out of all the songs featured on this list, this would be the one that I would urge you most to look up the lyrics on the internet.

Starting gently and working up to a spectacular crescendo as it ends, this is one of those songs that as soon as I heard it the first time, I wanted to listen to it over and over. I love the melody, the chorus is powerfully uplifting, and the drum part majestic.

When I think back my life and all the bad things that CF has thrown at me, I can reconcile those in my mind and just be thankful that I am still alive. Because all those things are memories now.

Here, in the present, when all is said and done and as the song rightly says, “this world is different now”. Despite all that has happened to me, all that’s left is love, hence the reason why that particular word is highlighted from all the others on the cover illustration of this book.

Live Forever (Oasis)

This song from the largest band around during the 1990s has always been my favourite Oasis track. The words, although relatively simple (with verse two simply repeating verse one as if to make a point so that the listener fully understands the message the Gallagher brothers *et al* are trying to convey) are beautifully crafted, dismissing the mundane (such as gardens growing) as if with a cursory waft of the hand, whist dreaming of bigger and better things – like wanting to fly, as the song puts it.

The words mean a lot to me, as if I should hold on to my dreams and don’t let CF drag me downwards, so that I can feel as though I might live forever. The penultimate sentence of the final chapter in this book includes these very words for a reason...

The Adventure (Angels and Airways)

Recorded in 2005, this is the second song from this band to feature on the playlist, the name of which could easily have been an alternative title for this book. The song is about living life to its fullest, and feeling rejuvenated and energised, despite what may have gone before.

A huge, pounding rock song that covers so many of the subjects found in the pages of this book. In particular, the opening verse talks about waking up, feeling alive and seeing “pure sunlight”, and ends with the profoundly upbeat message that despite everything, “you will be fine”.

The words of the chorus are also particularly apt to me and my story told within these pages – stating “here we go, life’s waiting to begin”. The second part of the chorus I dedicate to my wonderful wife, as they express exactly how I feel about her, us and our life together –

“I cannot live, I can’t breathe unless you do this with me.”

I absolutely love the energy and optimism of this song, and it takes up the final position on this playlist to bring everything nicely to a close. My life has been tough, fun, traumatic, exciting, frightening and rewarding – but above all, it has certainly been an adventure!

APPENDIX THREE – USEFUL LINKS

Cystic Fibrosis Australia

https://www.cysticfibrosis.org.au

Cystic Fibrosis Canada

www.cysticfibrosis.ca

Cystic Fibrosis Ireland

www.cfireland.ie

Cystic Fibrosis Foundation (USA)

www.cff.org

Cystic Fibrosis New Zealand

www.cfnz.org.nz

Cystic Fibrosis Trust (UK)

www.cysticfibrosis.org.uk

Live Life Give Life (UK-based transplant awareness charity)

www.livelifegivelife.org.uk

NHS Blood and Transplant UK

www.nhsbt.nhs.uk

Royal Brompton and Harefield Hospitals, Harefield, UK

www.rbht.nhs.uk

Royal Papworth Hospital, Cambridge, UK

www.royalpapworth.nhs.uk

Share Your Wishes (UK-based transplant awareness charity)

www.shareyourwishes.co.uk

The link for the Spotify playlist (Appendix Two) can be found at –

https://open.spotify.com/playlist/654Tl2FcrFs3JhwisNrQfU?si=OYsqLwDlRyiR7KwB0JBKPA

APPENDIX FOUR - ENDNOTES

1. The Day the Waiting Began

1. Published September 2017
2. England completed the legislative switch to an 'opt-out' system on 20th May 2020. Scotland will follow in March 2021.
3. According to the International Society for Heart and Lung Transplantation in 2016, out of a sample of 55,000 adult patients who underwent a lung transplant between 1990 and 2014, there was a mean survival time of 5.8 years, with broken down survival rates of 89% at three months (that is 89% of those who underwent a lung transplant remaining alive three months after the operation), 80% at one year, 65% at three years, 54% at five years and 32% at ten years following the receipt of new lungs.

2. Cystic fibrosis and me

1. UK Cystic Fibrosis Registry 2017

12. What's your name again?

1. In May 2019, Royal Papworth Hospital relocated to a brand new, purposely built new hospital on the Cambridge Biomedical Campus, close to the centre of Cambridge. This new hospital is on the same site as Addenbrookes Hospital, where my parents had both worked as I grew up and I had attended hospital as a child. The college where I took my A-Levels is also located adjacent to the campus. Despite my best efforts, all roads in my life lead to this small enclave of Cambridge, it seems.

25. The calm before the perfect storm

1. Climbing Uluru was finally prohibited by law in October 2019.

31. Darkest Hours

1. In the years since 2003, and thanks to advances in both scientific expertise and research techniques, sub-classification of NTM infections has become possible - research substantially driven following my personal experience. 'My' particular sub-type of NTM has since been given the nomenclature 'Mycobacterium abscessus' (also referred to as *M.abscessus*). Whilst other NTM infections had been identified in the CF community prior to 2003, it was this particular strain that caused the extreme symptoms I experienced, and proved to be so resistant to antibiotic treatment. This strain of NTM has since become far more prevalent in the CF community worldwide, although I was the first CF patient to be positively diagnosed with Mycobacterium abscessus in the UK. In the pursuit of brevity however, I continue to refer to it throughout this book as simply 'NTM'.
2. I was told in the months after my admission that as staff left the CF Unit at the end of their shifts, they were not expecting me to still be alive when they returned for their next.

ACKNOWLEDGMENTS

Acknowledgements

It would take an entire book on its own for me to personally thank the many people who have contributed in some way to me being still alive and having the opportunity to write my story down for others to share. But in the pursuit of brevity, I will do my best to whittle things down.

I must firstly thank all the NHS staff, whether they be doctors, nurses, physiotherapists, dieticians, surgeons, anaesthetists, pharmacists, or any other discipline, who have looked after me over so many years. Collectively, their dedication to follow their chosen occupation because they wish to spend their professional lives caring for other people is selfless and inspiring. They are all underpaid and underappreciated and deserve so much more than the conditions in which they are asked to perform, with poor facilities and limited resources. It is down to their dedication and caring spirit that I am still alive. I am in awe of you all.

Specifically, my very special thanks go out to the entire Cystic Fibrosis team at Royal Papworth Hospital in Cambridge (past and present) for their enduring support over the past twenty-six years and for looking after me through some of my darkest days with CF. I would like to mention Doctors Charles Haworth, Helen Barker, Chris Johnson, Uta Hill, and Professor Andres Floto, as well as the CF Specialist Nurse team of Samantha, Chi, and Susan. The words 'thank you' do not even begin to convey my gratitude towards you all for your care and support throughout my CF journey. I must also thank Professor Diana Bilton for her care and utmost professionalism during her time leading the CF team at

Royal Papworth, and for providing such a heartfelt and touching foreword to this book. I quite simply owe my life to you and you are the reason I am still here and still able to continue enjoying the opportunities that life affords me.

I must also thank the transplant team at Harefield Hospital, who navigated me through arguably the toughest period of my life and have brought me out the other side,. perhaps slightly bruised and definitely scarred, yet very much still alive and kicking, and ready to face whatever comes next on my journey.

Thanks go to Cara Thurlbourn for her patience and support during the process of writing this story down and for providing editorial services and transforming this dream of mine into reality. Thank you for believing in my abilities, and for giving me the motivation I needed to finish writing the book and to get the story of my journey 'out there'. You provided the inspiration I needed to believe in myself as a writer, and to overcome my 'imposter syndrome'. I am grateful for all your help, guidance, and support throughout the whole process. I should also thank my good friend Lucy Pettitt for introducing me to Cara.

Thanks go out to my all my friends but to Neil, Bill, and Alastair in particular. It was Neil, who by publishing his own book in 2015, gave me the kick I needed to finally start writing and to turn this project into reality. Additionally, Neil was the first person to read my first draft of this book and I am very grateful for all his comments and support. Thanks to all of you for your friendship over the years and for remaining with me after all this time, when so many others have drifted in and out of my life.

I would like to thank my very special and much-loved CF friends Ross and Sammie who have endured a similar journey to myself, yet always have time to give their support, love, and friendship despite what they may be going through themselves. They are always there with a smile and a joke regardless of the situation, a trait which I admire beyond measure. You are both amazing and if I could only emulate your enduring stoicism, determination and optimism, I would be a better person for it.

Although no longer with us, I wish to acknowledge my late friend Steve for giving me some of the most memorable moments of my life, for being there no matter what, and for just being one of the best friends anyone could have. I miss him greatly and will never forget either him or the fun and laughs we had together over the twenty-three years that we knew one another. I am so sorry that he didn't get the opportunity to undergo a lung transplant or to get the chance at another life with better lungs, but I hope that he is continuing to smile, breathing a bit easier and enjoying the beer wherever he may be.

Thanks go to my parents-in-law, John and Josie, who have always provided Aisling and myself with love, prayers and support throughout our times of adversity, and who have always treated me as part of their family.

To my dad, who ensured that my upbringing was always interesting, educational and fun; principles which I endeavour to impart on my own children's upbringing today. I love you, Dad.

To my two wonderful children, who keep me young at heart and give me so much to live for. I love you both so much and collectively, you will always provide the force that pulls me through the tough times so that we as a family can enjoy the good ones. I am also grateful to my son and my daughter for providing the wonderful illustrations that feature in this book, and my son for coming up with the initial concept for the front cover.

Finally, and most importantly of all, to my amazing wife, who has been through equally as much as I have with CF and has always dealt with the setbacks with the utmost resilience, composure and pragmatism. You are quite the most amazing person and I owe you everything. Your support has been steadfast, your strength and determination unwavering, and your love for me more than I could have ever wished for. I will never be able to thank you for all you have done for me and for remaining by my side throughout everything we have been through together. Quite simply, you have made my life complete and every day that I get to spend with you is a day worth living.

Supporters

Thanks go to all the supporters who made this book possible – both those listed below as well as those who did not wish for their name or names to appear in print.

Gareth and Tom Blake

Peter Blemings

Roisin and Craig Bowers

Rosamarie and Dickie Bowers

Kelly Bradley

Gary Broadhurst

Yvonne Burton

Heather Buxton

Anne and Michael Coyle

John and Josephine Coyle

Suzanne Daykin

Paul and Eimear Donaghy

Geraldine and Shane Donaghy

Audrey Eade

Martina Fay

Gwilym Funnell

Sharon Goudy

Kirsty Hawkins

Kim Hill

Ruth and Tim Hill

Prisca Jarf

Alastair and Emma Kiernan

Audrey Laidlaw

Vanessa Lancaster

Lucy Pettitt

James Pugh

Sammie and Ewan Read

Philip and Diana Rous

Chris and Victoria Silverwood

Lane Smith

Poppy Pennington-Smith

Hester Stuart

Anne Thomas

Jessica Twentyman

Anne Walker

Rachael and Bill Ward

Grahame Wardall

Pauline Willis

Emma and David Wooledge

ABOUT THE AUTHOR

Luke Peters is forty-eight years of age. He had a relatively normal upbringing living in Cambridge with his scientist father, midwife mother and two sisters. That said, following his birth in 1972, he was quickly diagnosed with the chronic condition cystic fibrosis. With this diagnosis, Luke was not expected to make it into double figures. Yet, with amazing care throughout his life from countless individuals within the NHS, huge advances in both treatment and medication for those with cystic fibrosis over several decades, as well as a substantial dose of good fortune, Luke remains alive today. Still going strong and whilst continuing to wish for more, Luke remains truly grateful for what he has and what his life, despite having CF, has brought him.

After a professional career spanning two decades working firstly in commercial aviation followed by a second career as a solicitor at a major London law firm, Luke took early retirement on medical advice. He moved out of the Surrey commuter belt and headed to live in the countryside closer to where he grew up, and to Royal Papworth Hospital in Cambridge, the world-renowned heart and lung hospital which has provided care for Luke since his early twenties.

Luke currently lives in the East of England with his wife of twenty years and his two young children. 'Coughing It All Up' is his first book.

You can contact Luke via *lukepeterswriter@gmail.com*

Printed in Poland
by Amazon Fulfillment
Poland Sp. z o.o., Wrocław

65560115R00263